AQA

Psychology

1

Jean-Marc Lawton
Eleanor Willard

Approval message from AQA

This textbook has been approved by AQA for use with our qualification. This means that we have checked that it broadly covers the specification and we are satisfied with the overall quality. Full details of our approval process can be found on our website.

We approve textbooks because we know how important it is for teachers and students to have the right resources to support their teaching and learning. However, the publisher is ultimately responsible for the editorial control and quality of this book.

Please note that when teaching the **AQA Psychology** course, you must refer to AQA's specification as your definitive source of information. While this book has been written to match the specification, it does not provide complete coverage of every aspect of the course.

A wide range of other useful resources can be found on the relevant subject pages of our website: www.aqa.org.uk.

Dedication

Jean-Marc Lawton: For my father – the mirror to my future
Eleanor Willard: Credit for this book must go to my supremely patient and supportive Olly and my Three Graces

Acknowledgements

p.viii t © Jean-Marc Lawton, b © Eleanor Willard; **p.1** © Mike Goldwater/Alamy; **p.2** t © NS-Dokumentationszentrum der Stadt Köln, b © Juergen Schwarz/Getty Images; **p.3** © Kenzo Tribouillard/AFP/Getty Images; **p.4** © fabiomax – Fotolia; **p.5** t © Mike Goldwater/Alamy, b © Christopher Dodson/iStockphoto.com; **p.6** © Cultura Creative (RF)/Alamy; **p.7** tr & br © Scientific American, bl Courtesy Kazuo Mori; **p.9** © Michal Heciak – Fotolia; **p.10** © Andrew Darrington/Alamy; **p.11** t © epa european pressphoto agency b.v./Alamy, bl © Pascal Eisenschmidt – Fotolia, br © Jana Lumley – Fotolia; **p.12** © ONOKY – Photononstop/Alamy; **p.13** With kind permission by Philip Zimbardo, Inc.; **p.17** tr © Arthur Turner/Alamy, bl © AP/Press Association Images, br © Hulton-Deutsch Collection/Corbis; **p.18** From the film Obedience © 1968 by Stanley Milgram; © 1993 renewed by Alexandra Milgram and distributed by Penn State Media Sales; **p.19** © Matt Archer/Getty Images; **p.20** © Jewish Currents; **p.22** © Gina Perry; **p.23** Courtesy NYC Municipal Archives; **p.24** © Gina Perry; **p.25** © Blend Images/Alamy; **p.26** t © National Geographic Image Collection/Alamy, b © Photo News/TopFoto; **p.28** Illustration from Kamptegnet, nr 17, 23. April 1942, page 6 "Rats: Destroy them" © Danish Royal Library; **p.30** © RTimages – Fotolia; **p.34** © Georgiy Pashin – Fotolia; **p.36** © Edyta Pawlowska – Fotolia; **p.37** © mstanley13 – Fotolia; **p.38** © Eric Hood/Getty Images; **p.41** © Sophie Bassouls/Sygma/Corbis; **p.44** © Alison Bowden – Fotolia; **p.46** t © Dominique Faget/AFP/Getty Images, b © Howard Jones/NEWZULU/Press Association Images; **p.47** © DOC RABE Media – Fotolia; **p.51** © Jonathan Selig/Getty Images; **p.52** © Thomas Boggan/East Valley Tribune; **p.54** © Natural Visions/Alamy; **p.55** l Courtesy Alan Baddeley, r Reproduced by kind permission of Royal Mail Group Ltd; **p.59** © Vidady – Fotolia; **p.61** l © John Dee/REX, r © The Wylie Agency UK Ltd; **p.64** © Jonathan Selig/Getty Images; **p.70** © Keith Beaty/Getty Images; **p.71** t © Giovanni Cancemi – Fotolia, b © Colin Anderson/Getty Images; **p.73** From: Phyllis Koenig et al: Categorization of Novel Animals by Patients With Alzheimer's Disease and Corticobasal Degeneration, Neuropsychology 2007, Vol. 21, No. 2, 193–206, figure 1 © APA (Publisher), reprinted with permission; **p.74** © photogerson – Fotolia; **p.77** t © Orestis Panagiotou/EPA/Corbis, b Map data © 2014 Google, reproduced with permission; **p.79** © jojje11 – Fotolia; **p.80** © Michael Stephens/PA Archive/Press Association Images; **p.85** © Kris Krug; **p.88** t © Cernan Elias/Alamy, b © Don Shrubshell/AP/Press Association Images; **p.89** © Courtesy Everett Collection/REX; **p.91** © Geoff Moore/REX; **p.95** © 67photo/Alamy; **p.101** © Nina Leen/The LIFE Picture Collection/Getty Images; **p.102** © David Crigger/AP/Press Association Images; **p.103** © Tom Wang – Fotolia; **p.105** © Monkey Business – Fotolia; **p.107** © Rob – Fotolia; **p.110** © Nina Leen/The LIFE Picture Collection/Getty Images; **p.111** t © Jeffrey Phelps/Aurora Photos/Corbis, b © Nina Leen/The LIFE Picture Collection/Getty Images; **p.115** © Monkey Business – Fotolia; **p.116** © Richard Bowlby; **p.122** Photo Courtesy U.Va. Public Affairs; **p.123** l Courtesy Marinus Van Ijzendoorn, r Courtesy Pieter Kroonenberg; **p.125** © John Warburton-Lee Photography/Alamy; **p.127** © Paul Kingsley/Alamy; **p.129** t © Carl Bromwich, Courtesy John D. Chapman, b © Firma V – Fotolia; **p.131** © Image Broker/REX; **p.132** © Scott Olson/Getty Images; **p.133** © Jackie Young; **p.136** © Mike Abrahams/Alamy; **p.138** © Here Media, Inc.; **p.139** © imtmphoto – Fotolia; **p.144** © Peter Macdiarmid/Getty Images; **p.145** © fotosmile777 – Fotolia; **p.149** © epa/Corbis; **p.151** © Howard Berman/Getty Images; **p.155** © Everett Collection/REX; **p.158** © Andrey Burmakin – Fotolia; **p.162** © Virtually Free (www.virtually-free.com); **p.163** © David Jones/PA Archive/Press Association Images; **p.164** No credit; **p.165** © Claudio Santisteban/Demotix/Press Association Images; **p.166** © Enigma/Alamy; **p.167** t © Nature Picture Library/Alamy, b © Lijuan Guo – Fotolia; **p.168** © Peter Hince/Getty Images; **p.169** © apops – Fotolia; **p.178** © fotosmile777 – Fotolia; **p.181** © Najlah Feanny/Corbis; **p.185** t © adimas – Fotolia, b © Kitty – Fotolia; **p.186** © Rock and Wasp – Fotolia; **p.187** © David Cole/Alamy; **p.189** © vladimirfloyd – Fotolia; **p.190** © Dr P. Marazzi/Science Photo Library; **p.192** © BSIP/UIG Via Getty Images; **p.197** © aphonua – Fotolia; **p.198** © orion_eff – Fotolia; **p.199** © Robyn Beck/AFP/Getty Images; **p.201** © Papirazzi – Fotolia; **p.207** © aphonua – Fotolia; **p.208** © Dusan Kostic – Fotolia; **p.213** With kind permission by Albert Bandura; **p.219** all © Simons, D. J., & Chabris, C. F. (1999). Gorillas in our midst: Sustained inattentional blindness for dynamic events. Perception, 28, 1059–1074.; **p.225** © dpa picture alliance/Alamy; **p.229** © Pictorial Press Ltd/Alamy; **p.236** Courtesy William D. "Scott" Killgore, Ph.D./SCAN Lab/Department of Psychiatry/University of Arizona; **p.241** © mrk28 – Fotolia; **p.235** © Everett Collection Historical/Alamy; **p.242** © Joss – Fotolia; **p.249** © AP/TopFoto; **p.251** © Christopher Furlong/Getty Images; **p.254** © dpa picture alliance/Alamy; **p.257** © Elenathewise – Fotolia; **p.258** t © George Silk/Time & Life Pictures/Getty Images, b © Quasarphoto – Fotolia; **p.260** © AF archive/Alamy; **p.263** © BORACAN/SIPA/REX; **p.267** © dalaprod – Fotolia; **p.269** © Glenda Powers – Fotolia; **p.270** © pesciolinorosso – Fotolia; **p.273** © luminastock – Fotolia; **p.277** © WavebreakmediaMicro – Fotolia; **p.279** © chrisdorney – Fotolia; **p.281** © Small Town Studio – Fotolia; **p.283** © Keystone/Getty Images; **p.284** © Bill Pierce/The LIFE Images Collection/Getty Images; **p.290** © Elenathewise – Fotolia; **p.302** t © 13/John Cumming/Ocean/Corbis, b © Antonioguillem – Fotolia.

Hachette UK's policy is to use papers that are natural, renewable and recyclable products and made from wood grown in sustainable forests. The logging and manufacturing processes are expected to conform to the environmental regulations of the country of origin.

Orders: please contact Bookpoint Ltd, 130 Milton Park, Abingdon, Oxon OX14 4SB. Telephone: +44 (0)1235 827720. Fax: +44 (0)1235 400454. Lines are open 9.00a.m.– 5.00p.m., Monday to Saturday, with a 24-hour message answering service. Visit our website at www.hoddereducation.co.uk

© Jean-Marc Lawton and Eleanor Willard 2015

First published in 2015 by

Hodder Education,

An Hachette UK Company

Carmelite House

50 Victoria Embankment

London EC4Y 0DZ

Impression number   10 9 8 7 6

Year   2019 2018

Cover photo © hitdelight – Fotolia

Illustrations by Aptara and Barking Dog

Typeset in 11/13 pt ITC Berkeley Oldstyle Std by Aptara, Inc.

Printed in Italy

A catalogue record for this title is available from the British Library

ISBN 9781471834882

Contents

*A-level only content
**Some A-level only content

Introduction

This book is aimed specifically at those students studying the AQA Psychology AS and A-level specifications, though hopefully it will prove of interest and use to any student of psychology.

The book details the course content as outlined by the AQA specifications, but should also serve as a learning aid in itself and not just be a basic textbook. To create ease of use, there is a standard format throughout the book, with the features designed specifically to help you with your studies.

The book is divided into seven chapters, reflecting the seven main topics that make up the AS course and the first year of the A-level course. Within these chapters is the basic text that describes the relevant theories and explanation required by the specifications, alongside the following regular features, which require some further explanation in order for you to understand and get the most from them.

Features

Understanding the specification

Found at the beginning of each chapter, this feature details the specific elements of topics that need to be studied.

IN THE NEWS

Written in the style of a newspaper story, this feature highlights topical news items that illustrate central psychological themes of the topics being discussed.

KEY TERMS

Concise and clear explanations of significant words and words associated with each topic. Key terms are highlighted within the text in the first instance and then fully explained and detailed within the text itself.

Evaluation

This regular feature can be found after a research section and at the conclusion of explanations/theories and consists of general evaluative and analytical points.

RESEARCH IN FOCUS

Using examples from the text, this feature gets you to focus on methodological aspects of research studies (how studies are carried out) and asks relevant questions to assist learning and understanding. This knowledge will also be useful for those progressing on to year two of the A-level. It will often be a good idea to reference material in Chapter 7 (Research methods) to get the most out of this feature.

This feature also focuses upon research methods, but this time from the viewpoint of the design of psychological studies. This will help to foster a greater understanding of why and how psychologists conduct research and help you to develop the necessary skills to plan your own research.

On the web

Take your learning and curiosity further by using this feature, which directs you to websites that provide a wealth of further information.

CLASSIC RESEARCH

As the title suggests, this feature focuses on famous psychological studies, taking you in some detail through the thinking behind such studies, as well as the aims, procedure, findings, conclusions and evaluation.

CONTEMPORARY RESEARCH

Similar in focus and presentation to the classic research feature, but this time featuring more recent cutting-edge research, providing an up-to-date account of the subject.

Increase your knowledge

A feature that provides extra learning material to form a useful and relevant source of elaboration for those who wish to take their learning a little further.

PSYCHOLOGY IN THE REAL WORLD

An occasional feature focusing upon practical applications of psychology that shows its usefulness within real-world settings and which will help to form a valuable source of AO3 evaluative material.

STRENGTHEN YOUR LEARNING

Found at the end of each element of a topic, this feature is designed to help you focus upon and appraise the material covered within the text. Acting as a form of comprehension exercise, the questions can be used as a means of revision before attempting the questions found at the end of each topic.

Assessment check

This feature consists of a variety of questions to help you with your studies.

SUMMARY

Each chapter concludes with a bullet-pointed review of the main points covered within the chapter.

A-level only content

This is indicated by a shaded blue background.

Assessment checks

Examination skills

The AQA examinations assess three examination skills. These are Assessment Objective 1 [AO1], Assessment Objective 2 [AO2] and Assessment Objective 3 [AO3].

AO1 assesses level of knowledge and understanding by asking candidates to demonstrate knowledge and understanding of scientific ideas, processes, techniques and procedures, such as by outlining and describing relevant theories/explanations and research studies.

AO2 requires students to apply knowledge and understanding of scientific ideas, processes, techniques and procedures, such as by providing students with some stimulus material and then asking them to apply their psychological knowledge to that material.

AO3 requires students to analyse, interpret and evaluate scientific information, ideas and evidence, such as by assessing the worth and meaning of theories/explanations. For example, by a consideration of what research findings suggest, support/lack of support from other research sources, methodological criticisms, relevant ethical points, as well as practical applications and implications of research.

The assessment check feature presents questions. There are several types of such questions you can be faced with.

1 'Choice' questions require you to select from options provided to complete the answer, for example, see question 1 on page 16 in Chapter 1 Social psychology: social influences.

2 'Scenario' questions describe a situation based on a topic area. Knowledge of that topic area must then be applied to the scenario, for example, see question 7 on page 16 in Chapter 1 Social psychology: social influences.

3 'Short answer' questions require specific answers, with elaboration (detail) needed to show fuller understanding, for example, see question 5 on page 32 in Chapter 1 Social psychology: social influences.

4 'Methodology' questions are based upon research studies associated with topic areas. Knowledge of methodology must then be applied, for example, see question 8 on page 16 in Chapter 1 Social psychology: social influences. Some of these questions will require mathematical skills in order to be successfully answered, for example, see questions 7(i) and 7(ii) on page 32 in Chapter 1 Social psychology: social influences.

5 'Essay' questions for the A-level qualification will never be worth more than 16 marks and 12 marks for the AS qualification. These may be in the form of 'outline and evaluate', for instance of an explanation or theory, for example, see question 3 on page 16 in Chapter 1 Social psychology: social influences.

About the authors

Jean-Marc Lawton is an accomplished lecturer of Psychology and a renowned author of books on the subject. Aside from teaching he regularly contributes to revision conferences and the professional development of teachers. He lives in the north-west Scottish Highlands and has a keen interest in hill running and unlistenable music.

Eleanor Willard is a chartered teacher of Psychology and examiner who was a department head in a school in Yorkshire. She's now loving life as a PhD researcher and lecturer in Leeds and spends any spare time she has catching up with her daughters and taking in the beauty of her beloved Yorkshire with her husband.

1 Social psychology: social influences

Introduction

Social psychology studies how people's thoughts, feelings and behaviour are affected by the presence of others. Focus can either be upon how others affect an individual or upon group interactions. The social psychology topic looked at here is that of social influence – how individuals affect and are affected by others. Several areas of social influence are focused upon:

- Majority influence – (types of conformity, explanations for conformity, variables affecting conformity and conformity to social roles)
- Obedience – (explanations for obedience, situational variables affecting obedience and dispositional explanations for obedience)
- Explanations of resistance to social influence
- Minority influence
- The role of social influence processes in social change.

Understanding the specification

- *Internalisation, identification and compliance* are types of conformity students must have knowledge of; they are referred to directly in the specification.
- *Informational and normative social influences* are also referred to directly as *explanations of conformity* and so again must be studied.
- A knowledge of *conformity to social roles* is additionally required, including the *research of Zimbardo* into this area.
- Another area to be studied is that of *explanations for obedience*, including the *agentic state* and *legitimacy of authority*. *Situational variables affecting obedience* will also need to be studied, including *proximity, location and uniform*. There will be a requirement to have knowledge of the research of *Stanley Milgram* to achieve this. There is an additional requirement to study the *dispositional explanation of the authoritarian personality*.
- Students are required to be able to explain *resistance to social influence*, especially *social support* and *locus of control*, as they are referred to specifically.
- *Minority influence* is another required area of study, which must include focus upon consistency, commitment and flexibility.
- Finally, a knowledge of the *role of social influence processes in social change* is required.

These are the basic requirements of the specification. However, other relevant material is included to provide depth and detail to your understanding.

Ψ The Psychological Enquirer

Pirates of independence

Figure 1.1 The Edelweiss Pirates (Jean Jülich, 1st left)

Figure 1.2 Jean Jülich as an older man

In November 2011 the press reported on Jean Jülich, who had died aged 82. He was one of the last surviving **Edelweiss Pirates** – working-class German teenagers who resisted the Nazis during the Second World War. Distinctive by their long hair, checked shirts, Edelweiss badges and their love of jazz music, by 1944 5,000 'Pirates' were living as outlaws in bombed-out cities throughout Germany.

Throughout the war Jean and his friends, both male and female, provided food and shelter to concentration camp escapees, fugitive Jews and German army deserters. They attacked Hitler Youth patrols, derailed ammunition trains, vandalised weapons factories and sabotaged machinery.

Jean was arrested at age 15, held in solitary confinement and tortured for four months. His 16-year-old friend, Barthel Schink, was hanged with 11 other Pirates, in public, without trial, on orders from Heinrich Himmler. Jean survived beatings, starvation and typhus in a concentration camp until he was freed by American troops in 1945.

One popular explanation for the atrocities committed by the Nazis in the Second World War, like the extermination of Jewish people and Gypsies, was that Germans had a personality defect that led them to unquestioningly obey and commit such horrific acts. However, the bravery of Jean and the Edelweiss Pirates in opposing the Nazis shows that blind obedience wasn't the response of all Germans; indeed there were groups of Pirates in most German cities. This goes against the dispositional explanation of obedience – that it was the internal characteristics of Germans which made them so obedient. Stanley Milgram's famous study suggested instead that it is situational factors – aspects of the environment – that leads to such behaviour. An element of normative social influence can also be seen in the hairstyle, clothing and music that the Pirates conformed to. The actions of the teenagers also highlight how social influence can be resisted. Indeed, it is heartening to realise that obedience with such destructive consequences can be resisted and that we are not doomed to commit immoral acts against our free will. However, the actions of the Pirates weren't appreciated. Due to their non-conformist nature, the conquering forces refused to recognise or reward their actions, and it wasn't until 2005 that their actions against the Nazis were no longer officially seen as criminal acts.

ON THE WEB

Want to know more about the Edelweiss Pirates and their resistance to the Nazis' attempts to control German society? Then go to:

www.raoulwallenberg.net/saviors/others/edelweiss-pirates-story/

1.1 Types of conformity

Conformity (majority influence)

'No man is an island, entire of itself, every man is a piece of the continent, a part of the main.'
John Dunne (1624)

'We are half ruined by conformity, but we would be wholly ruined without it.'
Charles Dudley Warner (1896)

Conformity is defined as yielding to group pressure. Conformity occurs when an individual's behaviour and/or beliefs are influenced by a larger group of people, which is why conformity is also known as **majority influence**. When conformity reduces a person's independence and leads to harmful outcomes, it can be a negative force. Generally though, conformity has positive outcomes, helping society to function smoothly and predictably. Much human activity is socially based, occurring in groups, so there is a need for individuals to agree in order for groups to form and operate efficiently. Conformity helps this process; by conforming we can make it easier to get along with each other.

Kelman (1958) made reference to three types of conformity, which vary in the amount to which they affect an individual's belief system.

1 **Compliance** – occurs when individuals adjust their behaviour and opinions to those of a group to be accepted or avoid disapproval. Compliance therefore occurs due to a desire to fit in and involves public, but not private, acceptance of a group's behaviour and attitudes. It is a fairly weak and temporary form of conformity, only shown in the presence of the group. For example, you may claim to support a certain football team, because many others of your age group do and you want to be accepted and not ridiculed by them. However, privately you may have little interest in this team, or indeed football at all.

2 **Identification** – occurs when individuals adjust their behaviour and opinions to those of a group, because membership of that group is desirable. This is a stronger type of conformity, involving private as well as public acceptance, but is generally temporary and is not maintained when individuals leave the group. For example, in the army you may adopt the behaviour and beliefs of fellow soldiers, but on leaving the army for civilian life, new behaviours and opinions will be adopted.

3 **Internalisation** – (also known as true conformity) occurs when individuals genuinely adjust their behaviour and opinions to those of a group. This involves individuals being exposed to the belief systems of others and having to decide what they truly believe in. If a group's beliefs are seen as correct, it will lead to public and private acceptance of the group's behaviour and opinions, which will not be dependent on the presence of the group or group membership for maintenance. For example, if you are influenced by a group's religious beliefs so that you truly convert to that faith, then your new religious way of life will continue without the presence or influence of the group. (Internalisation can also occur through minority influence, see page 41.)

KEY TERMS

Conformity – yielding to group pressure (also known as majority influence)

Compliance – publicly, but not privately, going along with majority influence to gain approval

Identification – public and private acceptance of majority influence in order to gain group acceptance

Internalisation – public and private acceptance of majority influence, through adoption of the majority group's belief system

Figure 1.3 A religious conversion would be an example of internalisation

3

Figure 1.4 'Which to use?' We have a better idea when we examine the behaviour of others

KEY TERMS

Informational social influence (ISI) –
a motivational force to look to others for
guidance in order to be correct

Normative social influence (NSI) –
a motivational force to be liked and
accepted by a group

1.2 Explanations for conformity

Explanations for conformity are an identification of the reasons why people conform.

Deutsch and Gerard (1955) distinguished between **informational social influence (ISI)** and **normative social influence (NSI)**. This distinction, they believed, was crucial to understanding majority group influence.

Informational social influence [ISI]

Humans have a basic need to feel confident that their ideas and beliefs are correct (a need for certainty). This helps people feel in charge of their lives and in control of the world. This is the motivation underpinning ISI. When individuals are uncertain about something, they look at the behaviour and opinions of others and this helps shape their own thoughts and behaviour. This generally occurs in unfamiliar situations, like knowing which cutlery to use when in a restaurant for the first time, or in ambiguous situations where there is no clear correct answer, like watching a film and not knowing what to make of it. Watching others to see which cutlery they use, or asking what they thought of a film, helps a person make up their own mind. When people conform because of ISI, they tend to believe the opinions adopted. As they are uncertain what to believe, they look to the opinions of others and become converted to their viewpoint.

For example, Jenness (1932) (see Classic research, page 5) gave participants a task with no clear answer: estimating how many jellybeans were in a jar. He found that individual estimates moved towards the estimates of others, showing that they genuinely (privately) believed these estimates, demonstrating an example of *internalisation* (true conformity).

ISI can be seen to have an evolutionary basis to it, as looking to others for guidance in new situations that are potentially dangerous could have a survival value.

Abrams *et al.* (1990) think that we are only influenced by others' opinions in ambiguous situations when we see ourselves as sharing characteristics with them. Thus we are much more likely to internalise the opinions of friends than strangers.

Normative social influence [NSI]

Individuals want others to like and respect them and not reject or ridicule them. This is the motivation underpinning NSI – the need to be accepted by others. The best way of gaining the acceptance of others is to agree with them. However, this does not necessarily mean that we truly agree with them.

Research

For example, Asch (1955) (see Classic research, page 6) got participants to conform to answers given by others that were obviously incorrect. If the participants gave the correct answers, they risked being ridiculed by the majority. A conflict had been created between an individual's opinion and that of the group. In the post-experimental debriefing, many said 'I didn't want to look stupid' or 'I didn't want to be the odd one out'. So they compromised, with what they *said* (publicly) and what they *believed* (privately) being completely different, demonstrating an example of *compliance*. Jenness' participants did not face this conflict, as in his study there was no obviously correct answer.

However, conflict is only experienced when individuals disagree with others whom they see as similar to themselves in some relevant way (as in ISI: see Abrams *et al.*, 1990).

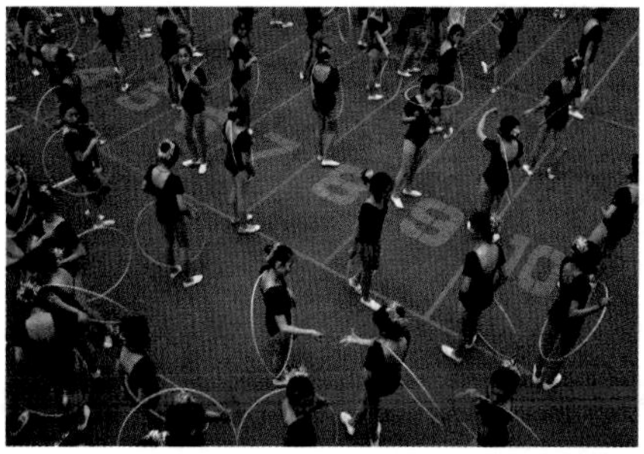

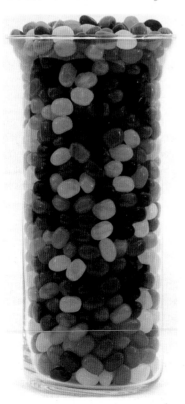

Figure 1.5 Normative social influence occurs because of a need to be accepted

INCREASE YOUR KNOWLEDGE

Cognitive dissonance

When individuals have two simultaneous contradictory ideas (cognitions), an unpleasant feeling occurs known as **cognitive dissonance**. Festinger (1957) suggested that altering these cognitions will reduce cognitive dissonance and this is best achieved through conforming. The fact that some examples of conformity cannot be explained by normative or informational social influence, but only by cognitive dissonance, supports this explanation. For example, Bogdonoff *et al.* (1961) found that the conflict created by participants performing an Asch-type procedure increased their stress levels (due to participants having opinions that went against those of the majority), but this was reduced by conforming. This also illustrates how conformity can be seen as a healthy response, as it reduces stress levels.

KEY TERM

Cognitive dissonance – an unpleasant feeling of anxiety created by simultaneously holding two contradictory ideas

CLASSIC RESEARCH

The role of discussion in changing opinion regarding a matter of fact – Arthur Jenness (1932)

Figure 1.6 How many jellybeans are in the jar?

Originally conducted as an investigation into social facilitation (the effect of the presence of others on performance), Jenness' research is now regarded as a groundbreaking study into informational social influence. The original focus was on how group discussion influenced the accuracy of judgement, but the most interesting result concerned how majority influence caused individual judgements to converge (move together). The task Jenness gave his participants, estimating the number of jellybeans in a jar, had no obvious answer; it was difficult to assess the amount. Therefore the conformity produced was motivated by informational social influence, where individuals in uncertain situations look to others for guidance as to how to behave.

Aim

To investigate whether individual judgements of jellybeans in a jar was influenced by discussion in groups.

Procedure

1. Participants made individual, private estimates of the number of jellybeans in a jar.
2. Participants then discussed their estimates either in a large group or in several smaller groups, discovering in the process that individuals differed widely in their estimates.
3. After discussion, group estimates were created.
4. Participants then made a second individual, private estimate.

Findings

1. Typicality of opinion was increased – individuals' second private estimates tended to converge (move towards) their group estimate.

2 The average change of opinion was greater among females – women conformed more.

Conclusions

The judgements of individuals are affected by majority opinions, especially in ambiguous or unfamiliar situations. Discussion is not effective in changing opinion, unless the individuals who enter into the discussion become aware that the opinions of others are different to theirs.

Evaluation

Although Jenness did not tell participants what the aims of the study were, the deception here was less severe than in other social influences studies. Therefore, the study could be regarded as more ethically sound.

This was a laboratory-based experiment using an artificial, unusual situation. It therefore lacks mundane realism, as it's not an everyday event to be asked how many sweets there are in a jar and so it does not reflect actual behaviour in real-life situations.

The study tells us little, if anything, about majority influence in non-ambiguous situations where people conform to obviously wrong answers (see Asch, 1955).

Jenness' study may involve NSI as well as ISI. After making initial individual estimates, participants then created group estimates, therefore their later second individual estimates may have moved towards their group estimates due to a desire for acceptance (NSI) as well as a desire to be correct (ISI).

KEY TERM

Confederates – (also known as pseudo-participants and stooges) individuals who pretend to be participants or researchers in research studies, but who are actually playing a part

YOU ARE THE RESEARCHER

Design a modification of Jenness' study that uses a different conformity task. For example, how could you use a library to conduct the study by asking participants to estimate the number of books? Or your local swimming pool by asking participants to estimate the volume of water? Or indeed a car filled with balloons? Try to think of an example of your own.

Figure 1.7 How could balloons in a car be used to study informational social influence?

What would be your independent variable (IV) and dependent variable (DV)? Write a suitable directional (one-tailed) and null hypothesis. Create some appropriate standardised instructions.

For more on research methods, see Chapter 7.

CLASSIC RESEARCH

Opinions and social pressure – Solomon Asch (1955)

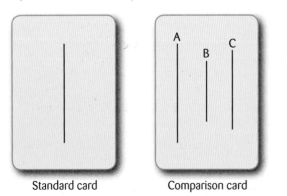

Standard card   Comparison card

Figure 1.8 Stimulus cards used in Asch's experiment

Solomon Asch, a Polish immigrant to the USA, transformed the study of social influence with his groundbreaking research at Harvard University. He also taught Stanley Milgram, who achieved later fame with his studies of obedience.

Asch was interested in testing conformity to obviously incorrect answers. He criticised research like Jenness' that only involved ambiguous tasks and uncertain situations. Beginning in 1951, Asch conducted a series of experiments, adding and publishing new data as he progressed.

Aim

To investigate the degree to which individuals would conform to a majority who gave obviously wrong answers.

Procedure

1 123 American male student volunteers took part in what they were told was a study of visual perception. Individual participants were placed in groups with between seven and nine others, sat either in a line or around a table, who in reality were pseudo-participants (**confederates**). The task was to say which comparison line, A, B or C, was the same as a stimulus line on 18 different trials. 12 of these were 'critical' trials, where pseudo-participants gave identical wrong answers, and

the naïve (real) participant always answered last or last but one.

2 There was also a control group of 36 participants who were tested individually on 20 trials, to test how accurate individual judgements were.

Findings

1 The control group had an error rate of only 0.04 per cent (3 mistakes out of 720 trials), which shows how obvious the correct answers were.

2 On the 12 critical trials, there was a 32 per cent conformity rate to wrong answers.

3 75 per cent of participants conformed to at least one wrong answer (meaning that 25 per cent never conformed).

4 5 per cent of participants conformed to all 12 wrong answers.

Post-experiment interviews with participants found three reasons for conformity:

● Distortion of action – where the majority of participants who conformed did so publicly, but not privately, as they wished to avoid ridicule.

● Distortion of perception – where some participants believed their perception must actually be wrong and so conformed.

● Distortion of judgement – where some participants had doubts concerning the accuracy of their judgements and so conformed to the majority view.

Conclusions

The judgements of individuals are affected by majority opinions, even when the majority are obviously wrong.

There are big individual differences in the amount to which people are affected by majority influence. As most participants conformed publicly, but not privately, it suggests that they were motivated by normative social influence, where individuals conform to gain acceptance or avoid rejection by a group.

Evaluation

Asch's method for studying conformity became a paradigm, the accepted way of conducting conformity research.

As only one real participant is tested at a time, the procedure is uneconomical and time-consuming. Crutchfield (1954) performed similar research, but improved on the procedure by testing several participants at once.

The situation was unrealistic and so lacked mundane realism. It would be unusual to be in a situation where you would disagree so much with others as to what was the 'correct' answer in a situation.

Asch's study was unethical, as it involved deceit; participants believed it was a study of visual perception. It also involved psychological harm, with participants put under stress through disagreeing with others (see Bogdonoff et al. (1961), page 5).

As the overall conformity rate on the critical trials was only 32 per cent (one-third of the participants), the majority of people are actually not conformist, but independent.

(a)

(b)

Figure 1.9a and b A minority of one faces a unanimous majority in Asch's study

---

CONTEMPORARY RESEARCH

Asch without the actors – Kazuo Mori & Miho Arai (2010)

Figure 1.10 Participants in the study by Mori and Arai

Asch's study became a paradigm study, but a major criticism was that of demand characteristics (see Chapter 7 Research methods) – the confederates weren't trained actors and therefore participants may have realised that the confederates' answers weren't real and so just pretended to conform, as that is what they thought the researcher wanted them to do. Mori & Arai's solution was the MORI technique (Manipulation of Overlapping Rivalrous Images by polarising filters). Participants wore filter glasses, allowing them to look at the same stimuli, but see different things. One participant in each group wore different glasses, thus perceiving a different comparison line to match to the stimulus line. Asch's study also only used males, while this study additionally used females.

ON THE WEB

Listen to a BBC Radio 4 programme about Asch's pioneering research into conformity as part of the *Mind Changers* series:

www.bbc.co.uk/programmes/ p00f8mzr

Search for the 'Asch Conformity Experiment' or the 'Asch Experiment' on YouTube to see some videos about the Asch procedure.

Aim

To reproduce the Asch experiment, but without a need for confederates.

Procedure

1 104 Japanese undergraduates were put in same-sex groups of four. Participants sat around a table, with the seat order randomised, and had to say aloud which of three comparison lines matched a stimulus line. The same comparison and stimulus lines were used as in Asch's study.

2 Participants wore sunglasses, supposedly to prevent glare, with the third participant in each group wearing different glasses, which made them see a shorter or longer comparison line to the other three participants on 12 out of 18 'critical' trials. The other six trials were neutral, where participants all saw the same thing.

3 Participants then answered a questionnaire containing 22 questions taken from the interview Asch used with his participants. Among the questions were ones asking whether participants were suspicious about the images seen, whether they noticed the others answering differently, whether they were sure of their answers and whether they were influenced by the others' answers if not confident of their own judgements.

Findings

1 The 78 majority participants who saw the correct-sized comparison lines answered incorrectly 8.2 per cent of the time (77 out of 936 tasks), with no significant gender differences.

2 The 26 minority participants who saw the different-sized comparison lines answered incorrectly 19.6 per cent of the time (61 out of 312 tasks). However, female minority participants answered incorrectly 28.6 per cent of the time, while for males it was only 5 per cent of the time.

3 With females, the results were similar to Asch's, with the minority conforming to wrong answers on the 12 critical trials an average of 4.41 times (3.44 times in Asch's study),

but male conformity was not noticeable. This is noteworthy because all participants in the Asch study were male.

Conclusions

Minority participants noticed their judgements were different, but none reported suspicions concerning the honesty of majority participants' answers, therefore it suggests demand characteristics did not occur.

Unlike Asch's findings, the frequency of conformity of minority participants was similar regardless of whether the majority answered unanimously or not. This suggests the number of people in a majority group has little effect on conformity levels (see Asch's variations, page 6).

As women conformed more than men, it suggests cultural or generational differences have occurred since Asch's study.

As no majority participants laughed at the performance of minority participants, conformity cannot have occurred due to fear of ridicule.

Evaluation

This new procedure could provide an effective means of examining conformity, especially in natural settings and in social situations where the use of confederates wouldn't be practical, such as with children.

The new procedure is still unethical, as participants were deceived into thinking the sunglasses were worn to prevent glare.

Conformity may have occurred due to both normative social influence (a desire to be accepted) and informational social influence (a desire to be correct).

Both Asch and Mori & Arai's studies lack mundane realism (can the results of a study be applied to real life), as comparing line sizes isn't something that is often done in real life.

Mori & Arai's study may be more externally valid, as the participants knew each other. Real-life conformity tends to occur among acquainted people, like family members, rather than in Asch-type situations where decisions are made among strangers.

ON THE WEB

You can read the full research paper of Mori & Arai's conformity study at:

http://dx.doi.org/10.4236/psych. 2013.411127

RESEARCH IN FOCUS

1 Studies of conformity tend to be laboratory experiments. Give one advantage and one disadvantage of this method.

2 What experimental design was used in Jenness' study? Give one advantage and one disadvantage of this design.

3 What are the independent variable (IV) and dependent variable (DV) in Jenness', Asch's and Mori & Arai's studies?

4 Mori & Arai's study is somewhat of a replication of Asch's paradigm. What is a replication and why would it be performed?

5 In what way can Asch's and Mori & Arai's studies be considered unethical? How would these ethical issues be addressed?

6 Mori & Arai's study was designed to reduce demand characteristics. What are demand characteristics and how did their study attempt to reduce them?

For information on research methods, see Chapter 7.

Figure 1.11 Better group cohesion can be achieved through informational social influence

One way in which knowledge of conformity can be used in a practical manner is in the formation of groups, for example sports teams. By giving potential members ambiguous tasks, where there is no clear correct answer, individuals will be drawn together through informational social influence into creating a group identity. This would involve identification (maybe even internalisation) and thus would create a stronger group bond than that done through compliance by simply creating normative social influence through getting new members to conform to group norms.

STRENGTHEN YOUR LEARNING

1 In what way does normative social influence differ from informational social influence?
2 What type of conformity is associated with normative social influence?
3 What type of conformity is associated with informational social influence?
4 Can you think of real-life examples of your own of informational social influence and normative social influence?
5 What aspect of Jenness' study involves informational social influence?
6 What aspect of Asch's study involves normative social influence?
7 What is cognitive dissonance? How can it be used as an explanation of conformity?

1.3 Variables affecting conformity

Situational variables

Research into majority influence has identified several **situational variables** – that is, qualities of an environment that influence levels of conformity – which have an influence over the degree to which individuals conform.

These include group size (the number of members within a social group), unanimity (to what degree the group members are in agreement with each other) and task difficulty (how obvious the correct answer/decision is when regarding a task). Asch performed several variations of his procedure that investigated these factors.

Size of group

Research indicates that conformity rates increase as the size of a majority influence increases, but there comes a point where further increases in the size of the majority doesn't lead to further increases in conformity.

KEY TERMS

Situational variables – features of an environment that affect the degree to which individuals yield to group pressures

Individual variables – personal characteristics that affect the degree to which individuals yield to group pressures

Figure 1.12 Even stickleback fish show conformist behaviour

Research

Asch (1956) found that with one real participant and one confederate conformity was low, rising to 13 per cent with two confederates and 32 per cent with three confederates (around the same rate as in his original study). Adding extra confederates (up to fifteen confederates) had no further effect on the overall conformity rate. Bond & Smith (1996) supported this idea by performing a meta-analysis (see Chapter 7) of 133 Asch-type studies from seventeen countries, and finding that conformity peaks with about four or five confederates. Gerard *et al.* (1968), however, questioned this, finding that conformity rates do rise as more confederates are added, though the rate of increase declines with each additional confederate. Pike & Laland (2010) gave support to Gerard by reporting that stickleback fish demonstrated conformity to feeding behaviour by showing an increased level of copying of a demonstrator fish eating at a food-rich site, but that the rate of conformity increase declined as the number of demonstrator fish increased. This additionally suggests an evolutionary basis to conformity due to its survival value.

Unanimity

Conformity rates have been found to decline when majority influence is not unanimous. The important factor though would seem to be the reduction in the majority's agreement, rather than an individual being given support for their opinions, as conformity drops if a rebel goes against the majority who don't support the rebel's viewpoint.

Research

Asch (1956) found if there was one confederate who went against the other confederates, conformity dropped from around 32 per cent to 5.5 per cent, but if the 'rebel' went against both the other confederates and the real participant, conformity still dropped to 9 per cent.

Task difficulty

Greater conformity rates are seen when task difficulty increases, as the right answer becomes less obvious. This means that individuals will look to others more for guidance as to what the correct response is, suggesting that ISI is the dominant force.

Research

Asch (1956) increased task difficulty by making the comparison lines similar to each other, finding that when he did so participants were more likely to conform to wrong answers, thus demonstrating the effect of task difficulty on conformity.

women to be more nurturing and co-operative and upon men to be more aggressive and confrontational.

Maslach *et al.* (1987) found that males tended to be more independent and assertive and therefore conform less. Females, however, were sensitive to others' needs and emotions and so conformed to maintain harmony. These differences in gender roles can therefore explain the varying levels of conformity found between the sexes.

Jenness (1932) (see Classic research, page 5) found that females conformed more. Perhaps this occurred as the research task was more male-orientated, making females less sure of their judgements, thus creating more ISI for females than males. Sistrunk & McDavid (1971) supported this view by finding that when tasks used had a traditionally male bias, such as involving cars rather than cooking, females felt more uncertain and conformed more.

Mood

Research suggests that humans will conform more when they're in a good mood, perhaps because when happy they are more amenable to agreeing with others. Research has also indicated that people will conform more readily when moving from a fearful to a more relaxed mood.

Tong *et al.* (2008) found that participants were more likely to conform to wrong answers to mathematical questions given by confederates when in a positive rather than neutral or negative mood, illustrating the effect mood can have on conformity levels.

Dolinski (1998) found evidence for a fear-then-relief phenomenon in both field and laboratory settings. Abrupt relief of anxiety states led to participants conforming more readily, again showing how mood states can effect conformity.

Culture

People from different cultures have been shown to conform to different levels, possibly because some cultures are more uniform in their structure, have shared values among their members and thus find it easier to agree with each other. Cultures can also be divided into collectivist ones, where

Figure 1.13 Norwegians are conformist as they share cultural values and norms

conformity to social norms is more socialised and expected, and individualist cultures that tolerate and encourage more deviance from social norms.

Smith & Bond (1993) found an average conformity rate among collectivist cultures of 25 to 58 per cent, while in individualist cultures it ranged from 14 to 39 per cent, which suggests culture does affect conformity to some extent.

Milgram (1961) found 62 per cent of Norwegian participants conformed to obviously wrong answers concerning the length of acoustic tones. Avant & Knudson (1993) argue that this is due to Norway being a very cohesive country with few ethnic minorities that values and promotes traditional values and frowns upon individualism.

Perrin & Spencer (1980), using the Asch paradigm, found a conformity level of only 0.25 per cent among Yorkshire science students, which suggests Britons have very low conformity levels, though a different explanation might be that science students are taught to question things and be independent thinkers. Indeed, the same researchers found a similar conformity rate to Asch's in young British criminals, who could be said to lack independent thought.

YOU ARE THE RESEARCHER

Psychology is centred on the designing and carrying out of practical research. Can you design a simple study to compare the level of conformity in Science students with PE students? What would the independent variable (IV) be? What experimental design would you use? You will need a measure of conformity to form your dependent variable (DV).

For more on research methods, see Chapter 7.

Figure 1.14 Who conforms more?

RESEARCH IN FOCUS

1 Bond & Smith (1996) performed a meta-analysis of Asch-type studies. What is a meta-analysis?
2 Bond & Smith found a positive correlation between conformity rates and the size of the majority influence. Explain how a positive correlation differs from a negative correlation.
3 Give one strength and one weakness of correlations.
4 What kind of graph would correlational data be plotted on?
5 Asch's variations, performed to identify important variables involved in conformity, involved the use of controlled conditions. What are controlled conditions and why are they used in experiments?

For information on research methods, see Chapter 7.

PSYCHOLOGY IN THE REAL WORLD

Figure 1.15 Individuals are heavily influenced by what peers think of products – advertisers use this as a form of NSI to get us to buy things!

Advertisers often use a knowledge of conformity to increase sales. One useful technique is the 'bandwagon effect', which focuses on the idea that individuals decide what to buy based on what their peers recommend, due to a need to fit in. If you feel everyone in a desirable social group has a product, such as a certain type of phone, then buying that type of phone will make you feel that you will be accepted into that group. Supporting evidence for this form of NSI comes from a Neilson Company study (2009) that surveyed 25,000 people from 50 countries and found that 90 per cent trusted their peers' opinions of products, significantly more than the 69 per cent who trusted media recommendations.

STRENGTHEN YOUR LEARNING

1 In relation to conformity what are:
   (i) individual variables
   (ii) situational variables?
2 Does increasing the size of a group always lead to greater conformity? Explain your answer.
3 What happens to conformity rates when majority influence isn't unanimous? What is the important factor here?
4 Why does conformity increase as task difficulty increases?
5 Why is conformity stronger when individuals identify with members of a group?
6 How might giving public and private answers affect conformity rates?
7 How can social norms affect conformity?
8 Do females or males generally conform more? Explain your answer.
9 How can mood affect conformity levels?
10 Explain why people from different cultures are thought to conform to different levels.

1.4 Conformity to social roles

Each social situation has its own social norms, an expected ways for individuals to behave, which will vary from situation to situation – for example, joining the back of a queue when arriving at the till in a shop. Individuals learn how to behave by looking at the **social roles** other people play in such situations and then conforming to them. These learned social roles become like internal mental scripts, allowing individuals to behave appropriately in different settings.

Conformity to social roles therefore involves *identification*, which is stronger than compliance, involving both public and private acceptance of the behaviour and attitudes exhibited.

Conformity to social roles isn't as strong as internalisation though, as individuals adopt different social roles for different social situations and only conform to particular roles whilst in those particular social situations. With each social role adopted, behaviour changes to fit the social norms of that situation, so as an individual moves to another social situation, their behaviour will change to suit the new social norms, played out through a different social role.

Conformity to social roles is therefore a useful way of understanding and predicting social behaviour, which brings a reassuring sense of order to our social interactions.

Philip Zimbardo's 1973 prison simulation study perfectly illustrates the role of social roles in conformity.

....

KEY TERM

Social roles – the parts individuals play as members of a social group, which meet the expectations of that situation

---

CLASSIC RESEARCH

A study of prisoners and guards in a simulated prison – Craig Haney, Curtis Banks, Philip Zimbardo (1973)

Figure 1.16 Zimbardo's study showed how people conform readily to social roles

Zimbardo's study was an attempt to understand the brutal and dehumanising behaviour found in prisons and reported on a regular basis in the American media. Two widely differing explanations were to be explored (see page 27). Firstly, there was the dispositional hypothesis that the violence and degradation of prisons was due to the 'nature' of the people found within the prison system – basically, that both guards and prisoners were 'bad seeds' possessed of sadistic, aggressive characteristics, which naturally led to endless brutality. Secondly, there was the situational hypothesis that saw violence and degradation as a product of 'the prison soil', the interactions between environmental factors that supported such behaviour – in essence that the brutalising and dehumanising conditions of prison led to the brutal behaviour of all concerned. To separate the effects of the prison environment from those within the prison system, Zimbardo built a mock prison that used 'average' people with no record of violence or criminality to play both prisoners and guards – roles that were determined completely randomly. If no brutality occurred, the dispositional hypothesis would be supported, but if brutality was seen, then it must be situational factors that were driving normal, law-abiding people to such behaviour.

Aims

● To investigate the extent to which people would conform to the roles of guard and prisoner in a role-playing simulation of prison life.
● To test the *dispositional* versus *situational* hypotheses that saw prison violence as either due to the sadistic personalities of guards and prisoners, or to the brutal conditions of the prison environment.

Method

1 75 male university students responded to a newspaper advertisement asking for volunteers for a study of prison life paying $15 a day. 21 students rated as the most physically and mentally stable, mature and free from anti-social and criminal tendencies were used (10 as guards and 11 as prisoners). Selection as to who would be guards and who would be prisoners was on a random basis. All participants initially expressed a desire to be prisoners. Zimbardo himself played the role of the prison superintendent.

2 The basement of the psychology department at Stanford University was converted into a mock prison and the experience was made as realistic as possible, with the prisoners being arrested by the real local police and then fingerprinted, stripped and deloused. **Dehumanisation** (the removal of individual identity) was increased by prisoners wearing numbered smocks, nylon stocking caps (to simulate shaved heads) and a chain around one ankle. Guards wore khaki uniforms, reflective sunglasses (to prevent eye-contact) and were issued with handcuffs, keys and truncheons (though physical punishment was not permitted).

3 9 prisoners were placed 3 to a cell and a regular routine of shifts, meal times etc. was established, as well as visiting times, a parole and disciplinary board, and a prison chaplain. The study was planned to run for two weeks.

Findings

1 Both guards and prisoners settled quickly into their social roles. After an initial prisoner 'rebellion' was crushed, dehumanisation was increasingly apparent with the guards becoming ever more sadistic, taunting the prisoners and giving them meaningless, boring tasks to do, while the prisoners became submissive and unquestioning of the guards' behaviour. Some prisoners sided with the guards against any prisoners who dared to protest. **De-individuation** was noticeable by the prisoners referring to each other and themselves by their prison numbers instead of their names.

2 After 36 hours, one prisoner was released because of fits of crying and rage. Three more prisoners developed similar symptoms and were released on successive days. A fifth prisoner developed a severe rash when his parole was denied.

3 Scheduled to run for 14 days, the study was stopped after 6 days when Zimbardo realised the extent of the harm that was occurring, and the increasingly aggressive nature of the guards' behaviour. The remaining prisoners were delighted at their sudden good fortune, while the guards were upset by Zimbardo's decision.

4 In later interviews, both guards and prisoners said they were surprised at the uncharacteristic behaviours they had shown.

Conclusions

The situational hypothesis is favoured over the dispositional hypothesis, as none of the participants had ever shown such character traits or behaviour before the study. It was the environment of the mock prison and the social roles that the participants had to play that led to their uncharacteristic behaviour.

Individuals conform readily to the social roles demanded of a situation, even when such roles override an individual's moral beliefs about their personal behaviour.

Both guards and prisoners demonstrated social roles gained from media sources (e.g. prison films) and learned models of social power (e.g. parent–child, teacher–student).

Evaluation

Individual differences are important, as not all guards behaved brutally. Some were hard but fair; some were brutal; others rarely exerted control over the prisoners. Prisoner behaviour was not identical either.

Zimbardo hoped his research would lead to beneficial reforms within the prison system. Beneficial reforms in the way prisoners were treated, especially juveniles, did initially occur. However, Zimbardo regards his study as a failure in the sense that prison conditions in the USA are now even worse than when he performed his study.

KEY TERMS

De-individuation – a state in which individuals have lower self-awareness and a weaker sense of personal responsibility for their actions. This may result from the relative anonymity of being part of a crowd

Dehumanisation – degrading people by lessening of their human qualities

ON THE WEB

Listen to a BBC Radio 4 programme about Zimbardo's prison simulation study as part of the *Mind Changers* series:

www.bbc.co.uk/programmes/b008crhv

A half-hour BBC television programme about Zimbardo's prison simulation study, including interviews with participants, can be seen on YouTube if you search for 'The Stanford Prison Experiment'.

NB Zimbardo's study contains elements of both conformity and obedience, so take care to use only the aspects that relate to conformity to social roles when answering questions.

RESEARCH IN FOCUS

1 Zimbardo used a self-selected sample.
   (i) Explain how this was achieved.
   (ii) Give one strength and one weakness of self-selected sampling.
2 In Zimbardo's study, guards and prisoners were selected by random sampling.
   (i) What is random sampling?
   (ii) How would it be achieved?
   (iii) Give one strength and one weakness of random sampling.
3 Zimbardo's study is not an experiment. What research method was used?
4 In what ways can Zimbardo's study be considered unethical? Justify your answer.

For information on research methods, see Chapter 7.

STRENGTHEN YOUR LEARNING

1 What are:
   (i) social roles
   (ii) social norms?
2 Why are different social roles adopted for different social situations?
3 Explain why conformity to social roles involves identification, but not internalisation.
4 Why, in Zimbardo's study, if no brutality had occurred, would the dispositional hypothesis have been supported?

ASSESSMENT CHECK

1 The following descriptions relate to conformity.

   A Looking to the group for information as to the correct behaviour

   B Going along with a group because we accept their belief system as our own

   C Going along with a group, even though privately we do not agree with them

   D Conforming to group norms publicly and privately, but only temporarily, as conformity is not maintained outside the presence of the group

   Copy and complete the table below by writing which description, A, B, C or D, describes which type of conformity. One statement will be left over. **[3 marks]**

Type of conformity	Description
Compliance	
Internalisation	
Identification	

2 Explain what is meant by identification. Give a real-life example. **[3 marks]**

3 Describe and evaluate explanations of conformity. **[16 marks]**

4 Discuss conformity to social roles. **[12 marks]**

5 **a)** Outline the aims and findings of one study of conformity to social roles. **[4 marks]**

   b) Describe one ethical issue associated with this study. **[2 marks]**

6 Zimbardo's prison simulation study uses a participant observation study method. Give one strength and one weakness of this type of study. **[2 + 2 marks]**

7 Priti has recently moved to a new school and has found it hard to make new friends, but she noticed that many fellow students support the local football team, Vale City. She bought a replica shirt of the team, even though she had little knowledge of or interest in football, and on wearing the shirt to school, soon found people being friendly to her and including her in their activities.

   a) What kind of conformity is being exhibited in the above passage? **[1 mark]**

   b) Refer to features of the passage to justify your answer. **[3 marks]**

8 Research studies of conformity generally involve experiments. Describe and evaluate the experimental method. **[6 marks]**

1.5 Obedience and the work of Milgram

Obedience

> *'I was only following orders.'*
> Adolf Eichmann (1961)

Obedience is a type of social influence defined as complying with the demands of an authority figure. Obedience generally has a positive influence, as society could not operate in an effective manner unless rules and laws are obeyed and people in authority are acknowledged as having the right to give orders.

However, obedience can also have negative consequences. During the Second World War, under the Nazis, some German citizens unquestioningly followed orders that saw the mass murder of millions of people like the Jews, the Gypsies and the disabled – an event that became known as the Holocaust. The American psychologist Stanley Milgram had a personal interest that motivated him to seek explanations for these despicable acts. Milgram came from a working-class, New York Jewish family that had fled Europe for America and escaped the Holocaust. He wanted to know whether Germans have a different personality that led them to blindly obey and commit acts of murder without question, or whether people are generally more obedient than they would care to believe. If Hitler and the Nazis had been a British phenomenon, would we have obeyed to the same extent? Milgram had been a student of Asch, whom he sought advice from in designing his classic obedience study.

As Milgram conducted his study, Adolf Eichmann, the Nazi responsible for carrying out *die Endlösung* (the Final Solution), the genocide of millions in the concentration camps, was abducted by Israeli secret service agents in Argentina and taken to Jerusalem to stand trial. Hannah Arendt, in her book *Eichmann in Jerusalem* (1963), famously reported on the *banality* (ordinariness) *of evil* – of how when Eichmann was led into court, instead of the expected inhuman monster, people were confronted by a mild-mannered, likeable man, who had 'merely been doing his job'. His defence for his behaviour was repeatedly to say 'I was only following orders.' A few days after Milgram completed his study, Eichmann was executed. Milgram had originally wanted to conduct his study in Germany after performing what was intended as a pilot study at Yale University. However, the results of this were so dramatic, there was no need.

KEY TERM

Obedience – complying with the demands of an authority figure

Figure 1.17 Obedience is seen as necessary for safety to be maintained

Figure 1.18 Adolf Eichmann: monster or obedient servant?

Figure 1.19 The Nazis dehumanized Jewish people, seeing them as sub-human

Behavioural study of obedience – Stanley Milgram (1963)

Figure 1.20 Stanley Milgram's shock generator

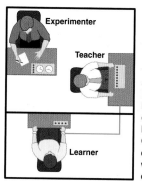

'I observed a mature and initially poised businessman enter the laboratory smiling and confident. Within 20 minutes he was reduced to a twitching, stuttering wreck, who was rapidly approaching nervous collapse. He constantly pulled on his ear lobe, and twisted his hands. At one point he pushed his fist into his forehead and muttered "Oh God, let's stop it". And yet he continued to respond to every word of the experimenter, and obeyed to the end.'

Figure 1.22 The Milgram experiment set up

Aims

- To test the 'Germans are different' hypothesis, which claimed that Germans are highly obedient and that Adolf Hitler could not have exterminated the Jewish people and other minority groups in the 1930s and 1940s without the unquestioning co-operation of the German population.
- To see if individuals would obey the orders of an authority figure that incurred negative consequences and went against one's moral code.

Procedure

1 40 American males aged 20–50 years responded to a newspaper advertisement to volunteer for a study of memory and learning at Yale University Psychology Department. They were met by a confederate experimenter wearing a grey lab coat (to give him the appearance of authority), who was actually a biology teacher. He introduced them to Mr Wallace, a confederate participant, a gentle, harmless looking man in his late 50s. The participants were told that the experiment concerned the effects of punishment on learning and that they would be either a 'teacher' or a 'learner', with the roles determined randomly. In fact this was rigged; Mr Wallace was always the learner and the real participant was always the teacher.

2 The experimenter explained that punishments would involve increasingly severe electric shocks. All three

went into an adjoining room, where the experimenter strapped a consenting Mr Wallace into a chair with his arms attached to electrodes. The teacher was told to give shocks through a shock generator in the next room. This generator had a row of switches each marked with a voltage level. The first switch was labelled '15 volts' and the verbal description 'slight shock'. Each switch gave a shock 15 volts higher than the one before, up to a maximum 450 volts, marked 'XXX'. The real participant received a real shock of 45 volts to convince him that everything was authentic.

3 Participants then read out a series of paired-associate word tasks, to which they received a pre-recorded series of verbal answers from the learner, with the real participant believing these to be genuine responses. The teacher was told by the experimenter to give a shock each time Mr Wallace got an answer wrong. His answers were given by him supposedly switching on one of four lights located above the shock generator. With each successive mistake, the teacher gave the next highest shock, 15 volts higher than the previous one.

4 At 150 volts the learner began to protest and demanded to be released; before this he had been quite willing to take part. These protests became more insistent and at 300 volts he refused to answer any more questions and said he has heart problems that are starting to bother him. At 315 volts he screamed loudly and from 330 volts was heard no more. Anytime the teacher seemed reluctant to continue, he was encouraged to go on through a series of verbal prods, such as 'the experiment requires you continue' and 'you have no choice, you must go on'. If the teacher questioned the procedure, he was told that the shocks will not cause any lasting tissue damage and was also instructed to keep shocking Mr Wallace if he stopped answering.

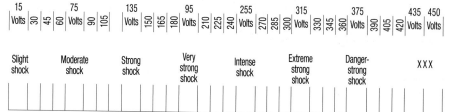

Figure 1.21 The levels of electric shock used in the Milgram experiments

Findings

1 Quantitative results – obedience was measured as the percentage of participants giving shocks up to the maximum 450 volts. In the main version of the experiment the obedience rate was 62.5 per cent (25 out of 40 participants). An earlier 'remote victim' version with no pre-recorded responses, but the victim pounding on the walls instead, gained an obedience rate of 65 per cent (26 out of 40 participants). 100 per cent of participants continued up to at least 300 volts.

2 Qualitative results – many participants showed distress, such as twitching, sweating or giggling nervously, digging their nails into their flesh and verbally attacking the experimenter. Three participants had uncontrollable seizures. Some participants showed little if any signs of discomfort, instead concentrating dutifully on what they were doing.

Conclusions

The 'Germans are different' hypothesis is clearly false – Milgram's participants were 40 'ordinary' Americans. Their high level of obedience showed that people obey those regarded as authority figures. If we had lived in Nazi Germany in the 1930s, we might have acted just as obediently. The results suggest that obeying those in authority is normal behaviour in a hierarchically organised society. We will obey orders that distress us and go against our moral code.

Evaluation

The **Milgram paradigm** – Milgram established the basic method, or paradigm, for studying obedience, which was adopted by many subsequent researchers.

It was intended as a pilot study – it is more useful to consider the research inspired by Milgram's study than the study itself. Milgram was so astounded by the results that he subsequently conducted 19 variations of the study, each time varying one aspect of the procedure, to try and identify the reasons why people were so obedient.

Practical application – it was hoped that Milgram's findings would help form strategies to reduce destructive blind obedience. Unfortunately, not much has changed since 1963; horrendous crimes are still committed by people operating under the excuse of 'simply following orders'.

Type of study – most people presume that Milgram's study is an experiment, indeed Milgram referred to it as such. However, there is no independent variable and in reality it is more of a controlled observation. It can, however, be considered an experiment if Milgram's variations of his study are considered. The independent variable (IV) then becomes which particular variation a participant performs, for example, having the experimenter not present in the room, as opposed to him being in the room.

INCREASE YOUR KNOWLEDGE

Milgram's work into obedience can help explain the abuse of Iraqi prisoners by US troops in the Abu Ghraib prison in Iraq in 2004. Several stages of abuse were involved. Firstly, *gradual commitment*, where initial abuses were minor, but paved the way for the acceptance of more serious abuse. This was similar to the initial shocks in Milgram's study only being minor ones and only increasing in small 15-volt increments. Secondly, *senior role*, where low-ranking troops, like the teacher in Milgram's study, were given important roles in controlling prisoners. Thirdly, *dehumanisation*, where the prisoners were degraded, making it easier to suspend morality and abuse them.

Figure 1.23 Lynndie England arrives at her trial for mistreatment of prisoners in Abu Ghraib

STRENGTHEN YOUR LEARNING

1 Define obedience.
2 What is meant by the Milgram paradigm?
3 What percentage of participants gave the maximum 450 volt shocks in Milgram's study?
4 Why can the 'Germans are different' hypothesis be rejected?
5 What practical application did Milgram hope would come from his study? Was this hope realised?

KEY TERM

Milgram paradigm – experimental procedure devised by Stanley Milgram for measuring obedience rates

To read an account of what it was like to be one of the 40 original participants, go to:

www.jewishcurrents.org/2004-jan-dimow.htm

Here you will find the personal account of Joseph Dimow.

You can also find a detailed account of Milgram's life and work at:

www.psychologytoday.com/ articles/200203/the-man-who-shocked-the-world

An excellent modern day replication of Milgram's study can be seen on YouTube if you search for 'Milgram's Obedience to Authority Experiment'.

A video of Milgram's actual study, including commentary from Milgram himself can be seen on YouTube if you search for 'Milgram Obedience Study'.

Figure 1.24 Joseph Dimow

RESEARCH IN FOCUS

1   Milgram's study produced both quantitative and qualitative data. What is the difference between these two forms of data?
2   Give one example of quantitative and qualitative data from Milgram's study.
3   Milgram's study was intended as a pilot study.
    (i) What is a pilot study?
    (ii) Why are pilot studies conducted?
4   Why is Milgram's original study not actually an experiment? At what point does his study become an experiment?

For information on research methods, see Chapter 7.

Ethical considerations

Milgram's study raised several ethical issues and indeed Milgram had his membership of the American Psychological Association (APA) suspended after his research was published. His work though was eventually ruled ethically acceptable, and he won a major award for it. Maybe what upset people was not the abuse of ethics, but the upsetting results that went against the accepted ideas of free will and personal responsibility for one's behaviour. It was the work of Milgram and similar psychologists, like Asch, which helped to identify the ethical issues that psychologists must consider when planning and conducting research. Without these studies of social influence, there would not be ethical codes and guidelines. Let us now consider the arguments for and against Milgram's study being unethical. (See also Burger (2009), page 24, for an attempt to conduct Milgram's paradigm in a more ethical manner.)

Psychological harm

For: Milgram is accused of exposing his participants to severe stress, which is supported by the extreme physical reactions many participants exhibited (three had seizures).

Against: Only 2 per cent had any regrets about being involved and 74 per cent thought that they had learned something useful about themselves. A thorough debriefing was carried out where participants met the unharmed learner and, a year later, all 40 participants received psychiatric assessments, none showing any signs of long-term damage. Therefore, the study can be justified by recourse to a cost–benefit analysis, where the short-term damage (stress reactions) is outweighed by the lack of long-term damage and the valuable results obtained.

For: However, Perry (2012) claims that debriefing of subsequent participants (Milgram eventually tested nearly 3,000 participants) didn't always occur, as Milgram was worried about news of the study becoming common knowledge before he finished his work. He believed a debriefing might confound his results, and that this was enough of a reason to deny debriefing directly after the experiment ended.

For: Baumrind (1964) accused Milgram of abusing his participants' rights and feelings.

Against: Baumrind's criticism assumes that the experimental outcome was *expected*. In fact, Milgram was surprised by the high obedience rate. Prior to the experiment, Milgram asked 40 psychiatrists what percentage of people would obey up to 450 volts. Their prediction was only 1 per cent.

Deception/informed consent

For: Milgram did deceive his participants. He said that the study was concerned with memory and learning. Only after volunteers had agreed to take part were the electric shocks mentioned. Also, Mr Wallace was an actor who never actually received any electric shocks and the researcher, Mr. Williams, was also a confederate. Therefore, participants could not give informed consent – they volunteered without knowing the true purpose or procedure.

Against: Milgram defended his use of deception by debriefing his participants. Also, deception was necessary if participants were to behave realistically – the participants had to believe they were real shocks; otherwise the results could not be generalised to real-life situations.

Right to withdraw

For: No explicit right to withdraw was given to the participants before the study started and indeed attempts to withdraw were met with the verbal prods that encouraged them to continue.

Against: Milgram argued that participants did have the right to withdraw, as 35 per cent of them exercised this option and refused to carry on.

Inducement to take part

For: The advert asking for volunteers for the study stated that they would be paid $4 each for taking part (plus 50 cents car fare), which may have led participants to believe they had to finish the study, i.e. give the shocks in order to receive the money.

Against: The advert also stated that monies would be paid upon arrival at the laboratory and no participant ever claimed they thought they had to obey to get paid.

Methodological criticisms

Several methodological criticisms have been made about Milgram's study concerning both how the study itself was conducted and the usefulness of the results it generated. Subsequent studies allow us to assess these criticisms.

Internal validity

Internal validity concerns the degree to which findings are attributable to the effect of the IV on the DV (see Research methods, page 259). Milgram's study would lack internal validity if participants didn't believe the shocks were real.

Orne and Holland (1968) criticised the internal validity of Milgram's study, as they believed participants delivered the shocks because they knew they were not real. However, 75 per cent of participants in post-study interviews said they believed them to be real. The extreme physical responses of many of the participants also suggest they believed them to be real. However, Perry (2012) traced as many original participants as she could and claimed the true figure was only about 50 per cent.

External validity

Can the results of Milgram's study be generalised beyond the experimental setting? The findings have been criticised in terms of whether they are representative of females, other cultures, people of today, and whether the results relate to real-life settings. Let us examine each of these in turn:

Androcentrism

As only males were used in Milgram's study, the accusation is that the results cannot be generalised to females. Many people would imagine that females would be much less obedient to orders with destructive consequences, yet research often surprisingly suggests that the opposite is indeed true. Maybe females can be more obedient and unquestioning of orders because their gender roles may dictate that they be more submissive, especially to assertive males.

Research

Sheridan & King (1972) got male and female participants to give real electric shocks to a puppy every time it responded to a command incorrectly, participants believing the shocks increased by 15 volts each time. The shocks were actually only mild ones (though severe enough to make the puppies jump and howl). Eventually, an undetectable anaesthetic gas was pumped in to render the puppy unconscious,

Figure 1.25 Gina Perry, in her book *Behind the shock machine*, has cast doubts on several of Milgram's claims

KEY TERM

Androcentrism – a bias in psychological research in which a male perspective is over-emphasised at the expense of a female one

making the participants think they had killed it. Although visibly upset, 54 per cent of males and 100 per cent of the females obeyed up to an apparent 450 volts, supporting the idea that Milgram's study was androcentric, as females can be more obedient.

Cultural bias

As Milgram's study only used American participants, the results can be said to be not necessarily generalisable to people of other cultures. Indeed, research has backed up this criticism, with varying levels of obedience found between different cultures. It may be that different cultures obey to different levels, because of cultural differences regarding authority.

Research

Meeus & Raaijimakers (1986) found the highest recorded obedience level with the Milgram paradigm of 90 per cent in Spanish participants, while Kilham & Mann (1974) used the Milgram paradigm to find the lowest cultural obedience rate of 28 per cent among Australians. This backs up the idea of obedience levels reflecting cultural attitudes to authority, as Australians have a traditionally negative view of authority. (Interestingly, Mantell (1971) used the Milgram paradigm to find a relatively high obedience rate of 80 per cent in Germany.)

Historical validity

It has been suggested that the high rate of obedience found in the Milgram study was a product of American culture being very authoritarian and obedient during the early 1960s, and, as such, doesn't reflect obedience levels today. Burger (2009) used an adaptation of the procedure to investigate whether this criticism is valid (see Contemporary research, page 24).

Ecological validity

Milgram's paradigm has been criticised for how unrepresentative it is of real-life occurrences (giving electric shocks to people). Hofling *et al.* (1966) performed a study to see if this was true (see Classic research, page 25).

INCREASE YOUR KNOWLEDGE

Milgram's shock machine still exists. It is kept at the Archives of the History of American Psychology at the University of Akron. For many years, it was part of a travelling psychology exhibit created by the American Psychological Association.

In 1949, at James Monroe High School in the Bronx, a tough 'ghetto' area of New York, two boys sat next to each other in class. One was Stanley Milgram and the other was Philip Zimbardo. Both had dreams of escaping the ghetto and doing something worthwhile with their lives and both went on to become world-renowned psychologists – Milgram for his obedience study and Zimbardo (1971) for his prison simulation study.

The man who played the learner in Milgram's original study suffered a heart attack three years later and was resuscitated by someone who had been a teacher in the study. Unfortunately, the man still died. Milgram himself would die aged just 51 in 1984 after his fifth heart attack.

Figure 1.26 James Monroe High School, where both Zimbardo and Milgram pledged to do something worthwhile with their lives

Replicating Milgram: Would people still obey today? – Jerry Burger (2009)

Figure 1.27 Jerry Burger has attempted to replicate Milgram's study in an ethically acceptable way

Milgram's study is one of the most famous psychology experiments ever undertaken, but would similar results be found today? Milgram's study would also be unethical under present-day guidelines; however, Burger developed a version of Milgram's procedure that addressed ethical concerns, so that a comparison could be made between obedience rates in the 1960s and now.

Aim

To develop a variation of Milgram's procedures allowing comparison with the original investigation while protecting the well-being of participants.

Procedure

Most of Milgram's procedure was followed, including the words used in the memory test and the experimenter's lab coat. However, important changes were made.

1 No one with knowledge of Milgram's study was used and the maximum apparent shock was 150 volts, the level at which the learner first cries in pain, in order to protect participants from intense stress.

2 A two-step screening process for participants was used to exclude any who might react negatively. No one with a history of mental problems or stress reactions was accepted. This excluded 38 per cent of potential participants.

3 Participants were told three times they could withdraw at any time and received only a 15-volt real shock, as opposed to the 45 volts applied in Milgram's study.

4 The experimenter was a clinical psychologist who could stop the procedure at any sign of excessive stress.

5 70 male and female participants were used. The relevant ethical monitoring body approved the procedure.

Findings

Burger found an obedience rate of 70 per cent, with no difference between male and female obedience rates. Another condition, where a second defiant confederate teacher was introduced, failed to reduce obedience significantly, unlike Milgram's findings.

Conclusions

It is possible to replicate Milgram's study in a fashion non-harmful to participants. Obedience rates have not changed dramatically in the 50-odd years since Milgram's study.

Evaluation

Burger's technique permits obedience research to be conducted that has not been possible for decades.

Burger's efforts to improve the ethics of the study are uncertain in their effectiveness and pose impractical demands.

The different procedures used by Milgram and Burger do not allow a clear comparison of results.

The study highlights the difficulties of extending research on destructive obedience in the context of contemporary ethical guidelines.

ON THE WEB

You can watch a 35-minute ABC television programme about Jerry Burger's study, including extensive footage from the study, if you search YouTube for 'ABC Milgram remake'.

There's also an in-depth review of the study from the American Psychological Association Monitor at:

www.apa.org/monitor/2009/05/ethics.html

An experimental study into the nurse–physician relationship – Charles Hofling *et al.* (1966)

Figure 1.28 Would nurses obey hospital rules or the commands of a doctor?

A number of naturalistic obedience studies in real-life settings have been carried out, but Hofling's study, carried out as part of a real hospital's normal routine, is significant because of its alarming findings.

Aim

To see whether nurses would obey orders from an unknown doctor to such an extent that there would be risk of harm.

Procedure

A confederate 'Dr Smith', allegedly from the psychiatric department, instructed 22 nurses individually by phone to give his patient 'Mr Jones' 20 mg of an unfamiliar drug called Astrofen (which was actually a sugar pill). Dr Smith was in a hurry and would sign the authorisation form later on. The label on the box stated the maximum daily dose was 10 mg. So if a nurse obeyed instructions, she would be giving twice the maximum dose. Also, hospital rules required doctors to sign authorisations before medication was given. Another rule demanded that nurses should be certain anyone giving medical instructions was a genuine doctor.

Findings

Of the 22 nurses, 21 (95.4 per cent) obeyed without hesitation. A control group of 22 nurses were asked what they *would have done* in that situation: 21 said they would not have obeyed without authorisation, or exceed the maximum dose.

Conclusions

Hofling *et al.* concluded that the power and authority of doctors was a greater influence on the nurses' behaviour than basic hospital rules. Also, that what people *say* they would do and what they *actually* do, can be very different.

Evaluation

Hofling's study suggests that nurses and institutional staff should have special training in following rules rather than orders from authority figures.

Hofling's study seems relevant to real-life settings. However, Rank & Jacobsen (1977) reported that the drug was unfamiliar to nurses and that they had not been allowed to consult with each other, as was normal practice. When a familiar drug, Valium, was used, and they were allowed to speak to their peers, only two out of 18 nurses (11 per cent) obeyed, suggesting that Hofling's study may not have external validity after all.

STRENGTHEN YOUR LEARNING

1 Why might Milgram's study lack internal validity? Does the evidence suggest it does?

2 In what ways might Milgram's study lack external validity? What does the evidence suggest?

YOU ARE THE RESEARCHER

A major problem with obedience studies is often their lack of relevance to real-life situations. However, one way of overcoming this difficulty is to carry out the following study looking at people's obedience rates in everyday life. You will need two signs with the same wording: *Use other bench. By order.* One sign should be printed professionally to give it an air of authority, and the other should be poorly made with scruffy writing.

Place one sign on a bench in an area where there are other benches people can use, and count how many people obey or disobey the sign in a given time period. If several people approach the bench simultaneously, you only count the behaviour of the first person, as the others may be influenced by the first person's actions. Repeat the procedure using the scruffy sign. If people do obey authority, more people should obey the neat sign. If you have not got suitable benches, then use two adjoining doors and have signs saying: *Please use other door.*

For more on research methods, see Chapter 7.

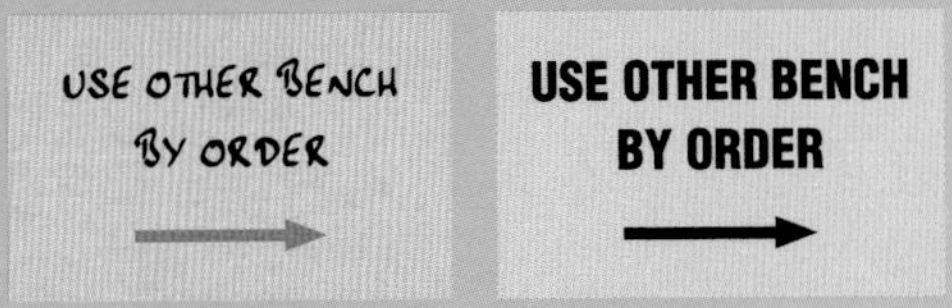

USE OTHER BENCH
BY ORDER

**USE OTHER BENCH
BY ORDER**

Figure 1.29 Which of these signs are you more likely to obey?

IN THE NEWS

Ψ The Psychological Enquirer

Plane crash kills 18: co-pilot dared not disobey captain

Figure 1.30 The town of Hibbing

On the 3rd of December 2003 the New York Times reported how Northwest Airlink Flight 5719 descended too quickly and crashed before it hit the runway in Hibbing, Minnesota. All 18 people on board died. The aircraft struck the top of a tree, continued for 634 feet, and then struck a group of aspen trees. Finally, the plane collided with two ridges and came to rest inverted and lying on its right side. The crash site was so isolated and the night so dark and thick with fog and freezing drizzle that no one saw the plane hit the side of the hill.

Investigators recovered the plane's cockpit voice recorder, which would turn out to be a crucial piece of evidence, for, rather than mechanical failure, the tragedy would prove to be a result of obedience to authority.

Investigators found that the captain had flown the plane inappropriately and given incorrect instructions, but had not been challenged in doing so by his co-pilot, a new probationary employee who knew that to challenge his captain could have a detrimental effect on his career. Further investigation revealed that other co-pilots had not previously reported that the captain often issued irregular commands, violated company policies by sleeping inflight and also flew with mechanical irregularities.

Why would co-pilots put passengers and themselves in such danger by not challenging the captain's behaviour and orders? Because he was perceived as a legitimate authority figure that his co-pilots had been trained to obey without question. This was not an isolated incident; Tarnow (2000) reported that a major contributory factor in 80 per cent of air traffic accidents was the power stemming from the captain's absolute authority, which led to co-pilots feeling unable to challenge wrong decisions. Similar disastrous consequences have occurred in other institutional settings for similar reasons (see the tragedy of Wayne Jowett, below). Through psychological research, such as that by Milgram (1963), obedience to authority has become better understood, leading to the formation of practical applications that may prevent such disasters occurring in the future.

PSYCHOLOGY IN THE REAL WORLD

Tragic incidents, like the crash of Northwest Airlink Flight 5719 (see 'In the News', above), caused through wrongful obedience to authority figures are all too common. In 2001, 18-year-old Wayne Jowett, on remission from leukaemia, died when a cancer drug was wrongly injected into his spine instead of a vein. He died one month later from creeping

Figure 1.31 Wayne Jowett

paralysis after being in such pain it sometimes took six nurses to hold him down. A junior doctor correctly injected a first drug, Cytosine, into Wayne's spine and was surprised when he was passed a second syringe of Vincristine and told to inject it by a more senior doctor into the boy's spine, as he was aware this wasn't the correct procedure. However, as with the nurses in Hofling's study (see page 25), he didn't challenge the decision on the assumption the more senior doctor knew what he was doing. In such institutional settings, there is a clear command structure and an expectation of unquestioning obedience, which can lead to terrible mistakes. Staff members need to be trained to follow official procedures, not authority figures, and to have confidence to challenge authority figures' commands if they believe them to be wrong or potentially harmful. As part of their training, aeroplane co-pilots now undergo simulations where captains issue them with wrongful orders, so that they are fully familiar with how to resist such instructions.

1.6 Explanations for obedience

Explanations of obedience attempt to give reasons as to why people obey. Such explanations include *situational* ones, which focus on environmental factors associated with obedience, as well as *dispositional* ones, which focus instead on personality characteristics that influence people to obey. Explanations do not necessarily work in isolation to each other, so it may well be that two or more explanations can be combined together to show why an individual obeys in a given situation.

The agentic state

Milgram (1974) proposed the idea of the agency theory, which argues that we are socialised from an early age to learn that obedience to rules is necessary to keep stability within society. However, in order to achieve this, an individual has to give up some of their free will (the ability to have conscious control over thoughts and actions). When an individual does have control and acts according to their own wishes, they are said to be in an **autonomous state** and thus see themselves as personally responsible for their actions. However, when an individual obeys an authority figure they give up some free will and enter an **agentic state**, where they see themselves as an agent of the authority figure giving the order. It is therefore the authority figure who is seen as responsible for the consequences of the individual's actions. In this way, a person becomes de-individuated, losing their sense of individuality, and so may obey orders that go against their moral code, because they don't see themselves as responsible for their behaviour.

The agency theory therefore sees obedience as occurring in hierarchical social systems (systems with people having different ranks to each other), where individuals will act as agents for and so obey those of perceived higher ranks than themselves. Adolf Eichmann, the Nazi responsible for the extermination of millions during the Second World War (see page 17), saw himself as in the agentic state with his defence that he was 'only following orders' – in other words, that he was merely complying with the orders of a higher-ranked authority than himself, and so was not himself responsible for the genocide.

KEY TERMS

Autonomous state – opposite side of the agentic state, where individuals are seen as personally responsible for their actions

Agentic state – the way in which an individual may obey an order, perhaps to do something that they see as 'wrong', because the individual hands over the responsibility for the outcome of the action to the authority figure. The individual sees themselves as acting as an agent for the authority figure and therefore does not feel responsible

Research

Milgram (1974) reported that in a 'remote authority' variation of his procedure when the confederate researcher wasn't in the same room as the teacher, but gave orders on a telephone link, obedience declined from 62.5 per cent to 20.5 per cent. This suggests participants were in the autonomous state and saw themselves as responsible for their actions.

Milgram (1963) reported that many participants in his study were under moral strain, as during debriefing many participants admitted they knew what they were doing was wrong (their physical reactions back this up too). However, they continued to obey, which suggests they were in an agentic state and felt they had to obey the orders of a higher-ranked authority figure.

Legitimacy of authority

Obedient individuals accept the power and status of authority figures to give orders; they are seen as being in charge. This again links to the agency theory that individuals are socialised to recognise the value of obedience to authority figures as helping to keep stability in society. From an early age, people experience examples of social roles relating to master and servant relationships, such as parent–child, teacher–student etc., where we learn that those higher in the social hierarchy should be obeyed. The emphasis here, therefore, is on doing one's perceived duty.

Research

Milgram (1963) reported that some participants in his study ignored the learner's apparent distress, showing little sign of harm themselves, but instead focused on following the procedure, for example by pressing the buttons properly. In this way, they could be seen to be doing their duty and thus recognising the **legitimate authority** of the researcher.

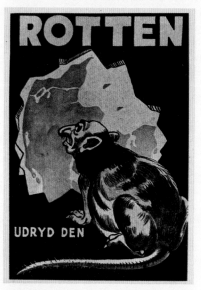

Figure 1.32 Nazi propaganda dehumanised Jewish people by portraying them as rats

INCREASE YOUR KNOWLEDGE

An additional explanation

Dehumanisation

This explanation argues that it is easier to obey orders that result in negative consequences if the recipients of the behaviour are first dehumanised – made lesser people in some way – so that they are perceived as somehow deserving of the treatment handed out to them. This also results in less moral strain being felt when carrying out such orders. The Nazis portrayed Jewish people as *Untermenschen* (subhuman) and themselves as *Übermenschen* (superior humans). They argued that inferior races were a threat to genetic purity and the natural superiority of the German Aryan race. Propaganda films of the time showed Jewish people as hordes of filthy rats invading German homes and spreading disease. Such dehumanisation made orders to murder Jews easier to obey. More recently, the massacre of hundreds of thousands of Tutsis by Hutus in the Rwandan civil war of 1994 can be seen in similar terms. The Hutus saw the Tutsis as *inyenzi*, or cockroaches – parasites that must be crushed. The resulting ethnic violence was made easier by this dehumanisation.

Milgram (1963) reported that some participants in his study made comments along the lines of '*That guy in there was so stupid he deserved to be shocked*', illustrating how dehumanisation can lessen the moral strain of obeying orders with destructive consequences.

1.7 Situational variables affecting obedience

The external explanation

Situational variables form an *external* explanation of obedience, where features of an environment (aspects of a situation) are seen as affecting obedience levels. Milgram's variations of his procedure, performed after his main study, identified several important situational factors.

Proximity

Proximity involves how aware individuals are of the consequences of their actions in obeying authority figures. When the physical distance between the teacher and the learner in Milgram's study was made closer, participants were less able to divorce themselves from the consequences of their actions and so obedience rates were lower. In a war situation, it could be argued that obeying an order to press a button from a remote location that releases a missile which kills thousands in a distant country is easier to do than obeying an order to shoot a single person standing next to you, where the consequences of your actions would be much plainer to see.

Figure 1.33 Proximity increases awareness of obeying an order: which of these orders to kill would be easier to comply with?

Research

Milgram (1974) found that when the teacher and learner were in the same room as each other, so that the teacher could see the learner's distress, obedience declined from 62.5 per cent to 40 per cent. When the teacher had to force the learner's hand onto an apparent shock plate, increasing the realisation of their actions, obedience fell further to 30 per cent. This illustrates the effect proximity has on obedience levels.

Location

The location of an environment can be relevant to the amount of perceived legitimate authority a person giving orders is seen to have. In locations that add to the perceived legitimacy of an authority figure, obedience rates will be higher. Obedience rates are often highest in institutionalised settings where obedience to authority figures is instilled into members. For example, in the army when a commanding officer orders a soldier to jump in the air, the expected response is 'how high?' not 'why?' It could be argued that a contributory factor to the high obedience rate seen in Milgram's study was the fact that the study took place at Yale University, an Ivy League, high-status institution.

Research

Milgram (1974) performed a variation of his study in an office block in a run-down part of town and found obedience dropped from 62.5 per cent to 47.5 per cent, which suggests the change in location from Yale University reduced the perceived legitimacy of the authority figure giving the orders, leading to a significant drop in the obedience rate.

Uniforms

The wearing of uniforms can give a perception of added legitimacy to authority figures when delivering orders, thus increasing obedience rates. In Milgram's experiment, the confederate researcher wore a lab coat to give him such an air of authority (he was also chosen for his tall height, which was thought to add to his status).

Research

Bickman (1974) found that when ordering people on a New York street to pick up rubbish, loan a coin to a stranger or move away from a bus stop, 19 per cent would obey his research assistant when he was dressed in civilian clothes, 14 per cent when dressed as a milkman, but 38 per cent when he wore a security guard's uniform. In a variation of the study, Bickman found people would even obey the guard when he walked away after giving the order, which suggests they obeyed not because they felt forced to do so, but because they believed he had legitimate authority.

The internal explanation

The dispositional explanation for obedience – the authoritarian personality

The **dispositional explanation** is an *internal* explanation, as the focus is on the idea that certain personality characteristics are associated with higher levels of obedience. This formed the basis of Milgram's research aim: to investigate whether Germans had a different personality type that made them unquestioningly obedient to authority figures.

The **authoritarian personality** was first proposed by Fromm (1941) as an attempt to explain those holding right-wing, conservative views and is a personality type characterised by a belief in absolute obedience, submission to authority and domination of minorities. It is probably best summed up by the phrase 'Might is right'. Adorno *et al.* (1950) saw people of this type as having insecurities that led them to be hostile to non-conventional people and having a belief in a need for power and toughness, which leads them to be highly obedient to authority figures. Adorno additionally saw the personality type as being shaped in early childhood by hierarchical, authoritarian parenting. To measure an individual's degree of authoritarian personality, Adorno constructed the F-scale questionnaire, which has 30 questions assessing nine personality dimensions. (The 'F' stands for 'fascist'.)

More recently, Jost *et al.* (2003) have claimed that the authoritarian personality is motivated by thought processes which underpin a desire to reduce the fears and anxieties that social change brings. Strict obedience to authority is seen as helping to prevent disruptive social change.

Research

Zillmer *et al.* (1995) reported that sixteen Nazi war criminals scored highly on three of the F-scale dimensions, but not all nine (as was expected), giving only limited support for the concept.

Elms & Milgram (1966) found that participants in Milgram's study, who were highly obedient, were significantly more authoritarian on the F-scale than disobedient participants, supporting the idea of a link between authoritarian personality type and obedience. Further support came from Altemeyer

Figure 1.34 Uniforms give a sense of legitimacy to authority

(1988) who reported that participants with an authoritarian personality type who were ordered to give themselves shocks, gave higher shocks than those without the personality type.

Evaluation

- Although the F-scale has some research support, supposedly authoritarian individuals do not always score highly on all the dimensions as the theory would predict.
- The F-scale suffers from response bias, as the scale is worded in a confirming direction. Therefore, if individuals agree with items they are rated as authoritarian. Altemeyer (1981) produced the less biased Right Wing Authoritarianism scale (RWA) which has an equal number of pro- and anti-statements.
- The theory is politically biased, as individuals with an authoritarian personality are seen as only existing on the conservative, right wing of political viewpoints.

STRENGTHEN YOUR LEARNING

1 How do the agentic and autonomous states differ from each other?
2 What is meant by legitimacy of authority?
3 How might dehumanisation have occurred in Milgram's study?
4 How do situational variables that affect obedience differ from dispositional ones?
5 In what ways might the following affect obedience rates?
   (i) proximity
   (ii) location
   (iii) uniforms.
6 Explain why those with an authoritarian personality might be more obedient to authority.

RESEARCH IN FOCUS

1 Bickman's (1974) obedience study was a field experiment. How does a field experiment differ from:
   (i) a laboratory experiment
   (ii) a natural experiment?
2 Give one strength and one weakness of a field experiment compared to a laboratory study.
3 The authoritarian personality is measured by the F-scale questionnaire.
   (i) What is the difference between open and closed questions in questionnaires?
   (ii) Explain two advantages and two disadvantages of a questionnaire such as the F-scale.
   (iii) In what way does a questionnaire differ from an interview?

For information on research methods, see Chapter 7.

ASSESSMENT CHECK

1 Which of the following terms best matches the descriptions below? Choose one term that matches each description and write either A, B, C, D or E in the box next to it. Use each letter once only. One term will be left over.

   A   Agentic state

   B   Situational variables

   C   The authoritarian personality

   D   Proximity

   E   Legitimacy of authority

   (i)   The degree to which individuals are seen as justified in having power over others **[1 mark]**

   (ii)   An individual with a belief in absolute obedience, submission to authority and domination of minorities **[1 mark]**

   (iii) Acting as a representative of another person who is therefore seen as responsible for the behaviour demonstrated **[1 mark]**

   (iv) Features of an environment that can affect individuals' level of compliance to authority figures **[1 mark]**

2 Discuss two explanations for obedience. **[16 marks]**

3 Outline and evaluate situational variables affecting obedience. **[12 marks]**

4 Outline and evaluate the findings and conclusions of one study of obedience. **[6 marks]**

5 Explain how proximity and location can affect obedience. **[2 + 2 marks]**

6 Yolanda dropped a crisp packet in the shopping centre and when told to pick it up by a fellow shopper she did nothing, but when told to do so by a security guard she immediately complied.

   With reference to the passage above explain why Yolanda obeyed the security guard, but not the fellow shopper. **[3 marks]**

7 Below is a table of data relating to the number of people who gave up a train seat when ordered to by a person dressing in different clothes:

	Number of people (out of 20) who obeyed an order to give up a train seat
Order issued by person in track-suit	3
Order issued by person in casual clothes	5
Order issued by person in train company uniform	16

   (i)   Calculate the mean number of people who obeyed the order to give up their seat across all three conditions. Show your calculations. **[2 marks]**

   (ii)   What would be an appropriate graph to plot the data? Explain why. **[3 marks]**

   (iii) The study used an independent groups design. Give one advantage and one disadvantage of this design. **[2 + 2 marks]**

1.8 Explanations of resistance to social influence

*'Whenever you find yourself on the side of the majority, it is
time to pause and reflect.'*
Mark Twain

*'It is necessary to distinguish between the virtue and the
vice of obedience.'*
Lemuel K. Washburn

Although social influence generally helps society to function in an effective
way, sometimes the consequences of conformity and obedience can be very
negative. The crash of Northwest Airlink Flight 5719 (see 'In the News',
page 26) is but one example of such negative consequences. If strategies are
to be constructed that help prevent such destructive types of conformity and
obedience, a thorough understanding of how social influence can be resisted
is required. This suggests that possibly the best way to resist the negative
effects of social influence is to train staff in institutional settings, where there
is generally a social expectancy of conformity and obedience, to conform
to and obey official guidelines and rules, rather than malevolent authority
figures and majority influences.

Resistance to social influence involves *disobedience* and *non-conformity*,
with non-conformity occurring in two ways:

1 Independence – involving a lack of consistent movement either towards
   or away from social expectancy (doing your own thing).
2 Anti-conformity – involving a consistent movement *away* from social
   conformity, for instance adopting the behaviour and norms of a
   minority group.

Social support

Research suggests that when there are others in social situations who defy
attempts to make them conform and obey, then it becomes much easier for
an individual to also resist such forms of social influence. With conformity,
the presence of others who *dissent* has proven to be a strong source of
defiance. In a variation of Asch's study (see page 6), if the naïve (real)
participants saw a dissenter disagreeing with the majority wrong answer on
critical trials, conformity dropped sharply. Dissenters provide the participant
with moral support, even if they give a different wrong answer from the
majority, 'freeing' the participant to give the correct answer. The dissenter
represents a form of **social support**. So, a major way of resisting conformity
is to break the agreement of the majority – if they do not all agree, their
impact is greatly reduced. It also seems that early social support is more
influential; if an individual finds themselves in a situation in which pressures
towards conformity are increasing and they feel they should be resisted, they
should try to speak out as soon as possible. The sooner they do, the greater
their chances of rallying others and resisting the majority.

KEY TERMS

Resistance to social influence – the ways
in which individuals attempt to withstand
perceived attempts to threaten freedom
of choice

Social support – the perception of
assistance and solidarity available from
others

Figure 1.35 Even dissenters with apparently poor vision reduced conformity in Asch's study

Research

Allen & Levine (1971) found that conformity was reduced on a task involving visual judgements if there was a dissenter, even if the dissenting 'partner' wore glasses with thick lenses and admitted to having a sight problem. This suggests dissenters help resist social influence even when dissenters are not skilled in particular situations.

Asch (1956) found that if there is a dissenter who answers correctly from the start of the study, conformity drops from 32 per cent to 5.5 per cent, but if the confederate only starts to dissent later in the study, conformity only drops to 8.5 per cent. This suggests that social support received earlier is more effective than support received later.

With obedience the presence of *disobedient models* has been shown to be a powerful source of social support. Similarly to dissenters with conformity, disobedient models reduce the unanimity of a group, making it easier for individuals to act independently. Such people also seem to demonstrate that disobedience is actually possible, as well as how to do it. In one of Milgram's variations, after confederate teachers had refused to obey, a real participant commented 'I didn't realise I could refuse to obey'. Disobedient models can additionally be seen as a form of conformity, as they create a group norm for individuals to follow suit.

Research

Milgram (1974) found that when two confederates paired with the real participant left the study early on, declaring that they would go no further, only 10 per cent of participants gave the maximum 450-volt shock. This suggests that the creating of a group norm of disobedience put the participants under pressure to conform to the behaviour of the confederates.

Mullen *et al.* (1990) found that when disobedient models broke the law by jay-walking (crossing roads illegally), participants were more likely to jay-walk themselves than when disobedient models weren't present, supporting the idea of disobedient models increasing resistance to social influence.

YOU ARE THE RESEARCHER

Would a dissenter who you identify with create more resistance to conformity than one you don't identify with? Design an Asch-type procedure where, in the experimental condition, all the confederates are wearing replica shirts of a football team different to the one the real participant supports, but with the dissenter wearing a replica shirt of the same team the real participant supports. What would the control condition be? What type of experimental design would be used? What would the IV and DV be? What would your experimental hypothesis be? Why would a non-directional (two-tailed) hypothesis be justifiable?

For more on research methods, see Chapter 7.

Figure 1.36 Would a dissenter who supported the same team as you make you more resistant to social influence?

Locus of control

Locus of control (LoC) was identified as a personality dimension by Rotter (1966). It concerns the extent to which people perceive themselves as being in control of their own lives. Individuals with a high internal LoC believe they can affect the outcomes of situations. Individuals with a high external LoC believe things turn out a certain way regardless of their actions.

Internal LoC refers to the belief that things happen as a result of an individual's choices and decisions, while external LoC refers to the belief that things happen as a result of luck, fate or other uncontrollable external forces. Rotter (1966) believed that having an internal LoC makes individuals more resistant to social pressure, with those seeing themselves in control of a situation more likely to perceive themselves as having a free choice to conform or obey.

Research into LoC and resisting conformity

Spector (1983) gave Rotter's locus of control scale to 157 university students and found that participants with a high external locus of control did conform more than those with a low external locus of control, but only in situations that produced normative social pressure. Both types of participants did not conform in situations that produced informational social influence. This suggests that people with less of a need for acceptance into a social group will be more able to resist social influence.

Shute (1975) exposed undergraduates to peers who expressed either conservative or liberal attitudes to drug taking. He found that undergraduates with an internal LoC conformed less to expressing pro-drug attitudes, supporting the idea that having an internal LoC increases resistance to conformity.

Moghaddam (1998) found that Japanese people conform more easily than Americans and have more of an external LoC. This suggests that differences in resistance to social influence across cultures can be explained by differences in LoC.

Avtgis (1998) performed a meta-analysis of studies involving LoC and conformity, finding that individuals with an internal locus of control were less easily persuadable and less likely to conform, supporting the idea of differences in LoC being linked to differences in the ability to resist social influence.

Research into LoC and resisting obedience

Holland (1967) tested for a link between LoC and obedience, but found no relationship between the two. However, Blass (1991) reanalysed Holland's data using more precise statistical analysis and found that participants with an internal LoC were more able to resist obedience than those with an external LoC. Those with an internal LoC were especially resistant if they thought the researcher was trying to force or manipulate them to obey. This suggests the aspect of personal control in a situation is important, as those with a high internal LoC like to feel they have choice over their behaviour.

Schurz (1985) found no relationship between LoC and obedience among Austrian participants, who gave the highest level of what they believed to be painful, skin-damaging bursts of ultrasound to a learner. However, participants with an internal LoC tended to take more responsibility for their actions than those with an external LoC, which again suggests that feelings of personal control may be related to resistance of social influence.

Jones & Kavanagh (1996) investigated the link between moral disengagement and individual differences in LoC. They found that those with a high external LoC were more likely to obey unethical authority figures. This is a possible explanation for corporate fraud and institutional abuses of power where junior staff members fail to resist immoral/criminal directives given to them by more senior managers.

ON THE WEB

Listen to a BBC Radio 4 programme on Julian Rotter's Locus of Control, which was part of the *Mind Changers* series:

www.bbc.co.uk/programmes/ b01gf5sr

To measure your own LoC go to:

www.psych.uncc.edu/pagoolka /LocusofControl-intro.html

KEY TERMS

Reactance – rebellious anger produced by attempts to restrict freedom of choice

Ironic deviance – the belief that other people's behaviour occurs because they have been told to do it lowers their informational influence

Status – an individual's social position within a hierarchical group

ON THE WEB

Read the full research paper of Lucian Conway & Mark Schaller on ironic deviance in conformity behaviour, including a review of similar research, at:

www2.psych.ubc.ca/~schaller/ ConwaySchaller2005.pdf

YOU ARE THE RESEARCHER

Design a correlational study to examine the relationship between LoC and degree of independent behaviour. You will need to measure participants' LoC. (Use the link in the 'On the web' feature on the left). You then need to measure participants' levels of conformity/obedience. Think about how this has been done in studies you have already studied. Plot your data on a scattergram to give an indication of the strength and direction of correlation.

For more on research methods, see Chapter 7.

INCREASE YOUR KNOWLEDGE

Other factors involved in the resistance of conformity

Reactance

When the freedom of choice of individuals is restricted, they may react with **reactance** (rebellious anger), such as when adolescents rebel against conforming to adult rules.

Hamilton (2005) found that Australian adolescents in a low-reactance condition, who were told it was normal to experiment with drugs as long as they were aware of health risks, were less likely to

Figure 1.37 Those in high reactance conditions are more likely to smoke

smoke than those in a high-reactance condition who were told to never smoke. This implies that when freedom of choice is threatened, resistance will occur (it could be argued to be obedience as well as conformity).

Ironic deviance

If the truthfulness of a source of informational social influence is doubted, then the chances of individuals conforming to the guidance given will be lessened.

Conway & Schaller (2005) found that office workers conformed and used a software product if other employees recommended it, but were less likely to conform if the colleagues had recommended it after being ordered by the office manager to use that particular software, rather than alternatives. In this instance, they attributed fellow office workers' behaviour as being determined by the boss's order. This supports the idea that if individuals believe a source of informational influence is not genuine, conformity to that influence will be resisted (**ironic deviance**).

Status

People of low **status** within a group, such as newcomers, are motivated to attain higher status by exhibiting conformist behaviour; therefore conformity is more able to be resisted if individuals perceive themselves as of higher status within a group. (See Contemporary research – Richardson, 2009, on page 37.)

Distinction defeats group member deviance. The unlikely relationship between differentiation and newcomer conformity – Erika Richardson (2009)

Status affects conformist behaviour, as people of lower status within a group are motivated to attain higher status by exhibiting conformist behaviour, while those who see themselves as of higher relative status will be more able to resist conformity.

Figure 1.38 Would low-status participants conform to poor investment advice from high-status people?

Aims

- To test the effects of information on newcomers' willingness to agree to group decisions.
- To assess how the status of individuals affects attempts to make them conform to obviously wrong answers.

Procedure

1 84 male and female students were assigned randomly to same-sex groups comprising of three people. Two of each group were confederates and one was a naïve (real) participant. The naïve participants were led to believe that they were newcomers to the teams. Within each team the group members introduced themselves, with the confederates always going first. In each team the confederates described biographical details (level of education, amount of experience and so on) as of high or low status. The teams then looked at some information about two stock companies and decided which one to invest money in (one stock company was clearly superior to the other).

2 Team members gave their opinion, with the real participant always answering last. The two confederates chose the weaker of the two stock companies.

Findings

In the teams where the confederates are believed to be of high status, participants conformed to the group decision. The reverse was true where confederates were believed to be of low status.

Conclusions

People of perceived lower status conform to the decisions of those group members of perceived higher status, even when they believe those decisions are suspect, in order to attain higher status. People use competence-based clues about the status of other group members to determine the level of their conformist behaviour. People of higher perceived status within a group are more able to resist attempts to make them conform.

Evaluation

The research has practical applications for the formation of groups. New group members should not be made to feel inferior, if they are to give honest opinions and be able to resist attempts to conform to obviously wrong/poor decisions.

The implication is that bad decisions made by people of high status are given additional support by the conformity to such decisions of junior group members. This is, therefore, similar to the findings of Tarnow (2000, see page 26) that aircraft accidents are often caused by junior co-pilots not questioning the wrong decisions of higher-status pilots.

The study is unethical, as it involved deceit. The confederates were not who they claimed to be, therefore informed consent could not be given.

Corporate fraud involves large commercial institutions performing illegal activities, such as paying bribes to get contracts and money laundering (disguising the proceeds of crime so that money cannot be traced to any wrongdoing). For example, the bank HSBC was fined £1.2 billion in 2012 for money laundering drug money in Mexico. There are also institutional abuses, where large organisations cover up evidence of their failures. The Healthcare Commission reported in 2009 that up to 1,200 'excess' deaths had been uncovered at Stafford hospital. Such frauds and abuses involve large groups of people working together within hierarchical structures. Evidence suggests that such frauds are possible where lower-status staff have external LoC, increasing the possibility of them complying with illegal orders given by authority figures within the hierarchy. Also, Chui (2004) suggests that 'whistle-blowing' – where individuals within a hierarchy report illegal activities at the risk of losing their jobs – is performed by individuals with high internal LoC. To prevent such incidents of fraud and abuses occurring again would require staff training that focuses on the recognition and resistance of such practices. Junior staff would need to be taught to obey official procedures, rather than the illegal demands of more senior authority figures.

Figure 1.39 Whistle-blowers who report illegal activities within institutions tend to have a high internal LoC

RESEARCH IN FOCUS

1 Holland (1967) performed a correlational study that examined the relationship between LoC and obedience. What were the two co-variables in this study?
2 In Hamilton's (2005) study into reactance, what were the IV and DV?
3 How can Richardson's (2009) study into status be considered unethical? How would these ethical issues be dealt with?
4 Richardson used a mixed gender sample. In what way is this an advantage?
5 Richardson randomly assigned participants to teams within her study. Does this guarantee a representative sample?

For information on research methods, see Chapter 7.

Other factors involved in the resistance of obedience

Systematic processing

Individuals are less likely to obey orders that have negative outcomes if they are given time to consider the consequences of what they have been ordered to do. However, the expectation in many institutional settings, such as the military, is that orders should be complied with immediately without thought; indeed much basic training in the military is concerned with achieving such a mindset, as conflict situations would generally require immediate obedience.

Research

Martin *et al.* (2007) found that when participants were encouraged and allowed to consider the content of an unreasonable order, they were less likely to obey, demonstrating the power of **systematic processing** in resisting social influence.

Taylor *et al.* (1997) reported that disobedience increases when people are encouraged to question the motives of the authority figure issuing an order.

KEY TERM

Systematic processing – analysis based upon critical thinking

This suggests that systematic processing helps resist obedience by lessening the legitimacy of authority figures.

Morality

Research has shown that individuals who make decisions on whether to obey or not based on moral considerations are more resistant to obedience than those who do not.

Research

Milgram (1974) reported that one participant who did not fully obey, stated in a post-study interview that he was a vicar and his disobedience had been based on his 'obeying a higher authority' (God). In other words, his religious **morality** had helped him resist the authority figure's commands to deliver the electric shocks.

Kohlberg (1969) gave moral dilemmas (a choice between two alternatives involving a moral decision, e.g. whether to keep or hand in money found on the street to the police) to participants from the Milgram study, finding that those who based decisions on moral principles were less obedient, supporting the idea that morality can be used to resist social influence.

Personality

Although there is little evidence to support the idea of there being **personality** characteristics which help resist social influence, research does suggest that individuals who can empathise with the feelings of others are more able to resist orders with destructive consequences.

Research

Oliner & Oliner (1988) compared a sample of 406 people who had sheltered Jews in Nazi Europe to a sample of 126 people who had also lived through the war, but hadn't sheltered Jews. It was found that those who rescued Jews reported an upbringing that stressed social norms of helping others and emphasised their empathy with the suffering of Jewish people. As sheltering Jews was against the law in Nazi-occupied countries, it illustrates the importance of empathy as a personality characteristic which helps resist destructive obedience.

KEY TERMS

Morality – decisions and behaviour based upon the perception of proper conduct

Personality – the combination of characteristics that forms an individual's distinctive nature

---

STRENGTHEN YOUR LEARNING

1 What is meant by resistance to social influence?
2 How do dissenters help reduce the likelihood of conformity?
3 How do disobedient models aid resistance to obedience?
4 What is meant by locus of control?
5 What is the difference between those with an internal LoC and those with an external LoC?
6 Why are individuals with an internal LoC more resistant to social pressure?
7 Does research support the idea of a link between LoC and likelihood of conformity/obedience?
8 Explain how the following can affect resistance to conformity:
  (i) reactance
  (ii) ironic deviance
  (iii) status.
9 Explain how the following can affect resistance to obedience:
  (i) systematic processing
  (ii) morality
  (iii) personality.

ASSESSMENT CHECK

1 Copy and complete the table below by writing which description, A, B, C or D, describes which term. One statement will be left over. **[3 marks]**

   A Rebellious anger produced by attempts to restrict freedom of choice

   B An individual's beliefs about the causes of successes and failures

   C The ways in which individuals attempt to withstand perceived attempts to threaten freedom of choice

   D The perception of assistance and solidarity available from others

Term	Description
Social support	
Resistance	
Locus of control	

2 Outline and evaluate two explanations of resistance to social influence. **[16 marks]**

3 Discuss social support as an explanation of resistance to social influence. **[12 marks]**

4 Explain how locus of control can affect resistance to social influence. **[3 marks]**

5 Jasper likes to wear his hat, but when getting on the bus home he noticed everyone else wearing a hat took theirs off, so he did too. The next day he was wearing his hat again and again all the other hat wearers took theirs off when getting on the bus, all except one boy in front of him, so Jasper kept his hat on too.

   With reference to the passage above, use resistance to social influence to explain why Jasper took his hat off on the first day, but kept it on the following day. **[4 marks]**

6 Research into locus of control and resistance to social support often involve correlational studies.

   (i) Describe the correlational study method. **[3 marks]**

   (ii) Give one strength and one weakness of the correlational study method. **[2 + 2 marks]**

   (iii) Sketch a scattergram showing a positive correlation between internal locus of control and resistance to social influence. **[2 marks]**

1.9 Minority influence

'Minorities are the stars of the firmament; majorities,
the darkness in which they float.'

Martin H. Fischer

Minority influence is a type of social influence that motivates individuals to reject established majority group norms. This is achieved through the process of *conversion*, where majorities become gradually won over to a minority viewpoint. Conversion involves the new belief/behaviour being accepted both publicly and privately and can be seen as a type of internalisation (see page 3), as it involves a change in an individual's belief system and as such is regarded as a strong (true) form of conformity.

Conversion through minority influence generally occurs through informational social influence (see page 4), where a minority provide new information and ideas to the majority. Minority influence therefore takes longer to achieve than majority influence based on compliance, where conformity is instantaneous and unthinking, because time will need to be taken for individuals to re-examine their beliefs and behaviour in light of the new information and beliefs that the minority are advocating.

The gradual process by which minority opinions become majority ones is called *social cryptoamnesia* (the 'snowball effect'). At first, converts to the minority viewpoint are few, but as more and more people change their attitude, the pace picks up and the minority gains status, power and acceptability.

Minority influence is a crucial factor in bringing about innovation and social change (see page 45) and research has suggested that behavioural style, especially consistency and commitment, as well as flexibility, are important factors in helping achieve minority influence.

KEY TERM

Minority influence – a type of social influence that motivates individuals to reject established majority group norms

Behavioural style – consistency and commitment

Minority influence will be persuasive if the minority is *consistent* (unchanging) with its opinion/behaviour, shows confidence in its beliefs, and appears unbiased. Consistency seems to be the most important feature here, as it shows the minority are committed, especially if the minority have had to resist social pressures and abuses against their viewpoint, and creates enough doubt about established norms to get individuals to re-examine their own beliefs and behaviour.

CLASSIC RESEARCH

Influence of a consistent minority on the responses of a majority in a colour perception test – Serge Moscovici *et al.* (1969)

Srul Hersh (Serge) Moscovici claimed that if majority influence was all-powerful, we would all think and behave the same. He pointed out that major social movements, like Christianity, start with an individual or small group and that without such influences, there would be no innovation in society. He set out to investigate this claim.

Figure 1.40 Serge Moscovici

Aim

To investigate the role of a consistent minority upon the opinions of a majority in an unambiguous situation.

Procedure

Participants were placed into 32 groups of six. In each group there were four real participants and two confederates. Participants were told that it was an investigation into perception. Each group was shown 36 blue slides, with filters varying the intensity of the colour. In the consistent condition, the confederates answered wrongly that the slides were green. In the inconsistent condition, the confederates said that 24 of the slides were green and 12 were blue. Answers were given verbally in the presence of the rest of the group.

Findings

There was an 8.2 per cent agreement with the minority in the consistent condition, with 32 per cent agreeing at least once. There was only 1.25 per cent agreement in the inconsistent condition.

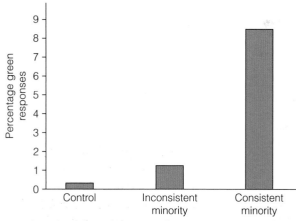

Figure 1.41 Bar chart showing conformity to inconsistent and consistent minority influence

Conclusions

Although the consistent condition finding of 8.2 per cent seems a small figure, it is significantly higher than the inconsistent condition figure of 1.25 per cent and so shows that although minority influence is relatively small, consistency is the important variable.

Evaluation

Consistent minorities have even greater influence on private attitudes. In a separate experiment where participants gave their answers *privately* in another consistent condition, there was even greater agreement.

Moscovici only used female participants as he thought that they would be more interested in colours – the results are not, therefore, generalisable to males. Generally, conformity research suggests females are more conformist.

Moscovici's study is unethical as it involved deceit, which means informed consent could not be given. Participants may also have endured mild stress.

The study does not identify important factors in minority influence, like group size, status or degree of organisation.

Research studies generally support Moscovici's findings. Meyers *et al.* (2000) found minority groups that were successful in affecting majorities were more consistent than those that were not.

Flexibility

Consistent minorities who are inflexible, rigid and uncompromising in their beliefs and behaviour will not be persuasive. If they are seen to be *flexible* by demonstrating an ability to be moderate, co-operative and reasonable, then they will be persuasive. Successful minority influence therefore seems to require the minority to compromise and be slightly inconsistent in its position.

Research

Nemeth (1986) created groups of three participants and one confederate who had to decide how much compensation to pay to the victim of a ski-lift accident. When the confederate, acting as a consistent minority, argued for a low amount and refused to change his position, he had no effect on the majority. However, when he compromised a little and moved to offering a slightly higher amount, the majority changed their opinion to a lower amount. This shows how minorities need to be flexible to be persuasive, while at the same time questions the importance of consistency. This was further supported by Mugny & Papastamou (1982) who got participants to respond to questions about responsibility for pollution. They were also exposed to a minority's extreme views on how to control pollution. When the minority refused to budge from their opinion they were not persuasive; however, when they appeared flexible by compromising, they were seen as less extreme, co-operative and reasonable and were more persuasive in changing majority opinions.

INCREASE YOUR KNOWLEDGE

Two other factors that are important in achieving minority influence are *style of thinking* and *identification*.

Style of thinking

A consistent, committed minority stand an increased chance of getting individuals to engage in *systematic processing*, where the minority viewpoint will be considered carefully and over time, rather than being instantly dismissed without any considered analysis through *superficial processing*.

Smith *et al.* (1996) found that if a minority could get a majority to consider an issue in terms of the arguments for and against the issue, then the minority became more influential, illustrating how style of thinking is important in determining the persuasiveness of a minority. This was further supported by Nemeth (2005), who reported that when a minority can get a majority to discuss and debate an issue, the persuasive influence of the minority becomes greater.

Identification

When a majority identifies with a minority, then the minority will be more persuasive in getting the majority to convert to its viewpoint. For example, if a minority consisted solely of males it would be more persuasive in converting the beliefs and behaviour of other males rather than females.

Maas *et al.* (1982) found that a homosexual minority arguing for homosexual rights were less persuasive in changing majority heterosexual opinions than a heterosexual minority arguing for homosexual rights. This suggests that the heterosexual majority identified with the heterosexual minority, making them more persuasive, while they perceived the homosexual minority as different from themselves and as having a self-interest in promoting their own particular cause.

ON THE WEB

Charlan Nemeth is one of the foremost researchers into minority influence. Go to:

www.charlannemeth.com/files/ MinorityInfluenceTheory.pdf

Here you can read a fascinating recent paper by her concerning the history of minority influence research, including details of her work with Serge Moscovici, and the importance of dissenters as a source of minority influence that encourages divergent thinking, leading to innovation and creativity.

STRENGTHEN YOUR LEARNING

1 Why might minority influence be regarded as a form of internalisation?
2 Why does minority influence take longer to achieve than majority influence?
3 What is social cryptoamnesia (the 'snowball effect')?
4 Explain how the following are important in making a minority persuasive:
   (i) behavioural style
   (ii) flexibility
   (iii) style of thinking
   (iv) identification.
5 What did Moscovici's study suggest is the most important factor in minority influence? Justify your answer.

IN THE NEWS

Ψ The Psychological Enquirer

Police investigate assisted suicide of paralysed rugby player

Figure 1.42 As with other contact sports, rugby carries a certain risk of injury

Daniel James, a 23-year-old England rugby player, committed suicide in a Swiss euthanasia clinic after being paralysed from the chest down in a training accident. Police investigated but no one was prosecuted.

Daniel, a hooker with Nuneaton rugby club, felt his body had become a 'prison' and lived in 'fear and loathing' of daily life. He tried to kill himself several times after a scrum collapsed on him in March last year, dislocating his neck vertebrae, trapping his spinal cord and rendering him instantly tetraplegic.

Assisted suicide is illegal in the UK and family or friends who help face up to 14 years in jail.

Dignity in Dying, which campaigns for a law change to allow terminally ill and mentally competent patients to choose assisted death, has supported several cases similar to Daniel's.

Dignity in Dying can be regarded as a minority group influence. Their argument that individuals should have the right to choose assisted suicide is not a mainstream one and has attracted criticism and even legal action. Increasingly, however, people are coming round to their viewpoint. Perhaps in a few years' time their view will be the majority one and euthanasia will be an accepted practice. If so, this would be an example of how minority influence leads to social change. Indeed, currently (2014), the House of Lords is considering the 'Assisted Dying Bill' with Dignity in Dying one of the official stakeholder groups.

1.10 The role of social influence processes in social change

> *'Do not follow where the path may lead. Go, instead, where there is no path and leave a trail.'*
> Ralph Waldo Emerson (1893)

> *'I can't understand why people are frightened of new ideas. I'm frightened of the old ones.'*
> John Cage (1988)

Social change

Social change involves the way in which society develops, through big shifts in people's beliefs, attitudes and behaviour. This process occurs continually, but at a gradual pace, with minority influence being the main driving force for social change through minority viewpoints slowly winning the majority over to what will become new social norms (expected ways of thinking and behaving).

Social change can be positive, such as the increased rights for women that developed in western cultures through the 1900s, but social change can also be negative, such as the adoption by society of eugenic beliefs, which saw people of different races as genetically inferior, leading to mass extermination of whole groups of people, such as that performed by the Nazis.

Majority influence's main role is to help maintain social order, to keep things the way they are. Majority influence can therefore be seen as a 'police officer' overseeing society, so that people know what behaviour and attitudes are expected of them and then stick to them. Majority influence is also more of an immediate, unthinking process and so can be broken down over time through minority influence affecting people's thought processes and belief systems to bring about social change.

Minority influence changes attitudes and behaviour over time, incurring a strong, long-lasting form of conformity, involving fundamental changes in belief systems (see Minority influence, page 41). This occurs by individuals directing their thinking at understanding why the minority hold a particular viewpiont. And conversion to the minority viewpoint then takes place, as individuals start to look at the issue in the same way as the minority. In this way innovation occurs and new ideas and behaviours become adopted as mainstream practices.

There comes during this process a moment of critical mass, where the minority viewpoint becomes that of the mainstream and the majority will begin to conform to this new viewpoint through compliance (see page 3). However, as this is only a public, but not private form of majority influence, people may still privately hold their original beliefs: for example, still privately holding sexist or racist beliefs, but not publically demonstrating them. For more permanent social change to occur, more people will need to conform to the new viewpoint through identification involving a change in their belief systems (see page 3).

KEY TERM

Social change – the process by which society changes beliefs, attitudes and behaviour to create new social norms (expected ways of behaviour and thinking)

Figure 1.43 Environmentalists are now the majority

As social change is generally a slow, gradual process of social cryptoamnesia (see page 41), it allows for change to occur in a manner that is not too disruptive to social order; rapid change would cause conflict within society that could be very harmful in the short term. The slowness of the process also allows for new ideas to be 'road-tested', to check their suitability for mainstream society. Once social change has occurred, conformity will serve to consolidate and maintain the new beliefs and behaviour, as part of a new social order.

Like conformity, obedience generally serves to maintain the existing social order. Therefore, as social change occurs, obedience (like conformity), will serve to oversee and uphold the new social order.

There is always the possibility that people who show resistance to conformity and obedience may become agents for social change, as they model the attitudes and behaviour necessary for such change to occur.

A good example of how social influence processes bring about social change would be that of the environmental group Greenpeace, which started in Canada in the early 1970s. Originally regarded as a bunch of cranks attracting ridicule and legal action, they slowly over time – through minority influence – changed more and more people's belief systems and so attracted more members and popular support, until finally becoming the mainstream, accepted, legitimate voice for environmental issues.

CONTEMPORARY RESEARCH

Resistance to persuasive messages as a function of majority and minority status – Martin, Hewstone & Martin (2003)

Figure 1.44 Would an argument against voluntary euthanasia be more resistant to change if supported by a minority or a majority group?

Aim
To see if opinions given by minority or majority group influence are more resistant to conflicting opinions.

Procedure
48 British university student participants who had an initial attitude of being supportive of voluntary euthanasia received two messages. The first message (the pro-attitudinal message) gave six arguments against voluntary euthanasia and was supported by either minority or majority group influence. The second message (counter-attitudinal message) conflicted with the first message by giving six arguments for voluntary euthanasia. Attitudes were measured after the presentation of both messages.

Findings
Attitudes following minority support for the pro-attitudinal message were more resistant to change following the counter-attitudinal message, than if the pro-attitudinal message had been given majority support.

Conclusions
Minority influence creates systematic processing (consideration) of its viewpoints, leading to attitudes that are resistant to counter-persuasion. The findings support Moscovici's belief that the opinions of minorities are subjected to a higher level of processing than those of majorities.

Evaluation
The results are consistent with the view that both majorities and minorities can lead to different processes and consequences under different situations. Minority influences have a much greater influence than was originally thought.

The results support the idea that minority influence can lead to social change, as systematic processing will cause changes in belief systems leading to fundamental changes in people's viewpoints and behaviour.

Martin & Hewstone (1999) found that minority influence leads to more creative and novel judgements than majority influence, supporting the idea of minority influence being a social force for innovation and change.

Burgoon (1995) argued that it is the deviant and unexpected behaviours of minorities that are alerting and arousing and which lead to a deeper-level analysis of the behaviour and ideas being presented. This suggests it is the violation of social norms by minorities which leads to systematic processing and, ultimately, social change.

Nemeth (2009) reported that it is the 'dissent' of minorities to established social norms that 'opens' individuals' minds to search for information, consider other options and ultimately become more creative and make better decisions. This illustrates how it is the resistance of minorities to conform to and obey social norms that acts as a catalyst (starting point) for social change.

STRENGTHEN YOUR LEARNING

1 What is meant by social change?
2 Explain how minority influence may bring about innovation.
3 Minority influence generally allows social change to occur in a slow, gradual fashion. How might this be a good thing?
4 Give a real-life example of your own of a minority group that has brought about social change. Using what you have learned about minority influence, explain how this social change occurred.

RESEARCH IN FOCUS

1 The aim of Martin, Hewstone & Martin's (2003) experiment was to see if opinions given by minority or majority group influence are more resistant to conflicting opinions. Explain how an aim differs from a hypothesis.
2 For Martin, Hewstone & Martin's study, construct a suitable:
   (i) non-directional hypothesis
   (ii) directional hypothesis
   (iii) null hypothesis.
3 Martin, Hewstone & Martin's study used an opportunity sample. What is meant by an opportunity sample? Give one strength and one weakness of this sampling method.

For information on research methods, see Chapter 7.

PSYCHOLOGY IN THE REAL WORLD

Research into minority influence and innovative change has had a big impact in the world of business and industry, where it has been realised that conformity and obedience within hierarchical social groups decrease the chances of beneficial change occurring. Companies that just place 'yes men' into work teams, individuals who quietly conform to usual practices and obey without question the directives of managers, will not experience any healthy dissent leading to meaningful analysis of work practices and ultimately beneficial innovation. More successful companies have used psychological knowledge and introduced minorities of genuine dissenters into teams to create an atmosphere of innovative social change.

Figure 1.45 Introducing dissenters into teams as a source of minority influence is an effective way of achieving innovation

ASSESSMENT CHECK

1 Which of the following terms best matches the descriptions below relating to minority influence? Choose one term that matches each description and write either A, B, C or D in the box next to it. Use each letter once only.

   A Flexibility

   B Compliance

   C Consistency

   D Commitment

   (i) Minorities who demonstrate an ability to be moderate, co-operative and reasonable **[1 mark]**

   (ii) Minorities who demonstrate resistance of social pressures and abuses against their viewpoint **[1 mark]**

   (iii) Minorities who are unchanging in their opinions and behaviour. **[1 mark]**

2 Discuss the role of social influence processes in social change. **[16 marks]**

3 Outline and evaluate minority influence. **[12 marks]**

4 With reference to minority influence, explain each of the following:

   (i) consistency **[2 marks]**

   (ii) flexibility **[2 marks]**

   (iii) commitment. **[2 marks]**

5 Ise and her partner have very strong views on the safety of children and they have always argued for and sent their children to school wearing high-visibility clothing. At first, their views and behaviour were ridiculed, but they stuck to it, though they compromised a bit by getting their children to just wear fluorescent jackets. Slowly, more and more parents started sending their children to school wearing high-visibility jackets, until the majority were doing so and it has even now become official school policy.

   With reference to the above passage, explain how social influence processes influence social change. **[6 marks]**

6 Explain three ethical issues psychologists must consider when researching into minority influence. **[6 marks]**

Conformity (majority influence)

SUMMARY

- Conformity involves yielding to group pressure. Kelman (1958) proposed three types of conformity: compliance, identification and internalisation, which differ in the degree to which they affect belief systems.

- Conformity is regarded as a form of majority influence, with minority influence regarded as a form of internalisation.

- One explanation for conformist behaviour is informational social influence, where individuals yield to majority influence in order to be correct. This was demonstrated in Jenness' (1932) study.

- A second explanation for conformist behaviour is normative social influence, where individuals yield to majority influence to be accepted/avoid rejection. This was demonstrated in Asch's (1955) study.

- Another explanation of conformist behaviour is cognitive dissonance, where conformist behaviour reduces the unpleasant feelings created by simultaneously holding two contradictory cognitions.

- There are several situational variables that affect rates of conformity, such as the size of the majority influence, the unanimity of the majority influence, task difficulty, group identity, whether responses are made publicly or privately, and social norms. There are also individual factors such as gender, mood, personality and culture.

- Social roles are the parts individuals play as members of a social group, which meet the expectations of a situation.

- Zimbardo found that individuals conform readily to the social roles demanded of a situation in his prison simulation study.

Obedience and the work of Milgram

- Obedience involves complying with the demands of an authority figure and Milgram's study identified several explanations for obedience, such as agentic state, legitimacy of authority and dehumanisation.

- Milgram also identified several important situational variations such as proximity, location and uniform.

- The authoritarian personality is a dispositional explanation of obedience that seeks to identify personality characteristics associated with obedience.

- Resistance to social influence involves the ways in which individuals attempt to withstand perceived attempts to threaten their freedom of choice and is influenced by factors such as social support and locus of control.

Resistance to social influence

- Resistance to conformity is additionally affected by reactance, ironic deviance and status, while resistance to obedience is affected by systematic processing, morality and personality.

Minority influence

- Minority influence is a type of social influence that motivates individuals to reject established majority group norms through the process of conversion, where majorities become gradually won over to a minority viewpoint.

- Important factors in the persuasiveness of minority influence are behavioural style, especially consistency and commitment, as well as flexibility, style of thinking and identification.
- Social change concerns the process by which society changes its beliefs, attitudes and behaviour to create new social norms, with minority influence as the main driving force.
- Minority influence allows innovation to occur, where new ideas and behaviours become adopted as mainstream practices.
- Minority influence provides the catalyst for social change, while majority influence and obedience reinforce existing social norms.

2 Cognitive psychology: memory

Introduction

Cognitive psychology concerns mental processes. The main emphasis is on information processing, with humans seen as taking in and analysing sensory information to initiate and monitor behaviour. The mental process featured here is memory, the retention of experience. Specific focus will be upon:

- Explanations of memory (the multi-store and working models)
- Different types of long-term memory
- Explanations for forgetting
- Factors affecting the accuracy of eyewitness testimony
- Strategies to improve memory recall.

Understanding the specification

- Both *the multi-store model and the working memory models of memory* must be covered, as they are referred to directly in the specification.
- *Semantic, episodic and procedural types of long-term memory* must also be studied.
- *Interference and retrieval-cue failure* are explanations for forgetting which must be learned, as they are explicitly named in the specification.
- *Eyewitness testimony* is to be covered in two ways. Firstly, through factors that affect it, including anxiety, leading questions and post-event discussion as types of misleading information. Secondly, through strategies to improve the accuracy of eyewitness testimony, including the cognitive interview.

These are the basic requirements of the specification. However, other relevant material is included to provide depth and detail to your understanding.

'Time moves in one direction, memory in another.'
William Gibson (2012)

'Memory is a net that one finds full of fish when it's taken from the brook, but a dozen miles of water have run through it without sticking.'
Oliver Wendell Holmes, Senior (1860)

IN THE NEWS

Ψ The Psychological Enquirer

The man who forgot everything, but not how to love

Figure 2.1 Scott Bolzan and wife Joan

46-year old Scott Bolzan had played American football for the New England Patriots and the Cleveland Browns,

before going on to run his own successful charter aeroplane business. Then, in December 2008, he slipped, banged his head and woke up blank. He didn't know his name or recognise his friends or family, or remember any past events. Scott had suffered severe retrograde amnesia, probably as he had had no blood flow to his right temporal lobe, a brain area associated with long-term memory. His memory loss was so severe that he had no understanding of concepts most people would take for granted, like the meaning of birthdays or what the relationship between a husband and a wife is. Fortunately, Scott was able to re-learn things, as his short-term memory ability was still intact, as was his ability to create new long-term memories.

Scott found it was not easy rekindling his love for his wife, a woman he no longer recognised. He had to be wooed and fall in love with her again. Eventually, they spent a night on a boat and re-started their sex life; he had retained a lot of procedural memory and 'thank goodness for that', said his wife.

Scott's case highlights how short-term and long-term memory involve different storage systems, as theorised by the multi-store model of memory. Indeed, other amnesia cases also support this explanation by showing the reverse: loss of short-term memory ability, but with long-term memories unaffected. Strangely, Scott could still understand written and spoken speech and perform old skills like riding a bicycle, which supports the idea that there are different types of long-term memory – Scott's accident hadn't affected them all.

KEY TERMS

Multi-store model (MSM) – an explanation of memory that sees information flowing through a series of storage systems

Sensory register (SR) – a short-duration store holding impressions of information received by the senses

Short-term memory (STM) – a temporary store holding small amounts of information for brief periods

Long-term memory (LTM) – a permanent store holding limitless amounts of information for long periods

Coding – the means by which information is represented in memory

Capacity – the amount of information that can be stored at a given time

Duration – the length of time information remains within storage

2.1 The multi-store model (MSM)

Kiss me goodbye and make it impressive; I have issues with my short-term memory.

Jennifer Delucy (2010)

The **multi-store model (MSM)**, devised by Atkinson & Shiffrin (1968) was the first cognitive explanation of memory; previous to the MSM, psychologists had mainly tried to study and explain memory through biological means. The model explains how information flows through a series of storage systems, with three permanent structures in memory: the **sensory register (SR)**, **short-term memory (STM)** and **long-term memory (LTM)**. Each stage differs in terms of:

- **coding** – the form in which the information is stored
- **capacity** – how much information can be stored
- **duration** – how long information can be stored for.

Information gathered by the sense organs enters the sensory register. Only the small amount paid attention to passes to short-term memory for further processing, the rest is lost very quickly. Information in short-term memory that is actively processed enough (thought about), mainly through rehearsal, transfers to long-term memory for more permanent storage.

The sensory register (SR)

The SR is not under cognitive control, but is an automatic response to the reception of sensory information by the sense organs and is the first storage system within the multi-store model (MSM). All information contained within LTM will have originally passed through the SR, though in an unprocessed form.

Coding in the SR

Information is stored in a raw, unprocessed form, with separate sensory stores for different sensory inputs: the *echoic* store for auditory information, the *iconic* store for visual information, the *haptic* store for tactile information, the *gustatory* store for taste information and the *olfactory* store for smell. Information that is paid attention to passes on to the STM, while the remainder fades quickly though trace decay, leaving no lasting impression.

Research

Crowder (1993) found that the SR only retains information in the iconic store for a few milliseconds, but for two to three seconds within the echoic store, which supports the idea of sensory information being coded into different sensory stores (it also suggests they have different durations).

Evaluation

- After-images of visual events provide good evidence of sensory memories. The light trail produced by a moving lighted stick was noted as early as 1740. Such phenomena led to early experiments into the SR in the 1960s.
- Sensory memory stores may consist of several sub-stores, for example, visible persistence and informational persistence within the iconic memory store.

Capacity of the SR

The capacity of each sensory memory store is very large, with the information contained being in an unprocessed, highly detailed and ever-changing format.

Research

Sperling (1960) flashed a 3 × 4 grid of letters onto a screen for one-twentieth of a second, and asked participants to recall the letters of one row. As the information would fade very quickly, he sounded different tones (high, medium or low) to indicate which row had to be recalled (1st, 2nd or 3rd). Recall of letters in the indicated row was high, which suggests all the information was originally there, indicating that the capacity of the SR (especially for the iconic store) is quite large.

Javitt *et al.* (1996) reported a biological basis to SR capacity, as the capacity of the iconic and echoic stores was found to be related to efficiency of the nervous system, which suggests there are individual differences in SR capacity.

Figure 2.2 Example of a 3 × 4 letter grid as used by Sperling (1960)

- Calculating the capacity of sensory memory stores often involves experiments where participants have to evaluate cues that suggest a change in random wave patterns. However, these only provide estimates of capacity and are highly artificial in nature and thus lacking in mundane realism.
- Although evidence exists that the iconic store can hold about fifteen to twenty images, the capacity of other sensory memory stores isn't well studied, as they last so briefly and generally only at a pre-conscious level.

Duration of the SR

It seems that all sensory memory stores have limited duration, though the actual duration of each store is not constant, with different types of information within each store decaying at different rates. Different sensory stores appear to have different capacities and there is some evidence that duration decreases with age.

Research

Walsh & Thompson (1978) found that the iconic sensory store has an average duration of 500 milliseconds, which decreases as individuals get older. This suggests duration of sensory memories is limited and dependent on age.

Treisman (1964) presented identical auditory messages to both ears of participants, with a slight delay between presentations. Participants noticed the messages were identical if the delay was two seconds or less, suggesting the echoic store has a limited duration of two seconds, while also illustrating the difference in duration from the iconic store.

Evaluation

- The brief duration of sensory memories is seen as due to their physical traces (engrams) fading quickly (see Explanations for forgetting, page 76). This suggests a biological explanation for the duration of information within the SR.
- The brief duration of the SR can be understood from an evolutionary perspective, as people only need to focus on perceptual information with an immediate survival value. Retaining non-useful information diminishes the ability to do this

Short-term memory (STM)

STM temporarily stores information received from the SR. It is an active (changing) memory system, as it contains information currently being thought about. STM differs from LTM especially in terms of coding, capacity and duration and how information is forgotten (see Explanations for forgetting, page 76). There are several Explanations for forgetting from STM (see Explanations for forgetting).

Coding in STM

Information arrives from the SR in its original raw form, such as in sound or vision, and is then encoded (entered into STM) in a form STM can more easily deal with. For example, if the input into the SR was the word 'platypus', this could be coded into STM in several ways:

Figure 2.3 Platypuses can be encoded into STM in several ways

- Visually – by thinking of the image of a platypus
- Acoustically – by repeatedly saying 'platypus'

- Semantically – (through meaning) by using a knowledge of platypuses, such as their being venomous egg-laying aquatic marsupials that hunt prey through electrolocation.
- Research suggests that the main form of coding in STM is acoustic (by sound), but other codes exist too.

CLASSIC RESEARCH

Influence of acoustic and semantic similarities on short- and long-term memory for word sequences – Alan Baddeley (1966)

Figure 2.4 and 2.5 Professor Alan Baddeley conducted research into postcodes and memory

Professor Alan Baddeley of York University started his research into memory when he received a grant from the Post Office to test how well different sorts of postcodes could be remembered. His preferred option wasn't adopted, but he did become famous for helping develop the working memory model (1974). He also carried out lots of other memory research, including the following experiment into coding in STM and LTM.

Aim

To assess whether coding in STM and LTM is mainly acoustic (by sound) or semantic (by meaning).

Procedure

1. 75 participants were presented with one of four word lists repeated four times.

   List A – acoustically similar words (sounded the same as each other) ('cat', 'mat', 'sat')
   List B – acoustically dissimilar words (sounded different to each other) ('pit', 'day', 'cow')
   List C – semantically similar words (meant the same as each other) ('big', 'huge', 'tall')
   List D – semantically dissimilar words (had different meanings to each other) ('hot', 'safe', 'foul')

2. To test coding in STM, participants were given a list containing the original words in the wrong order. Their task was to rearrange the words in the correct order.

3. The procedure for LTM was the same, but with a 20-minute interval before recall, during which participants performed another task to prevent rehearsal.

Findings

1. For STM, participants given List A (acoustically similar) performed the worst, with a recall of only 10 per cent. They confused similar-sounding words, e.g. recalling 'cap' instead of 'cat'. Recall for the other lists was comparatively good at between 60 and 80 per cent.

2. For LTM, participants with List C (semantically similar) performed the worst, with a recall of only 55 per cent. They confused similar-meaning words, e.g. recalling 'big' instead of 'huge'. Recall for the other lists was comparatively good at between 70 and 85 per cent.

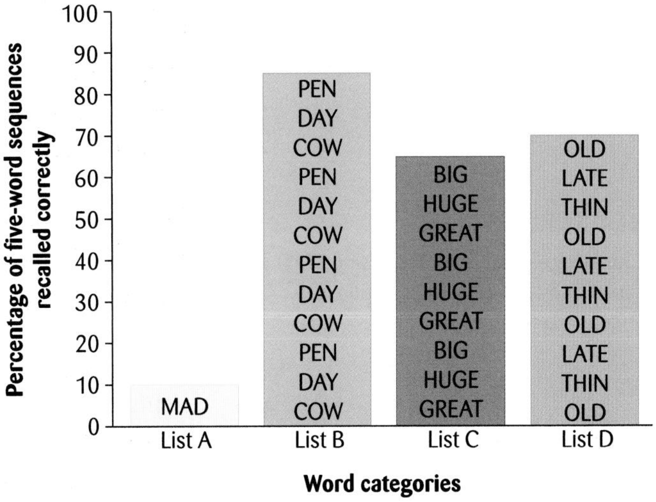

Figure 2.6 Baddeley's 1966 acoustic/semantic study findings

Conclusions

For STM, since List A was recalled the least efficiently, it seems there's acoustic confusion in STM, suggesting STM is coded on an acoustic basis.

For LTM since List C was recalled the least efficiently, it seems there's semantic confusion in LTM, suggesting LTM is coded on a semantic basis.

Evaluation

Baddeley's findings make 'cognitive sense'. For example, if you had to remember a shopping list, you'd probably repeat it aloud (acoustic rehearsal) while walking to the shops, but if you recall a book you've read, you remember the plot, rather than every single word.

The small difference in recall between semantically similar (64 per cent) and semantically dissimilar (71 per cent) lists, suggests there's also semantic coding in STM.

This was a laboratory study and therefore shows causality (cause and effect relationships), but may lack ecological validity (not representative of real-life activities).

As a laboratory study it can be replicated to check the results.

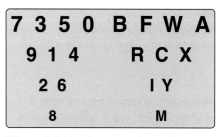

RESEARCH IN FOCUS
1. Baddeley's 1966 studies into coding in STM and LTM were experiments, but what type of experiment were they?
2. What type of experimental design was used?
3. Give one strength and one limitation of this design.
4. What were the IV and DV in the study?
5. What is a DV always a type of?

For information on research methods, see Chapter 7.

Research

Posner & Keele (1967) found participants were faster in assessing that 'A' followed by 'A' was the same letter than when 'A' was followed by 'a'. Because the visual code differs when 'A' is followed by 'a', the findings show that visual coding was occurring, which illustrates how codes other than the acoustic one occur in STM.

Figure 2.7 It is easier to decide that AA is the same letter repeated than is the case with Aa

Evaluation

- Although research shows that coding in STM is mainly acoustic, other sensory codes, such as visual, are used too. Indeed, some stimuli like faces or the smell of food would be difficult to code acoustically. What would the sound of treacle be?

Capacity of STM

STM has a limited capacity, as only a small amount of information is held in the store. Research indicates that between five and nine items can be held, though capacity is increased by **chunking**, where the size of the units of information in storage is increased by giving them a collective meaning. For example, chunking the twelve letters of SOSABCITVFBI into four chunks of SOS/ABC/ITV/FBI will increase capacity.

Research

Jacobs (1887) tested STM capacity with the serial digit span method, where participants are presented with increasingly long lists of numbers or letters and have to recall them in the right order. For example; '3, 9, 1' (followed by recall), '8, 5, 3, 9' (followed by recall), '2, 4, 7, 1, 3' (followed by recall) and so on. When participants fail on 50 per cent of tasks, they are judged to have reached their capacity. Jacobs found capacity for numbers was nine items and for letters seven items, which illustrates how the capacity of STM is limited. Numbers may be easier to recall as there are only nine single-digit numbers (0–9), compared to 26 letters in the English language (A–Z). One criticism is that experimental tasks such as recalling lists of letters have little relevance to everyday activities and so lack mundane realism.

Miller (1956) reviewed research to find the capacity of STM to be between five to nine items, but that the 'chunk' (pieces of information grouped together into meaningful sections) was the basic unit of STM. This means five to nine chunks can be held at any one time, increasing the store's capacity. Simon (1974) found that although STM capacity should be measured in terms of chunks, this varies with the type of material being recalled and the amount of information contained within the chunks.

KEY TERM

Chunking – method of increasing STM capacity by grouping information into larger units

```
7 3 5 0    B F W A
  9 1 4        R C X
    2 6          I Y
      8            M
```

Figure 2.8 Numbers may be easier to remember as there are only nine of them compared to 26 letters of the English alphabet

- Other factors, like age and practice, also influence STM capacity and nowadays STM limitations are mostly seen as due to processing limitations associated with attention.

Research

There may be individual differences in STM capacity. Daneman & Carpenter (1980) found capacity varied between five and twenty items between those with advanced and poor reading comprehension.

Duration of STM

The amount of time information remains within STM without being lost is limited to a maximum of about 30 seconds. This can be extended by rehearsal (repetition) of the information, which if done long enough will result in transfer of the information into LTM, where it will become a more long-lasting feature.

Research

Peterson & Peterson (1959) read nonsense trigrams (words of three letters that don't form recognisable words, like ZFB) to participants, and then got them to count backwards in threes from a large three-digit number (to prevent repetition of the letters) for varying periods of time. They found that around 90 per cent of trigrams were recalled correctly after three seconds, but only 5 per cent after 18 seconds, which suggests STM duration has a capacity of between 20 and 30 seconds. However, the results may be due to flawed methodology. Because different trigrams were used on each trial, this may have led to interference between items, leading to decreased recall. Also, recalling nonsense trigrams has little relevance to STM tasks in everyday life and therefore lacks mundane realism.

Marsh *et al.* (1997) found that if participants weren't expecting to have to recall information, STM duration was only between two and four seconds, which suggests duration of STM is affected by the amount of time taken to process information.

Evaluation

- Reitman (1974) suggested the brief duration of STM is due to displacement; as new information comes into STM it pushes out existing information due to its limited capacity (see Explanations for forgetting, page 76).
- There is little in the way of research evidence considering the STM duration of other forms of stimuli, like visual images.

YOU ARE THE RESEARCHER

Design and carry out an experiment into STM duration. You'll need some nonsense trigrams for your participants. You'll also need a stop-watch to time the intervals between presentation and recall. One condition will involve a short time interval and the other condition a longer time interval.

What experimental design will you use? What will be the IV and DV? How many participants are needed? Use Peterson & Peterson's study to work out whether you need a directional or non-directional hypothesis and then construct suitable experimental and null hypotheses.

Draw up a table to record your data. Calculate totals and relevant measures of central tendency and dispersion. What conclusions can you draw from your data?

For information on research methods, see Chapter 7.

Long-term memory (LTM)

LTM involves storing information over lengthy periods of time, indeed for a whole lifetime, with information stored for longer than 30 seconds counting as LTM. All information within LTM will have originally passed through the SR and STM, though may have undergone different forms of processing during the process. Research indicates that there are several different types of LTM (see Types of LTM, pages 69–74) and LTMs are not of equal strength. Strong LTMs can be retrieved easily, like when your birthday is, but weaker LTMs may need more prompting. LTMs are not passive (unchanging) – over time they may change or merge with other LTMs. This is why memories aren't necessarily constant or accurate. There are several explanations for forgetting from LTM (see Explanations for forgetting, pages 76–83). Research also indicates that the process of shaping and storing LTMs is spread through multiple brain regions.

Coding in LTM

Coding involves the form by which LTMs are stored – the means by which information is shaped into representation of memories. Coding of information will be stronger (and thus the memory more retrievable) the deeper the level of processing of a stimulus that occurs while it is being experienced.

With verbal material, coding in LTM is mainly semantic (based on meaning), though coding occurs in other forms too, research indicating a visual and an acoustic code. (See Classic research – Baddeley (1966) on page 55.)

Research

Frost (1972) gave participants sixteen drawings in four categories (e.g. animals), differing in visual orientation, like angle of viewing perspective. The order of recall of items suggested participants used visual and semantic coding, implying evidence for a visual as well as semantic code in LTM.

Nelson & Rothbart (1972) showed that acoustic coding also occurs in LTM, as participants made recall errors involving homophones, words that are pronounced the same but have different meanings, like 'night' and 'knight', again suggesting that coding in LTM has several varieties.

Evaluation

- It's difficult to see how smells and tastes could be coded semantically and reason suggests songs are encoded acoustically, supporting the idea of several forms of encoding in LTM.
- Different types of LTM involve different brain areas, with research suggesting that they are encoded in different ways, which implies that there are varying forms of coding within LTM.

Capacity of LTM

The potential capacity of LTM is unlimited. Information may be lost due to decay and interference, but such losses don't occur due to limitation of capacity.

Research

Anokhin (1973) estimated the number of possible neuronal connections in the human brain is 1 followed by 10.5 million kilometres of noughts. He concluded 'no human yet exists who can use all the potential of their brain', suggesting the capacity of LTM is limitless.

Wagenaar (1986) created a diary of 2,400 events over six years and tested himself on recall of events rather than dates, finding he too had excellent recall, again suggesting the capacity of LTM is extremely large. Diary studies, however, are a type of case study and therefore not representative of the general population and there could also be an element of bias as people are testing themselves.

Figure 2.9 Pigeons have an LTM; they can recall 1,200 picture response associations

Evaluation

- The capacity of LTM is assumed to be limitless, as research has not been able to determine a finite capacity.
- There may be an evolutionary basis to LTM; animal studies, like that by Fagot & Cook (1996), showed that pigeons can memorise 1,200 picture response associations. Baboons still hadn't reached their capacity after three years of training, memorising 5,000 associations. This suggests that an enlarged memory capacity has a survival value, which has been acted upon by natural selection.

Duration of LTM

Duration of LTM depends on an individual's lifespan, as memories can last for a lifetime; many elderly people have detailed childhood memories. Items in LTM have a longer duration if originally well coded and certain LTMs have a longer duration, like those based on skills rather than facts (see Types of LTM, page 69). Material in STM that isn't rehearsed is quickly forgotten, but information in LTM, doesn't have to be continually rehearsed to be retained.

Research

Bahrick et al. (1975) showed 400 participants aged between 17 and 74 years a set of photos and a list of names, some of which were ex-school friends, and asked them to identify ex-school friends. Those who'd left high school in the last fifteen years identified 90 per cent of faces and names, while those who'd left 48 years previously, identified 80 per cent of names and 70 per cent of faces, suggesting memory for faces is long lasting.

Goldman & Seamon (1992) asked participants to identify odours of everyday products experienced in the last two years and odours not experienced since childhood. Although identification (by name) was better for more recent odours, there was significant identification of less-recent odours, suggesting duration of olfactory (smell-based) information in LTM is very long lasting.

Evaluation

- Sometimes information in LTM appears to be lost, but may be a problem of access to the information rather than it not being in LTM (see Explanations for forgetting, page 76).
- The type of testing techniques used may affect findings from studies of duration of LTM. Recall is often better when asking participants to recognise stimuli, rather than getting them to recall stimuli.

Table 2.1 Summary of differences in coding, capacity and duration between the SR, STM and LTM

	Sensory register		Short-term memory		Long-term memory	
Coding	Separate sensory stores for different sensory inputs	Crowder (1993)	Mainly acoustic (by sound), other codes used too	Baddeley (1966): immediate recall study	Mainly semantic (by meaning), other codes used too	Baddeley (1966): delayed recall study
Capacity	Huge	Sperling (1960)	Small: 5–9 chunks of information	Jacobs (1887)	Huge	Anokhin (1973)
Duration	Brief: varies between different sensory stores	Walsh & Thompson (1978)	Short: maximum of 30 seconds	Peterson & Peterson (1959)	Potentially for a lifetime	Bahrick et al. (1975)

Evaluation

- The MSM was the first cognitive explanation of memory and thus was influential, inspiring interest and research, and formed the basis for the working memory model leading to a greater understanding of how memory works.

- There is considerable research evidence for the existence of the separate memory stores of the SR, STM and LTM (see studies of coding, capacity and duration).

- The model is supported by amnesia cases (loss of memory). Patients either lose their LTM or their STM abilities, but not both, supporting the idea that STM and LTM are separate memory stores (see 'Increase your knowledge', below).

- The serial position effect, Murdock (1962), supports the MSM's idea of there being separate STM and LTM stores. Words at the beginning and end of a list are recalled better than those in the middle. Words at the beginning of the list, the primacy effect, are recalled because they've been rehearsed and transferred to LTM, while words from the end of the list, the recency effect, are recalled as they're still in STM.

- The main criticism of the MSM is that it is over-simplified, as it assumes there are single STM and LTM stores. Research indicates several types of STM, like one for verbal and one for non-verbal sounds (see Working memory model, page 63), and different types of LTM, like procedural, episodic and semantic memories (see Types of LTM, page 69).

- Cohen (1990) believes memory capacity cannot be measured purely in terms of the amount of information, but rather by the nature of the information to be recalled. Some things are easier to recall, regardless of the amount to be learned, and the MSM doesn't consider this.

- MSM describes memory in terms of structure, namely the three memory stores and the processes of attention and verbal rehearsal. However, MSM focuses too much on structure and not enough on processes.

INCREASE YOUR KNOWLEDGE

Case studies of amnesia support the MSM, as retrograde amnesia affects **retrieval** from LTM abilities, while anterograde amnesia affects the ability to transfer information from STM to LTM. They also support the idea of there being separate types of LTM, as generally not all forms of LTM will be affected.

Scott Bolzan (see 'In the News', page 52) is an example of retrograde amnesia, where he lost access to his LTMs (though not his procedural LTM), but could still create new memories by transferring STMs to LTM.

Scoville (1957), in an attempt to treat HM's epilepsy, removed brain tissue that resulted in HM having anterograde amnesia, being unable to encode new long-term memories, although his STM seemed unaffected, supporting the idea of separate memory stores. HM donated his brain to science on his death in 2008 aged 82.

In 1985 musician Clive Wearing caught a virus that caused brain damage and amnesia that robbed him of the ability to transfer STMs into LTMs, as well as some LTM abilities. However, his procedural LTM was intact; he could still play the piano, though he had no knowledge that he was able to.

ON THE WEB

Watch a video lecture by Professor Jens Bo Neilsen on the amnesia case study of HM (Henry Molaison) on YouTube by searching for 'Intro to Memory/ Encoding Part 1a'.

You can also read more about HM, including how he gave permission for his brain to be studied after his death, at:

http://bigpictureeducation.com/brain-case-study-patient-hm

You can see a video about the case study of Clive Wearing on YouTube by searching for 'Clive Wearing Living Without Memory'.

Figure 2.10a and b Clive Wearing and Henry Molaison – two case studies of amnesia

ASSESSMENT CHECK

1 Following a viral infection Travis suffered damage to his memory. He was unable to learn new information and could not recall events occurring a short while before. However, his memory from before his illness was not affected. For example, he knew that he was married to Lois and he could still play the guitar, an ability learned as a child.

Use the MSM to explain the change in Travis' memory ability. **[4 marks]**

2 Explain how information is coded within short-term memory. **[3 marks]**

3 In the boxes next to the descriptions and statements below, write 'SR' next to the two that relate to the sensory register, 'STM' next to the two that relate to short-term memory and 'LTM' next to the two that relate to long-term memory. One description or statement will be left over. **[6 marks]**

A Coding is mainly acoustic.

B A short-duration store holding unprocessed impressions of information

C The first storage system within the MSM

D A slave system containing visual and spatial information

E Duration is for potentially a lifetime.

F Capacity is limited to between five and nine items.

G Information that is rehearsed sufficiently will be transferred here.

4 Outline and evaluate the multi-store model of memory. Refer to evidence in your answer. **[16 marks]**

5 Outline and evaluate the role of the sensory register and short-term memory within the multi-store model. **[12 marks]**

6 Research studies of the MSM are often conducted by laboratory experiments. Give a brief explanation of one strength and one limitation of laboratory experiments. **[2 + 2 marks]**

2.2 The working memory model (WMM)

Baddeley & Hitch (1974) questioned the existence of a single STM store (their model doesn't concern LTM), arguing STM was more complex than just being a temporary store for transferring information to LTM. They saw STM as an 'active' store, holding several pieces of information while they were being worked on (hence 'working' memory). Cohen (1990) described working memory as: 'the focus of consciousness – it holds information consciously thought about now'. The **working memory model (WMM)** should not be seen as a replacement for the MSM, but more as an explanation based upon the MSM.

To replace the single STM store of the MSM, Baddeley and Hitch proposed a multi-component **working memory (WM)** of initially three components. At the head of the model is the **central executive (CE)**, which oversees the two 'slave' systems, the **visuo-spatial sketchpad (VSS)** and the **phonological loop (PL)**, temporary stores that process specific types of information. A fourth component, the **episodic buffer (EB)** was added in 2000 to address shortcomings of the model.

The central executive (CE)

The central executive (CE) acts as a filter to determine which information received by the sense organs is and isn't attended to. It processes information in all sensory forms, directs information to the model's slave systems and collects responses. It's limited in capacity and can only effectively cope with one strand of information at a time. It therefore selectively attends to particular types of information, attaining a balance between tasks when attention needs to be divided between them, for example, talking while driving. It also permits us to switch attention between different inputs of information.

Research

Baddeley (1996) discovered participants found it difficult to generate lists of random numbers while simultaneously switching between pressing numbers and letters on a keyboard, suggesting the two tasks were competing for CE resources. This supports the idea of the CE being limited in capacity and only being able to cope with one type of information at a time.

D'Esposito *et al.* (1995) found using fMRI (functional magnetic resonance imaging – see Chapter 6) scans that the prefrontal cortex was activated when verbal and spatial tasks were performed simultaneously, but not when performed separately, suggesting the brain area to be associated with the workings of the CE.

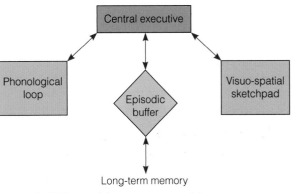

Figure 2.11 The working memory model

- Little is known about the central executive. It isn't clear how it works or what it does. This vagueness means it can be used to explain almost any experimental results. If two tasks cannot be performed together, then the two processing components are seen as conflicting, or it is argued that the tasks exceed the central executive's capacity. If two tasks can be done simultaneously, it's argued they don't exceed the available resources, in essence a circular argument (an argument that continually proves itself).

- The CE is probably better understood as a component controlling the focus of attention rather than being a memory store, unlike the PL and the VSS, which are specialised memory stores.

Phonological loop (PL)

The PL deals with auditory information (sensory information in the form of sound) and the order of the information, like whether words occurred before or after each other. The PL is similar to the rehearsal system of the MSM, with a limited capacity determined by the amount of information that can be spoken out loud in about two seconds. As it's mainly an acoustic store, confusions occur with similar sounding words.

Baddeley (1986) divided the PL into two sub-parts; the **primary acoustic store (PAS)** and the **articulatory process (AP)**. The PAS, or inner ear, stores words recently heard, while the AP, or inner voice, keeps information in the PL through sub-vocal repetition of information and is linked to speech production.

Research

Trojani & Grossi (1995) reported a case study of SC, who had brain damage affecting the functioning of his PL but not his VSS, suggesting the PL to be a separate system.

Baddeley *et al.* (1975) reported on the word length effect, where participants recalled more short words in serial order than longer words, supporting the idea that capacity of the PL is set by how long it takes to say words, rather than the actual number of words.

- PET scans show that different brain areas are activated when doing verbal and visual tasks, which suggests that the PL and the visuo-spatial sketchpad (VSS) are separate systems, reflected in the biology of the brain.

- The PL is strongly associated with the evolution of human vocal language, with the development of the slave system seen as producing a significant increase in the short-term ability to remember vocalisations. This then helped the learning of more complex language abilities, such as grammar and expressing meaning.

Visuo-spatial sketchpad (VSS)

The VSS, or inner eye, handles non-phonological information and is a temporary store for visual and spatial items and the relationships between them (what items are and where they're located). The VSS helps individuals to navigate around and interact with their physical environment, with information being coded and rehearsed through the use of mental pictures.

KEY TERMS

Primary acoustic store (PAS) – part of the phonological loop, stores words heard

Articulatory process (AP) – part of the phonological acoustic store, allows sub-vocal repetition of information within the store

Visual cache (VC) – part of the VSS, stores information about form and colour

Inner scribe – part of the VSS, stores information about the physical relationships of items

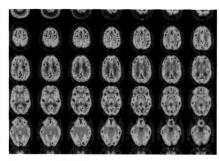

Figure 2.12 PET scans produce images that allow psychologists to see which brain areas are involved with different types of memory

Logie (1995) suggests sub-dividing the store into a **visual cache (VC)**, which stores visual material about form and colour, and an **inner scribe (IS)**, which handles spatial relationships and rehearses and transfers information in the visual cache to the CE.

Research

Gathercole & Baddeley (1993) found participants had difficulty simultaneously tracking a moving point of light and describing the angles on a hollow letter F, because both tasks involved using the VSS. Other participants had little difficulty in tracking the light and performing a simultaneous verbal task, as both tasks involve using the VSS and the PL, indicating the VSS to be a separate slave system.

Klauer & Zhao (2004) reported more interference between two visual tasks than between a visual and a spatial task, implying the existence of a separate visual cache and inner scribe.

Evaluation

- As well as showing the PL and the VSS to be located in different brain areas, PET scans also show brain activation in the left hemisphere of the brain with visual tasks and activation in the right hemisphere with spatial information, which further supports the idea of dividing the VSS into a separate VC and IS.
- Studies of the VSS (and the PL) often feature a dual task technique, where participants have to perform two simultaneous activities. However, the actual tasks performed are often not ones encountered much in everyday life and so such studies can be accused of being artificial and lacking in mundane realism.

YOU ARE THE RESEARCHER

Design an experiment to test whether participants can do two acoustic tasks at the same time. Firstly get someone to speak some numbers into a participant's ear; the participant has to add them up. Then get two people to simultaneously speak different numbers into both of the participant's ears and see if the participant can add them both up separately. What would be your IV? Your DV? How could you do something similar for: (i) two visual tasks; (ii) one visual and one acoustic task?

For more on research methods, see Chapter 7.

Figure 2.13 Can people perform two acoustic tasks at the same time?

The episodic buffer

Baddeley (2000) added a third slave system, the episodic buffer (EB), as the model needs a general store to operate properly. The PL and the VSS deal with the processing and temporary storage of specific types of information, but have limited capacity, and the CE has no storage capacity, and so cannot contain items relating to visual and acoustic properties. Therefore the EB was introduced to explain how it is possible to temporarily store information combined together from the CE, the PL, the VSS and LTM.

Research

Prabhakaran *et al.* (2000) used fMRI scans to find greater right-frontal brain activation for combined verbal and spatial information, but greater posterior activation for non-combined information, providing biological evidence of an EB that allows temporary storage of integrated information.

Alkhalifa (2009) reported on a patient with severely impaired LTM who demonstrated STM capacity of up to 25 prose items, far exceeding the capacity of both the PL and the VSS. This suggests the existence of an EB, which holds items in working memory until they are recalled.

PSYCHOLOGY IN THE REAL WORLD

Figure 2.14 Children with ADHD often have impairments in their working memory

The WMM suggests practical applications; especially for children with attention deficit hyperactivity disorder (ADHD) relating to impairments of working memory (WM). Alloway (2006) recommends several methods to help children focus on the task at hand:

1 Use brief and simple instructions so they don't forget what they're doing.
2 Break instructions down into individual steps.
3 Frequently repeat instructions.
4 Ask the child to periodically repeat instructions.

Klingberg *et al.* (2002) additionally report that computerised working memory training, using systematic exercises to produce cognitive gains, is beneficial to those with poor WM.

CONTEMPORARY RESEARCH

Exhibiting the effects of the episodic buffer (EB) on learning with serial and parallel presentations of materials – Ashaa Alkhalifa (2009)

As well as being a psychologist, Ashaa Alkhalifa is a member of the royal family of Bahrain, and has devised a method of testing for the existence of the episodic buffer as a general store for material integrated from other memory stores.

Aim
To determine the existence of the EB by seeing if parallel presented information overwhelms both the PL and the VSS, causing a reduction in learning, while the same information presented sequentially exhibits superior learning by being stored firstly in the PL and the VSS and then filtered to the EB, which should have a larger capacity.

Procedure
48 university students were presented with numbers on a screen given either as a sequence (e.g. 1, 2, 3, 4) or in parallel fashion where participants compare information in different parts of the screen simultaneously. Numbers of sufficient complexity were used to overwhelm the capacities of both the phonological loop and the visuo-spatial sketchpad. Participants were required to answer a number of problem-solving questions concerning the numbers presented.

Findings
Participants given numbers presented in a sequence got more problem solving questions right than those given numbers presented in parallel fashion.

Conclusions
As sequential processing was more effective, it suggests the total capacity of WM is larger than that determined by

the capacity of the phonological loop and the visuo-spatial sketchpad, implying the existence of the EB. There is a limit to the amount of information that can pass from perception to learning, as parallel processing causes a hindrance to learning.

Evaluation

The findings suggest practical applications in the designing of educational systems, as students will be able to learn more material with teaching methods that use sequential rather than parallel means.

As a laboratory study the findings may lack external validity, i.e. a lack of generalisability to other settings.

It may be that the EB provides the storage space and the CE the underlying processing of information that allows the separation of accurate recall from false memories and delusions.

The addition of the EB shows how the process of science works, with the model being updated after research highlighted shortcomings of the explanation. Therefore the addition of the EB 26 years after the model was first suggested can be seen as a strengthening of the model's ability to explain how memory works.

ON THE WEB

Professor Alan Baddeley is one of the most famous names in memory research and helped form the WMM. A video interview from 2010 that has him talking about all aspects of the WMM can be found at:

www.gocognitive.net/interviews/alan-baddeley-working-memory

STRENGTHEN YOUR LEARNING

1 Name the four main components of the WMM and briefly describe their functions.
2 What is the difference between:
   (i) the primary acoustic store (PAS) and the articulatory loop (AL)
   (ii) the visual cache (VC) and the inner scribe (IS)?
3 Give details of one research study that suggests that a visual and an acoustic task can be performed simultaneously.
4 Explain why the WMM doesn't work without the episodic buffer (EB).

ASSESSMENT CHECK

1 Walter is able to draw an accurate picture of his friend's face whilst simultaneously adding up numbers spoken aloud to him by his friend. Thinking he must be very talented, Walter was disappointed to find that he could not draw an accurate picture of his friend's face with one hand whilst at the same time tracing a moving dot of light with his other hand.

Refer to the WMM to explain why Walter is sometimes unable to perform two tasks at the same time. **[4 marks]**

2 Outline the central executive and episodic buffer components of the WMM. **[3 + 3 marks]**

3 Discuss features of the WMM. **[16 marks]**

4 Outline and evaluate the Working Memory Model. **[12 marks]**

5 Below is a list of components that relate to the WMM. Select from them to complete the table that describes different parts of the model. One component will be left over. **[4 marks]**

Central executive

Visual cache

Semantic memory

Episodic buffer

Articulatory process

Name of component	Description of component
	A filter determining which information is attended to
	Allows sub-vocal repetition of information stored in the phonological loop
	Stores information about form and colour
	A slave system dealing with processing and temporary storage of specific types of information

6 Research studies of the WMM sometimes use case studies of patients with brain damage that affects the functioning of their memory. Explain ethical considerations researchers would have to take into account when conducting such research. **[4 marks]**

2.3 Types of long-term memory

The WMM shows that the MSM is over-simplified as an explanation of memory, as there is more than one type of short-term memory store and the situation is the same with LTM; research indicates the existence of several types, each with a separate function and associated with different brain areas. The main sub-division of LTM is into explicit (also known as declarative, as it's easy to put into words) and implicit (also known as non-declarative, as it's not easy to express in words) types. Explicit LTMs are ones recalled only if consciously thought about, while implicit LTMs don't require conscious thought to be recalled. Explicit memories are also often formed from several combined memories.

Two types of explicit LTM are featured in this chapter: semantic and **episodic memories**, and one type of implicit LTM, procedural memory.

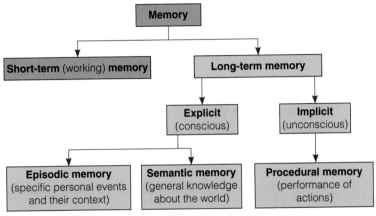

Figure 2.15 Types of long-term memory

Episodic LTM

Episodic LTM, first suggested by Endel Tulving (1972), is the memory that gives individuals an autobiographical record of personal experiences: when their birthday is, the circumstances of their children being born, etc. The strength of episodic memories is influenced by emotions present at the time a memory is coded, for example traumatic events are often well recalled due to their high emotional content. Strength of episodic memories is also affected by the degree of processing of information at coding, with highly processed episodic events recalled more easily. It is thought that episodic memory helps individuals to distinguish the difference between real events and imagination/delusions.

The prefrontal cortex brain area is associated with initial coding of episodic memories, with consolidation (strengthening) and storage of the memories associated with the neocortex. Memories of the different parts of an event are located in the different visual, auditory, olfactory, etc. areas of the brain, but are connected together in the hippocampus to create a memory of an episode rather than remaining a collection of separate memories.

Figure 2.16 Remembering when your birthday is, is an example of episodic LTM

Memory: performance, knowledge and experience – Endel Tulving (1989)

Figure 2.17 Endel Tulving

Early research into memory was concerned with identifying which brain areas were involved, but Estonian psychologist Endel Tulving was more interested in the mental processes occurring not just during retrieval of memories, but during storage too. Tulving wanted to assess memory as a conscious experience and not just document it as a form of performance. He therefore studied LTM from a much more cognitive approach than before.

Aims

- To investigate possible differences in the processing of episodic and semantic memory tasks.
- To assess the effectiveness of neuro-imaging as a means of investigating mental processes.

Procedure

1 Six volunteers were injected with a small amount of radioactive gold, which was scanned to detect its location with a gamma ray detector. Tulving was one of the participants, along with his wife and a colleague.

2 Each participant performed 8 successive trials, each lasting 80 seconds, involving 4 semantic and 4 episodic topics in randomised order.

3 Individual trials were separated by 2 minutes of rest each. A participant would lie, face up, on a couch with their eyes closed and indulge in either episodic or semantic LTM retrieval. The retrievals involved silent mental thought rather than physical stimulation or recording of behaviour.

Participants selected what topics they would think about: episodic ones involving personally experienced events, like a holiday, and semantic ones involving general knowledge acquired through learning, like by reading a book.

4 At a signal from a researcher a participant would begin thinking about a topic, the gold being injected in after 60 seconds and the scanning occurring about 8 seconds later, after the gold tracer had arrived in the brain. The scanning process took another 2.4 seconds.

Findings

Three participants produced inconclusive data for reasons that were not apparent. Data from the other three participants showed consistent differences in cortical blood flow patterns between semantic and episodic thinking. There was greater activation in the frontal lobes (anterior regions) of the cortex during thinking about episodic memories and greater activation in the posterior region of the cortex when retrieving semantic information.

Conclusions

Episodic and semantic LTMs appear to involve different brain areas and thus are separate forms of LTM.

The fact that episodic and semantic LTMs involve different brain areas suggests a biological basis to differences in LTM.

Evaluation

The identification of the involvement of the frontal lobes during episodic recall is supported by observations of the memory abilities of brain-damaged amnesiacs. Those with impaired episodic LTM tend to have damage to the frontal lobes.

The study provided, through successful use of neuro-imaging, an effective means of objectively studying and measuring cognitive processes within live participants.

As only 3 out of 6 participants showed differences between processing of episodic and semantic LTMs, the findings cannot be seen as conclusive or generalisable to the population as a whole.

As Tulving himself was one of the participants, plus his wife and another colleague, it may have been difficult to conduct the study and analyse the findings in an unbiased, objective manner.

ON THE WEB

A 5-minute video on the influential work of Endel Tulving, featuring the man himself, can be found on YouTube by searching for 'Dr Endel Tulving'.

Research

Herlitz *et al.* (1997) assessed explicit LTM abilities in 1,000 Swedish participants, finding that females consistently performed better than males on tasks requiring episodic LTM, although there were no differences in semantic LTM ability. This suggests that there are gender differences in episodic memory ability, which may be explained in part by females' generally having higher verbal ability.

Evaluation

- The extent to which episodic and semantic memory systems are different is unclear, as although different brain areas are involved, there is also a lot of overlap between the two systems, with semantic memories often clearly originating in episodic memory. Whether, therefore, the gradual transformation of an episodic into a semantic LTM means a change in memory systems cannot be certain.

- It may be that episodic memory differs from that of semantic memory in terms of different types of thinking and emotion; episodic memories are associated with conscious awareness of events and emotional feelings related to them, while semantic memories are associated with objective analysis of phenomena.

PSYCHOLOGY IN THE REAL WORLD

Figure 2.18 Scientists are attempting to programme episodic memory into a robot

Scientists at Vanderbilt University, USA, using knowledge of how memory works, are trying to programme episodic memory into their robot ISAC, the ultimate aim being to more closely mimic the brain functions of a human.

Already ISAC can recall specific past experiences to solve a current problem, just like a human would do and can indirectly affect the carrying out of tasks by influencing information placed in working memory. When given a new task, ISAC creates associations between the new task and stored experiences and then uses these associations to decide which information is entered into working memory. ISAC also uses episodic memory to relate past experiences of success and failure in different situations to decide preferences in new situations, which allows ISAC to influence goal and task setting.

Attempts are now being made to give ISAC an episodic buffer, so that it can combine information from separate memory channels involving different types of sensory input (just like the VSS and PL do in a human) into single memory chunks.

CONTEMPORARY RESEARCH

Using imagination to understand the neural basis of episodic memory – Demis Hassibis, Dharshan Kumaran, Eleanor Maguire (2007)

Figure 2.19 Episodic memories that use different brain areas may be the way individuals tell the difference between reality and fantasy

Episodic memory is generally seen as occurring through reconstructing experiences individuals have had, with research indicating that a number of brain areas are involved. However, Demis Hassibis and colleagues came up with a research variation whereby neuro-imaging of the brain would occur while participants thought about either true experiences they had had or imaginary ones.

Aim

To investigate whether different brain areas are involved in episodic LTM involving real and imagined experiences.

Procedure

1 10 male and 11 female participants aged between 18 and 31, recalled i) recent episodic memories, ii) fictitious experiences created during a pre-scan interview one week before and iii) constructed entirely new fictitious experiences whilst being scanned.

2 Interviews were conducted one week before scanning, with individual participants performing 4 tasks.
   Real objects condition (ROC) – participants were shown

on a computer screen images of 10 everyday objects (for instance a picture of a red fire extinguisher) along with written descriptions underneath the images (like 'a red fire extinguisher with black nozzle') for 20 seconds each.
Imagined objects condition (IOC) – 10 verbal descriptions of everyday objects were read out (like 'a fancy gold-plated pen with a silver nib and the initials JT engraved along the casing'); participants closed their eyes and tried to imagine visual images of the objects for 20 seconds each.
Imagined scene condition (ISC) – participants were asked to create 10 fictitious scenes prompted by short verbal cues of believable settings (like 'lying on a beach in a tropical sandy bay'). Participants had 2–3 minutes to describe each scene in as much detail as possible. (Each of these scenes could not be of a true or planned experience.)
Real memory condition (RMC) – participants were asked to describe 10 recent episodic memories.

3 During fMRI scans one week later, participants were given a one-word cue, flashed up onto a computer screen, that described what kind of trial type was being assessed.
'Recall' – a description of a real memory or object seen in the interview session (RM and RO conditions)
'Recreate' – reconstruction of scene/object created in the interview session (IS and IO conditions)
'Imagine' – construction of new fictitious scene or object (NS and NO conditions)
'Focus' – imagination of and focusing upon an imaginary white crosshair on a black background

4 Seven conditions (3 scene conditions: RMC, IS, NSC; 3 object conditions: ROC, IOC, NOC; and the low imagery baseline condition) with 10 trials per condition, yielding 70 trials in total. Scanning consisted of four main sessions

lasting around 11 minutes each during which 17 or 18 trials were randomly presented such that 2 or 3 trials were presented per condition, and never the same condition twice in a row. Text cues remained on the screen for 5.5 seconds and were then replaced by a 'close your eyes' text instruction.

Findings

By using comparisons of the fMRI scans for the different conditions, it was possible to identify that scene construction involved a wide range of brain areas, including the hippocampus, parahippocampal gyrus, and retrosplenial cortex and these were different from episodic memory-specific responses, which involved the anterior medial prefrontal cortex, posterior cingulate cortex and precuneus brain areas.

Conclusions

Episodic LTMs involving real and imagined experiences involve different brain areas.

The anterior medial prefrontal cortex, posterior cingulate cortex and precuneus brain areas are involved in familiarity processes that enable individuals to tell the difference between real and imaginary memories.

Evaluation

The study shows that imagining new experiences can be an effective experimental tool that may prove useful in increasing understanding of episodic memory and the processes underpinning it, as well as other related cognitive functions.

It may be that individuals who experience delusions and/or have difficulty in distinguishing between reality and fantasy, have suffered damage to particular brain areas.

Semantic LTM

Semantic LTM is another type of explicit memory and contains all knowledge (facts, concepts, meanings, etc.) an individual has learned (though of course not when the knowledge was learned). The strength of **semantic memories**, like episodic memories, is positively associated with the degree of processing occurring during coding, though in general semantic memories seem to be better sustained over time than episodic ones. Semantic LTMs are linked to episodic LTMs, as new knowledge tends to be learned from experiences, with episodic memory therefore underpinning semantic memory. Over time there will be a gradual move from episodic to semantic memory with knowledge becoming increasingly divorced from the event/experience that it was learned from.

There is disagreement over which brain areas are involved in semantic LTM; some evidence suggests involvement of the hippocampus and related areas, while others believe there is usage of several brain areas. Coding is mainly associated with the frontal and temporal lobes.

Research

Kroenig (2007) created 64 imaginary, but believable drawings of animals, one of which was the prototype for 'crutters' (animals that shared three particular features). Alzheimer sufferers and non-sufferers then had to decide which of the 64 drawings were of crutters. Participants had to use either direct comparison to make their assessments – judging which animals were crutters based on their similarity to the picture of the prototype – or they based their comparison on a stated rule that crutters matched the prototype on three of the four target features. Alzheimer sufferers were as good as non-sufferers when using direct comparison, but inferior when using the stated rule. As using a stated rule involves higher-level processing, it suggests semantic memory involves different processes and brain areas.

Vicari *et al.* (2007) reported on the case study of CL, an eight-year-old girl who suffered brain damage due to the removal of a tumour. She demonstrated deficiencies in her episodic LTM functions, especially in creating new episodic memories, but was still able to create and recall semantic memories. This suggests that episodic and semantic memory are separate systems using different brain areas, with the hippocampus associated with episodic memory and the perirhinal cortex with semantic LTM.

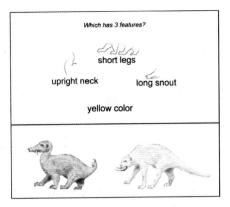

Rule-based training trial

Evaluation

- Semantic memory may involve more of a network of associated links performed in different brain areas, rather than being a single form of memory ability. Some links may be stronger than others or quicker to access, explaining why some semantic memories appear to be easier to recall than others.
- The fact that damage to different areas of the brain can affect semantic memory abilities differently supports the idea that semantic memory abilities are spread throughout brain structures, whilst also supporting the idea that semantic memory may consist of several interrelated memory abilities and therefore not be a single type of memory.

Similarity-based training trial

Figure 2.20 'Crutters' – make-believe animals used by Kroenig (2007) to investigate semantic LTM

Procedural LTM

Procedural LTM is a type of implicit memory permitting individuals to perform learned tasks with little conscious thought, for instance riding a bicycle. Although seemingly easy to do, procedural LTMs are difficult to explain in words (and so are classed as being non-declarative). Many procedural LTMs occur early in life, involving the learning of important motor skills, like walking, dressing, etc. Procedural LTM is also involved in language, helping individuals to speak automatically, using grammar and syntax without thinking how to. This shows how procedural and semantic memories work together. As **procedural memory** doesn't require conscious thought, it permits people to simultaneously perform other cognitive tasks that require attention.

Procedural LTM is associated mainly with the neocortex brain areas of primary motor cortex, cerebellum and prefrontal cortex, and unlike explicit forms of LTM, doesn't need the hippocampus to function.

Research

Finke *et al.* (2012) reported the case study of PM, a 68-year old professional cellist who suffered damage to various brain areas after contracting encephalitis, resulting in severe amnesia. His episodic and semantic LTM were very affected, but although he could not remember musical facts, such

KEY TERM

Procedural memory (PM) – type of LTM for the performance of particular types of action as the names of famous composers, his ability to read and play music was unaffected, including the learning of new complex pieces.

Figure 2.21 Knowing how to surf is an example of procedural LTM

Van Gorp *et al.* (1999) compared 37 heavy cocaine users with 27 non-abusing controls on memory ability for a 45-day period after abstaining from the drug. The interesting finding was that the former cocaine users showed a faster increase in procedural memory ability than non-users. As abstinence from cocaine causes dopamine production to be much increased, it suggests dopamine plays a part in procedural LTM.

Evaluation

- One problem in deciding which brain areas are involved in procedural memory is the relative lack of research. What is needed are case studies of people with brain damage that affects procedural memory but not explicit memory (semantic and episodic memory). However, such cases are rare.
- Procedural memories generally take longer to learn than explicit memory abilities. This may be because procedural memory involves motor functions and spatial abilities, while explicit memory tends not to (though the learning of procedural memories can also involve higher-level processing too).

STRENGTHEN YOUR LEARNING
1 What is the difference between semantic, episodic and procedural LTMs?
2 **(i)** Detail the findings and conclusions of Tulving's 1989 study of LTM.
   (ii) Give one strength and one limitation of the study.
3 Summarise the aims, procedure, findings and conclusions of Hassibis *et al.*'s 2007 study of episodic LTM.

ASSESSMENT CHECK

1 'I find it curious', said Mara, 'that when I try to remember the answers for my psychology test I have to think really hard, but when I ride my surfboard I don't have to think how to do it at all.'

   With reference to types of LTM, explain why Mara finds remembering the answers to her psychology test more difficult than remembering how to surf. **[4 marks]**

2 Explain what is meant by procedural long-term memory. **[3 marks]**

3 Discuss types of long-term memory. **[16 marks]**

4 Outline and evaluate episodic and procedural long-term memory. **[12 marks]**

5 Select from the descriptions A, B, C and D to complete the table concerning types of LTM below. One description will be left over. **[3 marks]**

   A Type of LTM for performing actions, tasks and skills

   B Type of LTM for facts, meanings and concepts

   C Type of LTM for events occurring in an individual's life

   D Type of LTM for emotional responses

Type of LTM	Description
Episodic	
Semantic	
Procedural	

6 For the data in the table below calculate:

   (i) the mean

   (ii) the median

   (iii) the mode

   (iv) the range. **[4 marks]**

Participant	Score on a LTM test
1	9
2	6
3	8
4	6
5	6
6	7
7	5

IN THE NEWS

Ψ The Psychological Enquirer

Discovering 'repressed' memories

In 1989 Laura B's sister Amy claimed to have discovered 'repressed' memories of sexual abuse by her own father, Joel Hungerford, when she was young. Laura B then attended 100 sessions of psychotherapy over nine months, often with her sister, building up a close relationship with her therapist. Five 'memories' of abuse were recovered that Laura B had no previous recollection of. These 'memories' would often start as unpleasant feelings (such as a dream of people walking in on her when on the toilet and feeling uncomfortable with it), which the therapist would then enlarge on through questioning, e.g. 'do you want to find out where that bathroom is?' Attempts to visualise the incident would occur and eventually actual sexual abuse by her father would be 'remembered', including being raped with a gun when

a little girl. Laura B recalled the abuse continuing until two days before her wedding. These revelations were then reported to the police and charges brought against her father; the sisters also broke off all contact with their father.

But Joel Hungerford was a lot luckier than many who had been in his position; in 1995 the Supreme Court of New Hampshire ruled that the recovered memories were not admissible as evidence, due to them being 'not scientifically reliable'. Joel then sued the psychotherapist. From this case came the term 'Hungerford's law'; whereby accusations involving recovered memories can only be heard in court if they pass strict criteria to ensure their validity. The problem with such

memories is the often highly suggestive questioning and methods used by therapists (e.g. 'guided visualisation'), leading to one accusation of them being a 'lobotomy for the modern age'. Before Joel Hungerford, many individuals, often loving fathers, had been publicly ruined and wrongly jailed for long periods over allegations of sexual abuse. Hundreds of accusers have subsequently withdrawn allegations of sexual abuse, many successfully suing their therapists. Work by psychologists like Elizabeth Loftus have helped to show how memories are not always accurate, this knowledge having huge implications for how court cases are conducted.

2.4 Explanations for forgetting

'As you get older three things happen, first your memory goes and the other two I can't remember.'
Norman Wisdom (2010)

KEY TERMS

Forgetting – the failure to retrieve memories

Retrieval failure – an explanation for forgetting when material is stored in the LTM but cannot be consciously recalled as a result of a lack of retrieval cues to 'jog the memory'

Interference/Interference theory (IT) – an explanation for forgetting when similar material is confused in recall from the LTM

Proactive interference – a form of interference that occurs when past memories inhibit an individual's full potential to retain new memories

Forgetting can be defined as a failure to retrieve memories (**retrieval failure**), with explanations varying between those that see information as no longer within storage, for example trace decay theory, and explanations that see forgetting as a failure to access stored information, i.e. the information is still within storage, but an individual cannot retrieve it – for example, **interference**.

Interference theory (IT)

IT sees forgetting as due to information in LTM becoming confused with or disrupted by other information during coding, leading to inaccurate recall. There are two forms of interference: proactive and retroactive.

1 **Proactive interference** – works forwards in time, occurring when information stored previously interferes with an attempt to recall something new, for example the memory of an old phone number disrupts attempts to recall a new phone number.

2 **Retroactive interference** – works backwards in time, occurring when coding new information disrupts information stored previously, for example the memory of a new car registration number prevents recall of a previous one.

Interference is generally researched by getting participants to learn two lists of word pairs, where the first word of each word pair is the same in both lists. After the lists have been memorised participants are given the first word of a pair and asked to recall which word goes with it. When proactive interference occurs, participants recall the first list of word pairs, while with retroactive interference the second list of word pairs is recalled.

KEY TERM

Retroactive interference – a form of interference that occurs when newly learned information interferes with the recall of previously learned information

List A	List B
Prince – Light	Prince – Record
Sock – Bench	Sock – Letter
Child – Moon	Child – Gravel
Carrot – Bird	Carrot – Shirt
Door – Knife	Door – Pudding

Figure 2.22 Example of lists of word pairs used to test for interference in memory

Figure 2.23 Confusing an old car registration number with a new one is an example of forgetting due to interference

CONTEMPORARY RESEARCH

Remembering the street names of one's childhood neighbourhood – Henk Schmidt *et al.* (2000)

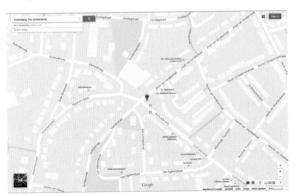

Figure 2.24 Street map of Molenberg in Holland

Many studies of interference use artificial laboratory conditions and thus have little relevance to real life. However, Henk Schmidt and his colleagues devised a method of testing for interference in a real-life setting by using childhood memories of street names.

Aim

To assess the influence of retroactive interference upon the memory of street names learned during childhood.

Procedure

1 700 names were selected randomly from a database of 1700 former students of a Dutch elementary school and were sent a questionnaire. 211 participants responded, ranging in age from 11 to 79 years, and were given a map of the Molenberg neighbourhood (where they had gone to school) with all 48 street names replaced with numbers and asked to remember as many of them as possible. Other relevant personal details were collected by questionnaire, such as how many times they had moved house, where they had lived and for how long, how often they visited Molenberg, etc.

2 The amount of retroactive interference experienced was assessed by the number of times individuals had moved to other neighbourhoods or cities (thus learning new sets of street names). This measurement was very variable; 25 per cent of participants had never moved, while one participant had moved 40 times.

Findings

There was a positive association between the number of times participants had moved house outside the Molenberg neighbourhood and the number of street names forgotten.

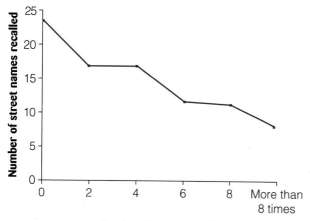

Figure 2.25 Number of street names recalled as a function of the number of times participants had moved to other neighbourhoods or cities

The findings suggest that learning new patterns of street names when moving house makes recalling an older pattern of street names harder to do.

Retroactive interference does seem able to explain forgetting in some real-life situations.

There are a number of extraneous variables that may have confounded results. For example, those who had played extensively in the neighbourhood or walked to school would probably have learned the street names to a greater degree than those who didn't play in the neighbourhood or who were driven to school.

The methodology used shows that it is possible to conduct research on retroactive interference in real-life settings; indeed the methodology could easily be adapted to test the influence of proactive interference too.

Research

Baddeley & Hitch (1977) got participants who had played a varying number of rugby union games to remember as many of the teams they had played against as possible. Interference theory was tested by assessing how recall was affected by the number of games played, while trace decay theory (see 'Increase your knowledge', page 81) was tested by assessing the amount of time that had passed between each game played. It was found that forgetting was due more to the number of games played rather than time passed between games, supporting interference theory rather than decay theory.

Abel & Bauml (2013) gave participants either a single list of word pairs to learn or two lists that would cause interference (the first word of each word pair being the same in both lists). Participants were tested on their memory of the lists after twelve hours of either wakefulness or sleep and it was found that sleep reduced both proactive and retroactive interference. This suggests that sleep helps to strengthen and stabilise memory content, making it less vulnerable to interference at recall.

Evaluation

- The main criticism of interference is that it only really explains forgetting when two sets of information are similar, for example when simultaneously learning French and Welsh at school. This does not happen very often and so interference cannot explain forgetting in the majority of real-life settings.
- Research into interference tends to use laboratory experiments based around artificial tasks, such as learning lists of word pairs, and as such can be accused of lacking mundane realism, not relating to real-life scenarios.
- Although studies show interference to be a real effect, they do not clearly identify the cognitive processes at work.
- There is more research support for **cue-dependent forgetting**, and other explanations of forgetting exist too, meaning IT cannot explain all examples of forgetting.

Cue-dependent forgetting (CDF)

CDF occurs when information is still in LTM, but can't be accessed. CDF sees recall as dependent upon retrieval cues – like the labels on files in a filing system. Recall is dependent upon accessing information by remembering the retrieval cue under which the information is stored. Tulving (1973) explained this as the encoding-specificity principle, where recall is hindered if the context of recall is different to that at coding. The effectiveness of a retrieval cue depends on how overloaded it is (the fewer the number of items associated with it, the more effective the cue), how deep the processing of the cue was and how well the cue fits the information associated with it.

There are two main forms of CDF: **context-dependent failure** and **state-dependent failure**.

● **Context-dependent failure** – occurs with *external* retrieval cues, with forgetting occurring when the external environment is different at recall from how it was at coding – for example, getting fewer marks in a test when sitting the test in a room you're not familiar with than when sitting the test in your normal classroom.

Research

Abernethy (1940) found that participants after learning some material recalled it less well when tested by an unfamiliar teacher in an unfamiliar room than participants who were tested by a familiar teacher in a familiar room. This supports context-dependent failure as an explanation of forgetting.

Godden & Baddeley (1975) got divers to learn material either on dry land or while underwater. Recall was found to be worse when it occurred in a different context to coding than the same context, for example recalling words learned under water were recalled better when under water than on dry ground. This gives further support to the cue-dependent failure explanation.

● **State-dependent failure** – occurs with *internal* retrieval cues, with forgetting occurring when an individual's internal environment is dissimilar at recall to when information was coded – for example, trying to recall information learned when sober while you are drunk.

Research

Overton (1972) got participants to learn material when either drunk or sober and found that recall was worse when participants were in a different internal state at recall than their internal state at coding – for example, recalling information learned when drunk was better if the information had been learned when drunk rather than sober. This suggests that state-dependent failure is a valid explanation of forgetting.

Darley *et al.* (1973) found that participants who hid money while high on marijuana were less able to recall where the money was when they were not high than when they were high again, providing additional support for the ability of state-dependent failure to explain forgetting.

Figure 2.26 Cue-dependent forgetting sees memory as like a filing cabinet, as you'll need to recall the name of the file as a retrieval cue to access a particular memory

KEY TERMS

Cue-dependent forgetting (CDF) – a type of forgetting based upon a failure to retrieve the prompts that trigger recall

Context-dependent failure – a form of CDF where recall occurs in a different external setting to coding

State-dependent failure – a form of CDF where recall occurs in a different internal setting to coding

RESEARCH IN FOCUS

1 How might Overton's 1972 and Darley's 1973 studies into state-dependent failure be considered unethical?

2 What is a cost–benefit analysis and how might it be used to justify unethical aspects of research?

For information on research methods, see Chapter 7.

Gems	Birds	Instruments
Sapphire	Stonechat	Trumpet
Ruby	Crow	Guitar
Emerald	Dipper	Saxophone
Opal	Wren	Drum

Figure 2.27 Example of category headings and lists used in retrieval cue research

Retrieval failure is often assessed by giving participants lists of items to learn, and then measuring recall after category headings of items on the lists are given or not.

Tulving & Pearlstone (1966) gave participants a written list of 48 words to learn organised into twelve categories of four words each. At the top of each category was a one-word heading (for example 'Fruit') followed by the names of four types of fruit. Participants were told they wouldn't have to recall the headings, just the words in the categories. Participants who weren't given the headings as cues to facilitate recall (free recall condition) remembered fewer words than participants given the headings as cues (cued recall condition). This supports the lack of retrieval cues as an explanation for forgetting.

Evaluation

- Many studies supporting CDF are laboratory-based and not like everyday memory tasks, such as ones based on procedural memory. The ability to perform learned skills, like riding a bike, isn't affected by state-dependent failure.

- Godden & Baddeley's findings only occurred when the divers had to free-recall items learned. When given a recognition test (involving saying whether a named item was in the learned list or not), the context-based effect wasn't seen, suggesting that cue-dependency can't explain all forms of forgetting.

- Cue-dependent forgetting fits the levels of processing theory of memory that states the more deeply information is processed when coded (how much thinking, what types of thinking, etc. occur) the more links and associations will be created between items in LTM, decreasing the chances for forgetting, as more retrieval cues will be available to aid recall.

- Many psychologists see CDF as the main reason for forgetting in LTM, due to the amount of research evidence supporting the importance of cues and how they trigger memory.

PSYCHOLOGY IN THE REAL WORLD

Figure 2.28 The reconstruction of the last moments of Danielle Jones

One practical use of knowledge gained by psychologists about cue-dependent forgetting is that of police reconstructions of unsolved crimes.

The aim is to jog the memory of witnesses by recreating the context of the incident through the use of retrieval cues, with participants wearing identical clothes and the reconstruction taking place in the same location and timescale as originally.

Danielle Jones was murdered in Essex in 2001, but her body was never found. Her uncle was eventually convicted, largely due to witness testimony that emerged after a reconstruction of the crime. Witnesses recalled seeing Danielle arguing with a man and getting into a blue transit van, a vehicle owned by her uncle. He was sentenced to life imprisonment.

INCREASE YOUR KNOWLEDGE

Several theories of forgetting in STM and LTM exist, with some theories explaining forgetting in either STM or LTM and some theories explaining forgetting in both.

Forgetting in STM

Two main theories have been put forward to explain forgetting in STM.

Trace decay (TD)

TD refers to a gradual fading of a memory. TD assumes that memories are stored as a physical trace called an engram and that memory traces decay over time.

Peterson & Peterson (1959) gave participants nonsense trigrams and found that if rehearsal of information was prevented by subtracting numbers aloud, short-term memories of the trigrams decayed almost completely after 18 seconds (see page 57). This suggests that the information was no longer in storage in line with TD.

Kandel (2006) found that structural changes occurred in neurons in the hippocampus of sea slugs when repeatedly stimulated, which suggests that physical memory traces are created in STM and that they're transferred to LTM when they become permanent, again supporting the idea of physical traces being created in memory.

Evaluation of trace decay

Maybe information in STM is displaced by other information, rather than decaying. For instance in Peterson & Peterson's study, the trigrams may have been displaced by the numbers recited to prevent rehearsal of the information.

Trace decay theory can explain forgetting in both STM and LTM, giving it the advantage of being a universal explanation, i.e. one that can be applied to all instances of forgetting.

Displacement theory (DT)

DT sees information as being lost from STM as it has a limited capacity (between five and nine items) and so new information displaces old information.

Waugh & Norman (1965) found that if a number (called the probe) from a list of numbers occurred nearer the end of a list than the beginning, recall of the next number was better. This suggests later numbers had displaced earlier ones from the limited-capacity STM store.

Shallice (1967) used the probe technique to assess both the displacement and decay theories, finding forgetting was less if numbers were presented faster (less chance for the information to decay), but also found that changing the probe's position had a stronger effect (affecting the chances for displacement to occur). This indicates that both displacement and decay cause forgetting in STM, but that displacement is more important.

Figure 2.29 Displacement is based on the idea of more recent items in STM pushing out older ones

Evaluation of displacement theory

Displacement can only explain forgetting in STM; as the capacity of LTM is believed to be practically endless it would therefore be impossible for LTM to be 'full' allowing newer material to displace older material.

Displacement theory can help explain the recent effect seen in the serial position effect (see 'You are the researcher', below), where the last few items in a list are still within the STM span (of five to nine items) and so have not yet been displaced. If individuals have to concentrate on other items given after the list of items, then the recency effect disappears, presumably as the more recent items displace the last few items in the original list (though decay theory could be the reason too).

YOU ARE THE RESEARCHER

The serial position effect involves the primacy and recency effects (see evaluation of the MSM – Murdock (1962), page 60). Design a study using a list of about fifteen unconnected words to investigate this phenomenon.

Previous research indicates more words from the beginning and the end of the list will be recalled, so what kind of hypothesis would you use?

If you wished to perform subsequent research that only investigated the recency effect, how could you prevent the primacy effect from occurring?

For more on research methods, see Chapter 7.

RESEARCH IN FOCUS

Much research into forgetting involves laboratory experiments, which allow extraneous variables to be kept to a minimum. What are extraneous variables and how do they differ from confounding variables?

For information on research methods, see Chapter 7.

Repression

Another important explanation of forgetting in LTM is that of repression. Repression is a type of motivated forgetting where emotionally threatening events are thought to be banished into the unconscious mind, to prevent the feelings of anxiety they might cause. Although the repressed memories continue to affect conscious thoughts, desires and actions, they are difficult to retrieve. This is a controversial area, as repressed memories 'recovered' during repressed memory therapy have often proved to be false, a phenomenon known as false memory syndrome. The accusation here is that such therapists are unwittingly suggesting and planting false memories in clients (see In the news, page 76).

Research

Williams (1994) investigated repression in women who had been diagnosed as suffering childhood sexual assaults. Thirty-eight per cent of the females had no recall of the earlier abuse and of those who did recall it, 16 per cent reported that at one time they hadn't been able to recall it, but had now 'recovered' the memories. Williams also found that the earlier the age the abuse had supposedly occurred, the more likely it was not be remembered. These findings suggest painful memories can be forgotten and then later 'recovered', supporting the concept of repression.

Karon & Widener (1997) found that many Second World War veterans who suffered battlefield trauma, repressed the memories, and the resulting mental disturbance was only relieved by these memories being recovered in therapy, giving further support to the validity of repression as an explanation of forgetting.

Holmes (1990) reviewed 60 years of research into repression and did not find any solid evidence of the phenomenon, weakening support for the explanation.

Bradley & Baddeley (1990) found that possibly anxiety and arousal depress STM, but enhance LTM. However, it may be that anxiety and arousal initially cause repression, but that it disappears over time, giving a different explanation as to why apparently forgotten memories are recovered.

Evaluation

- One criticism of Williams' study is that it is unknown if the original diagnoses of abuse were correct. It may be that some women didn't have a memory of the abuse, because it simply didn't occur, rather than having repressed the memory. It may also be possible that some women do remember being abused, but choose to pretend not to remember it, as they don't wish to talk about it.

- The idea of false memory syndrome is that it sees so-called 'recovered' memories as actually being false memories created through leading questions asked by therapists (questions that suggest certain false events may actually have occurred). Although some practitioners still argue that the technique is a valid one, the use of recovered memories as a psychotherapeutic technique is banned by the American Psychiatric Association and the British Psychological Society says there is no evidence to support the concept of recovered memories.

- Several successful court cases have been fought in the USA where people convicted on the basis of recovered memories have shown this to be false and have won huge sums in compensation, weakening support for the concept of repression.

ON THE WEB

Watch renowned psychologist Elizabeth Loftus talk about false memories and EWT at a lecture she gave in Edinburgh in 2013 by searching YouTube for 'Elizabeth Loftus: The fiction of memory'.

STRENGTHEN YOUR LEARNING

1 What is the difference between proactive and retroactive interference? Give an example of each.
2 Explain the technique by which interference is usually studied (hint: word pairs).
3 Detail the procedure and findings of Schmidt *et al.*'s 2000 study into interference.
4 What is the difference between context-dependent forgetting and state-dependent learning?
5 Explain the technique by which retrieval failure is usually investigated.
6 Why is cue-dependent forgetting a better explanation of forgetting than interference?
7 Explain what is meant by:
   (i) trace decay
   (ii) displacement
   (iii) repression.

1 Best friends Emma and Anneka get very similar scores on their psychology tests. However, recently when Anneka had to sit a test in an unfamiliar classroom, supervised by a teacher she'd never met before, she scored much worse than Emma, who sat the test in her usual classroom supervised by their usual teacher, even though the teacher didn't give her any help.

With reference to retrieval cues, explain why Anneka did worse than Emma in their recent psychology test. **[4 marks]**

2 Outline one explanation for forgetting. **[4 marks]**

3 Outline and evaluate two explanations for forgetting. **[16 marks]**

4 Discuss proactive and retroactive interference as explanations for forgetting. **[12 marks]**

5 Select from the descriptions A, B, C and D to complete the table concerning explanations for forgetting below. One description will be left over. **[3 marks]**

   A Forgetting based upon a failure to recover the prompts that trigger recall

   B Forgetting due to newly learned information interacting with and impairing the recall of previously learned information

   C Forgetting due to not chunking the material into meaningful sections

   D Forgetting due to interaction of material learned previously with that attempting to be remembered

Explanation for forgetting	Statement
Retroactive interference	
Absence of retrieval cues	
Proactive interference	

6 To test whether forgetting is due to retrieving information in a different context to that in which it was coded, a researcher reads a list of words to two groups of participants. Twenty minutes later one group recalls the list in the same room, while the other group recalls it in a different room.

Compose a suitable null hypothesis for this experiment. **[2 marks]**

IN THE NEWS

Ψ The Psychological Enquirer

Picking Cotton

Figure 2.30 'I was certain, but I was wrong' – Jennifer Thompson and Ronald Cotton

Back in 1984, college student Jennifer Thompson was confronted by an intruder in her flat. He overpowered her, held a knife across her throat and raped her. During the ordeal Jennifer carefully memorised every detail of his face, determined that if she survived she would ensure he was captured and imprisoned. She went straight to the police and constructed a sketch of the rapist, looking carefully through hundreds of images of facial features to get it absolutely right. A few days later she identified Ronald Cotton as the attacker. She was certain it was him and picked him out again at a police identity parade. On the strength of Jennifer's eye-witness testimony (EWT) Ronald was convicted and sent to jail – she said it was the happiest day of her life and she was so convinced of his guilt that she wanted him electrocuted, desiring to flip the switch herself.

But Ronald Cotton was innocent. Eleven years later in 1995 DNA samples proved it was another man that had committed the crime. Ronald was released from prison and Jennifer begged his forgiveness, which Ronald gave. The two have become close friends and given lectures on the unreliability of EWT. Unfortunately this wasn't an isolated case and there is a high probability that innocent people have been executed on the strength of false EWT. The Innocence Project in the USA has led to 214 men convicted of crimes they didn't commit due to false EWT. Ronald and Jennifer have written a book, *Picking Cotton*, about their experience, which illustrates the serious implications, especially in courts of law, for this area of psychology.

ON THE WEB

You can read a fuller account of Jennifer Thompson and Ronald Cotton's incredible story at:

http://faculty.washington.edu/gloftus/Other_Information/Legal_Stuff/Articles/News_Articles/Thompson_NYT_6_18_2000.html

Or for a video of a lecture Jennifer gave in Bristol about her ordeal, for the Innocence Project in 2012, search YouTube for 'Jennifer Thompson: Innocence and Forgiveness'.

KEY TERMS

Eyewitness testimony (EWT) – evidence provided by those recalling an event who were present when the event took place

Schema – a readiness to interpret sensory information in a pre-set manner

'There are lots of people who mistake their imagination for their memory.'
Josh Billings (1860)

'Memory is a complicated thing, related to truth, but not its twin.'
Barbara Kingsolver (2002)

Eyewitness testimony (EWT)

The guilt or innocence of people being tried in courts of law often depends upon the accuracy of the memories of eyewitnesses. Jurors often find **eyewitness testimony (EWT)** vitally important in making their decision and yet in 75 per cent of cases where individuals have been found by DNA evidence to have been wrongly convicted, the original guilty verdict was based on inaccurate EWT. Research into EWT is therefore vital, as it helps further understanding of how memory works, especially as to how inaccurate memories can be created, which then helps form practical applications as to how court cases should be conducted and how witness statements should be gathered – for instance, courts cannot convict an accused person on the basis of one uncorroborated eyewitness statement.

The influence of schema

Bartlett (1932) stated that memories aren't accurate 'snapshots' of events, but are 'reconstructions' of events, influenced by active **schemas**, ready-made

Figure 2.31 Schema involves seeing or remembering what you expect to see or remember: for example, here many people will see 'Paris in the Spring' (even though it doesn't state this) as that's what they expect to see

expectations based on previous experiences, moods, existing knowledge, contexts, attitudes and stereotypes. Schemas are used to make sense of the world, by 'filling in the gaps' in our knowledge and by simplifying the processing of information. This affects the reliability of EWT, because witnesses aren't merely recalling facts as they happened, instead they're reconstructing memories that are biased by schemas active at the time of recall, which can lead to false memories.

Research

Bartlett (1932) found that when Western cultural participants were told a Navajo Indian story, 'The War of the Ghosts', that didn't make sense from their cultural viewpoint, their memory of the story became distorted, with details of the story being changed to fit a Western cultural viewpoint. This illustrates how memory can be affected by cultural schemas, perceptions of what happened from a particular cultural viewpoint.

> **YOU ARE THE RESEARCHER**
>
> Design a study based on Bartlett's 'The War of the Ghosts' to investigate how schema can affect recall. You'll need to write a story that has no clear plot. Create some opportunities for participants to change the story using schemas. For example, you could include a librarian who likes to go out clubbing and a racing car driver who is shy and retiring, as the librarian may then get recalled as shy and retiring, as that fits the typical view of librarians.
>
> You'll need about eight participants. Only tell the story to the first participant, who then tells it to the second participant and so. The last participant writes down what they recall. How would you record and analyse data?
>
> *For information on research methods, see Chapter 7.*

2.5 Factors affecting the accuracy of eyewitness testimony (EWT)

Several factors have been identified as affecting the accuracy of eyewitness testimony (EWT); misleading information, in the form of leading questions and post-event discussion, will be featured here, along with anxiety factors.

Misleading information

Research regularly shows that EWT is affected by experiences occurring after a witnessed event. A key factor is the use of **misleading information**, particularly in the form of leading questions and **post-event discussion**. For instance, most people will have seen TV dramas set in courtrooms where barristers are accused of 'leading the witness' by asking questions that suggest a certain answer. Misleading information has been found to be more able to create false memories the more believable, emotionally arousing and subtle it is.

Leading questions are questions that increase the likelihood that an individual's schemas will influence them to give a desired answer.

Post-event discussion concerns misleading information being added to a memory after the event has occurred, with research indicating that false memories can be stimulated by misleading post-event experiences.

CLASSIC RESEARCH

Reconstruction of automobile destruction: an example of the interaction between language and memory – Elizabeth Loftus & John Palmer (1974)

Elizabeth Loftus would go on to forge a career based around research into EWT and the formation of false memories. In this early study she found that participants' memories of important details of an event witnessed on video could be influenced by the use of misleading questions.

Aim

To assess the extent to which participants' estimates of the speed of cars involved in accidents witnessed on video could be influenced by misleading questions.

Procedure

1 **Experiment one:** 45 university students were each shown 7 video clips of car crashes. After each accident participants wrote an account of what they could recall and answered specific questions, the key question being to estimate the speed of the vehicles. There were 5 conditions (with 9 participants in each condition), with the conditions varying through which verb was used in asking the key question.

Key question: About how fast were the cars going when they .... each other?

The blank space was filled with either 'contacted', 'hit', 'bumped', 'collided' or 'smashed'.

Participants' estimations of speed were then recorded.

2 **Experiment two:** 150 student participants viewed a video of a car crash. 50 were asked the key question with the word 'smashed' in it, 50 with the word 'hit' and a control group of 50 weren't asked at all. One week later they were questioned about their memory of the event, with the key question being 'Did you see any broken glass?' (There wasn't any.)

The number of participants who recalled broken glass was then recorded.

Findings

Experiment One:

Verb	Mean estimate of speed in miles per hour
Contacted	31.8
Hit	34.0
Bumped	38.1
Collided	39.3
Smashed	40.8

As the intensity of the verb used in the key question increased, so did the estimation of the speed of the cars.

Experiment Two:

Answer	Smashed	Hit	Control
Yes	16	7	6
No	34	43	44

Participants were twice as likely in the 'smashed' condition to recall the false memory of broken glass.

Conclusions

Experiment one showed that misleading information in the form of leading questions can affect memory recall of eyewitnesses.

Experiment two showed that misleading information in the form of post-event information can also affect memory recall of eyewitnesses.

Both studies suggest that at recall misleading information is reconstructed with material from the original memory.

Evaluation

The study is a laboratory experiment centred on an artificial task (watching videos) and as such lacks relevance to real-life scenarios. Witnessing real car crashes would have much more of an emotional impact and thus would affect recall differently.

The results may be due to demand characteristics, rather than genuine changes in memory; participants may have just given the answer they thought the researchers wanted, as suggested by which verb they heard in the key question.

RESEARCH IN FOCUS

1 A limitation of Loftus & Palmer's 1974 study is that demand characteristics may have caused the results. What are demand characteristics and how may they have occurred here?

2 How might including 'filler' questions as well as the 'key question' help reduce demand characteristics?

For information on research methods, see Chapter 7.

Research

Loftus (1975) found that 17 per cent of participants who watched a video of a car ride and were asked 'how fast was the car going when it passed the white barn?' (when there was no barn) recalled seeing a barn a week later, which supports the idea that post-event information added to a memory after the event has occurred, can affect recall.

Bekerian & Bowers (1983) showed slides of events leading up to a car crash, finding that participants' memories remained intact despite being asked leading questions, which suggests that post-event information affects the retrieval of memories rather than their storage.

Figure 2.32 Loftus & Pickrell planted false memories of being lost as a child into participants' memories. In another study they got people to remember meeting Bugs Bunny at Disneyland

Loftus & Pickrell (1995) gave 24 participants aged 18–53 four stories about their childhoods provided by relatives; three of the stories were true, but one was false, involving being lost in a department store aged five then rescued by an elderly lady before being returned to their family. Participants were then asked what they could remember of these incidents and to report 'I do not remember this' if they had no recollection of an event. 68 per cent of true incidents were recalled and 29 per cent of the false ones, with details and clarity of false memories being lower than for true ones. The findings imply that false memories can be created from suggestion.

Tomes & Katz (1997) found individuals who identify with others' moods, score highly on measures of imagery vividness and have poor recall are more affected by misleading questions, implying personality factors influence EWT.

CONTEMPORARY RESEARCH

Make my memory: How advertising can change our memories of the past – Loftus & Pickrell (2003)

Figure 2.33 Elizabeth Loftus

Inspired by their earlier success in creating false memories in individuals of being lost as a child in a shopping mall, Elizabeth Loftus and Jacqueline Pickrell were motivated to perform several studies centring on childhood memories of visits to Disneyland, an emotional experience that would presumably be remembered clearly. In this particular study the researchers showed how both verbal and pictorial suggestions created false memories of meeting Bugs Bunny at Disneyland – an impossibility, as he's a Warner Brothers character.

Aims

- To see whether false memories could be created through the use of suggestion.
- To investigate whether autobiographical advertising can make memories become more consistent with images evoked in advertising.

Procedure

120 students who had visited Disneyland in childhood were divided into four groups and instructed to evaluate advertising copy, fill out questionnaires and answer questions about a trip to Disneyland.

Group 1 read a fake Disneyland advert featuring no cartoon characters.

Group 2 read the fake advert featuring no cartoon characters and were exposed to a cardboard figure of Bugs Bunny placed in the interview room.

Group 3 read the fake Disneyland advert featuring Bugs Bunny.

Group 4 read the fake advert featuring Bugs Bunny and saw the cardboard figure of Bugs Bunny.

Findings

30 per cent of participants in group 3 and 40 per cent of participants in group 4 remembered or knew they'd met Bugs Bunny when visiting Disneyland.

A ripple effect occurred whereby those exposed to misleading information concerning Bugs Bunny were more likely to relate

Bugs Bunny to other things at Disneyland not suggested in the ad, such as seeing Bugs and Mickey Mouse together.

Figure 2.34 This image of Bugs Bunny was used in the fake advert

Conclusions

Through the use of post-event information, false memories can be created.

Both verbal and pictorial suggestions can contribute to false memories.

Memory is changeable and vulnerable to inaccuracy.

Evaluation

The study can be considered superior to Loftus' famous study of car crashes, as it uses memory of a real-life event rather than something watched on video.

The study shows the power of subtle association changes on memory.

A practical application is that of advertisers using nostalgic images to manufacture false positive memories of their products.

Evaluation

- The consequences of inaccurate memories are minimal in research settings compared to real-life incidents. Foster *et al.* (1994) showed EWT was more accurate for real-life crimes as opposed to simulations.

- Participants don't expect to be deliberately misled by researchers; therefore inaccurate recall should perhaps be expected since participants believe the researchers to be telling the truth.

- Misleading information often affects only unimportant aspects of memory. Memory for important events isn't as easily distorted when the information is obviously misleading. Subtle and plausible misleading information is much more influential.

- Studies of EWT that use potentially distressing stimuli bring ethical concerns of psychological harm. For instance, care should be taken not to include participants who may have experienced traumatic car accidents. Many studies of EWT also involve elements of deceit.

- Whether advertisers should be allowed to use techniques that deliberately try to create positive false memories of products so that people will buy them is debatable, as it could be argued to be a form of lying.

Anxiety

A main criticism of EWT research is that it often uses artificial scenarios that have no emotional involvement for witnesses. Real-life events, however, such as violent crimes, often have a high **anxiety** content that can greatly affect recall. One area of special interest is the degree to which anxiety might divert attention away from the important aspects of an event being witnessed. Loftus *et al.* (1987) argued for a 'weapons effect', whereby witnesses to violent crimes focus on the weapon being used, rather than the culprit's face, negatively affecting the ability to recall important details. Psychologists have performed lots of research, using both laboratory studies and real-life events, to identify the ways in which anxiety affects EWT.

The Yerkes-Dodson inverted-U hypothesis (IUH)

Deffenbacher (1983) used the IUH (originally a description of the relationship between arousal and performance) to explain how anxiety levels affect the accuracy of recall of events experienced. The IUH sees moderate amounts of anxiety as improving the detail and accuracy of memory recall up to an optimal (best) point, after which further increases in anxiety lead to a decline in the detail and accuracy of recall. The findings of research have been used to investigate whether this is true, though it is difficult to reach any firm conclusions.

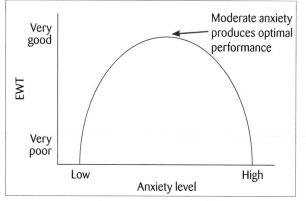

Figure 2.35 The Yerkes-Dodson inverted-U hypothesis

Repression

(See Explanations for forgetting, page 76.) Repression has also been offered up as an explanation of how anxiety can affect the accuracy of recall. Freud (1894) argued that anxiety hinders the recall of memories, as he saw forgetting as being motivated by the traumatic content of memories. Access to memories would be barred, so as to protect individuals from the emotional distress they would cause. Research evidence is not without criticism and some would argue whether the concept actually exists in reality.

Research

Loftus *et al.* (1987) found that if a person is carrying a weapon, then witnesses focus on the weapon rather than the person's face, negatively affecting their ability to recall facial details of armed criminals, supporting the idea that anxiety can divert attention from important features of a situation in line with the weapons effect.

Deffenbacher (1983) performed a meta-analysis of 21 studies examining the role of anxiety in the accuracy of EWT, finding heightened anxiety tended to negatively affect the memory of eyewitnesses. This again suggests that anxiety can divert attention away from important features of a situation. However, Christianson & Hubinette (1993) studied the recall of witnesses to real bank robberies, finding contradictory evidence, in that increased arousal led to improvements in the accuracy of recall, suggesting that anxiety-creating situations don't always divert attention from important features of a situation.

Research

Ginet & Verkampt (2007) produced moderate anxiety in participants by telling them fake electrodes attached to them would give electric shocks. Their recall of minor details of a traffic accident viewed on video was superior to participants with lower anxiety produced by being told the fake electrodes were purely for recording purposes. This implies moderate anxiety does increase EWT in line with the IUH. Peters (1988) provided further support by testing people attending their local health clinic for an injection. During the visit, they met a nurse, who gave them the injection, and a researcher for equal periods of time. Later on, using photographs, the researcher proved easier to recognise than the nurse, suggesting the heightened anxiety levels due to the injection led to a decrease in memory accuracy.

Oue *et al.* (2001) found that participants who were anxious from viewing emotionally negative events, recalled less details from the edge of a scene than participants witnessing emotionally neutral events; this suggests anxiety reduces witnesses' fields of view.

Koehler *et al.* (2002) found participants less able to recall stressful words than non-stressful words, lending support to Freud's concept of repression. However, Hadley & MacKay (2006) found stressful words were better recalled, as they were more memorable, suggesting repression may occur in some instances, but not always. (Other research on repression can be found on page 82.)

Figure 2.36 Witnessing a real-life incident often has much more emotional impact than a laboratory study

Evaluation

- Much research into anxiety and EWT is laboratory based, so do findings generalise to real-life scenarios? Yuille & Cutshall (1986) investigated the anxiety levels and accuracy of recall of thirteen witnesses to a fatal shooting in Vancouver, Canada, finding those with high anxiety had less accurate recall than those with lower levels, but those witnesses with very high anxiety had extremely accurate recall, which casts doubt on the inverted-U hypothesis, as those with very high anxiety should have shown less accurate recall. However, Fruzetti *et al.* (1992) point out that those with the highest levels of anxiety were actually closer to events and this might have helped their accuracy recall.

- Deffenbacher (2004) reviewed his earlier findings and found them over-simplistic. He performed a meta-analysis of 63 studies, finding that EWT performance increased gradually up to extremely high levels of anxiety, after which there was a catastrophic drop in performance with a negative impact on both accuracy of eyewitness identification and accuracy of recall of crime-related details. This supports an amended version of the IUH known as catastrophe theory.

- Care must be taken with studies of anxiety and EWT as, by their very nature, such studies could produce potentially high levels of psychological harm.

- Other factors could have a mediating effect on how anxiety affects the accuracy of memory recall; for instance, research indicates that age can have an effect on EWT accuracy and as individuals react differently to anxiety-creating situations it is highly possible that personality factors would play a mediating role too.

2.6 Improving the accuracy of eyewitness testimony

'I have a memory like an elephant, indeed elephants often consult me.'

Noel Coward (1959)

What psychologists have learned about the nature of memory and forgetting can be applied to the development of techniques that aid memory recall, either in everyday scenarios, or in specific situations, such as when interviewing witnesses to serious crimes. The general aim is to increase the accuracy of memories and the amount of accurate detail produced.

The cognitive interview (CI)

Table 2.2 Components of the cognitive interview

Component	Description
Change of narrative order	Recall the event in different chronological orders, e.g. from end to beginning
Change of perspective	Recall the event from different people's perspectives, e.g. from the offender's point of view
Mental reinstatement of context	Recall both the environmental and emotional context of the event, e.g. weather and personal feelings
Report everything	Recall all information, even that which seemingly has little relevance or that which is remembered less confidently or seems incomplete

KEY TERMS

Cognitive interview (CI) – a procedure for police questioning of witnesses that promotes accurate, detailed recall of events

The **cognitive interview (CI)** was developed by Fisher & Geiselman (1992) and is a series of memory retrieval and communication techniques designed to improve recall in police interviews. It is based on Tulving's (1974) idea that there are several retrieval paths to each memory and information not available through one pathway may be accessible through another.

Two such pathways are the 'change of narrative order' and 'change of perspective' components of the CI, which encourage interviewees to recall events in a variety of orders and different perspectives (viewpoints).

The CI also involves Tulving & Thomson's Encoding Specificity theory (1973), which suggests memory traces are made up of several features and, to enhance recall, as many retrieval cues as possible should be used. Context provides cues that increase feature overlap between initial witnessing and subsequent retrieval contexts. 'Context reinstatement' involves emotional elements of an event witnessed, i.e. how an individual was feeling, which work via state-dependent effects, for example returning to the scene of the crime and picturing how it smelt, what could be heard, etc. and sequencing elements, like what you were doing at the time. The final element, 'reporting everything', works on the basis that even seemingly trivial details can trigger more important memories.

The 'change of narrative order' and 'change of perspective' strategies are believed to aid recall because they reduce witnesses' use of prior knowledge, expectations and schemas, increasing witness accuracy.

Research

Geiselman *et al.* (1985) found that the CI procedure produced more accurate, detailed memories than the SPI technique and interviews conducted under hypnosis, suggesting the technique is relatively effective.

Geiselman & Fisher (1997) found that the CI works best when used within a short time following a crime rather than a long time afterwards, suggesting recall is enhanced best when CIs are conducted immediately after an incident has occurred.

Kohnken *et al.* (1999) conducted a meta-analysis of 55 studies comparing CI to a **Standard police interview (SPI)**, finding CIs produced more accurate detail, but also more inaccurate detail. No age differences were found, but recall was enhanced when witnesses were personally involved in the event being witnessed. The amount of correct detail produced seemed to decline the longer a CI was conducted after an event had occurred. This suggests the CI is relatively effective, but should be conducted immediately after an event and ways of reducing the production of inaccurate information need to be explored.

Milne & Bull (2002) found the 'report everything' and 'context reinstatement' components of the CI to be the key techniques in gaining accurate, detailed recall, which suggests modified versions of the CI should concentrate on these features.

The enhanced cognitive interview (ECI)

Fisher & Geiselman (1987) suggested an amended version of the CI known as the **enhanced cognitive interview (ECI)** that seeks to build a trusting relationship between interviewer and witness and improve the quality of communication between the two.

Important extra features of the ECI include:

- the interviewer not distracting the witness with unnecessary interruptions/questions
- the witness controlling the flow of information
- asking open-ended questions
- getting the witness to speak slowly
- participants being reminded not to guess and to use the 'don't know' option when necessary, in order to reduce confabulations (false memories)
- reducing anxiety in witnesses.

The ECI starts by getting the witness to control the flow of information through asking them open-ended questions on neutral topics. The next stage then involves context reinstatement, followed by the witness's free recall of events. During this time the interviewer stresses the importance of 'report everything' and not guessing if details are unknown. The interviewer then moves on to asking about the information recalled using focused memory techniques that involve asking the witness to concentrate on mental images of the memory, such as a person's face and using these to guide recall. The idea here is that details are most retrievable when they are perceptually related to the witness's mental image and so interviewers should time their questions accordingly.

ON THE WEB

For a 10-minute video on how a cognitive interview is conducted, search YouTube for 'Example of Cognitive Interview'.

KEY TERMS

Standard police interview (SPI) – the established method of police questioning

Enhanced cognitive interview (ECI) – an advanced method of questioning witnesses that overcomes problems caused by inappropriate sequencing of questions

Figure 2.37 The modified cognitive interview is often used to allow police officers to interview children

Modified versions of the CI and ECI have been produced for different reasons. Holliday (2003) produced a **Modified cognitive interview (MCI)** suitable for use with children, which stresses building a trusting relationship between interviewer and witness, gives control to the witness and removes the 'change perspective' component, as children are seen as being too young to effectively empathise with others (see things from another's point of view). Other MCIs are shortened versions, as many police forces have found that the CI and ECI take more time than they have available. These generally omit the 'change narrative order' and 'change perspective' components.

Research

Fisher *et al.* (1989) assessed the performance of police officers in gathering facts when using the ECI compared to a SPI, finding the ECI to be superior.

Coker (2013) found that an ECI technique that stressed the use of focused mental imagery produced increased accurate detail in comparison to the CI technique, especially concerning personal details of people being recalled and that this effect was greater if the ECI took place one week after an event rather than immediately afterwards. This suggests the ECI is an improvement on the CI, but that the timing of when an interview is conducted is vital to its success.

Holliday (2003) showed children, aged 4–5 and 9–10 years old, a five-minute video of a child's birthday party, with all children being interviewed the next day using either a SPI or a MCI specifically designed for use with children. The MCI produced more accurate detail than the SPI, illustrating the effectiveness of MCIs with specific groups of witnesses.

Verkampt & Ginet (2010) interviewed 229 children after a painting session, with either a CI, a SPI or one of four types of MCI, finding that the CI and MCIs were all superior to the SPI in producing accurate detail and that versions of the MCI that removed the 'change narrative order' component were superior, which supports the idea that MCIs are beneficial for specific types of witnesses.

Evaluation

- Although the CI was primarily designed for use by police interviewers, its success has led to calls for it be more widely used by other organisations and in situations where accuracy of memory recall is important.
- Although the ECI has proved a more effective technique, it's also more prone to producing confabulations, where incorrect items are recalled.
- As the CI is composed of several techniques, it makes working out which are the most effective components difficult.
- Comparison of CIs with SPIs isn't easy, as police interview techniques other than the CI are not standard, but actually use a lot of different techniques, for instance just asking 'what can you recall' or asking specific questions.
- A practical problem with the CI is it's time consuming, often requiring more time than officers have operational time for. Also, Memon *et al.* (1993) report that officers believe the 'change of perspective' component misleads witnesses into speculating about the event witnessed and due to this concern it's less frequently used.
- One limitation of cognitive interviews is that they are not generally effective as a form of memory-enhancement with regards to the recognition of suspects in identity parades and photographs.
- The development of MCIs means groups of witnesses, such as children and those with learning difficulties, can be interviewed effectively; 45 per cent of MCIs are designed for use with children.

CONTEMPORARY RESEARCH

The Cognitive Interview: A meta-analytic review and study space analysis of the past 25 years – Amina Memom, Christian Meissner & Joanne Fraser (2010)

Figure 2.38 How successful has the cognitive interview technique been?

Amina Memon and colleagues decided to commemorate the 25th anniversary since the introduction of the cognitive interview, by conducting a meta-analysis of studies into the effectiveness of the technique. They included studies used in the last major meta-analysis by Kohnken *et al.* (1999), as well as more recent ones, including those featuring the more recent modified cognitive interview, an amendment of the ECI.

Aims

- To assess the effective of the CI over a 25-year period as a vehicle for producing accurate, detailed information in the standard police interviewing (SPI) of witnesses.
- To see if the findings of the last major meta-analysis could be replicated to check their validity.

Procedure

1 57 studies (involving 65 experiments) to include in the meta-analysis were found through the online data bases PsycARTICLES and PsycINFO and also by contacting researchers in the field. All research had to involve experimental studies of the CI in comparison to a control or other interview technique, as well as being studies published, or accepted for publishing, in peer-reviewed journals.
2 64 per cent of the studies involved young adult witnesses, 28 per cent involved children, 8 per cent the elderly and 6 per cent learning disabled people.
3 32 per cent of the studies used the CI, 23 per cent the ECI and 45 per cent versions of the MCI.

Findings

1 The CI was seen to produce significantly more accurate detail than non-CI comparison techniques and the size of this effect was greater than that found by Kohnken *et al.* (1999). The effect was less evident with children, but more evident with the elderly in comparison to young adults.
2 As with the previous meta-analysis, a small but significant increase in inaccurate details was found between the CI and comparison techniques. The effect was less evident with children and at the same level for the elderly in comparison to young adults.
3 The CI and non-CI methods were seen as not to differ in the amount of confabulations (false memories) that they produced. The MCI, though, did produce slightly more confabulations.
4 The MCI produced significantly more inaccurate details than the CI and ECI, but there were no significant differences between all types in terms of the amount of accurate detail produced.

Conclusions

CIs are producing more accurate, detailed information than before, but also more inaccurate detail, with no differences in the amount of confabulated memories. These effects are more greatly evident among young adults and the elderly.

The CI and ECI seem superior in terms of the lesser amount of inaccurate detail produced compared to the MCI and the lesser number of confabulations produced.

The CI is an effective manner of conducting interviews in comparison to SPI techniques.

Evaluation

Although MCIs perform less well than the CI and the ECI, they are superior to the SPI procedure and may be more practical for police services to use in terms of time and cost–benefit considerations. The police don't always have the time or manpower to conduct full versions of the CI.

Increases in confabulations with the MCI may be due to interviewers overlooking a key component of the ECI: that witnesses shouldn't guess if they are unsure.

Several important factors have not been considered in the meta-analysis, such as how long after an event has occurred was an interview conducted, the number of times a witness was questioned and the degree of emotional involvement a witness had. All of these could have had large mediating effects.

RESEARCH IN FOCUS

1 Memon *et al.*'s 2010 study is an example of a meta-analysis. How is a meta-analysis conducted?
2 What is the main advantage of carrying out a meta-analysis?
3 What weaknesses of the method are there?

For information on research methods, see Chapter 7.

INCREASE YOUR KNOWLEDGE

Two other methods of increasing the accuracy of memory recall are **mnemonics** and **active processing**. Both techniques can be used to improve general recall or to facilitate recall in specific situations, such as being an eyewitness to a serious incident.

Mnemonics

Mnemonics are techniques that aid memory recall by the organisation of information. They work by developing links to existing memories in storage, so that retrieval of a familiar item leads to the recall of less familiar items. One proven method is to impose a common structure upon the material to be recalled.

Visual imagery mnemonics focus on visual images, for example a familiar route through the rooms of your house, whereby objects to be recalled are placed in each room. These objects are visualised within their visual settings and recall is aided by individuals imagining taking the familiar route.

Baltes & Kleigl (1992) that older adults should use verbal mnemonics rather than visual ones, as they increasingly find it harder to produce and recall visual images. This suggests the ability to use different forms of mnemonics changes throughout an individual's life.

Herrmann (1987) found interactive imagery, where two items are linked together, either visually or verbally, to be the most effective strategy, but the verbal mnemonic of creating a narrative story is most effective for recalling lists of items in any order. This implies different mnemonic techniques are more effective with particular types of memory tasks.

Evaluation of mnemonics

People differ in their abilities to visualise, and therefore the usefulness of visual imagery is dependent on how much an individual is a 'high-imager' or a 'low-imager'.

Visual imagery mnemonics often only work when trying to learn and recall actual objects rather than abstract concepts and ideas and so are not a universal means of improving memory.

Active processing

Active processing concerns procedures where learners go beyond mere passive, unthinking encoding of information and instead subject material to deep and meaningful processing. The deeper and more meaningful the processing, the better recall will be.

Craik & Lockhart (1972) found that if participants analysed material by meaning (semantics), recall was better, suggesting semantic processing draws upon many varied links between items in LTM, recall becoming easier as more recall pathways are created.

Arsenal 0	vs	Port Vale 6	
Manchester United 0	vs	Accrington Stanley 4	
Exeter City 2	vs	Plymouth 1	
Dagenham & Redbridge 3	vs	Barnet 0	
Inverness CT 1	vs	Ross County 5	

Figure 2.39 Active processing helps football fans to remember scores, for example by comparing scores to expected ones

Morris *et al.* (1985) found that football fans recalled more actual scores than non-fans, as they actively processed the information, for example comparing scores to expected ones and calculating the impact upon league positions. This suggests active processing is a useful strategy for memory improvement.

Evaluation of active processing

Active processing is a circular concept (proves itself). Not only is strongly processed information recalled better, but also information that's well recalled has been actively processed. This makes the concept untestable and non-scientific.

Active processing is a dynamic theory, seeing memory as a process, not a set of passive stores. It provides meaningful associations between memory and other cognitive areas, such as perception, language, etc.

STRENGTHEN YOUR LEARNING

1 Explain how schema can affect eyewitness testimony (EWT).
2 What is meant by:
   (i) leading questions
   (ii) post-event information?
3 Explain:
   (i) how in Loftus & Palmer's 1974 study of EWT demand characteristics may have affected the results
   (ii) what the main limitation of the study is.
4 How does Loftus & Pickrell's 2003 study of EWT suggest that advertisers can create false memories?
5 (i) How can the inverted 'U' hypothesis be used to explain the relationship between anxiety and memory?
   (ii) Does research suggest this is true?
6 Name and describe the four components of the CI.
7 What is the difference between the CI, ECI and MCI?
8 What does Memon *et al.*'s 2010 study suggest about the effectiveness of all types of cognitive interviews?
9 Explain what is meant by:
   (i) mnemonics
   (ii) active processing.

ASSESSMENT CHECK

1 Roland has been in court accused of causing a car crash by driving too fast. Witnesses to the crash questioned by the lawyer defending Roland recalled Roland driving at a lower speed than those witnesses questioned by the prosecuting lawyer.

Explain by reference to factors affecting the accuracy of eyewitness testimony why witnesses to Roland's car crash recalled him driving at different speeds. **[4 marks]**

2 Explain how anxiety can affect the accuracy of EWT. **[4 marks]**

3 Outline and evaluate how misleading information can affect the accuracy of EWT. **[16 marks]**

4 Outline and evaluate the use of the cognitive interview as a means of improving the accuracy of eyewitness testimony. **[12 marks]**

5 Following the recent tiddlywinks contest between the Dexterous Digits and the Knotted Knuckles there was a mass brawl between rival fans outside the tiddlywinks arena. Police interviewed witnesses by asking them what they could recall of the incident, but little of value was remembered.

Explain how police officers could possibly have gained more accurate and detailed information from the witnesses by using a cognitive interview. **[4 marks]**

6 The following are procedures of a cognitive interview:

A Change of narrative order

B Mental reinstatement of context

C Report everything

D Change of perspective

In the table below insert which procedure, A, B, C or D fits which description. One description will be left over. **[3 marks]**

Type of procedure	Description
	Recounting the scene in different chronological orders
	Recalling the scene as written bullet points
	Returning to the environmental and emotional context of the crime scene
	Recounting the scene from different perspectives
	Recalling all information, even if it appears to have little relevance or is accorded a lower level of confidence

Explanations of memory

Types of long-term memory

Explanations for forgetting

Factors affecting the accuracy
of eyewitness testimony

SUMMARY

- The MSM explains how information flows between the three storage systems of SR, STM and LTM.
- Memory stores within the STM differ in terms of coding, capacity and duration and the model is supported by research studies that illustrate these differences.
- The WMM is an explanation of STM that sees it as an active store holding several pieces of information simultaneously being worked on.
- The WMM has at its head the CE along with the three slave systems of PL, VSS and CE, with research supporting the idea that different tasks can be done simultaneously if they use different slave systems.
- LTM divides into the explicit types of episodic and semantic memory and the implicit type of procedural memory.
- Different types of LTM seem to perform separate tasks and are generally associated with different brain areas from each other.
- Explanations for forgetting focus on whether information is no longer in storage, or cannot be retrieved from storage.
- Interference sees newly-learned information interacting with, and impairing, the recall of previously learned information, with two apparent types: proactive and retroactive.
- Cue-dependent failure sees recall as dependent upon finding the correct retrieval cues.
- Other forms of forgetting include trace decay and displacement for STM, and trace decay and repression for LTM.
- Memories are reconstructions based on schemas, with the accuracy of EWT dependent upon several factors, such as misleading information in the form of leading questions, post-event information, as well as anxiety levels.
- The CI improved upon the SPI to produce greater accurate detail in police interviews, and is based upon the idea of using several retrieval paths to a memory.
- The ECI and the MCI are adaptations of the CI, designed to improve its effectiveness and usage with different types of people.
- Other ways of improving the accuracy of recall include mnemonics and active processing.

3

Developmental psychology: attachment

Introduction

Developmental psychology studies trends – how people change over time. Developmental influences can be biological (such as through genetics) or environmental (such as through parenting), with often several influences combining together. With much development occurring early in life, focus is often upon childhood and adolescence, like attachment behaviour, which will be concentrated on in this chapter. Focus will especially be upon:

- How attachments form
- Animal studies of attachment
- Types of attachment
- Explanations for attachments
- The consequences of disrupting attachments
- The influence of early attachments upon childhood and adult relationships.

Understanding the specification

- *Caregiver–infant interactions* must be studied as they are specifically listed on the specification, including *reciprocity and interactional synchrony*, as well as *Schaffer's stages of attachment formation*, *multiple attachments* and *the role of the father*.
- You also need to know about *animal studies of attachment*, as they are explicitly listed on the specification, especially those of Lorenz and Harlow.
- Two specific explanations of attachment are listed: *learning theory* and *Bowlby's monotropic theory* (including the concepts of a critical period and an internal working model).
- *Ainsworth's 'Strange Situation'* must be studied as it too is specifically included, with especial focus on types of attachment and cultural variations in attachment, including that of Van Ijzendoorn.
- *Bowlby's maternal deprivation theory* is also listed, along with *Romanian orphan studies* and *the effects of institutionalisation*.
- Final focus is upon *the influence of early attachment on childhood and adult relationships*, again including the role of an *internal working model*.

These are the basic requirements of the specification. However, other relevant material is included to provide depth and detail to your understanding.

IN THE NEWS

Ψ The Psychological Enquirer

The father who went to the ends of the earth for his daughter

Figure 3.1 Princess Emily Heaton, her father Jeremy and the flag of Bir Tawil

Jeremy Heaton, father of three children, can lay claim to be possibly the best dad in the world. Wanting to prove that he would literally go to the ends of the earth for his children, he gave daughter Emily a rather special 7th birthday present. Emily had always wanted to be a princess, so after conducting some research Jeremy discovered that there is an 800 square mile area of arid desert lying between Sudan and Egypt that doesn't officially belong to any country. So on June 16th 2014, Emily's dad made the long journey from the family home in Virginia, USA, to the North African area known to the locals as Bir Tawil and planted the flag he had made to claim the territory for Princess Emily. The delighted princess now wears her royal crown at all times. She is unsure when she will be able to visit her country, but would like it to become a centre for agriculture.

Psychologists have long argued over the role of fathers in parenting children. Some see them merely as sperm donors, others, such as John Bowlby, saw them as minor attachment figures, while some view them as figures of prime importance in the healthy development of children. It is important to know the truth, as figures released by the Office for National Statistics (2012) reveal that 42 per cent of marriages will end in divorce and about 90 per cent of single-parent families are female led with little or no involvement in parenting from biological fathers. Conversely, this means that in 10 per cent of single-parent households, parenting is being performed mainly by males. There are also an increasing number of children being raised by their biological mothers and a stepfather. To gain the truth as to what the role of fathers should be, research needs to be undertaken that is conducted in an unbiased and objective fashion, something that is difficult to achieve when so many people have deeply set views and opinions about this topic.

'The moment a child is born, the mother is also born.'
Rajneesh (1974)
'It goes without saying that you should never have more children than you have car windows.'
Erma Bombeck (1983)

3.1 Caregiver–infant interactions in humans

Precocial animals are born at a fairly advanced stage of development, for example, horses are able to walk and run around soon after birth. However, humans are *altricial*, born at a relatively early stage of development and so need to form attachment bonds with adults who will protect and nurture them.

An **attachment** is defined as 'an enduring, two-way, emotional tie to a specific other person', normally between a parent and child, which develops in set stages within a fairly set timescale. An attachment can be seen to have developed when an infant shows stranger anxiety (distress in the presence of unknown individuals) and separation protest (distress at the absence of a specific person).

As the attachment bond is not present at birth, let us first examine how such an attachment develops.

Attachment bonds are characterised by an infant's desire to keep close proximity to a particular individual and by the expression of distress if the infant is separated from that person. This particular individual gives an infant a sense of security and is usually the child's mother, though attachments can be provided by anyone who provides such comfort and security.

Interactions between a carer and an infant serve to develop and maintain an attachment bond between them. Even though an infant can't talk at this stage of its development, communication between carer and infant is rich and complex and occurs in several ways:

- **Bodily contact** – physical interactions between carer and infant help to form the attachment bond, especially in the period immediately after birth.
- **Mimicking** – infants seem to have an innate ability to imitate carers' facial expressions, which suggests it is a biological device to aid the formation of attachments.
- **Caregiverese** – adults who interact with infants use a modified form of vocal language that is high-pitched, song-like in nature, slow and repetitive. This aids communication between carer and infant and serves to strengthen the attachment bond.
- **Interactional synchrony** – infants move their bodies in tune with the rhythm of carers' spoken language to create a kind of turn-taking, as seen with two-way vocal conversations. This again serves to reinforce the attachment bond.
- **Reciprocity** – interactions between carers and infants result in mutual behaviour, with both parties being able to produce responses from each other, which also helps to fortify the attachment bond.

KEY TERMS

Attachment – a two-way, enduring, emotional tie to a specific other person

Interactional synchrony – the co-ordinated rhythmic exchanges between carer and infant

Reciprocity – the interaction of similar behaviour patterns between carer and infant

Figure 3.2 Interactions between carers and infants help to develop and maintain attachment bonds

YOU ARE THE RESEARCHER

Caregiverese, interactional synchrony, reciprocity, etc. appear to be early forms of communication that serve to create attachment bonds between carers and infants. Design a study that would suggest whether or not such forms of communication are biological in nature or learned. (**Hint:** see the section on cross-cultural studies on page 123).

For information on research methods, see Chapter 7.

Research

Klaus & Kennell (1976) compared mums who had extended physical contact with their babies lasting several hours a day with mums who only had physical contact with their babies during feeding in the three days after birth. One month later the mums with the greater physical contact were found to cuddle their babies more and made greater eye contact with them than the mums with lesser contact and these effects were still noticeable a year later. This suggests that greater physical contact leads to stronger and closer bond formation.

Meltzoff & Moore (1977) found that infants aged 2–3 weeks tended to mimic adults' specific facial expressions and hand movements, supporting the idea that infant mimicry is an innate ability to aid the formation of attachments, especially as it was subsequently seen in infants of less than three days old.

Papousek *et al.* (1991) found that the tendency to use a rising tone to show an infant that it was their turn in the interaction was cross-cultural, as American, Chinese and German mothers all exhibited the behaviour. This suggests that 'caregiverese' is an innate, biological device to facilitate the formation of attachments.

Condon & Sander (1974) analysed frame-by-frame video recordings of infants' movements to find they co-ordinated their actions in sequence with adults' speech to form a kind of turn-taking conversation, supporting the idea of interactional synchrony. Isabella *et al.* (1989) further strengthened the notion of interactional synchrony reinforcing attachment bonds, by finding that infants with secure attachments demonstrated more evidence of such behaviour during their first year of life.

Evaluation

- A practical application of Klaus & Kennel's findings was that hospitals placed mothers and babies in the same room in the days following birth, rather than the previous practice of rooming them apart, to encourage the formation of attachments.
- Durkin (1995) claimed Klaus & Kennell's findings were due not to increased physical contact, but instead due to the greater attention given to the mothers who were unmarried and poor. However, De Chateau & Wiberg (1984) found the same results with middle-class Swedish mothers, which gives support to Klaus & Kennell.
- 'Caregiverese' has been seen to be used by adults to all infants, not just those they have an attachment with, which suggests that although its usage aids communication between adults and infants it cannot be claimed to specifically help form attachments.
- The fact that interactional synchrony is not found in all cultures weakens support for the idea that it is necessary for attachment formation. Le Vine *et al.* (1994) reported that Kenyan mothers have little physical contact or interactions with their infants, but such infants do have a high proportion of secure attachments.

Stages of attachment development

Schaffer (1996) showed how the common pattern in the development of infants' attachments could be divided into several distinct stages (see Table 3.1).

Table 3.1 Schaffer's stages of attachment

Stage of attachment development	Descriptive features
Pre-attachment phase (birth to 3 months)	From six weeks of age, infants become attracted to other humans, preferring them to objects and events. This preference is demonstrated by their smiling at peoples' faces.
Indiscriminate attachment phase (3 to 7/8 months)	Infants begin to discriminate between familiar and unfamiliar people, smiling more at known people, though they will still allow strangers to handle and look after them.
Discriminate attachment phase (7/8 months onwards)	Infants begin to develop specific attachments, staying close to particular people and becoming distressed when separated from them. They avoid unfamiliar people and protest if strangers try to handle them.
Multiple attachments stage (9 months onwards)	Infants form strong emotional ties with other major caregivers, like grandparents, and non-caregivers, like other children. The fear of strangers weakens, but attachment to the mother figure remains strongest.

Multiple attachments

It is not disputed that most children form **multiple attachments**, emotional bonds with several people. But what is disputed is the relative importance of these different attachment figures. John Bowlby (see theory of monotropy, page 116) believed that children had one prime attachment and that although children had attachments to other people, these were of minor importance compared to their main attachment bond. However, Rutter (1995) proposed a model of multiple attachments that saw all attachments as of equal importance, with these attachments combining together to help form a child's internal working model (see page 118).

Multiple attachments are often formed to different people for different purposes, for example to mother for loving care, but additionally to father for exciting unpredictable play. Other attachments are often formed to grandparents, siblings and childminders.

Figure 3.3 Most children develop multiple-attachments to other people, such as grandparents

....
KEY TERM

Multiple attachments – the formation of emotional bonds with many carers

---

CLASSIC RESEARCH

The development of social attachments in infancy – Rudi Schaffer & Peggy Emerson (1964)

The researchers, realising that attachments weren't formed at birth, were interested in documenting the process of how attachments formed. To achieve this they studied a group of working-class Glaswegian children and their mothers on a regular basis.

Aims

- To assess whether there was a pattern of attachment formation that was common to all infants.
- To identify and describe the distinct stages by which attachments form.

Procedure

1 A longitudinal study was conducted upon 60 newborn babies and their mothers from a working-class area of Glasgow. Mothers and babies were studied each month for the first year of their lives in their own homes and again at 18 months. Observations were conducted, as well as interviews with the mothers, with questions being asked about whom infants smiled at, whom they responded to, who caused them distress, etc.

2 Attachment was measured in two ways:
   Separation protest – this was assessed through several everyday situations: the infant being left alone in a room, left alone with others, left in their pram outside the house,

left in the pram outside the shops, left in the cot at night, being put down after being held and being passed by while sitting in a chair/cot or pram.

Stranger anxiety – this was assessed by the researcher starting each home visit by approaching the infant to see if this distressed the child.

Findings

1 Most infants started to show separation protest when parted from their attachment figure at between 6–8 months, with stranger anxiety being shown around one month later.
2 Strongly attached infants had mothers who responded to their needs quickly and gave more opportunities for interaction. Weakly attached infants had mothers who responded less quickly and gave fewer opportunities for interaction.
3 Most infants went on to develop multiple attachments. At 18 months 87 per cent had at least two attachments, with 31 per cent having five or more attachments.
4 Attachments to different people were of a similar nature, with infants behaving in the same way to different attachment figures.
5 39 per cent of infants' prime attachment was not to the main carer.

Conclusions

There is a pattern of attachment formation common to all infants, which suggests the process is biologically controlled.

Attachments are more easily made with those who display sensitive responsiveness, recognising and responding appropriately to an infant's needs, rather than those spending the most time with a child.

Multiple attachments are the norm and of similar quality, which opposes Bowlby's idea that attachments are a hierarchy of one prime attachment and other minor ones. Schaffer commented that there is nothing to suggest that mothering can't be shared by several people.

Evaluation

Data was collected by direct observation or from the mothers, with both sources prone to bias and inaccuracy.

The study has mundane realism, as it was conducted under everyday conditions, meaning that the conclusions drawn about the formation of attachments can be seen as having high validity.

There were large individual differences in when attachments formed, casting doubt on the process of attachment formation being exclusively biological in nature.

KEY TERM

Stranger anxiety – the degree of distress shown by infants when in the presence of unfamiliar persons

Research

Carpenter (1975) presented infants with familiar and unfamiliar voices and faces. Sometimes face and voice would be of the same person and sometimes not. He found that two-week-old babies looked at a face longest when it was the mother's accompanied by her voice and were distressed by the sight of her face accompanied by a different voice. This suggests that babies can recognise and are attracted to their mothers from an early age, contradicting Schaffer & Emerson's belief that initially babies were attracted to any person interacting with them.

Evaluation of multiple attachment

- It can be argued that children with multiple attachments are at an advantage; they are more able to form and conduct social relationships, as they have the experience to do so and if a child loses an attachment figure, it has several others that it can turn to.

RESEARCH IN FOCUS

1 As they cannot talk, research using infants often involves interpreting their behaviour. Why might researcher bias be a problem with such research?
2 What strategies could be used to reduce the risk of researcher bias?
3 Shaffer & Emerson's (1964) study was a longitudinal study. How are longitudinal studies conducted and what do they show?
4 What are the strengths and weaknesses of longitudinal studies?

For information on research methods, see Chapter 7.

The role of the father

'The most important thing a father can do for his children is to love their mother.'
Theodore Hesburg (1973)

'She got her looks from her father. He's a plastic surgeon.'
Groucho Marx (1927)

Traditionally fathers have been seen to have played a minor role in the parenting of their children, indeed some would argue males are biologically unsuitable to raise children. In the past children were raised mainly by married couples, with the father going out to work to provide resources for his family, while the mother stayed at home to look after her children until they were of school age. But society has changed a lot. It is the norm now for mothers to have a job. According to the Office for National Statistics, in 2013 5.3 million British mothers were in employment, with males comprising nearly 10 per cent of those who care for children while their partner goes out to work. Another interesting statistic is that 9 per cent of British single parents (186,000) are male. Evidently many men are having a much bigger role in parenting than before, but let us examine psychologists' views about fathers and attachment.

Bowlby believed children have one primary attachment figure, usually the mother, though he conceded that this could in some cases be the father. Many researchers have seen the father less as a caregiver, but more of a playmate, as fathers' play is often more physical, unpredictable and exciting than mothers'.

Mothers have traditionally been seen, due to their perceived nurturing nature, as more able to show **sensitive responsiveness**, but it seems that males can quickly develop this ability when assuming the position of main care providers.

Several important factors have been identified that affect the relationship between fathers and children:

- **Degree of sensitivity** – more secure attachments to their children are found in fathers who show more sensitivity to children's needs.
- **Type of attachment with own parents** – single-parent fathers tend to form similar attachments with their children that they had with their own parents.
- **Marital intimacy** – the degree of intimacy a father has within his relationship with his partner affects the type of attachment he will have with his children.
- **Supportive co-parenting** – the amount of support a father gives to his partner in helping to care for children affects the type of attachment he will have with his children.

Research

Geiger (1996) showed that fathers' play interactions are more exciting and pleasurable than mothers', while mothers are more nurturing and affectionate, which supports the idea of fathers being playmates rather than caregivers. However, Lamb (1987) found that children often prefer

Figure 3.4 Do children attach to fathers just as playmates, or can the father fulfil a greater role?

....

KEY TERM

Sensitive responsiveness – recognising and responding appropriately to infants' needs interacting with fathers when in a positive emotional state and thus seeking stimulation (mothers are preferred when children are distressed and seeking comfort). This supports the idea of fathers being preferred as playmates, but only in certain conditions.

Hrdy (1999) reported that fathers are less able than mothers to detect low levels of infant distress, which suggests males are less suitable as prime attachment figures. However, Lamb (1987) found that fathers who become main care providers seem able to quickly develop more sensitivity to children's needs and become a safe base from which to explore, which suggests sensitive responsiveness isn't a biological ability limited to women.

Lucassen *et al.* (2011) performed a meta-analysis of studies involving observations and the Strange Situation technique (see page 120), to find that higher levels of sensitivity were associated with greater levels of infant–father attachment security. This supports the idea that more secure attachments are found in children whose fathers are more sensitive to their children's needs.

Bernier & Miljkovitch (2009) found that single-parent fathers' attachments with children aged 4–6 years was similar to the attachments the fathers had with their own parents. As no such effect was found with married fathers, it suggests continuity of attachments occurs more in fathers who are the main caregivers.

Belsky *et al.* (2009) found that high levels of marital intimacy was related to secure father–infant attachments, and that low levels of marital intimacy was related to insecure father–child attachments. This supports the idea that the closeness of relationships between fathers and partners affects the type of attachment a father has with his children.

Brown *et al.* (2010) assessed attachment patterns in 68 families with infants aged 12–13 months, finding that high levels of supportive co-parenting were related to secure attachment types between infants and fathers, but not between infants and mothers. This suggests that supportive co-parenting is important for fathers in developing positive attachments with their children.

Evaluation

- Children with secure attachments to their fathers go on to have better relationships with peers, less problem behaviours and are more able to regulate their emotions; illustrating the positive influence fathers can have on developmental outcomes.
- Children who grow up without fathers have often been seen to do less well at school and have higher levels of risk taking and aggression, especially in boys. This suggests fathers can help prevent negative developmental outcomes. However, Pedersen (1979) points out that most studies have focused on female single mothers from poor socio-economic backgrounds, so it may be social factors related to poverty that produce these outcomes, not the absence of fathers.
- Fathers are important not just for children, but mothers too. Supportive fathers provide mothers with much needed time away from childcare. This can help reduce stress in mothers, improve self-esteem and ultimately improve the quality of a mother's relationship with her children.

- Although evidence suggests that fathers are equally able as women to display sensitive responsiveness and form secure attachments with children, society has a long way to catch up. For example, many airline companies will not permit males to sit next to non-related children on aeroplanes, though no such restrictions apply to non-related females.

- When fathers spend more time with their children, the children develop more secure attachments, which suggests the amount of interaction is the important factor. However, it may be that fathers with more sensitivity to their children's needs interact with them more.

YOU ARE THE RESEARCHER

Design a case study to assess the degree of involvement and strength of attachment a father has with his child. Which people would you involve in the study? What methods would you use to generate and analyse your data? What methodological problems might there be with this study?

For information on research methods, see Chapter 7.

STRENGTHEN YOUR LEARNING

1 Define attachment.
2 Outline the different ways in which caregivers and infants interact.
3 At what age does an infant's first attachment generally form?
4 Explain why many children form multiple attachments.
5 Outline the procedure and findings from Schaffer & Emerson's 1964 study. What conclusions can be drawn from the findings?
6 Outline the factors that influence the relationship between fathers and their children.
7 What does research suggest about the role of fathers as attachment figures?

3.2 Animal studies of attachment

'*Ask researchers why they experiment on animals, and the answer is: "Because the animals are like us." Ask the researchers why it is morally okay to experiment on animals, and the answer is: "Because the animals are not like us."*'

Charles R. Magel (1981)

Much early research into attachments was conducted on animals; indeed John Bowlby, probably the most important psychologist in this area, was highly influenced by such studies in forming his theory of monotropy (see page 116) and his maternal deprivation hypothesis (see page 129), which explains the effects of disrupting attachment bonds. Such studies were often conducted on the basis that there was a biological continuity between humans and animals, so that what was true for animals would also be true for humans. Such studies were also regarded as being more ethical than if performed upon humans.

KEY TERM

Imprinting – a form of attachment where offspring follow the first large moving object

109

Imprinting – Konrad Lorenz (1935)

Even as a small boy Lorenz was intensely interested in animals, amassing a varied collection of them, including insects, dogs, fish, geese and a monkey. He noticed how a duckling transferred its affection to him – an observation that would later lead to his work on **imprinting**, for which he received a Nobel Prize (the most prestigious award in science).

Figure 3.5 Konrad Lorenz imprinted goslings onto himself back in 1935

Aim

To investigate the mechanisms of imprinting where the youngsters follow and form an attachment to the first large moving object that they meet.

Procedure

1 Lorenz (1935) split a large clutch of greylag goose eggs into two batches, one of which was hatched naturally by the mother and the other hatched in an incubator, with Lorenz making sure he was the first moving object the newly hatched goslings encountered. Following behaviour was then recorded.

2 Lorenz then marked all of the goslings, so he could determine whether they were from the naturally hatched batch of eggs or the incubated ones, and placed them under an upturned box. The box was then removed and following behaviour again recorded.

Findings

1 Immediately after birth, the naturally hatched baby goslings followed their mother about, while the incubator hatched goslings followed Lorenz around.

2 When released from the upturned box the naturally hatched goslings went straight to their mother, while the incubated goslings went to Lorenz, showing no bond with their natural mother. These bonds proved to be irreversible; the naturally hatched goslings would only follow their mother and the incubated ones would only follow Lorenz.

3 Lorenz also noted how imprinting would only occur within a brief, set time period of between 4 and 25 hours after hatching.

4 Lorenz subsequently reported on how goslings imprinted onto humans would, as matured adult birds, attempt to mate with humans.

Conclusions

Imprinting is a form of attachment, exhibited mainly by nidifugous birds (ones that leave the nest early), whereby close contact is kept with the first large moving object encountered.

Evaluation

The fact that imprinting is irreversible, suggests the ability is under biological control, as learned behaviours can be modified by experience.

The fact that imprinting only occurs within a brief, set time period influenced Bowlby's idea of a critical period in human babies (see page 117): a specific time period within which an attachment between infant and carer must form.

The fact that goslings imprinted onto humans exhibit sexual advances to humans when adult birds shows the importance of the behaviour upon future relationships, something that Bowlby incorporated into his continuity hypothesis (see page 138).

There are extrapolation issues with animal studies; the attachment behaviour of geese is not necessarily that of humans.

ON THE WEB

The idea of imprinting fascinated cartoonists and there are many examples of the phenomena being animated. A really good example is the 1955 *Tom & Jerry* episode 'That's my mommy'. Watch on YouTube by searching for 'Tom and Jerry – That's My Mommy 1955 (Episode 97)'.

INCREASE YOUR KNOWLEDGE

In 1938, Lorenz joined the Nazi party and stated 'my whole scientific work is devoted to the idea of the national socialists (Nazis)'. He worked as a military psychologist in the Second World War, deciding which 'half-breeds' would be sent to concentration camps, which led to the criticism that his involvement in Nazi eugenic policies (controlling breeding to increase desirable genetic characteristics) contaminated his work with researcher bias. However, it is widely believed that his research did retain scientific objectivity and he subsequently apologised for his involvement with the Nazis, going on to help form the Austrian Green Party in his later years.

PSYCHOLOGY IN THE REAL WORLD

Figure 3.6 Whooping cranes and their imprinted micro-light aircraft parents

In the 1996 film, *Fly Away Home*, 13-year-old Amy imprints some baby goslings onto herself. These birds are migratory with the parent birds normally teaching their young traditional migratory paths. As these birds have been orphaned, Amy and her father disguise two micro-light aircraft as huge geese and teach the birds to follow them in flight, taking them on a long migratory flight to an area of endangered wetland in the USA.

The following spring the young birds make their way back unassisted to Amy's home in Canada.

What many people might not realise is that the technique of imprinting migratory birds onto micro-light aircraft and teaching them migratory paths is one that is actually successfully used to reintroduce birds to areas where they have become extinct. Whooping cranes were reduced to just one flock of fifteen birds in eastern North America and they were declared an endangered species. However, using the micro-light migration technique their numbers are now in the hundreds and increasing.

Another practical application of imprinting is that used by sheep farmers. A newborn lamb whose mother has died will not normally be accepted by another ewe that has lost her own lamb, even though she is producing milk. However, if the dead lamb belonging to the ewe is skinned and its pelt tied to the orphaned lamb, there is a good chance that an attachment will occur. The imprinting here is olfactory (through smell).

ON THE WEB

Rare footage of Lorenz and his geese can be seen on YouTube by searching for 'Konrad Lorenz – Imprinting'.

There's also a half-hour interview with him, filmed in 1975, after he won his Nobel Prize in 1973. You can watch this on YouTube by searching for 'Konrad Lorenz – Ethology and Imprinting (1975)'.

CLASSIC RESEARCH

Even baby monkeys need comfort more than food – Harry Harlow (1959)

Figure 3.7 Harry Harlow and his surrogate mothers

Harlow used rhesus monkeys to see if attachments are primarily formed through food as explained by learning theory (see page 115). Newborn monkeys were separated from their mothers and raised in isolation in cages. In each cage was a 'baby blanket' and the infant monkeys became distressed whenever the blanket was removed, a similar reaction to when baby monkeys are separated from their mothers. This suggested that attachment was not based on association with food.

Aim

To test learning theory by comparing attachment behaviour in baby monkeys given a wire surrogate mother producing milk with those given a soft towelling mother producing no milk.

Procedure

1 Two types of surrogate mother were constructed – a harsh 'wire mother' and a soft 'towelling mother'. Sixteen baby monkeys were used, four in each of four conditions:

- a cage containing a wire mother producing milk and a towelling mother producing no milk
- a cage containing a wire mother producing no milk and a towelling mother producing milk
- a cage containing a wire mother producing milk
- a cage containing a towelling mother producing milk

2 The amount of time spent with each mother, as well as feeding time, was recorded.

3 The monkeys were frightened with a loud noise to test for mother preference during stress.

4 A larger cage was also used to test the monkeys' degree of exploration.

Findings

1 Monkeys preferred contact with the towelling mother when given a choice of surrogate mothers, regardless of whether she produced milk; they even stretched across to the wire mother to feed while still clinging to the towelling mother.
2 Monkeys with only a wire surrogate had diarrhoea, a sign of stress.
3 When frightened by a loud noise, monkeys clung to the towelling mother in conditions where she was available.
4 In the larger cage conditions, monkeys with towelling mothers explored more and visited their surrogate mother more often.

Conclusions

Rhesus monkeys have an innate, unlearned need for contact comfort, suggesting that attachment concerns emotional security more than food.

Contact comfort is associated with lower levels of stress and a willingness to explore, indicating emotional security.

Evaluation

This study involved animals and therefore we cannot necessarily extrapolate (generalise) the results to humans.

There are ethical issues involving the separation of baby monkeys and the stress caused to them.

Interestingly, over time, Harlow publicly distanced himself from the work of Bowlby and Ainsworth, as well as Lorenz's views on imprinting. He especially did not believe that his work supported Bowlby's belief of a child's innate need for mother love.

ON THE WEB

Two good videos about Harlow, containing original footage of the study, can be found on YouTube by searching for 'Harlow's Studies on Dependency in Monkeys' and 'Harlow's Monkeys'.

There you will find links to other relevant videos.

There's also a BBC programme about Harlow's experiments from the series *Mind Changers* at:

www.bbc.co.uk/programmes/b00ly7lp

Other research

Sluckin (1966) questioned whether there actually was a critical period, a set time period in which imprinting must occur or it never would do so. Performing a replication of Lorenz's famous study, but using ducklings instead of goslings, he successfully imprinted them onto himself, but kept one duckling in isolation well beyond (up to five days) Lorenz's reported critical period. He found it was still possible to imprint this youngster and concluded that the critical period was actually a **sensitive period**, a time period best for imprinting to perform, but one beyond which attachments could still be formed.

Harlow *et al.* (1965) raised newborn monkeys in total isolation from other living beings for 3, 6, 12 or 24 months. These monkeys displayed signs of psychological disturbance, hugging their own bodies and rocking repetitively. When eventually placed with other monkeys they were fearful of them and had no social interactions, other than to attack them. They also harmed themselves, biting their arms and legs and pulling out their hair. The degree of damage correlated positively with the amount of total isolation a monkey had endured. These monkeys, when adult, seemed to have no ability to engage in sexual courtship. Harlow, keen to see how they would cope as parents, devised an apparatus he called a 'rape rack' to which female monkeys raised in isolation would be tied and forcibly mated. As parents they were awful, abusing and neglecting their babies; one mother chewed off her own baby's feet and fingers, while another crushed her baby's head to a pulp. The findings suggest that social interactions are essential for normal social and emotional development to occur. Harlow & Suomi (1972) raised four

---

KEY TERM

Sensitive period – a best time period within which attachments can form, though they still can form with more difficulty outside this period

newborn male monkeys in total isolation for six months and then placed each one with a normally raised three-month-old female 'therapist' monkey for two hours three times a week, gradually increasing the amount of contact time. After twelve months their behaviour was almost normal and by three years of age they had totally recovered and were able to live among normally raised monkeys. This suggests that the effects of total isolation are reversible.

RESEARCH IN FOCUS

1 Why might it be difficult to generalise the findings of animal studies to humans? Refer to specific aspects of Lorenz's and/or Harlow's studies in your answer.
2 The ethics of experimenting on animals are also controversial. What aspects of Lorenz's and Harlow's studies could be considered unethical?
3 What is a cost–benefit analysis and could it be used to justify both Lorenz's and Harlow's studies?

For information on research methods, see Chapter 7.

Evaluation

- Harlow's isolation studies influenced Bowlby in devising his maternal deprivation hypothesis, where he saw any disruption of the attachment bond as having serious, irreversible effects.
- Sackett (2002), a student of Harlow's, believes that Harlow's research was so unjustifiably unethical that the American animal liberation movement was born out of it.

INCREASE YOUR KNOWLEDGE

Harlow's research raises serious ethical concerns as to the degree of harm it caused to monkeys, many of whom died. Harlow's wife died in 1971 from cancer, plummeting him into severe depression (treated with electroconvulsive therapy (ECT)), after which he developed a morbid interest in the origins of mental illness, which may explain his isolation studies and his inability to see the degree of harm they were causing. He fell into alcoholism, became estranged from his children, contracted Parkinson's disease and died from a brain tumour in 1981.

STRENGTHEN YOUR LEARNING

1 What is meant by imprinting?
2 Outline the procedure and findings of Lorenz's study into attachment.
3 What conclusions can be drawn from Lorenz's findings?
4 Explain one practical application of Lorenz's research into imprinting.
5 Why might Lorenz's research have been affected by researcher bias?
6 What does Harlow's surrogate mother study tell us about the learning theory explanation of attachments?
7 Give one strength and one weakness of using monkeys to study attachments.
8 Do findings from animal studies support the idea of a critical period? Explain your answer.
9 Is Harlow's total isolation study unethical? Give the case for and against.

ASSESSMENT CHECK

1 Select from the letters A, B, C, D and E to place the correct stage of attachment next to the descriptions in the table below. One letter will be left over. **[4 marks]**

   A Discriminate attachment phase

   B Pre-attachment stage

   C Post-attachment phase

   D Multiple attachments stage

   E Indiscriminate attachment phase.

Stage of attachment development	Descriptive features
	From six weeks of age, infants become attracted to other humans
	Infants smile more at known people, though they will still allow strangers to handle and look after them
	Infants avoid unfamiliar people and protest if strangers try to handle them
	Infants form emotional ties with other caregivers

2 A gust of wind blew a goose egg out of its nest and it came to rest against Breacan, an English Pointer dozing in the sunshine nearby; a few moments later the egg hatched. When Breacan got up and walked about, the baby gosling followed him wherever he went. As the day got hotter the dog went for a swim, followed closely by the gosling who completely ignored its mother swimming nearby with her other newly hatched chicks.

   Refer to the passage above to explain the gosling's behaviour in terms of imprinting. **[4 marks]**

3 Outline what psychologists have discovered about the role of the father in attachment behaviour. **[6 marks]**

4 Discuss caregiver–infant interactions in humans. **[16 marks]**

5 Outline and evaluate animal studies of attachment. **[12 marks]**

6 Explain what is meant by interactional synchrony. **[3 marks]**

7 Explain why Harlow's studies with monkeys could be considered unethical. **[4 marks]**

3.3 Explanations of attachment

'You don't have to be an at-home parent to be an attachment parent.'
Mayim Bialik (2012)

'Always be nice to your children because they are the ones who will choose your rest home.'
Phyllis Diller (2009)

We have already looked at how attachments develop, but now we turn our attention to the reasons why attachments form. Two explanations will be looked at here; **learning theory** and Bowlby's monotropic theory.

Learning theory

Learning theory (also known as behaviourism) sees all behaviour as acquired through experience via the process of association. Attachments are seen as developing through an infant learning to associate a caregiver with feeding. Two types of learning theory apply to the development of attachments: **classical conditioning** and **operant conditioning**.

As caregivers meet babies' physiological needs, learning theory is also known as a **cupboard love theory** (as the cupboard contains food).

Classical conditioning

Classical conditioning occurs when a response produced naturally by a certain stimulus, becomes associated with another stimulus that is not normally associated with that particular response.

Therefore attachments are learned by the stimulus of food (an unconditional stimulus), which produces a natural response of pleasure (an unconditioned response), being paired with a caregiver (a conditioned stimulus). After several paired presentations of caregiver and food, the infant learns to associate pleasure solely with the caregiver without any need for food.

Table 3.2 How attachments form due to classical conditioning

Before learning	Food (UCS) → Pleasure (UCR)
During learning	Food (UCS) + Caregiver (CS) → Pleasure (UCR)
After learning	Caregiver (CS) → Pleasure (CR)

Operant conditioning

Operant conditioning is based on the 'Law of Effect', where any action that has a pleasurable outcome will be repeated again in similar circumstances. Pleasurable outcomes are known as reinforcements (as they strengthen the behaviour, making it more likely to occur again). Positive reinforcements involve receiving something pleasurable for performing a certain behaviour (such as receiving pocket money for doing chores), while negative reinforcements involve not receiving something non-pleasurable for performing a certain behaviour (such as not being grounded for tidying your room).

KEY TERMS

Learning theory – the belief that attachments develop through conditioning processes

Classical conditioning – occurs when a response produced naturally by a certain stimulus, becomes associated with another stimulus that is not normally associated with that particular response

Operant conditioning – learning occurring via reinforcement of behaviour, thus increasing the chances of the behaviour occurring again

Cupboard love theory – the belief that attachments are formed with people who feed infants

Figure 3.8 Learning theory sees attachments as forming due to an association being developed between mother and feeding

Therefore attachments occur through caregivers becoming associated with reducing the unpleasant feeling of hunger (a negative reinforcement) so that the caregiver becomes a source of reinforcement (reward) themselves.

Research

Dollard & Miller (1950) argued that in their first year, babies are fed 2,000 times, generally by their main carer, which creates ample opportunity for the carer to become associated with the removal of the unpleasant feeling of hunger, a form of negative reinforcement. This gives support to the idea that attachments are learned through operant conditioning.

Schaffer and Emerson (1964) (see Classic research, page 105) found that in 39 per cent of cases, the mother (usually the main carer) was not the baby's main attachment figure, suggesting that feeding is not the primary explanation of attachment. This goes against learning theory.

Fox (1977) studied attachment bonds between mothers, babies and metapelets on Israeli kibbutzim (communal farms). Metapelets are specially trained, full-time carers of newborn children, allowing mothers to work (though some time is spent with parents). Generally children were more attached to their mothers than metapelets. As the metapelets did the majority of the feeding, this suggests learning theory is invalid.

Evaluation

- Conditioning best explains the learning of simple behaviours, but attachments are more complex behaviours with an intense emotional component. This, coupled with the fact that attachments develop with people who do not feed babies, casts doubt on the learning theory.
- Schaffer (1971) commented that 'cupboard love' theories put things the wrong way round. Babies do not 'live to eat', but 'eat to live', thus they actively seek stimulation, not passively receive nutrition.
- Bowlby (1973) argued that babies only need food occasionally, but constantly require the emotional security that closeness to an attachment figure provides. This suggests that food, and thus the learning theory, is not the main reason for formation of attachments. Conditioning and reinforcement through feeding probably do play a part in helping form attachments, but as Bowlby says, they're not the main reason.
- Behaviourist explanations are reductionist, as they explain complex behaviours in the simplest way possible. When explaining attachments as simply down to feeding, behaviourism does not consider internal cognitive (mental) processes or the emotional nature of attachments.

Bowlby's monotropic theory (1951, 1969, 1973)

John Bowlby (1907–90) had a lifetime interest in children's development, stemming from his early work with delinquent children and the growth of his own four children. In 1949 the World Health Organisation commissioned him to write a report entitled Maternal Care and Mental Health, concerning the mental health of homeless children (of which there were a lot after the Second World War). This led to his evolutionary

Figure 3.9 John Bowlby was a pioneer of research into children's attachments. He is buried in a quiet location on the Isle of Skye

explanation of attachment, the **monotropic theory**, which was formed and adapted over a number of years, and also his maternal deprivation hypothesis (see page 129), concerning the disruption of attachment bonds.

Bowlby was heavily influenced by animal studies, including Harlow's research with monkeys (see Classic research, page 111) and Lorenz's study of imprinting in goslings (see page 110), which led him to reject learning theory.

Bowlby applied the findings of these animal studies to humans to suggest that emotional bonds had evolutionary functions. He saw attachment bonds as developing during the Pleistocene (stone-age) era. Here humans faced the constant danger of predators and so attachments evolved via the process of natural selection to ensure that offspring stayed close to caregivers. Thus, through evolution infants became genetically programmed to behave towards their mothers in ways that increased their survival chances. These innate species-specific attachment behaviours are known as **social releasers** and include:

- **crying** – to attract parents' attention
- **looking**, **smiling and vocalising** – to maintain parental attention and interest
- **following and clinging** – to gain and maintain proximity (physical closeness) to parents.

Infants display these attachment behaviours from a very early stage. They occur in an automatic, stereotyped way to begin with and are triggered at first by many people. However, during the first year, these behaviours become focused on a few individuals and thus become organised into more flexible and sophisticated behaviour systems. Attachments, however, only form if carers respond to infant attachment behaviours in a meaningful way. Bowlby believed that the evolution of attachment behaviours involved a complementary system between infants and their carers, whereby carers would respond to infants' signals in a meaningful way. Although Bowlby saw this as generally occurring between infants and their biological mothers, he admitted this could, occasionally, occur with their fathers or even a non-biological figure (which explains how close attachments to adopted parents could occur).

Overall Bowlby saw attachment functioning as a control system to maintain proximity to the mother. When this state occurs, attachment behaviour is 'quiet' – infants have no need to cry or cling and so they can get on with playing and exploring (which aids mental and social development). When the state is threatened, such as when the mother disappears from view or a stranger approaches, attachment behaviours are activated to restore it. Generally, attachment behaviours are seen when children are upset, ill, scared or in strange surroundings; which particular responses are produced change as children grow and become more competent, cognitively and behaviourally.

Critical period

Bowlby believed that there is a **critical period** for the formation of attachments, whereby attachment behaviours between infant and carer must occur within a certain time period if children are to form attachments. He saw attachment behaviours as useless for most children if delayed until after twelve months and useless for all children if delayed until after two-and-a-half to three years.

KEY TERMS

Monotropic theory – the idea that infants have an inbuilt tendency to make an initial attachment with one attachment figure, usually the mother

Social releasers – innate, infant social behaviours that stimulate adult interaction and caregiving

Critical period – a specific time period within which an attachment must form

Internal working model

Bowlby sees attachments as monotropic, whereby infants have an innate tendency to become attached to the one particular adult who interacts with them the most sensitively, usually the biological mother. This attachment is unique: it is the first to develop and the strongest of all, forming a model for relationships, which the infant will expect from others. This is known as the **internal working model**, a template for future relationships based upon the infant's primary attachment, which creates a consistency between early emotional experiences and later relationships. For Bowlby, 'Mother love in infancy is as important for mental health as vitamins and proteins for physical health.' Although Bowlby acknowledged that infants could form attachments to other specific people, he saw these as secondary attachments. For Bowlby, attachment was a hierarchy with the prime attachment at the top and secondary attachments of minor importance below.

Research

Lorenz (1935) (see Classic research, page 110) found that certain animals have an innate tendency to respond immediately and consistently to specific forms of stimuli, like visual markings or sounds, usually displayed by a parent. They are attracted to these stimuli and will follow anyone displaying such stimuli and seem content when near them and distressed when not. This suggests that such innate 'pre-programming' provides an evolutionary advantage, as by staying close to such individuals, newborn animals are safer from predators and environmental danger. This therefore supports Bowlby's evolutionary theory.

Schaffer & Emerson (1964) (see Classic research, page 105) found that multiple attachments are the norm, which goes against Bowlby's idea of **monotropy**, as does the fact that 39 per cent of children had their main attachment to someone other than the main carer.

Rutter (1981) found that mothers are not special in the way Bowlby believed. Infants display a range of attachment behaviours towards attachment figures other than their mothers and there is no particular attachment behaviour used specifically and exclusively towards mothers, which lessens support for Bowlby's theory.

Lamb *et al.* (1982) studied the attachments infants had with people like fathers, grandparents and siblings and found that infants had different attachments for different purposes rather than attachments being a hierarchy. For example, infants go to fathers for play, but mothers for comfort, going against Bowlby's idea of monotropy.

INCREASE YOUR LEARNING

Kagan (1984) founded the temperament hypothesis, by finding that infants have an innate personality, such as being easy going or difficult, which influences the quality of their attachments with caregivers and later relationships with adults. This suggests that attachments form as a result of temperament not an innate gene for attachment, which goes against Bowlby's theory. Belsky & Rovine (1987) supported this by finding that infants in their first few days of life display characteristics that match their later attachment types; for example, calmer and less anxious infants went on to form secure attachments.

Evaluation

- Research evidence supports the continuity hypothesis (see page 138), that there is a consistency between early attachment types and later relationships in line with Bowlby's theory.
- Although Schaffer & Emerson (1964) found that children tended to have multiple attachments, they also tended to have one primary attachment figure, supporting Bowlby's idea of monotropy.
- Bowlby's theory has been used by right-wing political figures as scientific proof that women should be at home mothering children and not at work with their children in day care.
- Imprinting applies mainly to precocial animals (those mobile soon after birth). As humans are an altricial species (born at a relatively early stage of development), imprinting may not relate to humans.
- Bowlby's idea of attachment being a form of human imprinting suggests that mere exposure to another individual is sufficient for an attachment to develop. However, Schaffer & Emerson (1964) found that attachments occurred mainly with individuals displaying sensitive responsiveness, which goes against this idea.
- Bowlby sees fathers as minor attachment figures, but research (see The role of the father, page 107) suggests that fathers can be attachment figures in their own right.

STRENGTHEN YOUR LEARNING

1 How can the following explain the formation of attachments?
   a) Classical conditioning
   b) Operant conditioning
2 Give a brief evaluation of learning theory, giving points for and against.
3 Why is the learning theory explanation of attachment known as 'cupboard love theory'?
4 Explain why Bowlby's monotropy theory is an evolutionary explanation.
5 Explain what is meant by social releasers. Give some examples.
6 Explain how Kagan's temperament hypothesis opposes Bowlby's theory of monotropy.

3.4 Ainsworth's 'Strange Situation'

'Simply having children does not make mothers.'
John A. Shedd (1928)

American Mary Ainsworth (1913–99) worked with John Bowlby in the 1950s and then studied mother–child relationships in the Ganda tribe of Uganda. Over nine months she observed 26 mothers, with infants ranging in age from 15 weeks to 2 years, for hours at a time. In addition to her observations, Ainsworth carried out interviews with the mothers. From these data she identified three types of attachments (see Table 3.3).

Figure 3.10 The Strange Situation is a procedure for measuring the strength and type of infants' attachments to their mothers

Table 3.3 Ainsworth's attachment types

Type of attachment	Description
Type A: Insecure-avoidant	Infants are willing to explore, have low stranger anxiety, are unconcerned by separation and avoid contact at the return of their caregiver. Caregivers are indifferent to infants' needs.
Type B: Securely attached	Infants are keen to explore, have high stranger anxiety, are easy to calm and are enthusiastic at the return of their carer. Caregivers are sensitive to infants' needs.
Type C: Insecure-resistant	Infants are unwilling to explore, have high stranger anxiety, are upset by separation and seek and reject contact at the return of their caregiver. Caregivers are ambivalent to infants' needs, demonstrating simultaneous opposite feelings and behaviours.

In 1978 Ainsworth performed a similar study in Baltimore, USA, visiting 26 mother–child pairs every three to four weeks for the babies' first year of life. Each visit lasted three to four hours. Interviews and naturalistic observations were used, with the latter playing a greater role.

Ainsworth identified two important features of attachment, both with an adaptive survival value. Firstly, infants seek proximity to their mothers, especially when feeling threatened. Secondly, secure attachments allow infants to explore (behaviour that aids cognitive and social development), using their attached figure as a safe base to explore from and return to.

KEY TERMS

The Strange Situation – the accepted observational testing method for measuring attachment types

Separation anxiety – the degree of distress shown by infants when parted from attachment figures

---

CLASSIC RESEARCH

The Strange Situation – Mary Ainsworth et al. (1978)

The Strange Situation testing procedure was created to make sense of the data Ainsworth had collected and to create a valid method of measuring attachments.

Aims

- To assess how infants between 9 and 18 months of age behave under conditions of mild stress and novelty, in order to test stranger anxiety, **separation anxiety** and the secure base concept.
- To assess individual differences between mother–infant pairs in terms of the quality of their attachments.

Procedure

1 The Strange Situation comprised eight episodes. Each of these lasted for about 3 minutes, except episode one which lasted for 30 seconds.

2 Every aspect of participants' behaviour was observed and videotaped, with most attention given to reunion behaviours, the infants' responses to their mothers' return. Data were combined from several studies. In total 106 infants were observed.

3 The testing room was an unfamiliar environment (hence the name 'Strange Situation') comprising an 81 square foot (approx 7.5 square metres) area divided into 16 squares to help record movements.

4 Five categories were recorded:
   (i)   proximity- and contact-seeking behaviours
   (ii) contact-maintaining behaviours
   (iii) proximity- and interaction-avoiding behaviours
   (iv) contact- and interaction-resisting behaviours
   (v)   search behaviours.

5 Every 15 seconds, the category of behaviour displayed was recorded and scored on an intensity scale of 1 to 7.

Episode	Persons present	Brief description
1	Mother, infant, observer	Observer introduces mother and infant to experimental room, then leaves.
2	Mother, infant	Mother is passive while the infant explores.
3	Stranger, mother, infant	Stranger enters. First minute: stranger silent. Second minute: stranger converses with mother. Third minute: stranger approaches infant. After three minutes, mother quietly leaves.
4	Stranger, infant	First separation episode. Stranger's behaviour is geared towards that of the infant.
5	Mother, infant	First reunion episode. Stranger leaves. Mother greets and/or comforts infant, then tries to engage infant again in play. Mother then leaves, saying 'bye-bye'.
6	Infant	Second separation episode. Infant is alone.
7	Stranger, infant	Continuation of second separation. Stranger enters and gears her behaviour to that of the infant.
8	Mother, infant	Second reunion episode. Mother enters, greets and then picks up infant. Meanwhile, stranger quietly leaves.

Table 3.4 The eight episodes of the Strange Situation

Findings

1 Generally infants explored the playroom and toys more enthusiastically when just the mother was present than either a) after the stranger entered or b) when the mother was absent.

2 Reunion behaviours reflected three types of attachment:

Type A: Insecure-avoidant – 15 per cent of infants ignored their mother and were indifferent to her presence. Level of play wasn't affected whether by the mother's presence or absence. Infants displayed little stress when she left and ignored or avoided her when she returned. Infants reacted to the mother and stranger in similar ways, showing most distress when left on their own.

Type B: Securely attached – 70 per cent of infants played contentedly when their mother was present, whether or not a stranger was present, but were distressed when she left. On her return they sought comfort from her, calmed down and re-started to play. Mother and stranger were treated very differently

Type C: Insecure-resistant – 15 per cent of infants were fussy and wary, even with their mother present. They were distressed by her leaving and sought contact with her on her return, but simultaneously showed anger and resisted contact (for example, putting out their arms to be picked up, then fighting to get away once they had been picked up).

Conclusions

Sensitive responsiveness is the major factor determining the quality of attachments, as sensitive mothers correctly interpret infants' signals and respond appropriately to their needs. Sensitive mothers tend to have securely-attached babies, whereas insensitive mothers tend to have insecurely-attached babies.

Evaluation

The identification by Ainsworth of the importance of parental sensitivity in creating secure attachments is backed up by similar findings from studies using larger samples.

The Strange Situation testing procedure has become a paradigm, the accepted method of assessing attachments.

The Strange Situation assumes that attachment types are fixed characteristics of children, but classification can change if family circumstances, like mothers' stress levels, alter. Therefore attachment type is not a permanent characteristic.

The Strange Situation is an artificial way of assessing attachment, as it is laboratory based with mother and stranger acting to a 'script'. This is far removed from everyday situations and thus lacks ecological validity. Brofenbrenner (1979) found that infants' attachment behaviour is much stronger in a laboratory than when at home (because of the strangeness of the environment).

The Strange Situation focuses too much upon the behaviour of infants, and not enough on that of mothers, which could distort results.

The Strange Situation has been labelled unethical, as it deliberately stresses infants to see their reactions. However, it can be seen as justifiable, as the stress caused is no greater than that of everyday experiences like being left with an unfamiliar babysitter or childminder.

Main & Weston (1981) found that children acted differently in the Strange Situation depending on which parent they were with. Children might be insecurely attached to their mothers, but securely attached to their fathers, illustrating that attachment types are linked to individual relationships with carers and are not set characteristics of children.

This suggests that the Strange Situation might not be a valid measure of attachment types. The Strange Situation is reliable though, as children tested at different times generally have identical attachment types. Main *et al.* (1985) found all infants identified before 18 months of age, were still securely attached at 6 years of age and 75 per cent identified as insecure-avoidant still were.

Main & Solomon (1986) found an additional attachment type, insecure-disorganised (Type D), displayed by a small number of children, whose behaviour was a confusing mixture of approach and avoidance behaviours. Ainsworth (who had worked with Main) agreed with this extra type.

The Strange Situation may not be suitable for use in all cultures, as it contains elements unfamiliar to some cultures, like being left with strangers (see Cultural variations in attachment, page 123).

ON THE WEB

A reflection on the work of Ainsworth from the BBC series *Mind Changers*, focusing on her work in Africa and the Strange Situation can be found at:

www.bbc.co.uk/programmes/p00f8n6q

There's also a three-part programme about Ainsworth's life history and work on YouTube. Search for 'Ainsworth and Attachment Part 1', 'Ainsworth and Attachment Part 2' and 'Ainsworth and Attachment Part 3'.

INCREASE YOUR KNOWLEDGE

Figure 3.11 Just like her co-worker John Bowlby, Margaret Ainsworth had a poor relationship with her mother. Did this motivate their mutual interest in attachment theory?

John Bowlby and Mary Ainsworth are major figures in attachment theory, but their early life histories cast a fascinating light onto the origins of their interest in child psychology. Ainsworth had a close relationship with her father who performed, unusually for the time, many childcaring duties; she fondly recalled him reading to her and putting her to bed. However, he was away from home a lot as he worked as a travelling salesman. She did not have a close relationship to her mother, a woman who apparently showed little affection. Ainsworth married in 1950, but divorced ten years later, resulting in depression and long-term psychoanalytic therapy. She longed for children, but never had any. Bowlby was raised in an upper-middle-class family, who believed that too much parental affection and attention would spoil a child. As with Ainsworth he did not have a close relationship with his mother; he saw her for one hour each day at tea time. He was raised by a nanny, but he described her leaving when he was 4 years old as 'the tragic loss of my mother'. At age 7 he was sent to boarding school, which he recalled as a 'traumatic experience'. He did, however, enjoy a long and happy marriage that produced four children of whom he was immensely fond.

Perhaps Bowlby and Ainsworth's early experiences motivated them to try and find the path to true childhood happiness.

Cultural variations in attachment

If Bowlby's belief that attachments evolved and have a survival value is true then patterns of attachment types should be similar across different cultures, regardless of child-rearing styles used within those cultures. Secure attachments should dominate in all cultures, with equal amounts of insecure-avoidant and insecure-resistant types.

Belsky (1999) even proposes an evolutionary reason for the existence of similar attachment types in different cultures; he argues that insecure attachment types are associated with weak adult relationships and early sexual activity, which could be useful in certain situations, like after a famine or plague when many people have died, as people would need to reproduce by being sexually active at a young age and not getting too emotionally involved with people who may die young.

However, if different patterns of attachment types are found cross-culturally, it would mean that infants' attachment types are not biological, but learned through exposure to different cross-cultural child-rearing styles.

Child-rearing styles do vary across different cultures; in some cultures one person does most caregiving, while in others many carers are involved. There are also cross-cultural differences as to how different attachment types are regarded. For example, in Britain we view insecure-avoidant attachment negatively, as it is associated with weak attachments to people, but in Germany it is valued as it is associated with being independent from others, which is viewed positively in German culture. Not surprisingly, in Germany many more infants are classed as being insecure-avoidant.

KEY TERM

Cultural variations – differences in child-rearing practices and attachment types between different cultural groupings

CLASSIC RESEARCH

Cross-cultural patterns of attachment: meta-analysis of the Strange Situation – Marinus van IJzendoorn & Pieter Kroonenberg (1988)

Figure 3.12a and b Marinus van IJzendoorn & Pieter Kroonenberg

Several studies had used the Strange Situation procedure to assess similarities and differences in patterns of attachment types between cultures. However, these studies had comprised small sample sizes and hadn't considered intra-cultural against inter-cultural differences (whether differences between cultures are greater than those within cultures). The researchers' solution was to perform a meta-analysis of Strange Situation studies in different cultures.

Aims

- To assess whether within separate samples there was a pattern in the distribution of different attachment types.
- To assess the extent of inter- (between) and intra- (within) cultural differences in attachment types in separate samples.
- To assess similarities and differences in the amount of Type A, B and C attachment types in separate samples.

Procedure

A meta-analysis of 32 studies from 8 countries that used the Strange Situation procedure to assess mother–child attachments (and not father–child attachments, etc.) and which classified attachments as either Type A, B or C. 1,990 separate Strange Situation classifications were used. All studies comprised at least 35 mother–infant pairs with infants below 2 years of age.

Country	Number of studies	Number of mother–infant pairs	Percentage of Type A attachment type (insecure-avoidant)	Percentage of Type B attachment type (secure attachment)	Percentage of Type C attachment type (insecure-resistant)
Britain	1	72	22	75	3
China	1	25	25	50	25
Germany	3	136	35	57	8
Holland	4	251	26	67	6
Israel	2	118	7	64	29
Japan	2	96	5	68	27
Sweden	1	51	22	75	4
USA	18	1230	21	65	14

Table 3.5 Meta-analysis of 32 Strange Situation studies comprising 1,990 mother–child pairs

1 Overall attachment (drawn from all mother–infant pairs) was Type A = 21 per cent, Type B = 67 per cent, Type C = 12 per cent.

2 In samples from all cultures (except one sample from Germany) the modal attachment type was Type B (secure attachment).

3 The highest proportion of Type A attachment (insecure-avoidant) was found in German samples.

4 Intra-cultural differences (differences in attachment types between samples from one country) were often greater than inter-cultural differences (differences in attachment types between different countries). For example, in one USA sample there was 94 per cent Type A attachments, while in another USA sample there was only 47 per cent Type A attachments.

5 Type A attachment type was found more in Western cultures, while Type C attachment type was found more in Israel, China and Japan.

Conclusions

The data suggests there is a difference in the pattern of cross-cultural attachment types across cultures.

Intra-cultural differences in attachment types are often greater than inter-cultural ones.

Overall patterns of attachment types were similar to what Ainsworth found.

An important cross-cultural similarity is the predominance of Type B attachment in all cultures.

Evaluation

As intra-cultural differences were often found in different samples from the same researcher(s), it suggests such differences were not due to methodological differences.

Data drawn from cultures not represented in the meta-analysis, for example, African, South American samples, etc., would be required before universal conclusions could be drawn.

Some intra-cultural differences may be due to socio-economic differences, for instance some USA samples were of middle-class pairings, while other USA samples used pairings from poorer socio-economic backgrounds.

Cross-cultural studies like these can suffer from an **imposed etic**, where researchers analyse findings in a biased manner in terms of their own cultural beliefs, wrongly imposing cultural-specific beliefs onto other cultures. For instance, Ainsworth, an American, assumed that separation anxiety was an indication of secure attachment, but it may represent something else in other countries.

KEY TERMS

Cross-cultural studies – comparison of findings from people of different cultures

Imposed etic – using techniques that are only relevant to one culture to study and/or draw conclusions about another

YOU ARE THE RESEARCHER

Watch a video clip of the Strange Situation, such as the one you can find on YouTube by searching for 'Ainsworth Strange Situation'.

Watch it with the sound off and see if you can identify the type of attachment. You will need to create some behavioural categories first. Establishing inter-observer reliability would be important here; what is this and how would you establish it?

For information on research methods, see Chapter 7.

Infant–mother attachment among the Dogon people of Mali – Mary McMahon-True, Lelia Pisani, Fadimata Oumar (2001)

Figure 3.13 A Dogon mother with her child

Constantly keeping infants physically close, breastfeeding on demand and responding immediately to distress are common practices within Dogon culture, but very different from our own culture. Therefore this study gives a valuable insight into a culture where infants are raised by natural parenting practices and provides a contrast to the more usual studies performed on Western cultural samples.

Aims

● To assess whether infant attachment types are different in a culture that raises infants using natural parenting methods.
● To assess whether attachment security was related to the quality of mother–infant communications.
● To assess whether mothers of secure infants respond more sensitively to their infants than mothers of insecure infants.

Procedure

42 mother and infant pairs from rural Dogon villages were used as participants, with infants ranging in age from 10 months to 12.5 months at first assessment. The Strange Situation testing method was used to assess attachment styles. The results were compared to those from four North American samples, with a total of 306 mother–infant pairs tested.

Findings

Type of culture	Percentage of avoidant attachments (Type A)	Percentage of secure attachments (Type B)	Percentage of resistant attachments (Type C)	Percentage of disorganised attachments (Type D)
Dogon	0	67	8	25
North American	23	55	8	15

Table 3.6 Table showing comparison of attachment styles in Dogon and North American cultural samples

1 Many Dogon children had their grandmother as principal carer during the day, but attachment classifications were unaffected by the type of primary caregiver, because mothers remained closely involved with children through regular breastfeeding and co-sleeping during the night.

2 Positive correlations were found between maternal sensitivity and infant security ratings and the quality of mother–infant communications and infant security ratings.

Conclusions

Children raised by natural child-rearing practices have higher levels of secure attachment and no insecure-avoidant attachments. This is explained by the incompatibility of Dogon child-rearing practices with Western cultural child-rearing practices associated with insecure-avoidant styles. In Dogon culture there is no maternal rejection of attachment bids, intrusion or lack of physical contact.

Naturally parented children have greater attachment security and an absence of insecure-avoidant attachment, when compared to children of Western cultures.

Evaluation

The high proportion of secure attachments and no avoidant attachments found among the Dogon people is remarkable considering the mortality rate of around 45 per cent of infants before the age of 5 and the high rates of social and economic stressors, for example the high proportion of mothers with HIV and the high levels of poverty.

The findings are backed up by two similar studies. Tomlinson *et al.* (2005), using a South African sample, and Zevalkink *et al.* (1999), with an Indonesian sample, both found high levels of secure attachment and low levels of avoidant attachment.

Comparable studies are needed of infants naturally parented in Western cultures. Rates of secure attachment should be even higher here, because factors such as poverty, social stress and child mortality are less. One problem with such studies is the possibility that maternally sensitive mothers are more likely to choose natural parenting procedures, which could bias findings.

The Strange Situation procedure contains elements unfamiliar to Dogon infants, like being left with strangers, thereby creating a risk that infants are being wrongly classified as insecurely attached (see Psychology in the real world, page 127).

RESEARCH IN FOCUS

1 McMahon *et al.*'s (2001) study on Dogon mothers was a cross-cultural study with findings compared to those from North America. It is also a quasi experiment, using the naturally occurring independent variable (IV) of different child-rearing practices, with the dependent variable (DV) being the resulting attachment patterns.

   If behaviours are identical in different cultures, what does this suggest about the origins of those behaviours? If behaviours are different, what does this suggest?

2 The use of the Strange Situation in non-Western cultures is an example of an imposed etic. Explain what this means.

3 Why do some psychologists not consider quasi experiments to be true experiments?

4 In what situations would a quasi experiment be used?

5 Compile a list of the advantages and disadvantages of quasi experiments.

For information on research methods, see Chapter 7.

Research

Kyoung (2005) used the Strange Situation to compare 87 Korean families with 113 American families. There were notable differences: the Korean infants did not stay close to their mothers and when Korean mothers returned they were more likely to play with their infants. There were, however, a similar proportion of securely attached children in both cultures, suggesting that different child-rearing practices can lead to secure attachments.

Grossmann & Grossmann (1991) found that German infants tended to be classified as insecurely attached. This may be due to different child-rearing practices, as German culture requires 'distance' between parents and children. This indicates that there are cross-cultural variations in attachment.

Malin (1997) found that Aboriginal infants in Australia are discouraged from exploring by threats and distractions of food and so tend not to use their mothers as a safe base from which to explore, staying close to her at all times. This leads to the infants being incorrectly labelled as insecurely attached and often being put into care (see Psychology in the real world on page 127).

Evaluation

- The different patterns of reaction to the Strange Situation reflect cultural values and practices. For example, the greater frequency of insecure-avoidant children in Germany reflects a cultural emphasis on early independence training.

- The greater amounts of insecure-resistant attachment type in Japan may result from stress during the Strange Situation due to infants' unfamiliarity at being left with strangers. Japanese children are rarely separated from their mothers, so separation episodes are upsetting for these children. In contrast, Rogoff (2003) found that black American infants have many caregivers and are encouraged to be friendly to strangers and thus the Strange Situation activates their interest to explore. This shows that the Strange Situation has different meanings in different cultures and we need to examine child-rearing practices in order to interpret findings based on the Strange Situation.

- The facts that attachment patterns vary cross-culturally, and that the Strange Situation may not be applicable in all cultures, suggest that attachment theory is culture-bound and applicable only to Western cultures.

PSYCHOLOGY IN THE REAL WORLD

The use of the Strange Situation with Australian Aboriginal children

Figure 3.14 Is the use of the Strange Situation to determine whether Aboriginal children should be in care culturally appropriate?

Soo See Yeo (2003) has concerns about the use of the Strange Situation by the New South Wales Children's Court in determining whether Aboriginal children should be placed into care. Aboriginal children are nine times more likely to be in care than non-Aboriginal Australian children and Aboriginal children make up 25 per cent of Australian children placed in care since 2000. Yeo believes an imposed etic may be at work, as assessments are being made by what the dominant Australian culture sees as good parenting, with a disregard for Aboriginal cultural practices, resulting in life-changing decisions being made based on evidence that is culturally inappropriate.

Aboriginal children are often cared for and breastfed by many women within their community. Children are cared for by women interchangeably and are often brought up by women who are not their natural mothers. Aboriginal children are rarely left in the presence of strangers. Lewis (2005) argues that Aboriginal child-rearing practices create a network of multi-layered relationships that create an effective safety net for children, while attachment theory only focuses on the linear relationship between a mother and her infant. Therefore the assessment of Aboriginal children in line with Australian cultural values may lead to Aboriginal children being incorrectly assessed as having insecure attachments, taken away from their communities and placed in care. So what at first may seem an excellent practical use of psychology for the benefit of society may actually be having negative implications due to the use of inappropriate methodology. Yeo argues that assessments should be made on the basis of Aboriginal people's cultural values if they are to be seen as valid.

STRENGTHEN YOUR LEARNING

1. Outline the procedure of Ainsworth's Strange Situation.
2. Describe the characteristics of the following (be sure to include characteristics of the mother as well as the infant):
   a) secure attachment
   b) insecure-avoidant attachment
   c) insecure-resistant attachment.
3. Ainsworth believed sensitive responsiveness to be crucial to the development of attachments. What is sensitive responsiveness?
4. Evaluate the Strange Situation giving points for and against the technique.
5. What might the evolutionary purpose of insecure attachment types be?
6. Use findings from van IJzendoorn & Kroonenberg's study to assess whether attachment types are cross-cultural.
7. Explain why McMahan et al. (2001) found no evidence of insecure-avoidant attachments among the Dogon people.
8. Refer to Yeo's (2003) criticisms of the use of the Strange Situation to assess whether Aboriginal children should be put in care to explain why the technique might not be applicable to all cultures.

ASSESSMENT CHECK

1   Match the following descriptions to the correct type of attachment in the table below. There will be one description left over. **[4 marks]**

   A   A strong and contented attachment, developing through sensitive responsiveness

   B   An attachment type where infants seek and reject intimacy

   C   An attachment type characterised by a lack of a consistent pattern of social behaviour

   D   An attachment type where infants shun intimacy and social interaction

   E   An attachment type that develops through classical conditioning

Description	Type of attachment
	Insecure-avoidant attachment
	Insecure-disorganised attachment
	Secure attachment
	Insecure-resistant attachment

2   Manon was born a few months ago and for all of her life has been looked after at home by her mum who is very caring and loving towards her. Like most babies, Manon sleeps a lot, but when she is awake she gets hungry easily and this makes her very grumpy, causing her to cry. When this happens her mother always feeds her immediately and this soothes Manon and makes her feel very content.

   With reference to the above passage, explain how Manon may develop an attachment to her mother in terms of operant conditioning. **[4 marks]**

3   Explain what is meant by an internal working model. **[3 marks]**

4   Explain why the Strange Situation testing procedure may not be suitable for studying cultural variations in attachment. **[4 marks]**

5   Outline and evaluate Bowlby's monotropic theory. **[16 marks]**

6   Outline and evaluate learning theory as an explanation of attachment. **[12 marks]**

IN THE NEWS

Ψ The Psychological Enquirer

The monkey woman of West Yorkshire

(Adapted from Fortean Times, *June 2013)*

Figure 3.15 Marina Chapman with her family

63-year-old Marina Chapman of Bradford, West Yorkshire at first seems a relatively unremarkable woman, but her life history is anything but unremarkable. For Marina, born in Colombia, South America, was abducted by child kidnappers, abandoned, and then raised by a troupe of about thirty Weeper Capuchin monkeys. It is estimated that she spent in excess of five years among her monkey family. When found, she displayed many of their habits, including their eating behaviour, such as putting nuts into a hollow and then cracking them with a branch or rock, and their cleaning behaviour, such as wiping her bottom with moss. She also exhibited monkey vocalisations, using them to scare off snakes and express her emotions. When discovered, she was naked and black with dirt with hair down to her knees. Ultimately, Marina made a full recovery, came to Yorkshire as a children's maid and married her husband John in 1978, a relationship that produced two daughters. She can still scale trees in seconds, smell ripe fruit from afar and tends to open food tubs with her teeth, but apart from these remnants of her monkey past, few people would suspect Marina's unusual upbringing.

Feral children, like Marina, are not common and it is difficult to verify claims about their upbringing, but what interests psychologists is the degree to which such individuals can become 'normal' human beings, especially the extent to which they can develop relationships with other humans. The evidence, scant though it is, suggests that feral children can develop warm, emotionally secure relationships, and become good parents themselves. Perhaps it is the quality of the attachments to their animal carers which permits this to occur.

ON THE WEB

An excellent *National Geographic* film about feral children can be viewed in five parts. Search YouTube for 'Feral Children part 1', 'Feral Children part 2', and so on. You can also search for Marina Chapman Facebook.

3.5 Bowlby's maternal deprivation hypothesis (MDH) (1951)

Figure 3.16 Bowlby's maternal deprivation hypothesis is an explanation of what happens when attachments are broken

Bowlby's theory of monotropy (see page 116) believes that healthy psychological development is dependent upon attachments forming between infants and their mothers. Bowlby's maternal deprivation hypothesis (MDH) explains what happens if these attachments are broken. Bowlby argues that disruption of the attachment bond, even short-term disruptions, results in serious and permanent damage to a child's emotional, social and intellectual development.

KEY TERMS

Separation – short-term disruption of an attachment bond

Deprivation – long-term disruption of an attachment bond

Privation – never having formed an attachment bond

The best way to examine the validity of the MDH is to assess the effects of disruption to infants' attachments and see if Bowlby's predictions are true. Disruptions can occur in three basic ways: short-term **separation**, long-term **deprivation** and **privation**. Institutionalisation can also be examined to see its effects on infant development.

Short-term separation

Short-term separation consists of brief, temporary separations from attachment figures, like attending day care, being left with a babysitter or a short period of hospitalisation. Bowlby (1969) described the distress caused by short-term separation in terms of the PDD model (protest, despair and detachment):

- **Protest** – the immediate reaction to separation involves crying, screaming, kicking and struggling to escape, or clinging to the mother to prevent her leaving. This is an outward, direct expression of the child's anger, fear, bitterness and confusion.

- **Despair** – protest is replaced by calmer, more apathetic behaviour. Anger and fear are still felt inwardly. There is little response to offers of comfort; instead the child comforts itself, for example by thumb-sucking.

- **Detachment** – the child responds to people again, but treats everyone warily. Rejection of the caregiver on their return is common, as are signs of anger.

Research

Robertson & Robertson (1971) reported their 'Young Children in Brief Separation' research as five films that showed how brief separation from their mothers affected children's mental state and psychological development. One film (1969) featured John aged 17 months, who had a close and stable relationship with his mother. He experienced extreme distress while spending nine days in a residential nursery while his mother was in hospital having a baby. On his mother's return, John was thrown into confusion and struggled to get away from her. The negative effects of this separation were evident even years later. John had appeared to go through the three stages of the PDD model, suffering serious, irreversible damage, lending support to Bowlby's MDH.

Douglas (1975) found that separations of less than a week for children below 4 years of age were correlated with behavioural difficulties, giving further support to the MDH.

Quinton & Rutter (1976) found greater behavioural problems in samples of adolescents separated briefly from attachment figures before 5 years of age through hospitalisation, than among adolescents who weren't hospitalised, supporting Bowlby's prediction of long-term developmental damage.

Evaluation

- Robertson & Robertson (1971) took children facing short-term separations into their own home, providing them with an alternative attachment and a normal home routine and found this prevented the severe psychological damage, such as that seen with John. This suggests that negative outcomes are not inevitable, lessening support for Bowlby's MDH.

- Much evidence linking short-term separation to negative outcomes is correlational and doesn't show causality. Kagan *et al.* (1978) found no direct causal link between separation and later emotional and behavioural difficulties.

- Barrett (1997) argued that individual differences in reactions to short-term separation are important. For instance, securely attached children and more mature children cope better with separations, which suggests only some children experience distress.

PSYCHOLOGY IN THE REAL WORLD

James Robertson's film 'A Two-year-old Goes to Hospital' (1952) showed how separation from the primary attachment figure resulted in children experiencing distress. This work led to radical changes in hospital practices. Daily visiting for children was introduced, followed by unrestricted visiting and admission of the mother to hospital with the child. The Robertsons' 'Young Children in Brief Separation' research, reported in the five films 1967–1975, showed how a lack of opportunity to form alternative attachments resulted in the child experiencing extreme distress ('John, age seventeen months, for nine days in a Residential Nursery'). This research led to the closure of Residential Nurseries in favour of Foster Care for young children.

Figure 3.17 A cine-camera like the one the Robertsons used

ON THE WEB

A video clip from the Robertson & Robertson film, *The story of Laura*, can be seen on YouTube by searching for 'A two year old goes to hospital'.

A more detailed description of their films can be found at:

www.robertsonfilms.info/

Long-term deprivation

Long-term deprivation involves lengthy or permanent separations from attachment figures, most commonly due to divorce. Around 40 per cent of marriages in the UK end in divorce. Within two to three years of divorce, 50 per cent of divorced parents not living with their children (usually the father) have lost contact with their children. Long-term deprivation can also include death or imprisonment of a parent and resulting adoption by different caregivers.

Research

Rodgers & Pryor (1998) found that children experiencing two or more divorces have the lowest adjustment rates and the most behavioural problems, suggesting that continual broken attachments increase the chances of negative outcomes for children, supporting Bowlby's MDH.

Furstenberg & Kiernan (2001) found that children experiencing divorce score lower than children in first-marriage families on measures of social development, emotional wellbeing, self-concept, academic performance, educational attainment and physical health, suggesting that divorce has wide-ranging negative effects on children's development in line with Bowlby's MDH.

Schaffer (1996) found that nearly all children are negatively affected by divorce in the short term, though Hetherington & Stanley-Hagan (1999) found that only about 25 per cent of children experience long-term adjustment problems, with most children able to adapt. This suggests that negative outcomes to children's development are more short term than long term, lessening support for Bowlby's MDH.

- It seems logical that long-term separation has a greater negative effect upon children's development than short-term separation and research backs this up.

- Richards (1987) found that attachment disruption through divorce leads to resentment and stress, while the death of an attachment figure is more likely to result in depression than delinquency. This implies that separation through different causes produces different outcomes.

- Demo & Acock (1996) found that children vary widely in reactions to divorce, with some children developing better attachments to their parents after divorce. This may be due to the removal of the negative environment of marital conflict and also to parents being more attentive and supportive to children after divorcing. This suggests that divorce does not necessarily bring negative effects.

- Research has allowed psychologists to create strategies to help children cope with divorce. Some American states have a legal requirement for divorcing parents to attend an education programme that teaches them to understand and avoid the difficulties associated with disrupted attachments, like providing emotional warmth and support and keeping to consistent rules.

PSYCHOLOGY IN THE REAL WORLD

Figure 3.18 Is prison the best place for a young child? There are seven mother and baby units in English prisons

How can we apply what we know about the effects of attachment disruption to mothers and pregnant women in prison? Should young children be separated from their mothers in such circumstances or be allowed to stay with their mothers in prison? The facts make interesting reading. In England in 2013 there were 3,893 prisoners in thirteen women's prisons, seven of which have mother and baby units (MBUs). In 2006, 55 per cent of female prisoners had a child under 16 years and 33 per cent a child under 5 years of age. Between 2005 and 2008, 382 babies were born in prison. However, there are only places for 80 children in the mother and baby units, two of which allow babies to stay with their mothers up to 9 months of age and five up to the age of 18 months. Women with a poor past history of parenting are less likely to be given places, but each application is assessed on an individual basis by a multi-disciplinary team, focusing on the best interests of the child. For example, if a mother has an 18-month-old child in an MBU, but is due for release shortly, the child may stay with her. If a mother is serving a long sentence and is given a place on an MBU then in due course she will be separated from her child, though this is planned well in advance with social services and other family members involved.

Privation

Privation concerns children who have never formed an attachment bond. Privation is more likely than deprivation to lead to lasting damage, but research results are contradictory, with some individuals fully recovering, while others make little if any improvement. As cases of privation are relatively rare, they are generally researched through case studies.

Research

Freud & Dann (1951) reported on six children placed in a Nazi concentration camp, who were orphaned at a few months of age and had formed no maternal attachments. They were taken at age 3–4 to the Bulldog Bank Centre in West Sussex. They had little language, did not know what to do with toys and were hostile to adults. They were, however, devoted to each other and refused to be separated. Very gradually they became attached to their carers and made rapid developments in physical and intellectual capabilities. It was not possible to trace all the children as adults, but those that were traceable made good recoveries and had successful adult relationships, lessening support for Bowlby's MDH.

Koluchova (1972, 1991) reported on identical twins, Andrei and Vanya, whose mother died soon after their birth. When their father remarried, the stepmother locked them in a cellar for five-and-a-half years, giving them regular beatings. The father was mainly absent from the home due to his job. Discovered at age 7, the twins were underdeveloped physically, lacked speech and did not understand the meaning of pictures. Doctors predicted permanent physical and mental damage. The boys were given physical therapy and put into a school for children with severe learning difficulties and were then adopted by two child-centred sisters. At age 14 their intellectual, social, emotional and behavioural functioning was near normal. As adults, both married and had children; one worked as an instructor and the other was a computer technician. Both have enjoyed successful adult relationships and are still close to each other.

Curtiss (1977) and Rymer (1993) reported on Genie, a girl denied human interaction, beaten and strapped into a potty seat until discovered at age 13. She could not stand up or speak, spending most of her time spitting. She received years of therapy and was tested constantly, developing some language abilities and improving her IQ from 38 in 1971 to 74 in 1977. At 18 she returned to the care of her mother, staying for only a few months before moving to a succession of six different foster homes, where she was further abused. Genie then deteriorated physically and mentally, before going to live in a home for people with learning difficulties.

Figure 3.19 The Bulldog Bank children were survivors of Nazi concentration camps who had suffered extreme privation

Evaluation

- It may be that the close attachments the Czech twins and the Bulldog Bank children had to each other explain why they made lasting recoveries, while Genie, who had no attachments, made little progress. However, Moskowitz (1983) reports that the Bulldog Bank children were all individually adopted and never saw each other again and so should have exhibited the effects of disrupted attachment from each other.

- Case studies are usually used to study extreme privation, as it would be unethical or impractical to use most other research methods.

- Case studies are dependent upon retrospective memories that may be selective and even incorrect. There is no way of knowing fully what happened to these individuals before discovery. Genie's mother, for example, often gave conflicting stories of what happened to her daughter.

- Bowlby's viewpoint that the negative effects of maternal deprivation are irreversible seems overstated. The children whose privation experiences were followed by positive experiences made good recoveries.

RESEARCH IN FOCUS

1 For what reasons are case studies mainly used to investigate examples of privation?

2 Compile a list of the strengths and weaknesses of case studies.

For information on research methods, see Chapter 7.

Institutionalisation

Institutionalisation concerns the effects upon attachments of care provided by orphanages and residential children's homes, and Bowlby's MDH was largely upon studies conducted in the 1930s and 1940s of children raised in such institutions. **Institutional care** involves distinctive patterns of attachment behaviour and so can be regarded as a phenomenon in its own right; it often involves a mix of privation and deprivation effects. Institutionalised children often show a distinctive attachment behaviour called disinhibited attachment, characterised by clingy, attention-seeking behaviour and indiscriminate sociability to adults.

Research

Goldfarb (1943) compared fifteen children raised in social isolation in institutions from 6 months of age until $3\frac{1}{2}$ years of age with fifteen children who went straight from their natural mothers to foster homes. At age 3, the socially isolated children lagged behind the fostered children on measures of abstract thinking, social maturity, rule following and sociability. Between the ages of 10 and 14 years, they continued to perform poorly, with an average IQ of 72 compared to the fostered children's IQ of 95.

Spitz (1946) studied children raised in poor-quality South American orphanages. Members of staff were overworked and untrained and rarely talked to the children or picked them up, even for feeding. Children received no affection and had no toys. The children displayed anaclitic depression, a reaction to the loss of a love object, showing fear, sadness, weepiness, withdrawal, loss of appetite, weight loss, inability to sleep and developmental retardation.

Bowlby (1944) compared 44 juvenile thieves with a control group of non-thieves who had suffered emotional problems. Thirty-two per cent of the thieves exhibited **affectionless psychopathy**, lacking a social conscience. None of the control group was classed in this way. Eighty-six per cent of the affectionless psychopaths had experienced maternal separation compared to 17 per cent of the thieves who were not affectionless psychopaths. This supports Bowlby's idea that maternal deprivation can have serious and long-lasting negative effects.

Tizard & Hodges (1978) studied children placed into institutional care in the first four months of life. These children were privated as they had not formed attachments with their mothers. High staff turnover and the institute's policy of not letting carers form relationships with children prevented alternative attachments forming. Some children remained in the institution, some were adopted and some were restored to their natural homes. There was also a control group of children raised in their natural homes. The children were assessed at ages 4 and 8, and then again at age 16. Children who remained in the institution had no strong attachments and had problems relating to peers. Adopted children formed strong attachments within their adoptive families, but had problems with relationships outside their families. The restored children tended to have poor family and peer relationships and behavioural problems. This suggests that institutional care has long-lasting negative effects, though the development of close attachments is possible with loving care, as provided by adoptive parents.

Rutter (2006) found that the multiple carers provided by children's residential homes led to the formation of disinhibited attachments, supporting the idea of institutional care creating distinct attachment types.

RESEARCH IN FOCUS

1 In his study of juvenile thieves, Bowlby carried out interviews with children and mothers. Why is an interview a form of self-report?

2 What other forms of self-report are there?

3 Interviews can be structured, semi-structured or unstructured. Explain the differences between these types, giving advantages and disadvantages of each.

4 Although interviews are relatively easy to conduct and generate lots of data, they do have faults. Explain the following weaknesses:

   (i)   leading questions
   (ii) social desirability bias
   (iii) idealised answers (see the section on interviews, page 267).

For information on research methods, see Chapter 7.

Evaluation

- The early studies of children raised in institutions that Bowlby based his MDH on had serious methodological flaws. For example, the Goldfarb study did not use random samples, so it is possible that the fostered children were naturally brighter, more sociable and healthier than the socially isolated children and that is why they were fostered rather than placed in institutional care. Also, the institutions provided unstimulating environments and it may have been the lack of stimulation rather than the absence of maternal care that led to retarded development.

- In Tizard & Hodge's study the more socially skilled children may have been adopted and so found it easier to form attachments within their adoptive families. The study also suffered from atypical sample attrition, where, over time, a certain type of participant (for example, the more troubled children) drops out, thus affecting the reliability of the results.

YOU ARE THE RESEARCHER

In Bowlby's (1944) juvenile thieves study he compared thieves and non-thieves by interviewing the thieves, non-thieves and their mothers. Imagine you are conducting this study as a structured interview. Create a set of questions that are relevant to the factors being studied that generate both quantitative and qualitative data. How would both types of data be analysed?

For information on research methods, see Chapter 7.

The documentary film *Genie (Secret of the Wild Child)*, which tells the tale of her attempted rehabilitation, can be seen on YouTube by searching for 'Genie (Secret of the Wild Child)'.

'There can be no keener revelation of a society's soul than the way in which it treats its children.'

Nelson Mandela (1995)

Romanian orphan studies

In the 1990s media attention was directed to the horrific conditions endured by children in Romanian orphanages. There was a lack of nourishing food, toys and social interactions and little in the way of loving care. Divided into age groups, the orphans had little contact with older and more able peers. Many of these children were adopted and taken to more enriching environments in other countries where their progress has been monitored by psychologists in a series of research studies, generally to see if the effects of institutional care and privation can be overcome in the long term.

CONTEMPORARY RESEARCH

Developmental catch-up, and deficit, following adoption after severe global early privation – Michael Rutter *et al.* (1998)

Professor Michael Rutter and his team were interested in seeing whether the effects of institutional care and privation could be overcome by the long-term provision of a more nurturing and enriching environment. First reported in 1998, this is an on-going longitudinal study showing developmental trends (changes over time).

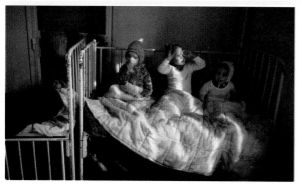

Figure 3.20 Professor Rutter's studies of Romanian orphans have aimed to see if the effects of institutionalisation can be overcome through loving care by adoptive parents

Aim

To assess whether loving and nurturing care could overturn the effects of privation the children had suffered in Romanian orphanages.

Procedure

1 This was a longitudinal study, incorporating a quasi experiment. The independent variable (IV) was the age of adoption, with three age groups being studied:
Condition 1: Children adopted before the age of 6 months
Condition 2: Children adopted between 6 months and 2 years
Condition 3: Children adopted after 2 years

2 The dependent variable (DV) was the children's level of cognitive functioning.

3 111 Romanian orphans were initially assessed for height, head circumference and cognitive functioning on arrival in Britain. All children were again assessed at age 4. A control group of 52 British adopted children were also assessed (to ascertain whether negative effects were due to separation from carers or the institutional conditions in Romanian orphanages).

Findings

1 Around 50 per cent of the Romanian orphans were retarded in cognitive functioning at initial assessment and most were underweight. The control group did not show these deficits.

2 At age 4 years, the Romanian orphans showed great improvements in physical and cognitive development, with the orphans adopted before 6 months of age doing as well as the British adopted children.

Conclusions

The negative effects of institutionalisation can be overcome by sensitive, nurturing care.

As the British adopted children (who had been separated from their mothers) did not suffer developmental outcomes, it can be seen that separation from carers will not on its own cause negative developmental effects.

Evaluation

Children have only been assessed up to the age of 4 years, so subsequent follow-ups will be required to assess the long-term effects of institutionalisation and the effects of subsequent enriching environments.

Only some of the children received detailed clinical investigations, so it is difficult to fully generalise the findings.

Because the children were not studied while in the Romanian orphanages, it is not possible to state which aspects of privation were most influential.

Follow-up and associated research

O'Connor *et al.* (1999) reported that the most enduring negative effects were difficulties making attachments, with many orphans displaying 'indiscriminate friendliness' (when children interact with strangers in the same way they would with a primary caregiver). These effects appear to be positively correlated with the length of time children were institutionalised.

O'Connor *et al.* (2000) performed a follow-up study at age 6 years, finding the improvements were maintained, though not advanced upon.

Rutter *et al.* (2001) performed a follow-up study, finding attachment problems, hyperactivity and cognitive impairment to be associated with institutionalisation, especially in children enduring long periods of institutionalisation, though 20 per cent of such children showed normal functioning. Emotional problems, poor peer relations and behaviour problems were not associated with institutionalisation. This suggests specific negative effects are related to long-term institutionalisation, but only in certain types of children.

Rutter (2007) followed up the same children at age 11, finding that many showed normal levels of functioning, but about 50 per cent of those showing disinhibited attachments at age 6 were still doing so.

Morison & Elwood (2005) found similar results with a group of Romanian orphans adopted by Canadian adoptive parents. This suggests Rutter's findings are reliable.

ON THE WEB

Watch Professor Michael Rutter talk about his Romanian orphans studies by searching YouTube for 'Professor Sir Michael Rutter'.

STRENGTHEN YOUR LEARNING

1 What is meant by the following? Give an example of each.
   a) Separation
   b) Deprivation
   c) Privation
2 Outline the PDD model.
3 How did the Robertsons discover that the effects of PDD could be avoided?
4 To what extent does research into the effects of short- and long-term disruption of attachment bonds support Bowlby's MDH?
5 Why is privation generally studied by the use of case studies?
6 Explain why the Czech twins and the Bulldog Bank children may have recovered from the effects of privation, but Genie didn't.
7 What distinctive attachment behaviour do institutionalised children often show and what are the characteristics of this behaviour?
8 What criticisms can be made of the early institutionalisation studies that Bowlby based his MDH upon?
9 What do studies of Romanian orphans tell us about whether the effects of institutional care can be overcome?

IN THE NEWS

Ψ The Psychological Enquirer

Can lesbians be good parents?

Figure 3.21 Sharon Bottoms had her child taken away from her as she was in a lesbian relationship

Sharon Bottoms and husband Dennis (of Virginia, USA) split up after a few months of marriage, only for Sharon to then discover that she was pregnant. Sharon moved back in with her mother and on July 5th 1991 her son Tyler Dovstov was born. Subsequently, Sharon started

dating April Wade and in late 1992 the couple held a 'commitment ceremony' and set up home together. Disgusted at her daughter's lesbian lifestyle, Sharon's mother Kay took her own daughter to court. Numerous witnesses, including her ex-husband, testified that Sharon was a good mother and Sharon also reported how her mother's partner had sexually abused her as a child. However, Judge Bruford Parsons stated that the gay couple's habit of kissing and cuddling in front of the boy would negatively affect him, even though court-appointed psychologists found no evidence of Tyler suffering ill effects. Kay won custody of her grandson.

A year later, an appeals court overturned the judgement, returning Tyler to his mother's care. But in 1995, the Virginia Supreme Court backed the original ruling, citing that Sharon 'refuses to subordinate her own desires and priorities to the child's welfare' and that growing up with lesbians would 'inevitably afflict the child's relationships with its peers and the community at large'.

Sharon Bottom's story was made into a film, *Two moms for Zachary*, but she never regained custody of her son and was only granted very limited visiting rights.

The issue over who makes good parents is a contentious one, with some arguing that parenting other than that by a man and a women, even indeed than that of a married man and woman, to be vastly inferior. However, psychological evidence suggests that it is the quality of parenting that is of prime importance not the gender, marital status or sexuality of the parents. Indeed, research from Birkbeck College, London, suggests same-sex couples make better parents, as their children can never be conceived accidentally. The rate of homosexuality among children raised by homosexuals is also reported to be no different to that of children raised by heterosexual parents.

3.6 The influence of early attachment on childhood and adult relationships

Psychologists have been interested in seeing whether attachments made in infancy have an effect on relationships individuals have in childhood and as adults. The **continuity hypothesis** sees children's attachment types being reflected in their later relationships. This idea is based upon the internal working model (see page 118), where an infant's primary attachment forms a model (template) for future relationships. In other words there will be continuity between early attachment experiences and later relationships.

Childhood relationships

Research indicates that there is continuity between early attachment styles and the quality of childhood relationships. Also, evidence suggests that children who form attachments to each other early in life will not generally go on to form adult sexual relationships with each other.

Research

Youngblade & Belsky (1992) found that 3–5-year-old securely attached children were more curious, competent, empathetic, resilient and self-confident, got along better with other children and were more likely to form close friendships.

Mullis *et al.* (1999) reported that in late childhood attachments that are made to peers reflect those made to parents in infancy. Laible (2000) backed this up by finding that in late childhood individuals transfer attachment behaviours learned in childhood to social situations and peer groups. This supports the idea of continuity from early attachments and the internal working model.

Westermarck (1891) reported that children who form close friendships in the first six years of life do not generally go on to form adult sexual relationships with each other, which suggests early attachments do affect childhood and adult relationships.

Shepher (1971) examined 3,000 Israeli marriage records to find that no children reared together on a kibbutz got married to each other, which backs up Westermarck's findings and supports the idea that early attachments influence later relationships.

Evaluation

- Attachments formed between infants and their carers have a large influence in determining the quality of subsequent childhood relationships, with those forming secure attachments seeming to profit best in terms of developing positive personal characteristics and social abilities.
- Early attachment types can be seen to influence the development of individual differences in cognitive ability, emotional responses and social skills, all of which influence the quality of later childhood relationships.
- Perceiving the quality of later relationships as being caused solely by the quality of early attachments is somewhat deterministic. It is likely that other factors are influential too, like financial pressures or age differences between partners.
- The fact that children who form attachments to each other in early life do not generally go on to form adult sexual relationships with each other, suggests it is an evolutionary anti-incest device that serves to stop related individuals breeding, as such relationships could lead to the birth of children with genetically transmitted disabilities.

Adult relationships

Research indicates an intergenerational continuity between adults' attachment types and their children, including children adopting the parenting styles of their own parents. There also appears to be continuity

Figure 3.22 Research suggests that individuals who form secure infant attachments go on to enjoy loving, long-lasting adult relationships

between early attachment styles and the quality of later adult relationships. However, those who fail to achieve secure attachments in childhood are not necessarily condemned to a life of broken relationships, divorce and a cycle of inadequate parenting, as research indicates that it is possible for such individuals to develop secure adult relationships. It should be noted though that not all evidence supports the idea of continuity between early attachments and later relationships.

CLASSIC RESEARCH

Romantic love conceptualised as an attachment process – Hazan & Shaver (1987)

The researchers were interested in examining the idea that early attachment styles would be reflected in adult romantic relationships, as predicted by Bowlby.

Aims/Hypotheses

To explore the possibility that attachment theory offers a perspective on adult romantic love and to create a framework for understanding love, loneliness and grief at different points in the life cycle.

It was predicted that:

1 There would be a correlation between adults' attachment styles and the type of parenting they received.

2 Adults with different attachment styles will display different characteristic mental models (internal representations) of themselves and their major social-interaction partners.

Procedure

1 Respondents to a 'love quiz' in a local newspaper were asked which of three descriptions best applied to their inner feelings about romantic relationships (see Table 3.7). These descriptions related to secure attachments, insecure-avoidant attachments and insecure-resistant attachments.

2 Participants also completed a checklist describing childhood relationships with parents, relating to the same attachment types. Two separate samples were tested.

3 Sample one comprised 205 men and 415 women, between 14 and 82 years of age, 91 per cent describing themselves as heterosexual. 42 per cent were married, 28 per cent were divorced or widowed, 9 per cent were co-habiting and 31 per cent were dating. (Some fitted more than one category.)

4 Sample two comprised 108 students (38 men and 70 women) who answered additional items focusing more on the 'self' side of the mental model (as opposed to their partner), as well as items measuring loneliness.

Findings

Table 3.7 below shows the percentage of respondents classified as securely attached, insecure-avoidant or insecure-resistant.

1 In both samples, those described as securely attached described the most important love relationship they ever had as 'happy, friendly and trusting'. These participants had longer lasting relationships and if they married tended not to divorce.

2 Securely attached participants expressed belief in lasting love. They found others trustworthy and had confidence in their self as likeable.

3 Insecure-avoidant participants were more doubtful about the existence or durability of romantic love. They also maintained they didn't need love partners to be happy.

4 Insecure-avoidant participants expressed more self-doubts, compared with both other types, but compared with the insecure-resistant participants didn't repress feelings of security.

5 Both insecure types were vulnerable to loneliness; the insecure-resistant (sample two) being most vulnerable.

Classification	% of respondents	Response
Securely attached	56 (Both samples)	I find it easy getting close to others and am comfortable depending on them and having them depend on me. I don't worry about being abandoned or about someone getting close to me.
Insecure-avoidant	23 (Sample one) 25 (Sample two)	I am uncomfortable being close to others; I find it difficult to trust them, difficult to depend on them. I am nervous when anyone gets close, and love partners want me to be more intimate than I feel comfortable being.
Insecure-resistant	19 (Sample one) 20 (Sample two)	I find others are reluctant to get as close as I'd like. I worry my partner doesn't really love me or won't stay with me. I want to merge completely with another person, and this desire scares people away.

Table 3.7 The percentage of respondents classified as securely attached, insecure-avoidant or insecure-resistant.

The percentages of adults in the different attachment types match those of children in Ainsworth's Strange Situation studies.

The correlation between adults' attachment style and their memories of parenting style they received is similar to Ainsworth's findings, where children's attachment styles were correlated with the degree of sensitivity shown by mothers.

Adults' mental models differ according to attachment styles. Securely attached are more positive and optimistic about themselves and (potential) love partners, compared with either insecurely attached types.

People with insecure attachment are vulnerable to loneliness.

Evaluation

The researchers provided a typical account of the processes involved in romantic attachment and an understanding of individual differences in adult relationship styles, as well as a connection between infant attachment theory and theories of romantic love, which stimulated research in the area.

The research showed continuity of childhood attachment style into adulthood doesn't always occur, i.e. insecurely attached children don't necessarily become insecurely attached adults. Continuity decreases as individuals progress further into adulthood. The average person participates in several important friendships and love relationships, providing opportunities for revising mental models of self and others. Main *et al.* (1985) support this optimistic view, finding that some adults insecure in relationships with parents produced securely attached children. They had mentally worked through their unpleasant experiences and now had mental models of relationships more typical of the securely attached.

Attachment types identified by the Strange Situation only relate to the quality of relationship with one person. Therefore an adult's choice of a paragraph describing their attachment style might only relate to their current relationship.

Research

McCarthy (1999) assessed the quality of adult relationships of 40 women aged 25 to 44 years with childhood insecure attachments. Women with insecure-avoidant attachments had less successful adult romantic relationships, while those with insecure-resistant attachments had problems forming non-romantic adult friendships, supporting the idea of an internal working model.

Kirkpatrick & Davis (1994) studied 300 dating couples for three years, finding that those identified as having secure childhood attachments were more likely to have stable and satisfying relationships, supporting the idea of continuity from an internal working model.

Belsky (1999) reported that women with childhood secure attachments experienced less conflict with husbands on topics related to time spent together and household division of labour than insecurely attached women. They were also more likely to manage conflict in mutually focused ways, explaining why they experience less conflict in the first place and why their relationships are mutually rewarding. This applied to both dating and married couples. Securely attached individuals were also more committed to relationships and felt greater love for their partners, consistent with Hazan and Shaver's 'secure' description of feelings about romantic relationships.

Brennan & Shaver (1995) found that individuals classified as insecure-avoidant were willing to engage in sex in the absence of strong feelings of love or an enduring relationship. Similarly, Hazan & Shaver (1994) found that such individuals were more likely to have one-night stands and sex outside established relationships and they preferred purely sexual contact, for example oral and anal sex, to more emotionally intimate sexual contact, such as kissing and cuddling. This again supports the concept of the internal working model.

Kunce & Shaver (1994) found that women classed as having childhood insecure-resistant attachments reported the highest levels of 'compulsive caregiving', that is, they were most likely to agree with statements such as 'I can't seem to stop from "mothering" my partner too much.'

- Wood *et al.* (2003) believes the quality of relationships results from the interaction of two people's attachment styles. Therefore insecurely attached people can have secure relationships if they are in relationships with securely attached people.

- The internal working model is not fully supported; Steele *et al.* (1998) found that only a small correlation of 0.17 between having a secure attachment type in childhood and early adulthood, while Zimmerman *et al.* (2000) found that attachment style at 12–18 months of age did not predict the quality of later relationships, while life events experienced, such as parental divorce, had a much larger influence. Also, Hamilton (1994) found that securely attached children went on to have insecurely-attached relationships if they had experienced negative life events.

- The **temperament hypothesis** sees the quality of adult relationships as being determined biologically from innate personality, suggesting that attempts to develop better quality relationships by changing people's attachment styles to more positive ones wouldn't work.

KEY TERM

Temperament hypothesis – the idea that the nature of infants' attachments is due to innate personality factors

YOU ARE THE RESEARCHER

Design a study that assesses whether early attachment types are reflected in later childhood and adult relationships. What kind of a study would this be? How would you measure attachment types in infancy, childhood and adulthood? How would you make sure your measurements were reliable?

For information on research methods, see Chapter 7.

STRENGTHEN YOUR LEARNING

1 What is the connection between an internal working model and the continuity hypothesis?

2 Why might children who form close early attachments to each other not go on to form adult sexual relationships with each other?

3 **a)** How did Hazan & Shaver (1987) investigate the relationship between early childhood and later adult relationships?

   b) What did Hazan & Shaver's findings suggest about the validity of an internal working model?

4 To what extent does research evidence support the continuity hypothesis?

ASSESSMENT CHECK

1 Place a letter 'I' next to the three statements below that relate to the effects of institutionalisation. Three statements will be left over. **[3 marks]**

Children are closely attached to one person. ☐

Children show a fear of strangers. ☐

Children display retarded cognitive abilities. ☐

Children are often underweight. ☐

Children display attention-seeking behaviour. ☐

Children are well-liked by their peers. ☐

2 Two-year-old Ruby has a secure, loving relationship with her mother, but her mother has to go into hospital for a few days to have a minor operation. During this time, her mother has made arrangements for Ruby to go and stay with someone she has never met before.

What strategies could be used to reduce any potential negative effects of Ruby's separation from her mother? **[4 marks]**

3 Outline the procedure and findings of one or more studies of Romanian orphans. **[6 marks]**

4 Outline one strength and one limitation of the case study method when studying privation. **[2 + 2 marks]**

5 Discuss the influence of early attachment on childhood and/or adult relationships. **[16 marks]**

6 Discuss Bowlby's theory of maternal deprivation. **[12 marks]**

SUMMARY

- Attachments are developed and maintained through interactions between carers and infants and develop in several distinct stages.
- Most children develop multiple attachments, with a debate between psychologists as to whether attachments are of equal value or whether there is one prime attachment.
- A debate also exists as to the importance of the father as an attachment figure.
- Bowlby was heavily influenced by animal studies, such as those by Harlow and Lorenz.
- The learning theory sees attachments as acquired through experience via the process of association.
- Bowlby's monotropic theory sees infants as having an innate tendency to become attached to one particular individual.
- Bowlby argued for a critical period, a specific time period within which an attachment must form.
- Bowlby also saw attachments as forming an internal working model, a template for future relationships.
- Ainsworth developed the 'Strange Situation', a method of assessing types of attachment.
- Cultural variations exist in attachment patterns and the Strange Situation may not be suited for use in all cultures.
- Bowlby's maternal deprivation hypothesis (MDH) argues that serious, irreversible damage will occur if attachment bonds are broken.
- Romanian orphan studies suggest that the negative effects of institutionalisation can be overcome by sensitive, nurturing care.
- Evidence suggests that a degree of continuity exists between early attachment types and the quality of later relationships.

How attachments form

Explanations for attachment

The Strange Situation

The consequences of disrupting attachment

The influence of early attachments upon childhood and adult relationships

4

Individual differences: psychopathology

Introduction

Psychology generally focuses upon the scientific outlook of finding what qualities people have in common. Most research even involves analysing data to find averages in order to establish 'truths' about the mind and behaviour. However, individual differences is a branch of psychology that focuses more upon how people differ from each other. The particular topic featured here is that of psychopathology, with specific focus on:

- Definitions of abnormality
- Characteristics of phobias, depression and OCD
- The behavioural approach to explaining and treating phobias
- The cognitive approach to explaining and treating depression
- The biological approach to explaining and treating OCD.

Understanding the specification

- Students are required to have knowledge of four named *definitions of abnormality*: *deviation from social norms, failure to function adequately, statistical infrequency and deviation from ideal mental health*.
- Three specified *mental disorders – phobias, depression and OCD –* must each be able to be described in terms of their emotional, cognitive and behavioural characteristics.
- Phobias must additionally be able to be explained from a *behaviourist viewpoint*, using the *two-process model of classical and operant conditioning*, with an additional knowledge also required of the behaviourist treatment of systematic desensitisation, including relaxation, use of hierarchy and flooding.
- *Depression* must be explained from a *cognitive viewpoint*, using Beck's negative triad and Ellis' ABC model, with an additional knowledge also required of *cognitive behavioural therapy*, including challenging irrational thoughts, as again this is directly referred to.
- *OCD* must be explained from a *biological viewpoint*, using genetic and neural explanations with an additional knowledge also required of drug therapy, as this is directly referred to.

These are the basic requirements of the specification. However, other relevant material is included to provide depth and detail to your understanding.

Ψ The Psychological Enquirer

The long walk home – naked

Figure 4.1 Stephen Gough's second naked ramble (with friend)

It is ex-Royal Marine Stephen Gough's heartfelt belief that being naked in public is a fundamental freedom and he wishes by doing so to separate nudity from sexual behaviour. So in 2003–04 and again in 2005–06 he walked from Land's End to John O'Groats in just his boots and occasionally (on sunny days) a hat. He was arrested 18 times and has spent 6 years in prison (naked) in isolation. His spells of freedom are often for a few seconds, with arrest following his refusal to wear clothes on leaving prison. The cost for his imprisonment now runs into several hundred thousand pounds. In 2012, he was allowed to walk home from Scotland to Hampshire, as long as he did so with 'consideration for others'. Three days later, he was arrested for walking naked past a children's playground in Fife and put back in prison, with Gough refusing to allow social workers to assess his mental health. The authorities have generally seen him as confrontational, intolerant and inconsiderate, and in January 2014, he was again jailed for 16 months for breaking an ASBO to not be naked in public.

Stephen Gough's behaviour by many definitions of abnormality would be seen as abnormal; he is deviating from the social norm of being dressed in public, displaying elements of failure to function adequately (such as displaying behaviour that causes offence to others), showing statistically infrequent behaviour (being naked in public) and deviating from ideal mental health (such as not having environmental mastery by not being competent in all aspects of life). But then again, many of us would say he's quite sane and is just behaving according to his principles, and that it's the objectors to his behaviour who have a problem.

ON THE WEB

Watch a BBC documentary about Stephen Gough by searching for 'Stephen Gough Naked Rambler' on YouTube.

4.1 Definitions of abnormality

'To study the abnormal is the best way to understand the normal.'
William James (1890)

'Perfect sanity is a myth propagated by straitjacket salesmen.'
Rebecca McKinsey (2013)

'. . . and then I decided I was a lemon for a couple of weeks.'
Ford Prefect in *The Hitchhiker's Guide to the Galaxy* by Douglas Adams (1978)

KEY TERM

Abnormality – a psychological or behavioural state leading to impairment of interpersonal functioning and/or distress to others

Abnormality is difficult to define; psychologists disagree about the causes of mental disorders and how they reveal themselves. One point of view sees abnormality resulting from flawed biology, another that abnormality is due to 'incorrect' learning or defective thought processes. Others argue that mental disorders originate from problems of the mind and personality. Different viewpoints have been favoured at different times and across different cultures. Rosenhan & Seligman (1995) believe that normality is merely an absence of abnormality. This means that by defining abnormality, decisions are being made about what is normal.

Four criteria for defining abnormality are examined here, each with its strengths and weaknesses.

The deviation from social norms definition

Each society has norms, unwritten rules for acceptable behaviour, for example not being naked in public. Any behaviour that varies from these norms is abnormal, so abnormal behaviour is, therefore, behaviour that goes against social norms (**deviation from social norms**). The definition draws a line between desirable and undesirable behaviours and labels individuals behaving undesirably as social deviants; it allows interference into their lives in order to help them, for instance putting them into a mental hospital. These norms will vary across cultures, situations, ages and even gender, so that what is seen as acceptable/normal in one culture, situation, age group or gender type will not be in others. One important consideration is the degree to which a social norm is deviated from and how important society sees that norm as being.

KEY TERM

Deviation from social norms – behaviour violating accepted social rules

Strengths of the definition

- **Helps people** – the fact that society gives itself the right to intervene in abnormal people's lives can be beneficial, as such individuals that need it may not be able to get help themselves.
- **Social dimension** – the definition gives a social dimension to the idea of abnormality, which offers an alternative to the isolated 'sick-in-the-head' individual.
- **Situational norms** – the definition considers the social dimensions of behaviour; a behaviour seen as abnormal in one setting is regarded as normal in another, for instance while being naked in town is seen as abnormal it's regarded as normal on a nudist beach.
- **Developmental norms** – the definition establishes what behaviours are normal for different ages, for example filling a nappy aged 2 is considered normal, perhaps not so if you're 40.
- **Distinguishes between normal/abnormal** – the definition gives a clear indication of what is and isn't seen as normal behaviour.
- **Protects society** – the definition seeks to protect society from the effects an individual's abnormal behaviour can have on others.

Limitations of the definition

- **Subjective** – social norms are not real, but are based on the opinions of ruling elites within society rather than majority opinion. Social norms are then used to 'control' those seen as a threat to social order. A true definition of abnormality should be objective and free from subjective factors. Szasz (1960) sees the term 'mental illness' as a form of social control. Those labelled as abnormal are discriminated against. Some countries, for example China, have been known to label political opponents as abnormal and confine them to mental institutions.
- **Change over time** – the norms defined by society often relate to moral standards that vary over time as social attitudes change. As an example,

homosexuality was not removed from the International Classification of Diseases classification of mental disorders until 1990.

- **Individualism** – those who do not conform to social norms may not be abnormal, but merely individualistic or eccentric and not problematic in any sense.

- **Ethnocentric bias in diagnosis** – Western social norms reflect the behaviour of the majority 'white' population. Deviation from these norms by ethnic groups means that ethnic minorities are over-represented in the mental illness statistics. Cochrane (1977) found that black people were more often diagnosed as schizophrenic than white people or Asians. However, while this high rate of diagnosis for black people is found in Britain, it is not found in such countries as Jamaica where black people are the majority, suggesting a cultural bias in diagnosis among British psychiatrists.

- **Cultural differences** – social norms vary within and across cultures and so it is difficult to know when they are being broken. If a male wears a skirt does it indicate abnormality? Would the same be true of a Scottish male wearing a kilt? Therefore this definition of abnormality is an example of **cultural relativism**.

The failure to function adequately definition

The **failure to function adequately** definition sees individuals as abnormal when their behaviour suggests that they cannot cope with everyday life. Behaviour is considered abnormal when it causes distress leading to an inability to function properly, like disrupting the ability to work and/or conduct satisfying interpersonal relationships. Such people are often characterised by not being able to experience the usual range of emotions or behaviours. The definition focuses on individual suffering, thus drawing attention to the personal experiences associated with mental disorders.

Rosenhan & Seligman (1989) suggest that personal dysfunction has seven features. The more an individual has, the more they are classed as abnormal (see Table 4.1).

Table 4.1 Rosenhan & Seligman's features of personal dysfunction

Features of personal dysfunction	Descriptions of features
Personal distress	A key feature of abnormality. Includes depression and anxiety disorders
Maladaptive behaviour	Behaviour stopping individuals from attaining life goals, both socially and occupationally
Unpredictability	Displaying unexpected behaviours characterised by loss of control, like attempting suicide after failing a test
Irrationality	Displaying behaviour that cannot be explained in a rational way
Observer discomfort	Displaying behaviour causing discomfort to others
Violation of moral standards	Displaying behaviour violating society's moral standards
Unconventionality	Displaying unconventional behaviours

To assess how well individuals cope with everyday life, clinicians use the Global Assessment of Functioning scale (GAF), which rates their level of social, occupational and psychological functioning.

KEY TERMS

Cultural relativism – the way in which the function and meaning of a behaviour, value or attitude are relative to a specific cultural setting. Interpretations about the same behaviour may therefore differ between cultures

Failure to function adequately – an inability to cope with day-to-day living

Strengths of the definition

- **Matches sufferers' perceptions** – as most people seeking clinical help believe that they are suffering from psychological problems that interfere with the ability to function properly, it supports the definition.

- **Assesses degree of abnormality** – as the GAF is scored on a continuous scale, it allows clinicians to see the degree to which individuals are abnormal and thus decide who needs psychiatric help.

- **Observable behaviour** – it allows judgement by others of whether individuals are functioning properly, as it focuses on observable behaviours.

- **Checklist** – the definition provides a practical checklist individuals can use to assess their level of abnormality.

- **Personal perspective** – it recognises the personal experience of sufferers and thus allows mental disorders to be regarded from the perception of the individuals suffering them.

Limitations of the definition

- **Abnormality is not always accompanied by dysfunction** – psychopaths, people with dangerous personality disorders, can cause great harm yet still appear normal. Harold Shipman, the English doctor who murdered at least 215 of his patients over a 23-year period, seemed to be a respectable doctor. He was abnormal, but didn't display features of dysfunction.

- **Subjective nature of the features of dysfunction** – although GAF measures levels of functioning, it doesn't consider behaviour from an individual's perspective. What is normal behaviour for an eccentric, like wearing flamboyant clothes, is abnormal for an introvert.

- **Normal abnormality** – there are times in people's lives when it is normal to suffer distress, like when loved ones die. Grieving is psychologically healthy to overcome loss. The definition doesn't consider this.

- **Distress to others** – behaviour may cause distress to other people and be regarded as dysfunctional, while the person in question feels no distress, like Stephen Gough, the naked rambler (see page 146).

- **Personally rewarding abnormality** – an individual's apparently dysfunctional behaviour may actually be rewarding. For example, a person's eating disorder can bring affection and attention from others.

- **Cultural differences** – what is considered 'normal functioning' varies from culture to culture and so abnormal functioning of one culture should not be used to judge people's behaviour from other cultures and subcultures.

Figure 4.2 Harold Shipman

RESEARCH IN FOCUS

A problem with interpreting behaviour from different cultures is that of *imposed etics*. What is an imposed etic and what effect can it have?

For information on research methods, see Chapter 7.

ON THE WEB

Harold Shipman was a psychopath and yet was never seen as abnormal. Read an in-depth review about him at 'Crime library', including a mental profile at:

www.crimelibrary.com/serial_killers/notorious/shipman/30.html

Deviation from the ideal mental health definition

This definition perceives abnormality in a similar way to how physical health is assessed, by looking for signs of an absence of wellbeing, but in terms of mental rather than physical health. Therefore any deviation away from what is seen as normal is classed as abnormal.

The definition needs a set of characteristics of what is required to be normal and these were provided by Marie Jahoda (1958), who devised the concept of ideal mental health. She described six characteristics that individuals should exhibit in order to be normal (see Table 4.2). An absence of any of these characteristics indicates individuals as being abnormal, in other words displaying **deviation from ideal mental health**.

Table 4.2 Jahoda's characteristics of ideal mental health

Characteristics of ideal mental health	Descriptions of characteristics
Positive attitude towards oneself	Having self-respect and a positive self-concept
Self-actualisation	Experiencing personal growth and development. 'Becoming everything one is capable of becoming'
Autonomy	Being independent, self-reliant and able to make personal decisions
Resisting stress	Having effective coping strategies and being able to cope with everyday anxiety-provoking situations
Accurate perception of reality	Perceiving the world in a non-distorted fashion. Having an objective and realistic view of the world
Environmental mastery	Being competent in all aspects of life and able to meet the demands of any situation. Having the flexibility to adapt to changing life circumstances

The more characteristics individuals fail to meet and the further they are away from realising individual characteristics, the more abnormal they are.

Like the deviation from social norms and the failure to function adequately definitions, this definition focuses on behaviours and characteristics seen as desirable, rather than what is undesirable.

Strengths of the definition

- **Positivity** – the definition emphasises positive achievements rather than failures and distress and stresses a positive approach to mental problems by focusing on what is desirable, not undesirable.
- **Targets areas of dysfunction** – the definition allows targeting of which areas to work on when treating abnormality. This could be important when treating different types of disorders, such as focusing upon specific problem areas a person with depression has.
- **Holistic** – the definition considers an individual as a whole person rather than focusing on individual areas of their behaviour.
- **Goal setting** – the definition permits identification of exactly what is needed to achieve normality, allowing creation of personal goals to work towards and achieve, thus facilitating self-growth.

Limitations of the definition

- **Over-demanding criteria** – most people do not meet all the ideals. For example, few people experience personal growth all the time. Therefore, according to this definition, most people are abnormal. Thus the criteria may actually be ideals (how you would like to be) rather than actualities (how you actually are).

- **Subjective criteria** – many of the criteria are vague and difficult to measure. Measuring physical health is more objective, using methods like X-rays and blood tests. Diagnosing mental health is more subjective, relying largely on self-reports of patients who may be mentally ill and not reliable.

- **Contextual effects** – mental health criteria are affected by context. Spitting while out jogging is quite normal, but is not considered normal in the college cafeteria.

- **Changes over time** – perceptions of reality change over time. Once seeing visions was a positive sign of religious commitment, now it would be perceived as a sign of schizophrenia.

- **Cultural variation** – the criteria used to judge mental health are culturally relative and should not be used to judge others of different cultures. Some types of abnormality exist only in certain cultures, like Koro, which is a syndrome found in South East Asia, China and Africa, where a man believes that his penis is fatally retracting into his body.

- **Non-desirability of autonomy** – collectivist cultures stress communal goals and behaviours and see autonomy as undesirable. Western cultures are more concerned with individual attainment and goals, so the definition is culturally biased.

Figure 4.3 The deviation from ideal mental health definition may be more about the ideal self than the actual self

YOU ARE THE RESEARCHER

Design a questionnaire to measure Jahoda's characteristics of ideal mental health. Include questions that produce both *qualitative* and *quantitative* data. How would you use *content analysis* to make sense of your qualitative data?

For information on research methods, see Chapter 7.

The statistical infrequency definition

The idea here is that behaviours that are statistically rare should be seen as abnormal. Statistics are gathered that claim to measure certain characteristics and behaviours, with a view to showing how they are distributed throughout the general population.

What is regarded as statistically rare depends on normal distribution. A normal distribution curve can be drawn to show what proportions of people share the characteristics or behaviour in question. Most people will be on or near the mean for these characteristics or behaviours with declining amounts of people away from the mean (either above or below it). Any individuals who fall outside 'the normal distribution', usually about 5 per cent of a population (two standard deviation points away from the mean) are perceived as being abnormal. So, for example, individuals whose moods were elevated above or below that of the normal distribution would be classed as abnormal.

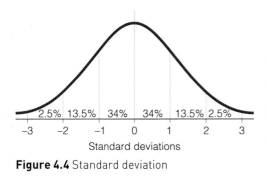

Figure 4.4 Standard deviation

The definition goes no further than declaring which behaviours are abnormal and makes no judgements about quality of life or the nature of mental disorders.

Strengths of the definition

- **Can be appropriate** – in many situations statistical criteria can define abnormality, for example mental retardation.
- **Objective** – once a way of collecting data about a behaviour/characteristic and a 'cut-off point' has been agreed, it becomes an objective way of deciding who is abnormal.
- **No value judgements** – no judgements are made, so, for example, homosexuality, which was defined as a mental disorder under early versions of diagnostic criteria used by psychiatrists, would not be seen under this definition as 'wrong' or 'unacceptable', but merely as less frequent than heterosexuality.
- **Evidence for assistance** – statistical evidence that a person has a mental disorder can be used to justify requests for psychiatric assistance.
- **Based on real data** – the definition relies on real, unbiased data and so again is an objective means of defining abnormality.
- **Overall view** – the definition gives an overview of what behaviours and characteristics are infrequent within a given population.

Limitations of the definition

- **Where to draw the line** – it's not clear how far behaviour should deviate from the norm to be seen as abnormal. Many disorders, like depression, vary greatly between individuals in terms of their severity.
- **Not all infrequent behaviours (those showing statistical infrequency) are abnormal** – some rare behaviours and characteristics are desirable rather than being undesirable. For example, being highly intelligent is statistically rare, but desirable.
- **Not all abnormal behaviours are infrequent** – some statistically frequent 'normal' behaviours are actually abnormal. About 10 per cent of people will be chronically depressed at some point in their lives, which suggests depression is so common as to not be seen as abnormal under this definition.
- **Cultural factors** – the definition doesn't consider cultural factors. What is statistically normal in one culture may not be in another. This can lead to the problem of judging people of one culture by the statistical norms of another culture.

STRENGTHEN YOUR LEARNING

1 What is cultural relativism? How might it apply to each definition of abnormality?
2 Outline the strengths and limitations of the deviation from social norms definition of abnormality.
3 Describe Rosenhan & Seligman's features of personal dysfunction.
4 Describe Jahoda's characteristics of ideal mental health.
5 Explain the idea of normal distribution in relation to defining abnormality.

ASSESSMENT CHECK

1 David has been feeling rather low lately and his absences from work are threatening his chances of promotion. His sudden outbursts of rage can be quite scary to others and yesterday he turned up at work with his hair dyed purple.

Explain David's behaviour by reference to the failure to function adequately definition of abnormality. **[4 marks]**

2 Explain one strength and one limitation of the deviation from social norms definition of abnormality. **[2 + 2 marks]**

3 The following statements relate to definitions of abnormality. Copy and complete the table below by inserting the statement, A, B, C, D or E, which describes each definition of abnormality. One description will be left over. **[4 marks]**

   A   Abnormal behaviours are ones that are very rare.

   B   Behaviours that are not acceptable to society are abnormal.

   C   People who can't cope with everyday activities are abnormal.

   D   Yielding to group pressures is abnormal.

   E   A lack of autonomy is abnormal.

Definitions of abnormality	Descriptions of abnormality
Deviation from social norms definition	
Deviation from ideal mental health definition	
Failure to function adequately definition	
Statistical infrequency definition	

4 Outline and evaluate definitions of abnormality. **[16 marks]**

5 Outline and evaluate the statistical infrequency and deviation from ideal mental health definitions of abnormality. **[12 marks]**

6 To conduct research into definitions of abnormality, psychologists often conduct interviews with participants. Explain one strength and one limitation of conducting such interviews. **[2 + 2 marks]**

4.2 Characteristics of phobias, depression and OCD

'The only thing we have to fear is fear itself.'
Franklin D. Roosevelt (1933)

'There's nothing funny about a clown in the moonlight.'
Lon Chaney (1925)

Phobias

Phobias are a type of anxiety disorder. Anxiety is an emotion all people experience and is a natural response to potentially dangerous stimuli, but phobias are characterised by uncontrollable, extreme, irrational and enduring fears and involve anxiety levels that are out of proportion to any actual risk. As many sufferers attempt to deal with their phobias themselves, it is difficult to estimate what the occurrence rate is, but about 10 per cent of people will suffer from a phobia at some point, with females having twice the incidence of phobias as males. Phobias can be very long lasting, enduring over many years.

Most phobias originate in childhood, but lessen in strength during adulthood. Generally people with phobias have insight into their condition, as they realise their fear reactions are irrational, but they cannot consciously control them.

Symptoms

Behavioural

Avoidant/anxiety response – as confrontation with feared objects and situations produces high anxiety responses, efforts are made to avoid the feared objects and situations in order to reduce the chances of such anxiety responses occurring. For instance, if someone has a fear of ghosts they do not take a short-cut home through the graveyard at midnight.

Disruption of functioning – anxiety and avoidance responses are so extreme that they severely interfere with the ability to conduct everyday working and social functioning. For example, a person with a social phobia will find it very hard to socialise with others, or indeed interact meaningfully with them at work.

Emotional

Persistent, excessive fear – phobias produce high levels of anxiety due to the presence of or anticipation of feared objects and situations.

Fear from exposure to phobic stimulus – phobias produce an immediate fear response, even panic attacks, due to the presentation of the phobic object or situation.

Cognitive

Recognition of exaggerated anxiety – generally phobics (people who suffer from phobias) are consciously aware that the anxiety levels they experience in relation to their feared object or situation are overstated.

Sub-types

Phobias are divisible into:

1 simple phobias
2 social phobias
3 agoraphobia.

Simple phobias (also known as *specific phobias*) occur where sufferers have fears of specific things and environments, like astraphobia, the fear of thunderstorms, and coulrophobia, the fear of clowns. Simple phobias are further divisible into:

- animal phobias – for example, arachnophobia (fear of spiders) and mottephobia (fear of moths)
- injury phobias – for example, haematophobia (fear of blood) and scotomaphobia (fear of blindness)
- situational phobias – for example, aerophobia (fear of flying) and gephydrophobia (fear of bridges)
- natural environment phobias – for example, hydrophobia (fear of water) and nephophobia (fear of clouds).

Social phobias are a commonly experienced type of phobia, and involve being over-anxious in social situations, like having to talk in public. Social phobias involve the perception of being judged and feeling inadequate. Social phobics therefore often find conducting meaningful relationships difficult. Social phobias are further divisible into:

- performance phobias – being anxious about performing in public, like playing at a concert or eating in a restaurant with others
- interaction phobias – being anxious about mixing with others, like going on a date or having an interview
- generalised phobias – being anxious about situations where other people are present, like being in a crowd at a football match.

Agoraphobia, the fear of leaving home or a safe place, is another common type of phobia, and often occurs with panic attacks, where sufferers experience panic first and the anxiety generated makes them feel vulnerable about being in open spaces. Agoraphobia can also be brought on by simple phobias such as a fear of contamination or social embarrassment. The natural avoidance response to make in such situations is to find and stay in a safe place, generally at home.

Animal phobias tend to have the earliest onset, followed by other simple phobias, social phobias and then agoraphobia. Phobias can either be learned from experience or genetically transmitted (see The behavioural approach to explaining and treating phobias, page 163).

Figure 4.5 Coulrophobia is a fear of clowns

ON THE WEB

To watch an informative BBC *Explorations* programme (in five parts) on phobias, including types, explanations and treatments, go to YouTube and search for 'Primal Fears BBC Explorations Storyteller Media'.

YOU ARE THE RESEARCHER

Design a questionnaire that determines whether there's a gender difference in the experience of phobias. Ensure your questions measure the intensity of phobias and what types of phobia people experience. Compile a suitable results table and draw relevant conclusions and a graph from it.

For information on research methods, see Chapter 7.

Depression

'Depression comes in bouts. Like boxing. Dad is in the blue corner.'

Joe Dunthorne (2011)

'There are wounds that never show on the body that are deeper and more hurtful than anything that bleeds.'

Laurel K. Hamilton (2006)

KEY TERMS

Depression – a mood disorder characterised by feelings of despondency and hopelessness

Unipolar depression – a form of depression occurring without mania

Bipolar depression – a form of depression characterised by periods of heightened moods and periods of despondency and hopelessness

Depression is an affective mood disorder involving lengthy disturbance of emotions. About 20 per cent of people will suffer from some form of depression, with women twice as vulnerable as men. Females are especially vulnerable to depression in mid to late adolescence, a time when many experience body dissatisfaction, low self-esteem and resistance to achieving. Depression can occur in cycles, symptoms coming and going over time, with an episode of depression generally lasting between two and six months. There's a high suicide rate among depressives; 10 per cent of severely depressed people commit suicide and 60 per cent of all suicides are related to mood disorders.

Depression can begin any time from adolescence onwards, with average age of onset being in the late twenties, though age of onset has decreased over the past 50 years, as the number of people with the disorder has increased.

At least five symptoms (see later for a full list of symptoms) must be apparent every day for two weeks for depression to be diagnosed by a doctor, with an impairment in general functioning also evident that is not accountable for by other medical conditions or events, for instance mourning a loved one. To be diagnosed with major depression one of the five symptoms must be a constant depressed mood or lessened interest in daily activities. A distinction is made between *major depression* and *dysthymic depression* (chronic depression), the difference being in the duration, type and number of symptoms. Patients meeting the criteria for dysthymic depression have three or more symptoms, instead of the five required for major depression, including depressed mood, but not suicidal thoughts, and show these symptoms for more than two months.

YOU ARE THE RESEARCHER

Design a correlational study to assess the relationship between level of stress and strength of depression. What would be your co-variables? How would you measure level of stress and strength of depression? Compose and justify the use of a suitable directional correlation hypothesis. Identify one confounding variable that could occur in this study.

For information on research methods, see Chapter 7.

Depression is divisible into two main types, **unipolar depression** and **bipolar depression** (also known as manic-depression), but can also be broken down into *endogenous* depression, related to internal biochemical and hormonal factors, and *exogenous* (reactive) depression, related to stressful experiences, though sufferers can have elements of exogenous and endogenous depression combined.

Unipolar depression

Unipolar depression (also known as *major depression*) is a form of depression occurring without mania that differs from bipolar depression by its sufferers only experiencing depression and not the manic episodes sufferers of bipolar depression experience. Up to 25 per cent of women will suffer from unipolar depression and as much as 12 per cent of men, with up to 9 per cent of women and 3 per cent of men suffering from it at any one time. Unipolar depression is characterised by clinical symptoms, usually occurring in cycles. A more severe version is where sufferers also experience delusions; these patients generally experience more social impairment and episodes of depression occur more frequently. Such sufferers don't respond well to antidepressants, but do respond favourably to a combination of antidepressants and antipsychotics.

Symptoms

Behavioural

Loss of energy – depressed people can have reduced amounts of energy, resulting in fatigue, lethargy and high levels of inactivity.

Social impairment – there can be reduced levels of social interaction with friends and relations.

Weight changes – significant decreases or increases in weight are often associated with depression.

Poor personal hygiene – depressed people often have reduced incidence of washing, wearing clean clothes, etc.

Sleep pattern disturbance – depression is often characterised by constant insomnia or oversleeping.

Emotional

Loss of enthusiasm – depression is often characterised by a lessened concern with and/or lack of pleasure in daily activities.

Constant depressed mood – a key characteristic is the ever present and overwhelming feelings of sadness/hopelessness.

Worthlessness – those suffering from depression often have constant feelings of reduced worth and/or inappropriate feelings of guilt.

Cognitive

Delusions – some depressives will experience delusions, generally concerning guilt, punishment, personal inadequacy or disease. Some will also experience hallucinations, which can be auditory, visual, olfactory (smell) or haptic (touch).

Reduced concentration – there can be difficulty in paying/maintaining attention and/or slowed-down thinking and indecisiveness.

Thoughts of death – depressives can have constant thoughts of death and/or suicide.

Poor memory – some depressives will have trouble with retrieval of memories.

Figure 4.6 Bipolar depression involves swinging between bouts of mania and depression

ON THE WEB

An excellent BBC documentary, *The Truth about Depression*, can be seen on YouTube if you search for 'The Truth about Depression BBC Full Documentary 2013'.

KEY TERM

OCD – anxiety disorder characterised by persistent, recurrent, unpleasant thoughts and repetitive, ritualistic behaviours

Bipolar depression

Bipolar depression (also known as *manic depression*), is less common than unipolar depression, with about 2 per cent of people suffering from it, equally divided between the sexes. Bipolar depression usually appears in a person's twenties and before the age of 50. Mixed episodes of mania and depression are more common than mania alone.

The onset of depression has been strongly linked with cognitive factors, though biological and other psychological factors are also known to play a part (see The cognitive explanation of depression, page 172).

Symptoms

In addition to the symptoms of unipolar depression, sufferers of bipolar depression also have alternating manic episodes, characterised by the following symptoms.

Behavioural

High energy levels – the condition is characterised by boundless energy resulting in increased work output, increased social interactions/sexual activity.

Reckless behaviour – the condition is also often characterised by dangerous behaviour and risk-taking.

Talkative – the condition is generally characterised by fast, endless speech without regard for what others are saying.

Emotional

Elevated mood states – constant 'high' moods are common, with intense feelings of euphoria.

Irritability – sufferers are often frustrated and irritable if they don't get their own way immediately.

Lack of guilt – the condition is characterised by social inhibition and a general lack of guilt concerning behaviour.

Cognitive

Delusions – many ideas sufferers get will be delusional and grandiose; they can also believe others are persecuting them.

Irrational thought processes – the condition is often characterised by reckless and irrational thinking and decision-making.

Obsessive–compulsive disorder (OCD)

'I put gloves on before I put gloves on, so I don't get my gloves dirty.'

Jarod Kintz (2007)

OCD is an anxiety disorder where sufferers experience persistent and intrusive thoughts occurring as obsessions, compulsions or a combination of both. Generally speaking, obsessions are things people think about and compulsions are what people do as a result of the obsessions. Obsessions comprise forbidden or inappropriate ideas and visual images that aren't based in reality, such as being convinced that germs lurk everywhere, and which lead to feelings of extreme anxiety, while compulsions comprise intense, uncontrollable urges to repetitively perform tasks and behaviours, like repetitively washing your hands to get rid of germs. The compulsions are an attempt to reduce distress or prevent feared events, even though there's little chance of them doing so. Most sufferers realise their obsessive ideas and compulsions are excessive and inappropriate, but cannot consciously control them, resulting in even higher levels of anxiety. Sufferers can also realise their compulsions are only a temporary solution, but have no other way of coping, so rely on them as a short-term solution. Compulsions can also include avoiding situations that trigger obsessive ideas or images. The symptoms of OCD can overlap with other conditions, such as Tourette's syndrome and autism, which has led some to question whether OCD really exists as a separate disorder.

A sufferer's obsessions and compulsions become very time-consuming, thus interfering with the ability to conduct everyday activities. OCD occurs in about 2 per cent of the population, with no real gender differences in the prevalence of the disorder, though there are gender differences in the types of OCD suffered. Preoccupations with contamination and cleaning are more common in females, while males focus more on religious and sexual obsessions. OCD is more common among male children than females, as males tend to have an earlier, gradual onset with more severe symptoms. Females generally have a later, sudden onset with fewer severe symptoms.

Symptoms: obsessions

Behavioural

Hinder everyday functioning – having obsessive ideas of a forbidden or inappropriate type creates such anxiety that the ability to perform everyday functions is severely hindered – for example, being able to work effectively.

Social impairment – anxiety levels generated are so high as to limit the ability to conduct meaningful interpersonal relationships.

Emotional

Extreme anxiety – persistent inappropriate or forbidden ideas create excessively high levels of anxiety.

Cognitive

Recurrent and persistent thoughts – sufferers experience constantly repeated obsessive thoughts and ideas of an intrusive nature.

Recognised as self-generated – most sufferers understand their obsessional thoughts; impulses and images are self-invented and not inserted externally.

Realisation of inappropriateness – most sufferers understand their obsessive thoughts are inappropriate, but cannot consciously control them.

Attentional bias – perception tends to be focused on anxiety-generating stimuli.

Common obsessions include:

- Contamination, for example by germs
- Fear of losing control, for example through impulses to hurt others
- Perfectionism, for example fear of not being the best
- Religion, for example fear of being immoral.

Symptoms: compulsions

Behavioural

Repetitive – sufferers feel compelled to repeat behaviours as a response to their obsessive thoughts, ideas and images.

Hinder everyday functioning – the performance of repetitive, compulsive behaviours can seriously disrupt the ability to perform everyday functions.

Social impairment – the performance of repetitive, compulsive behaviours can seriously affect the ability to conduct meaningful interpersonal relationships.

Emotional

Distress – the recognition that compulsive behaviours cannot be consciously controlled can lead to strong feelings of distress.

Cognitive

Uncontrollable urges – sufferers experience uncontrollable urges to perform acts they feel will reduce the anxiety caused by obsessive thoughts, such as cleaning door handles to remove the threat of contamination.

Realisation of inappropriateness – sufferers understand their compulsions are inappropriate, but cannot consciously control them.

Common compulsions include:

- Excessive washing and cleaning, for example hair-brushing
- Excessive checking, for example that doors are locked
- Repetition, for example of bodily movements
- Mental compulsions, for example praying in order to prevent harm
- Hoarding, for example of magazines.

Research has suggested a genetic component to the cause of OCD, though other psychological factors are also seen as making a contribution (see The biological approach to explaining and treating OCD, page 184).

Figure 4.7 OCD involves repetitive behaviour to reduce the anxiety caused by obsessive thoughts

STRENGTHEN YOUR LEARNING

1 Describe the behavioural, emotional and cognitive characteristics of phobias, depression and OCD.
2 Explain what is meant by:
   a) simple phobias
   b) social phobias
   c) agoraphobia.
3 Explain how unipolar depression differs from bipolar depression.
4 Describe common obsessions and compulsions associated with OCD.

ON THE WEB

A two-part BBC documentary about OCD, *Extreme OCD Camp*, where sufferers confront their disorder, can be found on YouTube if you search for 'Extreme OCD Camp 2013 BBC Three documentary'.

ASSESSMENT CHECK

1 Ever since her house was flooded a few years ago Betty has developed a fear of running water. She always tries to make sure she doesn't go near any rivers or other sources of running water and her phobia causes problems at work and home as she is unable to use the taps to wash or clean her teeth. Betty gets very fearful if she feels there's a risk of being placed in a situation where there will be running water. Betty knows her fear is unreal, but it will not go away.

   Making reference to the situation above, identify behavioural, emotional and cognitive characteristics of phobias. **[4 marks]**

2 Describe one behavioural and one cognitive characteristic of OCD. **[2 marks]**

3 Use the numbers next to the following list of characteristics to complete the table below concerning characteristics of phobias and unipolar depression. One characteristic will be left over. **[4 marks]**

   1 Loss of energy

   2 Compulsions

   3 Delusions

   4 Avoidant response

   5 Recognition of exaggerated anxiety

Type of characteristic	Phobias	Unipolar depression
Behavioural		
Cognitive		

4 Describe the behavioural, cognitive and emotional characteristics of depression and OCD. **[6 marks]**

5 A team of researchers wishes to conduct an observational study to examine the behavioural characteristics of people with OCD. Explain the following. **[2 + 2 marks]**

   (i) Why it would be necessary to establish inter-observer reliability in the study

   (ii) How inter-observer reliability could be established

The explanation and treatment of mental disorders

KEY TERMS

Behavioural approach – the perception of phobias as occurring through learning processes with treatments based upon modifying maladaptive behaviour through substitution of new responses

Cognitive approach – the perception of depression as determined through maladaptive thought processes with treatments based upon modifying thought patterns to alter behavioural and emotional states

Biological approach – the perception of OCD as determined by physiological means with treatments based upon chemical means

In the following sections we shall consider how various psychological approaches can be used to explain and treat different mental disorders. Those especially focused on will be:

- the **behavioural approach** to phobias
- the **cognitive approach** to depression
- the **biological approach** to OCD.

For each disorder, alternative explanations and treatments will be offered, as these can be a useful source of evaluation. However, care should be taken to use these only to highlight the comparative strengths and weaknesses of the approach under scrutiny. Avoid merely describing an alternative explanation and then evaluating it in terms of research support, practical applications, etc.

IN THE NEWS

Ψ The Psychological Enquirer

Using technology to overcome a fear of spiders

Figure 4.8 The first stage 'cute' spider

Psychiatrist Dr Russell Green is terrified of spiders. A colleague once brought a tarantula's skin into work and he fled the hospital hardly able to breathe. Dr Green's arachnophobia, an exaggerated fear of spiders, is so bad even pictures of spiders scare him. But now Dr Green, along with Dr Fonseca, has created a company called Virtually Free and invented a smartphone app, 'Phobia Free', to help others with a similar phobia. Users first play a series

of games with cartoon spiders; initial ones are cute and harmless looking, but gradually become more realistic. In the second stage a 'low-fear' spider appears with scary features removed, before the third stage presentation of a 'low-fear' spider in a real outdoor environment. The fourth stage progresses onto a 'medium-fear' spider (with some scary features) in a real home-setting, before the fifth stage presentation of a 'high-fear' spider (with all its scary features). The last two stages involve an image of a tarantula and then presentation of a spider using augmented reality via the phone's camera. Dr Green believes it would be possible to cure arachnophobia in as little as four hours, but most sufferers would take about two weeks. Different forms of the app could be developed for different phobias; a version that reduces agoraphobia (fear of open spaces) is currently being developed.

The arachnophobia app is based on a behavioural treatment called systematic desensitisation, where phobias are gradually reduced by introducing a sufferer in stages of rising intensity to their phobic object or situation. Sufferers work through a hierarchy of anxiety-producing stimuli, with the central idea being that fear and relaxation can't co-exist, so relaxation strategies are used to remove the fears any stage causes, before moving on to the next stage. Psychologist Elizabeth Gray warns that the app isn't a replacement for real therapy, as part of that process is treatment by a real therapist. For some patients this is the case but others admit having overcome the phobia with the app and on their own.

4.3 The behavioural approach to explaining and treating phobias

Explaining phobias

A wide range of both biological and psychological explanations have been offered as the cause of phobias. Several of these are probably valid, but the focus here will be on behavioural (or behaviourist) explanations though other explanations will also be featured as a means of evaluation.

Behaviourist explanations see phobias as being learned through experience via the process of association. In **classical conditioning (CC)** a stimulus becomes associated with a response, while **operant conditioning (OC)** involves learning behaviour due to the consequences of that behaviour (see Chapter 3, page 115). There is also social learning theory (SLT), where learning occurs vicariously by observation and imitation of another. CC is associated with behaviour not under conscious control, while OC and SLT are associated with voluntary behaviour.

Via the **two-process model**, CC and SLT are used to explain the acquisition (onset) of phobias and OC is used to explain how phobias are maintained.

The two-process model

1 *The acquisition (onset) of phobias* is seen as occurring directly through classical conditioning, for example by the experience of a traumatic event, like being bitten by a dog, or indirectly through social learning, for example through observing or hearing about a fearful event happening to another, like seeing someone else bitten by a dog

2 *The maintenance of phobias* is seen as occurring through operant conditioning, where avoiding or escaping from a feared object/situation acts a negative reinforcer (the reward being the reduction of anxiety). This reinforces the avoidance response (makes it more likely to occur again).

Classical conditioning

CC is based upon the work of Ivan Pavlov (1903), who explained how dogs learned to salivate in anticipation of being fed rather than when actually being fed (see Chapter 5, page 207). The process by which Pavlov explained this as occurring can be also used to explain the acquisition of phobias, where a natural response that causes fear becomes associated with a neutral stimulus, so that the neutral stimulus by itself causes a fear response. For example, a single pairing of the neutral stimulus of night-time with a frightening experience that produces a natural fear response, such as being mugged, leads to a phobia of the dark.

Operant conditioning

OC involves learning through the consequences (outcomes) of behaviour. A behaviour that is rewarding *reinforces* the chances of the behaviour being repeated in future similar circumstances. An outcome of a behaviour that is pleasant is known as a *positive reinforcement,* while an outcome of a behaviour that results in escaping something unpleasant

Figure 4.9 Being bitten by a dog can lead to a phobia of dogs through classical conditioning

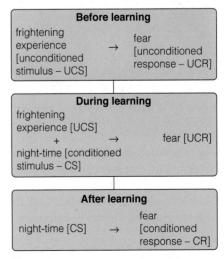

Figure 4.10 The process of acquiring a phobia of the night-time via classical conditioning

163

is known as a *negative reinforcement.* As detailed by the two-process model, OC explains how phobias are maintained, as when avoidance responses (behaviours that lessen the chances of contact with the feared object or situation) are made the fear response is reduced, reinforcing the avoidance responses, making them more likely to occur again. If a person has a phobia of the dark, because they had a traumatic experience, like being mugged at night-time, then the person might sleep with the lights on, which is *negatively reinforcing,* as it reduces the fear response associated with being in the dark. This reinforces the behaviour, in other words it increases the chances of the person sleeping with the lights on again because anxiety is not experienced. Phobias therefore become very resistant to extinction (dying out), because of the sufferer constantly making reinforcing avoidance responses.

INCREASE YOUR KNOWLEDGE

Along with CC, SLT can also explain the acquisition of phobias. SLT sees behaviour as learned by *modelling* through observation and imitation. Watching someone else experience a traumatic event can cause the observer to subsequently experience the fear response in the presence of the same stimulus. For example, seeing someone else being bitten by a dog could cause the observer to develop a phobia of dogs.

Ost & Hugdahl (1981) reported the case of a boy who witnessed his grandfather vomit while dying and subsequently developed a persistent vomiting phobia, and even contemplated suicide when feeling nauseous, supporting the idea that phobias can be acquired vicariously through social learning.

ON THE WEB

A good site for information on phobias, including a vast list of different types, explanations, treatments, etc., can be found at:

http://phobialist.com/

CLASSIC RESEARCH

The case of 'Little Albert' – John Watson & Rosalie Rayner (1920)

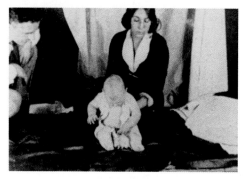

Figure 4.11a A rare photograph of John Watson and Rosalie Raynor during the conditioning of Little Albert

The researchers developed the idea, from real-world observations, that fear could be conditioned into children through the use of loud noises. Their participant was an 11-month-old boy, 'Little Albert', and the study took place at Johns Hopkins University, Baltimore, USA.

Aim

To provide empirical evidence that human emotional responses could be learned through classical conditioning.

Procedure

1 A laboratory experiment was conducted with one participant, an 11-month-old boy who lived in the hospital where his mother was a nurse. Albert was presented with various stimuli, including a white rat, a rabbit and some cotton wool, and his responses were filmed. He showed no fear reaction to any stimuli.

2 A fear reaction was then induced into Albert by striking a steel bar with a hammer behind his head. This startled Albert, making him cry. He was then given a white rat to play with, of which he was not scared. As he reached to touch the rat, the bar and hammer were struck to frighten him. This procedure was repeated three times. Variations of these conditioning techniques continued for 3 months.

3 It was intended that Albert's fear reactions would be 'de-conditioned', but he was removed from the hospital by his mother before this could occur.

Findings

Subsequently, when shown the rat, Albert would cry, roll over and crawl away. He had developed a fear towards the white rat, which he also displayed to similar animals with less intensity and to other white furry objects, like a white fur coat and Santa Claus beard.

Before learning
hammer and bar [UCS] → fear [UCR]

During learning
hammer and bar [UCS] + rat [conditioned stimulus – CS] → fear [UCR]

After learning
rat [CS] → fear [CR]

Figure 4.11b Learning a phobia of rats

Conclusions

Conditioned emotional responses, including love, fear and phobias, are acquired as a direct result of environmental experiences, which can transfer and persist, possibly indefinitely, unless removed by counter-conditioning.

Evaluation

The extent of Albert's fear response is disputed. There are mentions in the original paper that Albert's fear reactions were only 'slight'. By today's standards the study was unethical: it was performed without his mother's knowledge or consent and the participant was subjected to unnecessary distress. It would not, therefore, be possible to replicate the study to verify the findings.

(Footnote: It is believed that the real 'Little Albert' died of illness at only 6 years old.)

RESEARCH IN FOCUS

Identify the following in the Watson & Rayner study:
 (i) the unconditioned stimulus
 (ii) the conditioned stimulus
 (iii) the unconditioned response
 (iv) the conditioned response.

For information on research methods, see Chapter 7.

Research

Bagby (1922) reported on a case study of a woman who had a phobia of running water that originated from her feet getting stuck in some rocks near a waterfall. As time went by she became increasingly panic-stricken. Although she was eventually de-conditioned, the neutral stimulus of the sound of the running water became associated with the fear she had felt and thus her phobia of running water was acquired.

King *et al.* (1998) reported that case studies showed that children tended to acquire strong phobias through a traumatic experience, which further supports the idea of phobias being acquired through CC.

Di Gallo (1996) reported that around 20 per cent of people experiencing traumatic car accidents developed a phobia of travelling in cars, especially of travelling at speed, which can be explained by CC, whereby the neutral stimulus of a car became associated with the naturally occurring fear response to the crash. They then tended to make avoidance responses involving staying at home rather than making car journeys to see friends, which can be explained by OC, whereby the avoidance response of staying at home was negatively reinforcing and was thus repeated, making the phobia resistant to extinction.

Mowrer (1960) found that by making a few presentations of an electric shock to rats immediately following the sound of a buzzer, he could produce a fear response just by sounding the buzzer. The rats had acquired a phobia of the buzzer through CC. Then through OC he trained the rats to escape the electric shocks by making the avoidance response of jumping over a barrier when the buzzer sounded. As this was negatively reinforcing, the rats repeated the behaviour every time the buzzer sounded, maintaining their fear of the sound of the buzzer.

Figure 4.12 Twenty per cent of people involved in serious traffic accidents will develop a phobia of travelling in cars

- Rachman (1984) put forward the *safety signals hypothesis* to explain that avoidance responses made to reduce the chances of exposure to phobic objects/situations are not motivated by a reduction in anxiety as stated by the two-process model, but by positive feelings associated with safe places. He used the example of agoraphobics who will leave their home in the presence of certain people, or travel to work using particular roads, because these people and roads are ones that are trusted and thus represent *safety signals*.

- Bounton (2007) argues that the two-process model neglects the influence of *evolution history*, whereby avoidance responses are learned more rapidly if the required response resembles an animal's natural defensive behaviour.

- The effectiveness of behaviourist treatments, like systematic desensitisation, in addressing phobic symptoms, lends support to behaviourist explanations of phobias.

- The behaviourist viewpoint is weakened by the fact that not everyone experiencing traumatic events, like car accidents, goes on to develop a phobia.

- A strength of behaviourist explanations is that they can be combined with biological ones to give a better understanding of phobias. For instance, the idea of *genetic vulnerability* shows how some individuals are more susceptible to developing phobias through environmental experiences.

INCREASE YOUR KNOWLEDGE

Alternative explanations of phobias

Cognitive explanations

Behaviourist explanations focus on maladaptive (faulty) behaviours, but neglect the cognitive processes that occur between a stimulus and a response. Thus cognitive explanations focus on the idea that phobics have an *attentional bias* to focus more upon anxiety generating stimuli, for example the teeth of a dog rather than its other features. Phobics are also seen as having maladaptive thoughts and beliefs about stimuli, like believing open taps will lead to flooding, which generalises to a phobia of flowing water.

Figure 4.13 The cognitive explanation sees phobics as having an attentional bias to focus upon anxiety generating stimuli, like the teeth of a dog rather than its other features

Thorpe & Salkovskis (2000) assessed conscious beliefs related to exposure to phobic stimuli, finding a major role in specific phobics for cognitions (thinking) related to harm, suggesting the nature of specific phobias to be cognitive rather than behavioural in origin.

Tomarken *et al.* (1989) showed people with snake phobias slides of snakes and neutral objects and asked how many snakes, trees, etc. there had been. Snake phobics over-estimated the number of snakes compared to a control group, which shows the role distorted thinking plays, an element the behaviourist explanation neglects.

Evaluation of the cognitive explanation

Cognitive explanations may be superior to behaviourist ones as they detail the thought processes underpinning phobias. However, phobias are still dependent in many instances on the role of direct conditioning experiences.

The cognitive viewpoint can explain how a phobia is maintained, but not why it originated in the first place. For example, a phobia could be caused by conditioning (or genetics) and then is perpetuated by faulty thinking.

Evolutionary explanation

The evolutionary explanation sees phobias as having an adaptive (survival) value and so they have become commonplace in the population through the process of natural selection.

Garcia & Koelling (1966) found that rats quickly learned not to drink a sweet tasting liquid paired with an injection that made them sick, as it's a natural adaptive response. They did not develop such a taste aversion as quickly when the sweet tasting liquid was paired with an electric shock, as it's not an adaptive response, electric shocks not being apparent in the environment of evolutionary adaptiveness (EEA). This supports the idea that some phobias are more evolutionary in nature and others more behaviourist.

Cook & Mineka (1989) provided additional support for this idea by demonstrating to laboratory-raised monkeys a wild monkey's fear response to a snake and a rabbit. Subsequently the laboratory-raised monkeys showed a similar fear response to a toy snake, but not a toy rabbit, suggesting an evolutionary readiness to fear snakes, but not rabbits.

Evaluation of the evolutionary explanation
Phobias explain adaptive functions that behaviourist explanations can't, for instance the fear element of phobias can immobilise individuals, aiding concealment from predators, as would a flight response help individuals to outrun predators. Fear responses even cause the release of hormones aiding the clotting of blood, helping heal wounds, as well as stimulating the liver to release glucose to provide energy, important in facilitating flight or fight.

Biological preparedness sees animals having an inherited ability to display certain fears, because they have an adaptive value. Therefore animals develop some conditioned fears more easily, for instance a fear of snakes, as they would have posed a serious threat in the Pleistocene era when most evolution occurred. This shows how the evolutionary and behaviourist explanations can be combined, as phobias have to be learned from environmental experience, with the predisposition to learn the fear being the inherited component.

PSYCHOLOGY IN THE REAL WORLD

Gustafson *et al.* (1976) demonstrated how learning phobias through classical conditioning could be used as a humane method of stopping wolves and coyotes attacking sheep.

Wild wolves and coyotes were fed mutton wrapped in sheepskins dosed with lithium chloride. This made them vomit and the predators quickly learned to associate sheep with the nauseous chemical; instead of attacking sheep, they began to show submissive behaviour towards them.

Figure 4.14 Wolves can be taught using classical conditioning to fear sheep

---

Treating phobias

If phobias are maladaptive behaviours acquired by learning, it should be possible to replace them with adaptive behaviours acquired through treatments using conditioning techniques based on behaviourist principles.

Systematic desensitisation

Systematic desensitisation (SD) is the main behaviourist treatment for phobias. Developed by Wolpe (1958), SD is based on classical conditioning, with patients learning in stages to replace fear responses with feelings of calm, rather than previous associations between phobic objects/situations and fear. The two opposing emotions of anxiety and relaxation are perceived as incapable of co-existing simultaneously (*reciprocal inhibition*). SD uses a progressive, step-by-step approach to feared objects or situations and takes about a month to advance through the entire desensitisation hierarchy.

The hierarchy is constructed before treatment commences, going from least to most feared types of contact with phobic objects/situations, and patients are taught relaxation strategies for each stage of contact. Contact is normally achieved by imagining scenarios (*covert desensitisation*), but sometimes involves actual contact (*in vivo desensitisation*). Snake phobics may begin SD treatment by looking at a picture of snakes in a sealed tank and progressively work through to actually holding one.

KEY TERM

Systematic desensitisation – a behavioural therapy for treating anxiety disorders in which the sufferer learns relaxation techniques and then faces a progressive hierarchy of exposure to the objects and situations that cause anxiety

Figure 4.15 Systematic desensitisation involves a step-by-step approach to a feared object or situation

Flooding

KEY TERM

Flooding – a behavioural therapy used to remove phobias through direct confrontation of a feared object or situation

Another behaviourist therapy is **flooding** (also known as implosion), where instead of a step-by-step approach patients go straight to the top of the hierarchy and imagine, or have direct contact with, their most feared scenarios. The idea is that patients cannot make their usual avoidance responses and anxiety peaks at such high levels it cannot be maintained and eventually subsides.

CONTEMPORARY RESEARCH

The treatment of technophobia by systematic desensitisation – Mark Brosnan & Sue Thorpe (2006)

Technology pervades our occupational, educational and leisure lives and so technophobia, a fear of interacting with technology like computers, has a major negative impact on the life of sufferers. Indeed, technophobia is comparable in severity to more traditional phobias. The researchers investigated whether technophobia is treatable by psychological means.

Figure 4.16 Technophobia is a fear of interacting with modern technology

Aim

To see whether a fear of computers could be successfully treated by systematic desensitisation.

Procedure

In the first study, a sample of 16 participants was used: 8 computer-anxious participants and a control group of 8 non-anxious participants. A 10-week systematic desensitisation programme was delivered to the computer-anxious participants.

In the second study, 30 computer-anxious participants were assigned to a treatment group or a non-treatment group. There was also a non-anxious control group of 59 participants.

Findings

In the first study, computer anxiety and coping strategies were significantly improved in the computer-anxious group, becoming comparable to the non-anxious controls.

In the second study, testing established over the period of an academic year that the reduction in anxiety was three times greater in the treated group than the non-treated group. By the end of the year the treated group no longer differed from the control group, while the non-treated group remained significantly more anxious.

Conclusions

The behavioural therapy of systematic desensitisation is effective in reducing technophobia.

Evaluation

It is not known whether the therapy had a long-term benefit in reducing technophobia of computers, nor whether it is effective against other forms of technophobia. The success of the therapy suggests a major benefit in allowing technophobes to participate in an increasingly technologically-orientated world.

RESEARCH IN FOCUS

Previous research suggests SD is effective in treating phobias. Compose a suitable one-tailed (directional) hypothesis for Brosnan & Thorpe's study into the treatment of technophobia. What would the null hypothesis be?

For information on research methods, see Chapter 7.

Research

Jones (1924) used SD to eradicate 'Little Peter's' phobia of white fluffy animals and objects, for example rabbits and cotton wool. The rabbit was presented to the patient at closer distances each time his anxiety levels subsided to permit movement onto the next stage and Peter was rewarded with food to develop a positive association towards the rabbit. Eventually he developed affection for the rabbit, which generalised onto similar animals and objects.

Rothbaum *et al.* (1998) reported on virtual reality exposure therapy where patients are active participants within a computer generated three-dimensional world that changes naturally with head movements. The advantage of this over normal SD and implosion is that treatment occurs without ever leaving the therapist's office, more control is gained over phobic stimuli and there's less exposure of patients to harm and embarrassment.

Wolpe (1960) used flooding to remove a girl's phobia of being in cars. The girl was forced into a car and driven around for four hours until her hysteria was eradicated, demonstrating the effectiveness of the treatment.

Ost (1997) found that flooding is a rapid treatment that often delivers rapid, immediate improvements, especially when a patient is encouraged to continue self-directed exposure to feared objects and situations outside of therapy sessions.

Barlow (2002) reports that flooding has been shown to be equally as effective in treating phobias as SD, but SD is preferred, as it is better tolerated by most patients.

Solter (2007) reported on the case study of a 5-month old baby who showed signs of traumatic stress after a three-day hospital stay for surgery to correct the shape of his head. Flooding was used, whereby the child was allowed to have a full-blown emotional response during several treatment sessions. The outcome was positive, with the disappearance of some symptoms of traumatic stress disorder after the first week, and no remaining symptoms after two months. Follow-up evaluations for one year revealed normal development with no return of symptoms. This suggests flooding is an effective therapy and can be used with very young children.

Figure 4.17 Wolpe removed a girl's fear of cars by flooding – direct confrontation with the feared object

Evaluation

- SD is mainly suitable for patients who are able to learn and use relaxation strategies and who have imaginations vivid enough to conjure up images of feared objects/situations.
- Although patients can gradually confront phobias in an imaginary sense, there's no guarantee this will work with actual objects/situations, suggesting in vivo treatment to be superior to covert desensitisation.
- Behaviourist treatments work best in treating simple phobias, but are less effective with agoraphobia and social phobias, which suggests these types of phobias may not be best explained through behaviourist means.
- There are ethical considerations with both SD and flooding, as they can both be psychologically harmful, though cost–benefit analyses may regard long-term benefits of eradicating the phobia as outweighing the short-term costs of distress.
- Flooding is not suitable for patients who are not in good physical health, as the extreme anxiety levels caused by confrontation with feared objects/situations, although short-lived, can be very stressful on the body, incurring risks of heart attacks, etc.

INCREASE YOUR KNOWLEDGE

Other treatments

Drug treatments

Although phobias tend to be treated mainly by psychological means, drug treatments that reduce symptoms of anxiety have proven useful. Anxiolytic drugs, such as the Benzodiazepines (BZs) like Valium and Librium, work by increasing the effect of the neurotransmitter GABA. Phobias are also treated with anti-depressants: selective serotonin re-uptake indicators (SSRIs) elevate serotonin levels, while monoamine oxidase inhibitors (MAIOs) increase serotonin and noradrenaline levels.

Slaap *et al.* (1996) treated 30 social phobics with the anti-depressant SSRIs, finding 72 per cent of patients had reduced heart rate and blood pressure, suggesting drug treatments are effective in lowering the physical symptoms of the disorder in the short term.

Den Boer *et al.* (1994) reported considerable evidence indicating MAOI inhibitors, like moclobemide, to be effective in reducing social anxiety and social avoidance phobias.

Evaluation of drug treatments

A disadvantage of drugs compared to behaviourist treatments is their potential side-effects; BZs can cause drowsiness and addiction, MAOI inhibitors have an increased risk of hypertension with their usage, while SSRIs can lead to stomach and sleep pattern disturbance and loss of sexual ability.

Drug therapies are more cost-effective than behaviourist therapies and don't require the presence of a therapist, but as well as the risk of side-effects, they do not address the cause of anxiety – once the drugs are withdrawn anxiety levels will increase again.

Cognitive behavioural therapy (CBT)

The aim of CBT is to help patients identify irrational and maladaptive thinking patterns and change them to rational, adaptive ones. Thinking is seen as underpinning feelings and behaviour, so by modifying modes of thought, feelings and behaviour should also change for the better.

Spence *et al.* (2000) assessed the value of CBT in treating 50 children with social phobias aged between 7 and 14 years. Child-focused CBT and CBT plus parental involvement were found to be effective in reducing social and general anxiety levels and these improvements were retained at a one-year follow-up, suggesting CBT has a long-term effectiveness with phobic children, and illustrating its effectiveness in comparison to behaviourist therapies.

Kvale *et al.* (2004) conducted a meta-analysis of 38 treatment studies for people with dental phobias, finding CBT resulted in 77 per cent of patients regularly visiting a dentist four years after treatment, again showing the treatment's long-term effectiveness in comparison to behavioural therapies.

Evaluation of CBT

CBT is the most frequently used treatment for phobias, testament to its effectiveness in comparison to behaviourist and other therapies.

Behaviourist therapies merely address the observable symptoms of phobias, while CBT targets the maladaptive thinking that underpins phobias, making them a more effective treatment than behaviourist ones, though both treatments have the advantage of not incurring side-effects, like drug therapy does.

One specific form of CBT used with phobics is cognitive-behavioural group therapy (CBGT), where other group members offer support as a hierarchy of fears is worked through, using relaxation strategies at each step. This of course has similarities with the behavioural therapy of SD, but with the additional cognitive element of replacing irrational beliefs that generate anxiety, with rational ones.

STRENGTHEN YOUR LEARNING

1 How can classical and operant conditioning be combined to explain the acquisition and maintenance of phobias?

2 Outline the procedure and findings of Watson & Rayner's study of 'Little Albert'.

3 How do alternative explanations account for phobias?

4 Explain the difference between SD and flooding in treating phobias.

5 Explain how Bosnan & Thorpe used SD to treat technophobia. To what extent were they successful?

6 Outline other treatments for phobias. How successful are they compared to behavioural treatments?

ASSESSMENT CHECK

1 Seumas was walking home after a night out in town when a man suddenly grabbed him and swung a punch at him. Ever since then Seumas has been scared of the dark and cannot get to sleep unless the light is on. He now refuses to go out at night-time and prefers to stay at home. Use classical conditioning to explain how Seumas has developed a phobia of the dark. **[3 marks]**

2 Explain how relaxation and the hierarchy components of systematic desensitisation are used to treat phobias. **[4 marks]**

3 Place a 'C' next to the two descriptions below that relate to classical conditioning and an 'O' next to the two descriptions that relate to operant conditioning. One descriptions will be left over. **[4 marks]**

Description	Type of conditioning
Involves observation and imitation	
Involves a stimulus becoming associated with a response	
Involves learning through the consequences of a behaviour	
Involves the use of reinforcements	
Explains the acquisition of phobias	

4 Outline and evaluate systematic desensitisation as a treatment for phobias. **[16 marks]**

5 Outline and evaluate the behavioural approach to explaining phobias. **[12 marks]**

6 The table below shows degree of anxiety scores for snake phobics when confronted by a snake. From the data shown calculate the following: **[3 marks]**

(i) the mean

(ii) the median

(iii) the mode.

Participant	Degree of anxiety score
1.	9
2.	7
3.	6
4.	7
5.	4
6.	7
7.	6
8.	5
9.	8
10.	3
11.	4

Table showing degree of anxiety score (out of 10) for snake phobics when confronted by a snake

4.4 The cognitive approach to explaining and treating depression

Explaining depression

A wide range of both biological and psychological explanations have been offered as the cause of depression, with each having a degree of evidence to support it, but the focus here will be on the cognitive approach, though other explanations will also be featured as a means of evaluation.

The **cognitive approach** generally explains depression in terms of faulty and irrational thought processes and perceptions. Where behaviourist explanations would focus on maladaptive (faulty) behaviours, the cognitive approach focuses on the maladaptive cognitions that underpin such maladaptive behaviours.

Beck's negative triad

Beck (1987) believes people become depressed because the world is seen negatively through *negative schemas* (see below), which dominate thinking and are triggered whenever individuals are in situations that are similar to those in which negative schemas were learned. Beck perceived negative schemas as developing in childhood and adolescence, when authority figures, such as parents, place unreal demands on individuals and are highly critical of them. These negative schemas then continue into adulthood, providing a negative framework to view life in a pessimistic fashion.

These negative schemas fuel and are fuelled by cognitive biases, causing individuals to misperceive reality.

Negative schemas

- **Ineptness schemas** – make depressives expect to fail
- **Self-blame schemas** – makes depressives feel responsible for all misfortunes
- **Negative self-evaluation schemas** – constantly remind depressives of their worthlessness.

Cognitive biases

- **Arbitrary inference** – conclusions drawn in the absence of sufficient evidence. For example, a man concluding he's worthless because it's raining the day he hosts an outdoor party
- **Selective abstraction** – conclusions drawn from just one part of a situation. For example, a worker feeling worthless when a product doesn't work, even though several people made it
- **Overgeneralisation** – sweeping conclusions drawn on the basis of a single event. For example, a student regarding poor performance on one test as proof of his worthlessness
- **Magnification and minimisation** – exaggerations in evaluation of performance. For example, a man believing he's ruined his car due to a small scratch (maximisation) or a woman believing herself worthless despite many praises (minimisation)

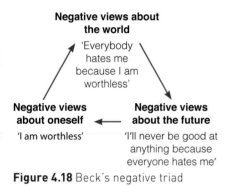

Figure 4.18 Beck's negative triad

Negative schemas, together with cognitive biases/distortions, maintain the *negative triad*, which sees negative thoughts as being about:

1 **The self** – where individuals see themselves as being helpless, worthless, and inadequate, i.e. 'nobody loves me'

2 **The world** – where obstacles are perceived within one's environment that cannot be dealt with, i.e. 'everything is beyond my control'

3 **The future** – where personal worthlessness is seen as blocking any improvements, i.e. 'I will always be useless'.

Ellis' ABC model

Ellis believed that depressives mistakenly blame external events for their unhappiness. He thought, however, that it is their interpretation of these events that is to blame for their distress. To explain this process, Ellis developed what he referred to as the **ABC model**:

A – Activating event: Something happens in the environment around you, for example your teacher tells you that she's unhappy with your work.

B – Beliefs: You hold a belief about the event or situation, for example you see yourself as a failure.

C – Consequence: You have an emotional response to your belief, for example a feeling of worthlessness.

The activating event triggers an emotion that is seen as true and the consequence is that the individual becomes depressed because they have a negative view about themself and no confidence in their ability.

Other people who do not tend towards depression may react completely differently. For instance, when being told the boss is unhappy with their work, the belief may be that they did their best with the consequent emotion of being motivated to do better. The difference between depressed and non-depressed people, therefore, is how they perceive themselves.

Rational emotive behaviour therapy (REBT) (see page 177) was formed from Ellis' ABC model.

(see page 177)

KEY TERM

Ellis' ABC model – an explanation that sees depression occurring through an *activating agent*, a *belief* and a *consequence*

INCREASE YOUR KNOWLEDGE

Abramson *et al.* (1978) proposed another cognitive explanation by revising learned helplessness in terms of *depressed attributional style*, based on three dimensions:

- **internal/external locus** – whether cause of an event concerns the individual or not
- **stable/unstable** – whether the cause is a permanent feature or temporary
- **global/specific** – whether the cause relates to the whole person or just one feature.

This explanation is based on the way individuals *attribute* reasons to events that occur in their lives. Those who see themselves as having little control over their lives tend to attribute reasons as due to negative occurrences and perceive such failures as due to an internal locus of control ('It's my fault and I'm responsible'), global features of their personality ('that's how I am with everything in my life') and stable features ('that's how I will always be'). Such individuals have low self-esteem and lack motivation and so are vulnerable to developing depression.

Seligman (1979) created the *attributional style questionnaire (ASQ)* comprising a series of hypothetical situations for which individuals identify the cause. Depressives tend to demonstrate an attributional style whereby positive events are perceived as caused by other people and negative events by themselves.

- Seligman (1979) reported that students making global, stable attributions remained depressed for longer after examinations, supporting the cognitive explanation of attributional style.
- Peterson & Seligman (1984) found that people identified by the *attributional style questionnaire* as being vulnerable to depression explained negative life events as being due to internal, global, stable factors and were more likely to develop depression when experiencing stressors, demonstrating support for the concept of depressed attributional style.

CONTEMPORARY RESEARCH

Depression symptoms and cognitive control of emotion cues: A functional magnetic resonance imaging study – Beevers, Clasen, Stice & Schnyer (2010)

Previous research has indicated, in line with Beck's negative triad, that patients with depression tend to respond more to negative stimuli than to neutral or positive ones. However, in this novel study the researchers used fMRI scanning to assess possible links between depressive symptoms and alterations in brain areas associated with cognitive control, with a view to seeing if this could be used as a means to predict those at risk of developing more severe forms of depression.

Aims

- To assess whether brain areas associated with cognitive control are affected by emotional stimuli in individuals with mild depressive symptoms.
- To assess whether ventral lateral pre-frontal cortex function is altered in individuals with mild to moderate depressive symptoms during cognitive control of stimuli.
- To see whether neural mechanisms can show the degree of vulnerability to developing severer forms of depression.

Procedure

Figure 4.19 Happy and sad facial types used in the study

1 27 females aged 18–27 years responded to advertisements to form a self-selected sample.
2 Depression in all participants was measured with the well-established Centre for Epidemiologic Studies Depression scale (CESD) with 13 participants being placed in a low depression symptoms group (LDG) and 14 in a high depression symptoms group (HDG).
3 The mean CESD score for the HDG group was indicative of mild to moderate symptoms of depression.
4 Cue stimuli consisted of three facial types, happy, sad and neutral, along with a control condition of geometric shape cues.
5 432 trials were conducted where a single facial or geometric shape cue was presented on a screen along with one of two target stimuli (either * or ** on the screen in the same location as the shape cue). Participants pressed a button to indicate which target stimuli was presented and the time measured to do this was recorded.
6 Participants simultaneously had their brains scanned with an fRMI scanner.

Findings

Different brain activation was recorded between the LDG and the HDG during presentation of happy or sad faces, in brain areas requiring cognitive control over emotional stimuli (ventral lateral pre-frontal cortex function). There was no difference in brain activation with neutral facial and geometric shape cues.

Conclusions

Individuals with mild to moderate levels of depression have difficulty in activating brain areas associated with cognitive control of emotional information.

Depressive symptoms are associated with impaired engagement of lateral pre-frontal cortex (PFC) and parietal brain regions during cognitive control of emotional information.

Poor cognitive control of emotional information may indicate levels of vulnerability to more severe forms of depression.

Evaluation

The findings do not generalise to males, as only females were tested. The age range of participants was also relatively narrow and so results do not generalise to children or older adults.

Participants' menstrual cycles were not assessed and so it is not known if hormonal fluctuations associated with menstrual cycle activity may have affected the findings.

The CESD scale for measuring depression is regarded as highly reliable and valid, giving added support to the findings.

Longitudinal research would be needed to assess if deficits in cognitive control of emotional information are a cause or consequence of mild to moderate depressive symptoms and whether such symptoms do predict the onset of severer forms of depression.

If the findings are true, then improving cognitive control may help prevent the onset of more severe forms of depression.

Research

McIntosh & Fischer (2000) tested the negative cognitive triad to see if it contains the three proposed distinct types of negative thought. They found no clear separation of negative thoughts, but instead a single, one-dimensional negative perception of the self, suggesting retention of all three areas of the triad as separate dimensions is unnecessary for representing the structure of depressive cognition.

Boury et al. (2001) monitored students' negative thoughts with the Beck depression inventory (BDI), finding that depressives misinterpret facts and experiences in a negative fashion and feel hopeless about the future, giving support to Beck's cognitive explanation.

Saisto et al. (2001) studied expectant mothers, finding that those who didn't adjust personal goals to match specific demands of the transition to motherhood, but indulged instead in negative thinking patterns, had increased depressive symptoms, supporting Beck's cognitive theory.

Koster et al. (2005) presented participants with either a positive, negative or neutral word on a screen, after which a square appeared and participants pressed a button to say which area of the screen the square appeared in. Depressed participants took longer to disengage from the negative words than non-depressed participants, which suggests the depressives were focusing more on the negative words in line with Beck's theory.

Evaluation

- There is lots of research evidence supporting the idea of cognitive vulnerability being linked to the onset of depression, with depressives selectively attending to negative stimuli.

- The cognitive explanation of depression is based upon scientific principles that permit objective testing, allowing improvement of the model and thus greater understanding of the disorder.

- A high degree of success has been achieved in treating depression with cognitive therapies in comparison to therapies based on other explanations, thus providing support for such explanations. Most evidence linking negative thinking to depression is correlational and doesn't indicate negative thoughts causing depression. Beck came to believe it was a *bi-directional relationship,* where depressed individuals' thoughts cause depression and vice versa.

- A big strength of the theory is that it acknowledges that other aspects, such as genes, development and early experiences, can lead to certain thinking patterns which then lead to depression.

- The cognitive approach has had less success in explaining and treating the manic component of bipolar depression, lessening support for the model as a global explanation of depression.

- Some critics believe that not all depressed people have a distorted view of their own abilities and that while they may focus on negative elements of events they do actually understand such events accurately and therefore don't show the negative biases that Beck believes they should.

RESEARCH IN FOCUS

Most evidence linking negative thinking to depression is correlational.

1 Why would such evidence not show causality?

2 Would the relationship be a positive or a negative one?

3 What kind of graph is used to plot correlational data?

For information on research methods, see Chapter 7.

Alternative explanations of depression

Genetic explanation

The genetic explanation centres on the idea that vulnerability to depression is inherited. The explanation is generally researched through twin and adoption studies, though more recently gene-mapping studies have been used that compare genetic material from those with high and low incidences of the disorder.

Research

Wender *et al.* (1986) found that adopted children who develop depression were more likely to have a depressive biological parent, even though adopted children are raised in different environments, implying biological factors are more important than cognitive ones.

Plomin *et al.* (2013) used gene-mapping techniques with a sample of 3,154 pairs of 12-year-old twins, to find that genetics accounted for about 66 per cent of the heritability of cognitive abilities. This suggests that the cognitive features of depression, such as negative schemas, may have a large genetic component to them, which illustrates how the genetic and cognitive explanations can be combined together to give a better understanding of the origin of the disorder.

Evaluation

- The similarity of symptoms across gender, age and cultural groups, plus the similarity in physical symptoms, suggests a genetic rather than a cognitive influence, though of course the cognitive features of depression may be genetically mediated, which again suggests the two explanations can be combined rather than seen as separate.

- If the genetic explanation was solely true, then concordance rates between MZ (identical) twins would be 100 per cent and all depressives would share genetic material, which they don't. So although research does indicate a genetic influence, other influences, such as cognitive factors, must also play a role.

Behavioural explanation

The behavioural explanation sees depression as a learned condition. Lewinsohn (1974) proposed that negative life events may incur a decline in positive reinforcements and even lead to learned helplessness, where individuals learn through experience that they seemingly can't bring about positive life outcomes. Depression could even result from social learning, through the observation and imitation of depressed others.

Research

Maier & Seligman (1976) found that participants placed in a situation where escape from noise or shocks was impossible didn't try to escape from future similar situations where escape was possible, lending support to the concept of learned helplessness.

Coleman (1986) found that individuals receiving low rates of positive reinforcement for social behaviours became increasingly passive and non-responsive, leading to depressive moods, which provided support for Lewinsohn's learning theory.

Evaluation

- Overall, there is little research evidence that solidly backs up behaviourist explanations, while the cognitive approach is supported by a body of research based evidence, which strongly suggests the cognitive explanation to be superior.
- Kanter *et al.* (2008) state that behaviourism cannot offer an account of depression that addresses its complexity satisfactorily. Cognitive explanations are more able to do this, as they can account for the irrational thought processes that are seen as underpinning the condition.

Treating depression

Cognitive behavioural therapy (CBT)

CBT is the main psychological treatment used to help treat depression and is based on the cognitive model, which sees abnormal behaviour as caused by disordered thought processes. The idea behind CBT is that beliefs, expectations and cognitive assessments of self, the environment and the nature of personal problems affect how individuals perceive themselves and others, how problems are approached and how successful individuals are in coping and reaching goals. Therefore CBT assists patients to identify irrational and maladaptive thoughts and alter them. As behaviour is seen as being generated by thinking, the most logical and effective way of changing maladaptive behaviour is to change the maladaptive thinking underlying it. Thoughts are perceived as affecting emotions and behaviour and so are modified to reduce depressive symptoms.

CBT is an umbrella term for a number of different therapies, the two best known being *rational emotive behaviour therapy* (REBT) and *treatment of negative automatic thoughts* (TNAT). The central idea of both is to challenge and restructure maladaptive ways of thinking into adaptive, rational ones.

Rational emotive behaviour therapy (REBT)

Rational emotive behaviour therapy (REBT) was developed by Albert Ellis and modified over a number of years until his death in 2007. According to Ellis, *people are not disturbed by things but rather by their view of things* and so he believed the way people feel is largely influenced by how they think.

Ellis saw irrational thoughts as causing emotional distress and behaviour disorders. Irrational thoughts cause negative self-statements and so REBT involves making patients' irrational and negative thoughts more rational and positive. Ellis identified eleven basic irrational *musturbatory beliefs* that are emotionally damaging and can lead to psychological problems. These include: 'I must be loved by everybody . . . otherwise everyone hates me' and 'I must be excellent in all respects . . . otherwise I am worthless'. The therapist's aim is to challenge patients' thinking and show how irrational their thoughts are. Patients are told to practise positive and optimistic thinking. A central part of the therapy involves using the ABC model as a technique to record irrational beliefs.

A = Activating event: patients record events leading to disordered thinking, such as exam failure.

B = Beliefs: patients record negative thoughts associated with the event, such as 'I'm useless and stupid.'

C = Consequence: patients record negative thoughts or behaviours that follow, such as feeling upset and thinking about leaving college.

Figure 4.20 The ABC model

Figure 4.21 REBT involves trying to see things more optimistically

REBT involves *reframing*, in other words challenging negative thoughts by reinterpreting the ABC in a more positive, logical way. For example, the exam was difficult, or there was not enough time for revision. Basically, REBT involves looking on the bright side and seeing things more optimistically.

Treatment generally involves one or two sessions of therapy every two weeks for about fifteen sessions. Therapists and patients work together to verify reality. If a patient makes the negative statement 'I'm a poor parent, because my children misbehave', the therapist gets the patient to assess its truth and examine the idea that someone's a bad parent because children are sometimes naughty. Patients therefore become more realistic, more able to distinguish fact from fiction and don't perceive things in extreme terms.

After the *education phase,* where individuals learn relationships between thoughts, emotions and behaviour, *behavioural activation* and *pleasant event scheduling* are introduced, aimed at increasing physiological activity and participation in social and other rewarding activities, for instance socialising with others. Cognitive factors are then addressed after patients have experienced improvement in mood or energy, by being taught to identify faulty thinking responsible for low mood and to challenge these thoughts. Between sessions patients are given goals to boost self-esteem. These involve *hypothesis testing* of negative thoughts through behavioural coping skills, for instance testing the belief that they're incapable of being included in conversations, by talking to strangers in social situations. Therapists only set tasks they're confident patients can succeed at; failure reinforces the ineptness patients believe in. To prevent relapse, a few 'booster' sessions are given in the subsequent year.

CONTEMPORARY RESEARCH

The effectiveness of cognitive behavioural therapy in depression – Sandra Embling (2002)

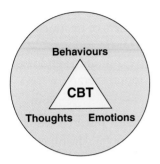

Figure 4.22 How effective is CBT in treating depression?

The effectiveness of CBT has been scrutinised in many studies, but most compared CBT against other treatments and, while showing that CBT works, they don't provide insight into who benefits most. In an age where available resources are being financially restricted it is important that resources are targeted at those who would benefit most from them.

Aims

- To assess which types of depressive patients benefit most and least from CBT.
- To explore the relationship between emotions and depression to assess which patients benefit most from CBT.

Procedure

1 An opportunity sample of 38 patients, aged between 19 and 65 years and suffering from depression as diagnosed by ICD-10 criteria, were the participants.
2 A waiting list group of 19 patients receiving antidepressant medication formed the control group, who were seen once a week by a trained clinician for between 10 and 20 minutes to review symptoms and side-effects and provide advice. Both treatment and control group patients continued to receive drug therapy during the study.
3 Participants in the treatment group received 12 sessions of CBT from trained therapists, each session lasting between 60 and 90 minutes. They received 2 sessions per week for 4 weeks, followed by 1 session a week for 4 weeks.
4 Patients recorded dysfunctional thought records (DTRs) to monitor and record mood changes. Using a 1–100 scale patients rated the negative emotions of anger, anxiety and sadness. As DTRs are an important part of CBT they weren't used with the control group.
5 The Beck depression inventory version 2 (BDI-II) was used to assess level of depression in all patients, pre-study and at one-week intervals throughout the study.

Findings

1 The treatment group's mean BDI-II scores decreased over the course of the treatment. The control group's mean scores remained the same.
2 The treatment group expressed more negative emotions at the end of the study than the beginning, which is part of CBT's success. Expressing negative emotions is necessary for recovery to occur.
3 Those who did not improve with CBT had high levels of *sociotropy* (the need to be liked by others, please others and to seek the approval of others) and *perfectionism*, low levels of *autonomy* and *high external locus of control* (see Chapter 1, page 35).

Conclusions

Depressed patients are less likely to readily express negative emotions.

CBT combined with drug therapy is more effective than drug therapy alone.

Personality characteristics are associated with suppressing emotions and affect CBT outcomes. People with perfectionist traits, high in sociotropy and with high external locus of control and low levels of autonomy have poorer outcomes from CBT, while people with self-orientated perfectionism, with high levels of autonomy, an internal locus of control and low levels of sociotropy benefit most from CBT.

Evaluation

A lack of expressed emotions may be a causal factor of depression or an effect of being depressed.

The improvement in condition of the treatment group may be due to them being seen more frequently and for longer than the control group.

Depressed patients should be psychologically measured to assess their suitability for CBT as it may not be appropriate for everyone.

RESEARCH IN FOCUS

Embling's study into CBT used an opportunity sample.

1 How would this sample be gathered?
2 Give one strength and one limitation of an opportunity sample.

For information on research methods, see Chapter 7.

Research

Lincoln *et al.* (1997) used a questionnaire to identify stroke victims who had developed clinical depression. Nineteen patients were then given CBT sessions for four months, resulting in reduced symptoms, suggesting CBT to be a suitable treatment for specific groups of depressives.

The Department of Health (2001) reviewed research papers of treatments for depression, including behavioural, cognitive, humanistic and psychotherapeutic ones, finding CBT the most effective, but didn't endorse the use of CBT alone, as other treatments, like behavioural therapy, were effective too.

Whitfield & Williams (2003) found CBT had the strongest research base for effectiveness, but recognised there's a problem in the National Health Service being able to deliver weekly face-to-face sessions for patients and suggested this could be addressed by introducing self-help versions of the treatment, like the SPIRIT course, which teaches core cognitive behavioural skills using structured self-help material.

Hollon *et al.* (2006) found that 40 per cent of moderately to severely depressed patients treated with CBT for sixteen weeks relapsed within the following twelve months, compared to a relapse rate of 45 per cent for patients treated for the same period with drug therapy and 80 per cent for patients treated with a placebo (given a pill containing no medication). This suggests that CBT is slightly more effective, long term, than drug therapy and much better than no treatment at all.

David *et al.* (2008) found, using 170 patients suffering from major depressive disorder, that patients treated with fourteen weeks of REBT had better treatment outcomes than those treated with the drug fluoxetine six months after treatment. This suggests that REBT is a better long-term treatment than drug therapy.

Evaluation

- CBT is the most effective psychological treatment for moderate and severe depression and one of the most effective treatments where depression is the main problem. It is also very effective in stopping mild depression from developing into severe depression. It also has few side-effects.
- The better trained the therapist, the better the therapeutic outcomes, which illustrates how the use of trained therapists is essential to the treatment's effectiveness.
- The application of CBT occurs over relatively short time periods compared to other treatments and is more cost effective than such treatments. CBT also has long-term benefits, as the techniques involved are used continually to stop symptoms returning.
- One problem with CBT is whether the theory behind it is correct. Is a depressed person's disordered thinking a cause or an effect of depression? Many cognitive behavioural therapists believe the relationship works both ways.
- There are ethical concerns with CBT as it can be too therapist centred. Therapists may abuse their power of control over patients, forcing them into certain ways of thinking and patients can become too dependent on therapists.

- CBT is difficult to evaluate. Senra & Polaino (1998) found that the use of different measurement scales to assess CBT produced different measures of improvement among patients.

- For patients with difficulty concentrating, often problematic with depressives, CBT can be unsuitable, leading to feelings of being overwhelmed and disappointed, which strengthens depressive symptoms rather than reducing them.

- CBT, as with all 'talking therapies', isn't suitable for patients who have difficulties talking about inner feelings, or for those without the verbal skills to do so.

INCREASE YOUR KNOWLEDGE

Other treatments

Drugs
While CBT addresses maladaptive thought processes, antidepressants have a physical effect on the brain by increasing serotonin production. There are three types of antidepressants used to treat depression: *monoamine oxidase inhibitors* (MAOIs), *tricyclics* and *selective serotonin re-uptake inhibitors* (SSRIs).

There's no best drug, as patients respond differently to different drugs and drug choice is also affected by symptoms displayed and side-effects exhibited.

Hirschfield (1999) reported tricyclics are effective in the treatment of mild and severe depression and are the first choice of treatment in the latter. Sixty to sixty-five per cent of patients taking tricyclics experience improvement in symptoms, which compares favourably to CBT, but relapse rates are relatively higher after treatment ceases.

DeRubeis *et al.* (1999) compared antidepressants and CBT in four clinical trials for the treatment of severe depression, finding a small advantage for CBT, which suggests CBT is a more appropriate treatment for severe forms of depression.

Cuijpers *et al.* (2008) performed a meta-analysis of trials that compared more modern versions of SSRIs against CBT and found a small but significant difference in favour of SSRIs. While this indicates that the effectiveness of drug therapies has improved to a more favourable level than with CBT, drug therapies still have much higher relapse rates than CBT, making overall effectiveness more difficult to calculate, especially when the lower cost of drug therapies is also considered.

Evaluation of drug treatment
Comparison of the relevant effectiveness of drugs and CBT isn't easy to assess, as there are different forms of antidepressants and CBT, which have different success rates with different types of depression. As well as the effectiveness of the treatments, the relapse rates for both forms of treatment must also be considered, though CBT is generally seen as superior here. Then there is the question of cost-effectiveness; drugs don't require a therapist to administer them (which CBT does) and are generally a cheaper treatment, but are they more cost-effective when relapse rates are considered?

An advantage of CBT is that it brings improvement in condition very quickly, while drugs take time to act, usually kicking in after ten to fourteen days, making it difficult to persuade patients to keep taking them, and medication must continue after improvements in mood are achieved or relapse may occur. Drugs also have to be withdrawn slowly: sudden cessation causes restlessness, insomnia, anxiety and nausea and they have side-effects, which CBT doesn't, such as possible cerebral haemorrhage with MAOIs, possible cardiovascular effects with tricyclics (and death from overdose) and risk of suicide with Prozac.

ECT
ECT (electroconvulsive treatment) involves electrically stimulating the brain through electrodes on the head and is believed to produce changes in neurotransmitter levels including sensitivity to serotonin and an increase in GABA, noradrenaline and dopamine levels. It is generally used when other treatments have failed.

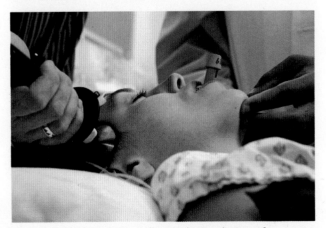

Figure 4.23 ECT involves electrical stimulation of the brain

Fenton et al. (2006) gave six patients twelve weeks of CBT after a course of ECT treatment and found five out of six had further symptom reductions. This suggests CBT may prolong improvements produced by ECT, illustrating how the two treatments can be effectively combined.

Shelton & Hollon (2012) report that ECT is highly effective, with 60 per cent of patients resistant to other forms of treatment showing significant improvements in the short term. However, 84 per cent relapse within six months. This suggests that overall ECT is less effective than CBT, but for these patients CBT may already have proved of little worth.

Evaluation of ECT

Although ECT may only have a relatively short-lived positive effect, it does give an opportunity for other proven therapies, such as CBT, to then be applied. The reduction in symptoms produced by ECT may allow CBT to now be effective when before symptoms were too severe for this to occur.

Although ECT may seem brutal and can produce side-effects, such as memory loss, it does save lives, as patients given ECT have generally failed to respond to other treatments like CBT and are often suicidal.

STRENGTHEN YOUR LEARNING

1 What are:
   (i) negative schemas
   (ii) cognitive biases?
2 Describe the three components of the negative triad.
3 Outline the procedure and conclusions of Beevers et al.'s study into depression.
4 How well are the genetic and behavioural explanations able to account for depression in comparison to the cognitive explanation?
5 How is CBT thought to work?
6 How is Ellis' ABC model included into REBT?
7 Outline the aims and conclusions of Embling's study into CBT and depression.
8 How do drug therapies and ECT attempt to treat depression? In comparison to CBT how effective are they?

ASSESSMENT CHECK

1 Oonagh has been feeling emotionally low for some time now. She feels that nobody really likes her and that she has no positive qualities to offer, nor does she feel that things will improve, as she will always be useless.

   Explain in terms of Beck's negative triad why Oonagh may be suffering from depression. **[3 marks]**

2 Explain how cognitive behavioural therapy is used to treat depression. **[4 marks]**

3 Use the numbers next to the following statements to complete the table below concerning Beck's negative triad. One statement will be left over. **[3 marks]**

   1 Individuals see themselves as having little worth.

   2 Individuals see things as beyond their control.

   3 Individuals see personal defects as preventing them from improving.

   4 Individuals see others as thinking differently to them.

Component of Beck's negative triad	Statement number
The self	
The future	
The world	

4 Outline and evaluate the cognitive approach to explaining depression. **[16 marks]**

5 Discuss cognitive behaviour therapy as a means of treating depression. **[12 marks]**

6 Explain two ethical issues that should be taken into account when conducting research into patients with depression. **[4 marks]**

IN THE NEWS

Ψ The Psychological Enquirer

'Obsessed with control' – a battle with OCD

Figure 4.24 Melissa Blinstock's OCD was so bad that before starting work she had to close her eyes and touch the tip of each pencil five times

Melissa Binstock's troubles began aged 8 when the unpredictable movements of her Tourette's syndrome left Melissa feeling not in control of her life. So control became her obsession; first it was her belongings at school, books and pencils, perfectly sharpened of course, had to be arranged in order. Before starting work she had to close her eyes and touch the tip of each pencil five times. Her desire was for a safe, predictable world which she felt her

rituals could provide; without them she was consumed with overwhelming anxiety. However, control over the external world then progressed onto controlling herself. So her rituals now included wearing the same T-shirt every day, it gave her a sense of power and stability. Then she moved on to what she ate; 12 grams a day of fat, 12 grams of sugar per item, only eating at one restaurant. By the time she went to high school, rituals controlled every moment of her life: the way she dressed, undressed, only eating white foods. At university Melissa spiralled out of control, the constant battle between the comfort of her rituals and a great desire to be 'normal' became too much and she collapsed from lack of food; she'd been surrounded by people all day and her rule was that she could only eat in private. Her saving moment came when, during a lecture about CBT, Melissa realised it might be possible for her to change her thoughts and feelings.

Through practice exposure and response prevention (ERP), she forced herself repetitively into anxiety-provoking activities until they no longer produced feelings of fear. Eventually, Melissa, aged 22, was free of her obsessions and compulsions and the anxiety that came with them.

Melissa was suffering from obsessive–compulsive disorder (OCD), an anxiety disorder characterised by persistent unpleasant thoughts and repetitive behaviours. Sufferers generally realise their thoughts and behaviour are inappropriate, but can't control them. Like Melissa, sufferers often have symptoms of Tourette's syndrome too. Research has brought a greater understanding of the condition, allowing effective therapies, like that received by Melissa, to be developed.

4.5 The biological approach to explaining and treating OCD

The **biological approach** is also known as the medical model and sees abnormal conditions as being similar to physical illnesses caused by abnormal biological processes. Two possible biological explanations are firstly hereditary influences through genetic transmission and secondly the occurrence of OCD through damage to neural (brain) mechanisms.

Genetic explanations

The explanation here centres on OCD being inherited through genetic transmission, with research originally centring on twin and family studies to assess whether this viewpoint is valid and, if so, to what extent genes do play a part. However, as in other areas of psychology, the problem with twin studies is separating out the relative influences of genes and environment.

With the introduction of DNA profiling, more recent attention has been upon gene-mapping studies, which involve comparing genetic material from OCD sufferers and non-sufferers. Such studies also permit researchers to see whether OCD truly is a separate disorder, as OCD sufferers often also have Tourette's syndrome. Results from both forms of study indicate a genetic link to OCD, with particular genes being involved that make some individuals more vulnerable to developing the disorder than others. It is unlikely that single genes cause OCD; more likely is that it is a combination of genes that determine an individual's level of vulnerability to the condition. Although there seems to be some genetic similarity between OCD and Tourette's syndrome, current thinking is that they are two separate disorders. One interesting finding is the possibility that the genetic contribution to the disorder varies among different age groups. Future research in this area needs to be done to identify whether there are varying rates of genetic influence upon different sub-types of OCD.

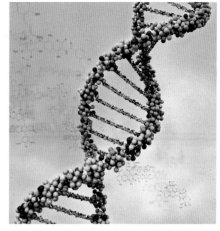

Figure 4.25 Gene-mapping studies allow researchers to test the genetic explanation

CONTEMPORARY RESEARCH

Twin studies on obsessive–compulsive disorder: A review – Grootheest, Cath, Beekman & Boomsma (2005)

Figure 4.26 Can twin studies help us to see if OCD is inherited through our genes?

Twin studies of OCD began in 1929 and varying degrees of genetic influence have been suggested. In this meta-analysis the researchers assessed 70 years of twin studies into OCD. In a twin study MZ (identical) twins are compared against DZ (non-identical) twins. If the chances of both twins in an MZ pair having OCD is greater than that of both twins in a DZ pair having the disorder, it suggests a genetic component, as MZ twins are 100 per cent genetically similar, while DZ twins are only 50 per cent genetically similar. Case studies of single pairs of twins were also included in the review.

Aims

- To see if there is any indication of the extent to which OCD is inherited.
- To see if there is any difference in the extent to which OCD is inherited between children and adults.

Procedure

1 Twin studies of two broad types were reviewed:
  - 'Old literature' – comprising studies performed between 1929 and 1965, where it is not known if patients

would be diagnosed with the disorder under modern diagnostic criteria.
  - 'Studies meeting modern criteria' – comprising studies where patients were diagnosed under DSM criteria.

2 In all 10,034 twin pairs included in 28 twin studies formed the review. There were 9 studies from 1929 to 1965 comprising 37 twin pairs, and 19 modern-era studies comprising 9,997 twin pairs.

Findings

1 From studies where methodology and statistical analysis were deemed sufficiently objective to gain useful data, it was estimated that in children, obsessive–compulsive symptoms are heritable, with genetic influences ranging from 45 to 65 per cent.

2 From studies where methodology and statistical analysis were deemed sufficiently objective, it was estimated that in adults, obsessive–compulsive symptoms are heritable, with genetic influences ranging from 27 to 47 per cent.

Conclusions

Twin studies indicate a genetic component to the transmission of OCD.

Heritability of OCD appears to be greater in children than among adults.

Evaluation

The majority of twin studies of OCD were not performed in large enough numbers or under methodological conditions sufficient to gather objective data, therefore there is a need for further properly controlled twin studies to investigate the heritability of OCD.

There is a need to assess whether the different sub-types of OCD have different levels of genetic transmission.

There is a need to include, along with MZ–DZ twin comparisons, data from more gene-mapping studies, which look for similarities in genetic material in the DNA of sufferers and non-sufferers.

Research

Lenane *et al.* (1990) performed a study into the prevalence of OCD among related family members, finding evidence for the existence of heritable contributions to the onset of the disorder, lending support to the genetic viewpoint.

Samuels *et al.* (2007) used gene mapping to compare OCD sufferers who exhibited compulsive hoarding behaviour with those who didn't, finding a link to chromosome 14 marker D14S588, implying a genetic influence to compulsive hoarding behaviour, which may also indicate the existence of separate OCD sub-type.

Stewart *et al.* (2007) performed gene mapping on OCD patients and family members, finding that a variant of the OLIG-2 gene commonly occurred, which suggests a genetic link to the condition.

Davis *et al.* (2013) used a study method called genome-wide complex trait analysis, which allows simultaneous comparison of genetic variation across the entire genome, rather than the usual method of testing genes one at a time. The genetic datasets of 1,500 participants with OCD were compared against 5,500 non OCD-controls (the study also compared the datasets of 1,500 Tourette's syndrome sufferers with 5,200 non-Tourette's controls). The results showed that both OCD and Tourette's syndrome had a genetic basis, though more so in Tourette's syndrome, and that although there were some shared genetic characteristics, the two disorders had distinct genetic architectures. This suggests the two are separate disorders, though with some overlap.

Tang *et al.* (2014) decided that as complex genetics hinder attempts to understand their role in OCD in humans, they would perform research using dogs. Dogs suffer from naturally occurring compulsive disorders that closely model human OCD, but the limited diversity within dog breeds makes identifying genetic influences easier. Gene analysis showed that OCD-affected dogs had significantly higher levels of particular gene variants than dogs without the condition, which suggest a genetic link to OCD. The extent to which findings can be generalised to humans is debatable.

Figure 4.27 Dogs can have OCD as well as humans and so are used in research into the disorder

Evaluation

- Although research suggests a genetic component to OCD, there must be some environmental influences upon the disorder, or else the concordance rate between MZ twins would be 100 per cent.

- There does not appear to be a single gene involved in the transmission of OCD, instead what research suggests is that many genes scattered throughout the genome each contribute a small amount to an individual's overall risk of developing the disorder. Whether an individual does go on to develop the disorder is then dependent on the degree of environmental triggers that an individual encounters.

- Pato *et al.* (2001) report that a substantial amount of evidence suggests that OCD is a heritable condition, but that few details are understood about actual genetic mechanisms underpinning the disorder, indicating the need for more focused research.

- As evidence indicates genetic factors are at work in the expression of some forms of OCD, especially obsessions about contamination, aggression and religion, and compulsions involving washing, ordering and arranging, it may well be that some types of OCD are more genetic in nature than others.

- As studies like Grootheest *et al.* (2005) find, OCD originating in childhood is more genetic in nature than that originating in adulthood, suggesting there may be different types of OCD with different causes.

- The fact that family members often display dissimilar OCD symptoms, for example a child arranging dolls and an adult constantly washing dishes, weakens support for the genetic viewpoint, as if the disorder was inherited then surely exhibited behaviours would be the same?

Neural explanations

Some forms of OCD have been linked to breakdowns in immune system functioning, such as through contracting streptococcal (throat) infections, Lyme's disease and influenza, which would indicate a biological explanation through damage to neural mechanisms. Such onset of the disorder is more often seen in children than adults.

PET (positron emission tomography) scans also show relatively low levels of serotonin activity in the brains of OCD patients and as drugs that increase serotonin activity have been found to reduce the symptoms of OCD, it suggests that the neurotransmitter may be involved with the disorder.

PET scans also show that OCD sufferers can have relatively high levels of activity in the orbital frontal cortex, a brain area associated with higher-level thought processes and the conversion of sensory information into thoughts. The brain area is thought to help initiate activity upon receiving impulses to act and then to stop the activity when the impulse lessens. A non-sufferer may have an impulse to wash dirt from their hands; once this is done the impulse to perform the activity stops and thus so does the behaviour. It may be that those with OCD have difficulty in switching off or ignoring impulses, so that they turn into obsessions, resulting in compulsive behaviour.

Figure 4.28 Lyme's disease, caused by tick bites, is associated with OCD through damage to neural mechanisms

KEY TERM

Neural explanation – the perception of OCD as resulting from abnormally functioning brain mechanisms

Research

Pichichero (2009) reported that case studies from the US National Institute of Health showed that children with streptococcal (throat) infections often displayed sudden indications of OCD symptoms shortly after becoming infected. Such children also often exhibited symptoms of Tourette's syndrome. This supports the idea that such infections may be having an effect on neural mechanisms underpinning OCD.

Fallon & Nields (1994) reported that 40 per cent of people contracting Lyme's disease (a bacterial infection spread by ticks) incur neural damage resulting in psychiatric conditions including OCD. This suggests that the **neural explanation** can account for the onset of some cases of OCD.

Zohar *et al.* (1987) gave mCPP, a drug that reduces serotonin levels, to twelve OCD patients and twenty non-OCD control participants, finding that symptoms of OCD were significantly enhanced in the OCD patients. This suggests that the sufferers' condition was related to abnormal levels of serotonin.

Hu (2006) compared serotonin activity in 169 OCD sufferers and 253 non-sufferers, finding serotonin levels to be lower in the OCD patients, which supports the idea of low levels of serotonin being associated with the onset of the disorder.

Saxena & Rauch (2000) reviewed studies of OCD that used PET, fMRI and MRI neuro-imaging techniques to find consistent evidence of an association between the orbital frontal cortex brain area and OCD symptoms. This suggests that specific neural mechanisms are involved with the disorder.

Evaluation

- It is thought that infections which reduce immune system functioning don't actually cause OCD, but may instead trigger symptoms in those more genetically vulnerable to the disorder. The onset of the disorder generally occurs very quickly after infection, usually within one to two weeks.

- To what extent abnormal levels of serotonin and activity within the frontal orbital cortex are actual causes of OCD or merely effects of the disorder has not been established.

- There may well be a genetic connection to neural mechanisms, through such mechanisms (for example, levels of serotonin activity) being regulated by genetic factors. An NIMH (National Institute for Mental Health) study examined DNA samples from sufferers and found OCD to be associated with two mutations of the human serotonin transporter gene (hSERT), which led to diminished levels of serotonin.

- Despite the fact that research indicates there are neural differences between OCD sufferer and non-sufferers, it is still not known how these differences relate to the precise mechanisms of OCD.

- Not all sufferers of OCD respond positively to serotonin enhancing drugs, which lessens support for abnormal levels of the neurotransmitter being the sole cause of the disorder.

ON THE WEB

A useful site for comprehensive information about OCD, including its causes and treatments, can be found at:

www.mind.org.uk/information-support/types-of-mental-health-problems/obsessive-compulsive-disorder-ocd/#.VLArLU2zWP8

INCREASE YOUR KNOWLEDGE

Alternative explanations of OCD

Evolutionary explanation

This explanation sees OCD as being beneficial by having an adaptive survival value. OCD involves repetitive behaviours like washing and grooming and these would have been useful against infection. Other similar behaviours may have increased vigilance and alertness, again incurring a survival value. Therefore behaviours like continually cleaning door handles may merely be exaggerations of prehistoric adaptations.

Chepko-Sade *et al.* (1989) found rhesus monkeys who performed the most grooming of others were retained within a group following group in-fighting, suggesting that OCD tendencies have an adaptive value, as continued group membership is crucial to survival.

Abed & Pauw (1998) believe OCD is an exaggerated form of an evolved ability to foresee situations and predict the outcome of one's own thoughts and behaviour, so that dangerous scenarios can be coped with before they happen, suggesting that OCD helps in the avoidance of harm.

Figure 4.29 Compulsive behaviours, like repetitive hair brushing, may be an exaggeration of evolutionary acquired behaviours that incur a survival value

Evaluation of the evolutionary explanation

The explanation is a biological one that can be seen as an extension to the genetic explanation rather than an opposing explanation, as genes are the medium by which evolution occurs. There's a common-sense value to OCD having occurred through the process of evolution and thus having a genetic basis, leading to neuro-anatomical and biochemical influences.

Behavioural features of OCD, like precision and hoarding, would be beneficial in hunting and foraging and therefore useful in the EEA (see page 167) and remain now due to genome lag, where genes take time to evolve and fit current environments.

The cognitive explanation

The cognitive explanation sees OCD sufferers as having faulty, persistent thought processes that focus upon anxiety-generating stimuli, such as assessing the risk of infection from an environment as much higher than it is in reality. Behaviours that lessen impaired obsessive thoughts become compulsions because of their anxiety-reducing qualities.

Rachman & Hodges (1987) report that some individuals are more susceptible to obsessional thinking because of increased vulnerability due to genetic factors, which links cognitive factors to the genetic explanation.

Gehrig et al. (2000) found that the irrational thought processes of nine OCD patients were associated with activity within the orbital frontal cortex that was not seen in non-OCD control patients. This illustrates how the neural and cognitive models can be combined to explain the occurrence of OCD.

Evaluation of the cognitive explanation

OCD sufferers have impaired thought processes that could be due to them having impaired neural functions, which allows the cognitive explanation to be put into a biological framework by being seen as linked to the neural explanation rather than being a separate explanation.

The fact that there are different sub-types of OCD, each focusing upon different forms of anxiety arousal and impaired thought processes (for example emotional contamination, where people fear that by associating with people with negative emotions they will become like them, or sexual identity, where sufferers fear being of an opposite sexual orientation), supports the idea of OCD being largely determined by cognitive rather than biological factors.

The biological approach to treating OCD

Biological treatments are based on the idea of correcting the biological abnormalities seen as causing OCD. Drugs are the most common form of biological therapy, though psychosurgery (see below) is also occasionally used as a treatment.

Drug therapy

Antidepressants are used to treat OCD, such as SSRIs, which elevate levels of serotonin and cause the orbital frontal cortex to function at more normal levels. The most common SSRI used with adults is fluoxetine (Prozac). For children aged 6 years, sertraline is usually prescribed and fluvoxamine for children aged 8 years and older. Treatment usually last for between twelve and sixteen weeks. Anxiolytic drugs are also used due to their anxiety lowering properties. Antipsychotic drugs that have a dopamine lowering effect have also proven useful in treating OCD, though they are only generally given after treatment with SSRIs hasn't proved effective (or incurs serious side-effects).

KEY TERM

Drug therapy – the treatment of OCD through chemical means

Olanzapine augmentation for treatment-resistant obsessive–compulsive disorder – Koran, Ringold & Elliott (2000)

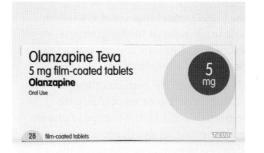

Figure 4.30 Antidepressants are the most common drug used to treat OCD

Research had shown that combining the antipsychotic drug risperidone with a serotonin re-uptake inhibitor (SRI) benefits patients with forms of OCD that don't respond to treatment. So the researchers here decided to assess the ability of another atypical antipsychotic, olanzapine, to do the same, as it has a similar effect on serotonin and dopamine levels.

Aims

To assess the ability of olanzapine augmented with an SRI to alleviate treatment resistant forms of OCD.

Procedure

1 10 adult OCD patients, whose condition had not responded to treatment of at least 60 mg a day for 10 weeks of the SRI drug fluoxetine, consented to act as participants.
2 All participants had OCD for at least one year, as diagnosed by the Yale-Brown obsessive compulsive scale (Y-BOCS) and had not been diagnosed with any other disorder.
3 Participants had failed a mean of 3.3 SRI trials and had a mean Y-BOCS score of 29.0

4 Administration of fluoxetine continued, but 2.5 mg a day of olanzapine was added to the treatment for two weeks. The olanzapine was then increased to 5 mg a day and two weeks later to 10 mgs a day for four more weeks.

Findings

1 9 participants completed the trial.
2 Mean Y-BOCS scores were 24.4 (−4.6, a 16 per cent reduction).
3 One patient's Y-BOCS score dropped by 68 per cent, another by 30 per cent and a third by 29 per cent
4 Only one patient was rated as 'much improved', but this improvement was maintained over the next 6 months taking 5 mg daily of olanzapine.
5 6 patients experienced the side-effect of significant weight increase.

Conclusions

Augmenting SRI treatment with olanzapine has some positive effect with treatment of resistant forms of OCD.

The administration of simultaneous drug therapies can be more effective than single drug treatments.

Evaluation

Results would need to be confirmed by double-blind, placebo controlled trials to be confirmed (see page 259). There is also a need to compare the effectiveness of risperidone and olanzapine when added to SRI treatments to see which is superior.

A negative of the trial is that 60 per cent of participants put on considerable weight, which may lead to psychological harm. A cost–benefit analysis here would need to consider the extent of the improvement in patients' condition, weighed against the degree of harm caused through side-effects.

The response of patients to a biological treatment supports the idea of a biological cause to OCD, though the treatment aetiology fallacy warns that just because a disorder responds to a treatment doesn't necessarily mean the treatment is addressing the cause.

PSYCHOLOGY IN THE REAL WORLD

Research suggests that drugs are an effective therapy, but critics accuse the drugs companies of suppressing evidence that drugs often aren't effective and indeed are dangerous. They pay clinicians to promote their products and have an unhealthy influence over politicians who control mental health services. Sales of antipsychotic drugs globally topped £10 billion in 2008 and new generation drugs cost on average £75 compared to £17 for older versions, yet evidence suggests they are no more effective. Dr David Healey (2013), a leading expert, reports that by 2003 six million Europeans were taking antidepressants semi-permanently while the number of prescriptions for them increases at about 10 per cent a year. Prozac is linked by Bergquist et al. (1999) to suicidal urges in some people and Healey estimates that up to 2,500 extra suicides a year in Europe are triggered by antidepressants, with other serious side-effects including 6,000 birth defects and 30,000 miscarriages from taking antidepressants in pregnancy (about 1 in 10 pregnant women are prescribed antidepressants). The accusation remains that profit is being put before people's health.

Research

Pigott & Seay (1999) reviewed studies testing the effectiveness of drug therapies, finding SSRIs to be consistently effective in reducing OCD symptoms. While the tricyclic antidepressant drug clomipramine proved slightly more effective, it had more serious side-effects. This suggests that SSRIs should be given as a first attempt drug treatment and clomipramine should only be used when SSRIs have not proven effective.

Ciccerone et al. (2000) investigated the effect of low doses of the antipsychotic drug risperidone in treating OCD, finding treatment effective due to the drug's dopamine lowering effect.

Julien (2007) reported that studies of SSRIs show that although symptoms do not fully disappear between 50 and 80 per cent of OCD patients improve, allowing them to live a fairly normal lifestyle, which they wouldn't be able to do without the treatment.

Soomro et al. (2008) reviewed seventeen studies of SSRIs versus placebo treatments involving 3,097 patients and found SSRIs to be moderately effective in the short term in treating OCD of varying duration in adults, lending a degree of support to the treatment.

Evaluation

- Generally drugs don't 'cure' OCD, but reduce obsessive thoughts and compulsive behaviour to such a level that a more normal lifestyle can be achieved.

- A limitation of drug therapy is the side-effects that patients may experience. Loss of sexual appetite/ability is common, as is irritability, sleep pattern disturbance (insomnia/drowsiness), headaches and loss of appetite.

- Antidepressant medication may be more suitable for adults, as they are more able to tolerate and understand side-effects.

- It's not sure if drug treatments effective in treating OCD reduce obsessive symptoms, or instead lessen the depressive symptoms that often accompany the condition.

- Drug treatments are widely used to treat the symptoms of OCD as they are relatively cheap, don't require a therapist to administer them and are a user-friendly form of treatment, as people are used to taking medicines for illnesses.

- Some would argue that because of the risk of side-effects and the tendency of antidepressants to produce heightened levels of suicidal thinking, plus the effectiveness of psychological treatments, drug treatments shouldn't be used to treat OCD.

PSYCHOLOGY IN THE REAL WORLD

Mainly we have been considering the effectiveness of single treatments for mental disorders by comparing their success rates with each other, yet a more interesting approach is that of *eclectic treatments*, where different treatments are combined together for greater effectiveness. For depression a combination of drugs and psychotherapy is effective, especially when antidepressants are given during the acute phase of depression and then psychotherapy to prevent relapse.

OCD and phobias are both anxiety disorders and treating them with drugs can incur a high relapse rate, while CBT often isn't tolerated due to the high anxiety levels it causes, but a combination of the two cancels out each other's weaknesses: drugs ease anxiety levels and CBT decreases relapse rates. So even though two treatments is more costly than one, it may be cost-effective if it results in long-term improvements in condition, rather than having to repeatedly treat a recurring condition.

YOU ARE THE RESEARCHER

Design an experiment to test the effectiveness of antidepressant drugs against placebo treatment. What experimental design would be used? What would be your independent variable (IV) and dependent variable (DV)? How would you establish a double-blind procedure?

For information on research methods, see Chapter 7.

Other treatments

Psychosurgery

Psychosurgery involves destroying brain tissue to disrupt the cortico-striatal circuit by the use of radio-frequency waves. This has an effect on the orbital frontal cortex, the thalamus and the caudate nucleus brain areas, and is associated with a reduction in symptoms. There's been a recent movement towards using deep-brain stimulation, which involves the use of magnetic pulses on the supplementary motor area of the brain, which is associated with blocking out irrelevant thoughts and obsessions.

Research

Richter *et al.* (2004) reported that 30 per cent of OCD patients had a 35 per cent or greater reduction in symptoms, but there were occasional complications, such as urinary incontinence and seizures. As these were patients at risk of suicide who hadn't responded to drug therapies, the treatment can be considered relatively effective.

Mallett *et al.* (2008) evaluated deep-brain stimulation as a therapy for treatment resistant OCD, comparing it with sham (pretend) stimulation and found significant symptom reduction, which suggests the treatment to be effective.

Figure 4.31 Psychosurgery involves irreversible destruction of brain tissue to treat OCD

Evaluation

- Although psychosurgery has a relatively small success rate and can cause serious side-effects, it can be seen as an acceptable treatment, as it's only used on severe forms of OCD that have not responded to other treatments, such as drug therapies, for about ten years and where there is severely diminished quality of life and/or risk of death to the patient.

- About 10 per cent of OCD patients actually get worse over time, even with drug treatments (and psychological therapies), and so psychosurgery can be deemed a valid treatment for such patients.

RESEARCH IN FOCUS

1 Why might it not be possible for individuals with severe OCD to give informed consent for psychosurgery?
2 Who would give consent for them?
3 Who else cannot give informed consent?

For information on research methods, see Chapter 7.

CBT

While drugs address the physical counterparts seen as underpinning OCD, CBT is instead focused on changing obsessional thinking, like with *habituation training* (HT), where sufferers relive obsessional thoughts repeatedly to reduce the anxiety created. Intrusive thoughts are shown to be normal and patients come to understand that thinking about a behaviour isn't the same as actually doing it. Sufferers are taught to focus on their estimations of potential risks and realistically assess the likelihood of them occurring. Sufferers are encouraged to practise their new adaptive beliefs and to disregard their former maladaptive ones. Although CBT is seen as the most effective treatment for OCD, even higher success rates are found when it is combined with drug treatments.

Research

O'Connor et al. (1999) assessed the effect of combining CBT with drug medication. Patients received either drugs and CBT together, CBT only, drugs only or no treatment. Patients in all groups, except the no-treatment group, showed improvements, but most symptom reduction was seen when drugs were combined with CBT, especially if drugs were given for a period first. This suggests that the most effective treatment is to first administer drugs to reduce symptoms, especially anxiety levels, so that CBT can then have a more beneficial effect.

O'Kearney et al. (2006) assessed the ability of CBT to treat children and adolescents with OCD, finding it effective, but more so when combined with drug treatments, demonstrating how drugs and CBT can work together to alleviate the condition.

Jonsson & Hougaard (2009) found that CBT was better than drug treatments in reducing OCD symptoms, which suggests it's a more effective treatment than drug therapy.

Evaluation

- Although CBT was acknowledged to be more effective and not to have the side-effects of other treatments associated with OCD, it isn't suitable for patients who have difficulties talking about inner feelings, or for those who don't possess the verbal skills to do so. Maybe such patients would be more suited to drug therapies.

- Although drugs may not 'cure' OCD they may reduce anxiety and symptoms sufficiently for CBT to be successfully introduced, showing how the two treatments can be successfully combined.

- Drug treatments are lengthy in comparison to CBT. Even if a patient shows improvements with drugs, they should continue taking the medication for at least twelve months to ensure their symptoms continue to improve.

STRENGTHEN YOUR LEARNING

1 Why is the biological approach also known as the medical model?
2 How do gene-mapping studies work?
3 Outline the procedure, results and conclusions of Grootheest et al.'s study into OCD.
4 What neural influences are thought to cause OCD?
5 Compared to the biological approach, how do the evolutionary and cognitive explanations account for OCD?
6 What types of drugs are used to treat OCD and how are they each thought to work?
7 Outline the aims and conclusions of Koran et al.'s study into OCD.
8 In comparison to drug therapy, how effective are psychosurgery and ECT in treating OCD?

ASSESSMENT CHECK

1 Just after his tenth birthday, Roscoe developed a nasty throat infection and a few weeks later he started to have persistent thoughts about being infected by germs, which caused him a lot of anxiety. He began repetitively washing his hands many times a day. He was diagnosed as suffering from OCD, a condition several members of his family have had. However, since he has begun taking medication that increases the level of serotonin in his brain, his symptoms have decreased.

Referring to the situation above, show how genetic and neural explanations may account for Roscoe's OCD. **[4 marks]**

2 Outline the neural explanation for OCD. **[3 marks]**

3 Place a 'G' next to the two descriptions below that relate to the genetic explanation of OCD and an 'N' next to the two descriptions that relate to the neural explanation. One description will be left over. **[4 marks]**

Description	Type of explanation
Sees OCD as occurring due to faulty brain mechanisms	
Is seen as occurring due to repressed memories	
Sees OCD as linked to abnormal levels of serotonin	
Is tested by the use of twin studies	
Sees OCD as an inherited condition	

4 Outline and evaluate drug therapy as a means of treating OCD. **[16 marks]**

5 Discuss the biological approach to explaining OCR. **[12 marks]**

6 The tables below show data for reduction of OCD symptoms in patients treated with drug therapy or a placebo. **[3 marks]**

(i) What type of graph would be appropriate to plot this data?

(ii) Describe two features of this graph.

Participant	Score for reduction of OCD symptoms after treatment with drug therapy
1	28
2	36
3	62
4	29
5	38

Participant	Score for reduction of OCD symptoms after treatment with placebo
1	13
2	3
3	4
4	8
5	12

Definitions of abnormality

SUMMARY

- The deviation from social norms definition sees abnormality as behaviour violating accepted social rules.
- The failure to function adequately definition sees abnormality as an inability to cope with day-to-day living.
- The statistical infrequency definition sees abnormality as behaviours that fall outside of normal distribution.
- The deviation from ideal mental health definition sees abnormality as a failure to meet the criteria for perfect psychological wellbeing.

Characteristics of phobias, depression and OCD

Explaining and treating phobias

- Phobias, depression and OCD are all mental disorders that can be described in terms of their behavioural, emotional and cognitive characteristics.
- The behavioural approach explains phobias as occurring through the two-process model, where phobias are acquired through classical conditioning and social learning, and are then maintained through operant conditioning.
- Alternative explanations include the cognitive approach that focuses upon vulnerability through attentional bias and the evolutionary explanation, which sees phobias as having an adaptive value.
- Systematic desensitisation is a behavioural treatment that modifies phobias by constructing and working through hierarchies of anxiety-producing stimuli.
- Other treatments of phobias include drugs, which seek to reduce anxiety levels, and CBT, which seeks to modify the irrational thought processes associated with the condition.

Explaining and treating depression

- The cognitive approach explains depression in terms of maladaptive thinking, with Beck's negative triad seeing depression as occurring through three types of maladaptive thinking about the self, one's environment and the future.
- Alternative explanations include the genetic explanation that sees depression as an inherited condition and the behavioural explanation, which sees it as a condition learned from experience.
- CBT seeks to treat depression by modifying thought patterns to alter behavioural and emotional states.
- Other treatments include drug therapies, which treat the physical symptoms of depression through chemical means, and ECT, which treats the condition by providing electrical stimulation to the brain.

Explaining and treating OCD

- Biological explanations of OCD include seeing it as an inherited condition and as a condition associated with abnormal neural functioning.
- Alternative explanations include the evolutionary explanation that sees OCD as having an adaptive value, and the cognitive approach of explaining it in terms of maladaptive thought processes.
- Drug therapy attempts to treat OCD by addressing its physical symptoms.
- Other treatments include psychosurgery, which involves irreversible destruction of brain tissue, and CBT, which attempts to modify irrational thought processes.

5 Approaches for AS Psychology

Introduction

The 'approaches' are the varying ways that any one area of psychology considers behaviour.

This chapter will cover the following areas of the specification:

- Origins of psychology: Wundt, introspection and the emergence of psychology as a science
- The biological approach
- The learning approaches
- The cognitive approach.

In Year 1 you will study the basic assumptions of the three approaches listed above.

In Year 2 you will study the psychodynamic approach, humanistic psychology and a comparison of the approaches. These will be covered in Book 2.

Understanding the specification

- Origins of psychology: you need to have an awareness of the early history of psychology, particularly the work of *Wundt*.
- For the biological approach, the influence of *genes, biological structures* and *neurochemistry* on behaviour can be asked about separately from each other. You also need to be clear what the terms *genotype* and *phenotype* mean, including how to apply those terms to a behaviour example. Again, *the genetic basis of behaviour* and *evolution* and *behaviour* can each be asked about separately.
- Regarding the learning approaches, each aspect also needs to be known, as they are all named specifically. You also need to know about *imitation, identification, modelling, vicarious reinforcement* and *the role of mediational processes*, as well as *Pavlov's, Skinner's* and *Bandura's* research studies because they are named on the specification.
- It is stated clearly what you need to know for the cognitive approach. Where it states '*make inferences about mental processes*', it is the ability of the theoretical and computer models that need to judged, not your ability to make inferences. However, you will need to be able to understand results of experiments and be able to write about schemas.

These are the basic requirements of the specification. However, other relevant material is included in this chapter to provide depth and detail to your understanding.

5.1 Origins of psychology: Wundt, introspection and the emergence of psychology as a science

Figure 5.1 Wilhelm Wundt

Wundt

The origin of psychology as a discipline is widely thought to have occurred in Germany from the work of Wilhelm Wundt. In 1875, Wundt established the first psychology laboratory. He worked at Leipzig University and had a room dedicated to conducting psychological experiments. He later founded the Institut für Experimentelle Psychologie (the Institute of Experimental Psychology) in 1879 with his colleague Gustav Fechner. It is at this point in time when the discipline moved from the realms of philosophy, biology and physiology into psychology.

Introspection

Wundt used **introspection** in his work. Introspection is the examination of one's own thought processes and Wundt's researchers were trained to examine theirs for feelings, emotions and sensations. This would be done in Wundt's room at the university in a controlled environment. The researchers would then report back to him what they had experienced and their analysis of that experience. Wundt found that these reports could not be replicated, and were therefore unreliable, as the experience was too subjective (meaning it was based solely on one person's opinion/viewpoint).

The emergence of psychology as a science

Psychology today is seen as a scientific discipline and, as such, uses a variety of methodologies, many of which are empirical (scientific), to investigate human and animal behaviour. The legacy of the biological and physiological origins means that many psychologists apply the scientific method to their work and use empirical methods to test their hypotheses. This is not the case for all of psychology and some psychologists are not focused as much on the scientific aspects with their work. They argue that there will always be an element of subjectivity, as witnessed by Wundt.

One of the results from these varying viewpoints on whether psychology can be truly scientific is the differing methods used by psychologists to test behaviour. This means that they consider behaviour through varying viewpoints. They may look at it at a neuronal level or at a more social level. These viewpoints are called approaches and it is this aspect that we will be examining in this section of the book.

The approaches

Behaviour can be explained in lots of different ways. These differing ways of seeing and testing behaviour and thought are called the approaches.

The very different ways in which a behaviour can be understood can be demonstrated by the case of Elliot Rodger (see below).

IN THE NEWS

Ψ The Psychological Enquirer

Elliot Rodger's Retribution

Figure 5.2 Elliot Rodger

On 23rd May 2014 Elliot Rodger, aged 22, shot dead seven people, including himself, and injured seven more, after making a YouTube video in which he said he was going to stage a revenge attack. The shootings took place in Isla Vista, near the University of California-Santa Barbara.

His first victims were three men who lived in his apartment block and were known to him. He then proceeded to drive around in his car shooting people at random and killing three more people who he did not know, before finally driving his car into a parked car and shooting himself in the head.

The YouTube video, called *Elliot Rodger's Retribution,* that he made of himself the day before the shootings showed him talking about how he had been rejected by women and how he hated them for that. The attack was revenge for that rejection. He stated in the video: 'Tomorrow is the day of retribution. The day in which I will have my revenge.'

This event has been explained by some as being due to Elliot being a 'misfit', whose advances towards women were repelled.

This behaviour can be explained in many different ways and at many different levels. Psychologists see and explain behaviour this way and the approaches are those alternative perspectives.

So, Elliot's behaviour can possibly be explained by:

- his hormones/neurotransmitters or brain physiology (biological approach)
- his learning from experience (learning approach)
- his thought processes (cognitive approach)
- his unconscious mind (psychodynamic approach)
- his need for fulfilment (humanistic approach).

All these approaches have a different way of explaining the same behaviour. Three approaches, namely the biological, learning and cognitive approaches, will be outlined in this chapter, whereas the psychodynamic and humanistic approaches, together with a comparison of all the approaches discussed in both books, will be explained and discussed in Book 2.

The basic assumptions of the biological approach will be outlined in the following section. In Chapter 6 (from page 225), we will consider biopsychology in more detail.

5.2 The biological approach

> *'We are survival machines – robot vehicles blindly programmed to preserve the selfish molecules known as genes. This is a truth which still fills me with astonishment.'*
> Richard Dawkins, *The Selfish Gene* (1991)

This approach sees behaviour as rooted in the physiology and biology of the body. It examines the processes that occur, and looks for how that may affect an individual.

Basic assumptions

The core assumptions of biopsychologists are that behaviour is affected by:

1) Genetics

Biological psychologists believe that the genes an individual possesses influence his or her behaviour. This also means that there is a belief in the process of evolution. It is believed that behaviour evolves the same way as physical characteristics through the process of evolutionary adaptation. This then leads to the idea that the examination of animals can also usefully tell us about our own behaviour.

2) The central nervous system, which comprises the brain and spinal cord

The brain is seen as the main focus when explaining behaviour, as it is seen to be the origin of how the world is seen and acted upon by an individual.

3) The chemistry of the body

Varying levels of the chemicals in the bodies found both in the brain (neurotransmitters) and the body (**hormones**) are thought by biological psychologists to be related to an individual's behaviour. They are believed to influence reactions to the environment.

The chemistry of the body is a rapidly advancing approach in psychology due to the progression of technology and understanding of researchers about how the brain and body work.

The influence of genes on behaviour

There are two key terms which help show how genetics can influence the development of an individual:

Genotype

The **genotype** is an individuals' genetic make-up, which occurs at conception and provides the genetic code for how that individual will develop. Each individual is thought to have around 100,000 genes. The genotype dictates such characteristics as eye and hair colour. Each individual (apart from identical twins) has a genotype which is unique to them.

Phenotype

The **phenotype** of an individual is the product of what happens when the genotype interacts with the environment. With a physical characteristic such as height the genotype dictates the maximum height an individual can reach but environmental factors such as nutrition will affect how likely the person is to achieve their potential height.

So, an individual's genotype might be that they have the genetic potential to be tall. The genotype relates to these genetic instructions. However, much like a planted seed, if the environment does not provide the optimum conditions then the individual will not fulfil their potential to become tall. For example, there may be a period of poor nutrition or they may take a drug which inhibits their growth. This means that the phenotype is the height they actually become, not their genetic potential. This is the same for psychological characteristics in that there may be a genetic predisposition to a behaviour but it may not express itself due to the environment inhibiting its development.

Genetic basis of behaviour

Each individual is born, typically, with 23 pairs of chromosomes which have been inherited from their birth parents. These are our genotype and form the basis for our development. The work of geneticists and psychologists has suggested that there may be a genetic underpinning for certain behaviours.

Often the work is carried out on pairs of twins. As monozygotic (MZ or identical twins) are 100 per cent genetically similar, the likelihood of them both having a behaviour/disorder compared with the likelihood of non-genetically identical twins (DZ or dizygotic twins) gives an indication of how much the behaviour may be genetic.

Figure 5.3 Research with identical twins is useful for investigating the basis of certain behaviours

If the MZ twins show a *higher* likelihood of sharing behaviours/disorders than DZ twins then there is argued to be a genetic component. This is thought to be because the only difference between the two pairs of twins is how genetically similar they are. If the shared behaviour is greater when they are more genetically similar, then the argument is that this is due to shared genetics.

Examples of concordance rates (shared behaviour) from twin research are shown in Table 5.1 below.

Table 5.1 Examples of concordance rates

Behaviour/ Disorder	Research	Concordance rate for MZ (identical) twins	Concordance rate for DZ (non-identical) twins
Schizophrenia	Gottesman (1991)	48%	17%
Bipolar depression	Craddock & Jones (1999)	40%	5–10%
Anorexia nervosa	Walters & Kendler (1995)	23%	9%

It should be noted that these are merely examples. There will be other research that shows differing concordance rates. It is also significant that the rate for MZ twins is not 100 per cent in any of these pieces of research. This suggests that, although there may be a genetic influence, it is not the sole reason for the behaviour/disorder occurring. If it was entirely due to genes you would expect the concordance rate for identical twins to be 100 per cent as they are 100 per cent genetically similar. It seems that some behaviours could be a mix of both genetics and environment.

Evolution and behaviour

The evolution of human behaviour is thought, by biological psychologists, to develop in the same way as the physical characteristics of humans. The idea is based around adaptiveness.

Initially, there is a random change, a mutation, in the genetic make-up of an individual which leads to a characteristic or behaviour occurring. If that change means that the survival and/or chance of reproduction are reduced for the organism then the gene is not passed on. If it, however, increases their chance of survival and reproduction then it gets passed on when they reproduce. This means the mutation has been adaptive for the individual and it then has every chance of being adaptive for subsequent organisms.

Biological psychologists believe that psychological characteristics such as intelligence and aggression were adaptive at the outset and therefore became part of the evolutionary process.

This process takes many generations to occur and so the process of one behaviour becoming part of the genetic make-up of humans is lengthy.

The behaviour in animals occurs, it is argued, in much the same way. Biological psychologists believe therefore that examination of non-human behaviour is useful.

In the case of humans, the organism is the individual. We may have a genetic mutation which makes us physically more able and attractive and therefore the mutation is adaptive. It is argued to be the same for behaviours.

Aggression is widespread in animal behaviour and can be seen to be adaptive in that it can improve survival rates in some situations and increase access to resources. It also helps protect territory. In finding a mate this can mean that the individual becomes more attractive to potential mates, and this therefore increases the individual's chance of reproduction.

Evolution works in the same way for humans. In simple terms, for example, being aggressive will, at some point in our ancestry, have been advantageous in terms of survival and increased chances of reproduction for an individual. This was perhaps due to acquisition of resources and protection of family. This in turn increased attractiveness to potential mates. This made the likelihood of passing the gene on much greater as there would have been more available and receptive mates. The genetics could then have been passed on to subsequent generations and the behaviour became more widespread.

There is research now into the genetic basis of aggression and the MAOA (or Warrior) gene, which is found in one-third of men (Lea *et al.* 2005 and 2006). This research is ongoing and is looking for potential genetic underpinning to aggressive and risk-taking behaviour.

Biological structures

The human body is a collection of systems which integrate to help us live. There are key structures within those systems which are particularly useful in terms of explaining the behaviour and psychology of the individual. These are outlined briefly below.

The nervous system

The nervous system is divided into two parts: the central and the peripheral nervous system. These are described in greater detail in Chapter 6 (Biopsychology for AS and A-level), but they are outlined here in summary form to help lay the foundations of what is needed for you to access the rest of the text.

The central nervous system

The **central nervous system** consists of the brain and the spinal cord. These are pivotal in transferring messages to and from the environment but perhaps more importantly, they act as the centre from which all the physiology of the individual is controlled. Breathing, eating, the heart beat and the senses are all co-ordinated from the central nervous system. This is why biological psychologists look to the brain for behaviour as most actions and reactions are generated from the central nervous system.

The peripheral nervous system

The **peripheral nervous system** sends and receives information to the central nervous system as it is the nervous system for the limbs and torso which collect information from the environment in terms of temperature, pain and threat. The autonomic system is important for survival of the individual and affects the reaction to threat, along with returning the body to normality (called homeostasis) after an acute reaction. The somatic system within the peripheral nervous system comprises the muscles attached to the skeleton and is therefore very important in movement. The somatic system also receives information from the skin, for example temperature of the environment.

The neuron

The **neuron** is a nerve cell which transfers information between the nervous systems. There are billions within the human body and they vary depending on their job. What neurons do and what their structure looks like is described in more detail in Chapter 6.

The endocrine system

The **endocrine system** is not part of the nervous system but is important in terms of the biochemistry of the body. Its main job is to maintain levels of hormones in the blood and other bodily fluids. This is done by using the glands in the body. The most important gland is argued to be the pituitary gland, which is located in the brain. This is sometimes called the 'master gland' because it instructs the other glands to secrete hormones when necessary. Biological psychologists argue that the level of a hormone in the system can affect the behaviour of an individual.

Neurochemistry

Neurochemistry is the biochemistry of the central nervous system. Hormones (see page 200) are the chemicals which travel through the blood. However, in the brain, the transmission of chemicals is via the cerebral fluid (the fluid in the brain). These chemicals are called **neurotransmitters** and are seen to be very important by biological psychologists as they are thought to affect behaviour. An example of this is that high levels of a neurotransmitter called dopamine are related to schizophrenia. (See Chapter 6 for more on the process of synaptic transmission and neurotransmitters, page 228.)

KEY TERMS

Central nervous system – this system is made up of the brain and spinal cord

Peripheral nervous system – this system is the accompanying system running throughout the body which acts with the central nervous system

Neuron – a nerve cell which transfers information throughout the nervous system

Endocrine system – this is the system which affects the transfer and secretion of hormones throughout the body

Neurotransmitters – chemicals within the cerebral (or brain) fluid that transmit signals

- The biological approach adopts scientific methods for investigation using measures which are largely objective (not subject to opinion) such as brain scanning and biochemical levels.

- It is one of the strongest supporters of the nature perspective in the nature–nurture debate as it argues for genetic influence on behaviour.

- Biopsychology research can result in practical applications being developed such as drugs that help the symptoms of people struggling with psychological problems.

- It is argued that some of the explanations are too simplistic and do not do the complexity of human behaviour justice. This means they are reductionist as they can often fail to acknowledge the role of the environment in behaviour.

STRENGTHEN YOUR LEARNING

1 What is the function of a neuron?
2 Where would you find neurotransmitters?
3 What is the difference between the central and the peripheral nervous systems?
4 What is the job of the endocrine system?
5 What is the difference between genotype and phenotype?
6 Why might certain behaviours be thought to be passed from generation to generation?
7 Does research support the idea that any one behaviour is completely genetic?
8 Explain how twin studies show that a behaviour might be genetic.
9 Explain the strengths of the biological approach.
10 What is meant by evolution?

ASSESSMENT CHECK

1 Explain what introspection is. **[2 marks]**

2 Outline and evaluate the biological approach to explaining behaviour. **[12 marks]**

3 Complete the table below by writing which definition A, B, C or D describes which term. One definition will be left over. **[3 marks]**

   A This system acts with the central nervous system and transmits/receives information in most of the body.

   B This is the system which affects the transfer and secretion of hormones throughout the body.

   C This system is made up of the brain and spinal cord.

   D This system helps digest food.

Term	Definition (A,B,C or D)
Central nervous system	
Endocrine system	
Peripheral nervous system	

4 Describe how evolution might explain IQ scores increasing across generations. **[4 marks]**

5 Identical twins sometimes do not achieve similar grades at school despite being very similar in lots of ways. With reference to the terms genotype and phenotype, explain how this could occur. **[4 marks]**

6 Researchers investigating the possible genetic cause of a mental illness decided to use data on twin concordance rates to ascertain the possible level of genetic influence.

   MZ (identical) twins were 30% concordant and DZ (non-identical) twins were 15% concordant. The researchers used these figures to conclude that there is a genetic influence on developing the illness.

   Explain why they were justified in reaching this conclusion. **[3 marks]**

7 Discuss the biological approach to understanding human behaviour. Use at least two alternative approaches as a comparison in your answer. **[16 marks]**

5.3 Learning approaches

'Give me a dozen healthy infants, well-formed, and my own specified world to bring them up in and I'll guarantee to take any one at random and train him to become any type of specialist I might select – doctor, lawyer, artist, merchant-chief, and, yes, even beggarman and thief, regardless of his talents, penchants, tendencies, abilities, vocations, and race of his ancestors.'

John B. Watson, *Behaviorism* (1930)

The learning approach takes a very different focus on behaviour to the biological, and indeed, other approaches. It focuses on how we are a product of our learning and incorporates both behaviourism and the social learning approach. Experience and environment are all-important for the learning approaches.

The behaviourist approach

The basic assumptions of the behaviourist approach are as follows:

- Behaviour is learned from experience.
- Only observable behaviour is measureable scientifically and it is only these behaviours that should be studied. Thought processes are subjective and difficult to test.
- It is valid to study the behaviour of animals as they share the same principles of learning (i.e. classical and operant conditioning).
- According to the behaviourist approach we are born a blank slate, so there is no genetic influence on behaviour.

Classical conditioning

Classical conditioning is one of the behaviourist principles of learning and is learning by association (see page 115). Both humans and animals can be classically conditioned and this is one of the ways they interact with their environment to learn behaviour.

The key idea is that learning occurs when an association is made between a previously neutral stimulus and reflex response. This reflex response can be positive or negative. If the association of the stimulus is with a positive feeling, then that positive feeling will arise whenever the person comes into contact with that specific stimulus. The same is true for negative associations.

For example, imagine that Catherine, an 18-year-old student, has started university and is having great fun in her fresher's week. A particular song is being played a lot during this time whilst she is out and she often dances to it. She will make a positive association with that song, and for years to come whenever she hears that song she will feel positive and happy. Similarly, if Catherine was miserable and homesick in that time she would feel bad whenever she heard the song.

The process can be seen in Figure 5.4 below.

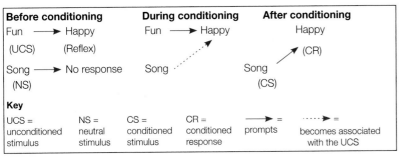

Before conditioning	During conditioning	After conditioning
Fun ⟶ Happy	Fun ⟶ Happy	Happy
(UCS) (Reflex)		(CR)
Song ⟶ No response	Song	Song
(NS)		(CS)

Key

UCS = unconditioned stimulus	NS = neutral stimulus	CS = conditioned stimulus	CR = conditioned response	⟶ = prompts	⋯⟶ = becomes associated with the UCS

Figure 5.4 Classical conditioning

Classical conditioning can be applied to many different situations and you can probably think of a time when you have been classically conditioned in some way. One of the most memorable ways that someone can be conditioned is when they acquire a phobia (see page 154). They will make an association between an object/situation and fear.

This is illustrated by the rather unethical work of Watson & Rayner (1920) who classically conditioned a boy named 'Little Albert' to become phobic of rats (see page 164). Little Albert was his research name not his actual name. This was done by the presentation of an unconditioned stimulus of a loud noise at the same time as the rat. After following this procedure several times, Little Albert started to cry whenever he was shown a rat, even though he had previously not been scared of it.

Pavlov's research

Classical conditioning was documented for the first time by Ivan Petrovich Pavlov (1849–1936). He was a physiologist whose research work initially focused on the digestive system of dogs. To do this he had a dog harnessed to a bench with a tube coming out of its mouth and going into a jar. When his assistant came into the laboratory with the food for the dog Pavlov noticed that the dog salivated upon hearing the sound of the door. Dogs salivate automatically when they see food, but Pavlov's dog had clearly made an association with the imminent arrival of food when the door was opened. Pavlov decided to look at this association as his research.

When dogs hear a bell there is no reflex response (apart from maybe pricking up their ears). So, Pavlov rang a bell whenever the dogs were given food. The sound of the bell then became associated with the food. This meant eventually that whenever he rang the bell, the dogs would salivate, even if there was no food present.

This is illustrated in Figure 5.5 below.

Figure 5.5 Statue of Pavlov with his dog

Before conditioning	During conditioning	After conditioning
Food ⟶ Salivate	Food ⟶ Salivate	Salivate
(UCS) (Reflex)		(CR)
Bell ⟶ No response	Bell	Bell
(NS)		(CS)

Key

UCS = unconditioned stimulus	NS = neutral stimulus	CS = conditioned stimulus	CR = conditioned response	⟶ = prompts	⋯⟶ = becomes associated with the UCS

Figure 5.6 Pavlov's experiment

Stimulus generalisation – when a stimulus becomes generalised to other related stimuli which are also associated with the conditioned response

Stimulus discrimination – when a stimulus is not associated with the conditioned response as it is too different from the original stimulus

Operant conditioning – learning due to the positive or negative consequences of the behaviour

Positive reinforcement – a behaviour is more likely to reoccur because of positive consequences

Negative reinforcement – a behaviour is more likely to reoccur because of avoidance of negative consequences

Punishment – a behaviour is less likely to reoccur because of negative consequences

Pavlov also found out several other points about the process.

Stimulus generalisation

Pavlov found that if he varied the bell pitch and tone, the dogs would still salivate. This meant that if a stimulus has characteristics close to the conditioned stimulus, then the association would also be made to that new stimulus.

In the case of Watson & Rayner's 'Little Albert' study (see page 164) the little boy was not only frightened by the original white rat but also other small furry animals and white fluffy objects. This is an example of how the stimulus can be generalised to other similar things.

Stimulus discrimination

At some point there has to be cut-off point where the association will not be made and the **stimulus generalisation** will not occur. This is called **stimulus discrimination** and happens when the characteristics of the conditioned stimulus and an object become too different to be generalised.

Using the Little Albert case study as an example, he would not associate a large brown dog with fear as, although it is an animal, it varies in terms of size, colour and type.

Time contiguity (temporal contiguity)

Pavlov found that the association only occurs if the unconditioned stimulus and neutral stimulus are presented at the same time, or around the same time, as each other. If the time lapse between presentations is too great then there will be no association made.

Operant conditioning

Operant conditioning is another learning principle of the behaviourist approach. It works on the principle of learning by consequence. There are three key ways this can occur: positive reinforcement, negative reinforcement and punishment (see key terms).

If you apply this to a school-based example of whether to complete a piece of homework or not, you would find that the:

- **positive reinforcement** would be potential better grades, teacher approval and praise
- **negative reinforcement** would be avoiding disapproval from teachers and parents, avoiding a detention, teacher's anger.

Both these would be more likely to make you do the work.

However:

- **punishment** for not completing homework would be disapproval from teachers and parents, detention and the teacher's anger.

This makes NOT doing the homework less likely.

Operant conditioning is used widely in society as a principle in schools, prisons and the home.

Figure 5.7 Punishment is designed to make certain behaviour less likely in future

PSYCHOLOGY IN THE REAL WORLD

Tranquility Bay was a co-educational behaviour modification school in rural Jamaica. Its intake was adolescents aged from 12 to 19 who were mainly American and sent by their parents because they were out of control at home. Parents paid annual tuition fees of $25,000 to $40,000.

Tranquility Bay used various other methods to help 'modify' behaviour following behaviourist principles.

The school held group therapy sessions with students, who were encouraged to comment on what their peers said. The comments could be negative or positive.

There were two types of punishments used at Tranquility Bay:

- **Study Hall:** This was a form of detention where students stayed in a room for three hours and had to write an essay. This was a common punishment given for less severe infractions. It required students to stay in a small, non-air-conditioned room on lawn chairs for three hours. The idea was that the students would subsequently behave so that they could avoid the punishment (negative reinforcement of good behaviour).
- **Observation Placement:** Students had to lie flat on the floor, face down for a period of time decided by the staff. They were allowed to move around for ten minutes of each hour. This again was designed to negatively reinforce good behaviour.

Good behaviour was rewarded by a points system. If a student gained enough points they could move to the next level, which gave them more privileges such as being able to talk, when they were previously kept in silence or, at level 3, being able to phone home. Another form of punishment was the removal of points, making progression to the next level harder.

The school operated from 1997 until it was closed in 2009 for economic reasons and due to poor publicity.

(Information summarised from an article by Decca Aitkenhead, The Observer, *Sunday 29 June 2003)*

This is an example of operant conditioning used within education, in an extreme form. Schools are often governed by behaviourist principles where good behaviour is rewarded with commendations, gold stars, reward trips, etc. Punishment varies from institution to institution, with some schools using detentions, sin bins and exclusions.

These methods vary in their effectiveness and are dependent on the ages of the students. Take a moment to consider what forms of positive reinforcement and punishment you have encountered in your time at school. Did they work?

Research on operant conditioning

The 'Law of Effect' (see page 115) was generated from work by Thorndike (1898) and underpinned the principles of operant conditioning. Thorndike's work observing how cats managed to escape a puzzle box where they were required to pull on a latch was pivotal in formulating operant conditioning. The first time the cats were put in the box it took them time to escape as it happened by chance, but once they had learned that they could escape by pulling the latch they did so straight away in subsequent trials. This was because pulling the latch was positively reinforced as it led to them escaping. There was also a fish within sight outside the box, which acted as further reward once they were out of the box.

Skinner's research

B.F. Skinner was influenced by Thorndike's work and was a major force in the behaviourism movement. His work was prolific and focused around work in laboratories on animals, investigating the role of reward and punishment in shaping behaviour.

Skinner's box was important in this work and, just like Thorndike's work using the puzzle box, it was designed to be able to observe animal response in contrived situations. Skinner worked predominantly on animals such as rats and pigeons, but did conduct some experimentation on humans.

Skinner's box for rats contained a response lever which could prompt the release of a pellet down a chute so that the rat could eat it. There were

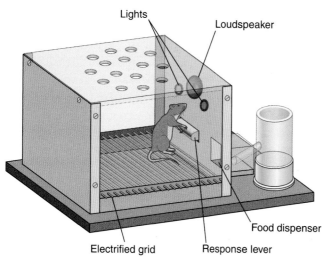

Lights
Loudspeaker

Food dispenser

Electrified grid
Response lever

Figure 5.8 Skinner's box for rats

also loudspeakers and lights which acted as visual and auditory signals when needed, which acted as cues in some of the trials. Finally, the floor was metal and had the capacity to be electrified so that an electric shock could be administered to the rat if the experiment so required. The electric shock provided punishment to the rats. Actions to avoid the shocks would then be reinforced, an example of negative reinforcement.

Using the terms of operant conditioning in Skinner's research we can say that the pellet is the positive reinforcement, the electrified floor is the punishment and the negative reinforcement is the avoidance of the electrified floor or punishment.

Skinner observed that as soon as a rat learned that it would get a pellet when pressing the lever it would keep doing so (as the behaviour was positively reinforced). The pressing of the lever then becomes a learned behaviour as the rat learns that it will be rewarded with a pellet every time it presses the level. This is called continuous reinforcement.

RESEARCH IN FOCUS

Skinner's work was conducted primarily on animals such as rats and pigeons.

1 What are the advantages of using animals in research?
2 What are the problems with using animals in research?
3 What ethical issues could occur with this kind of research were it to be conducted on humans?

For more on research methods, see Chapter 7.

ON THE WEB

Skinner's work on operant conditioning was used in the Second World War, for training pigeons to guide and release missiles onto enemy targets.

There are various films on this use of his research available on YouTube. One worth watching to give you a feel for how operant conditioning was used can be found by searching for 'Skinner's Project Pigeon'.

YOU ARE THE RESEARCHER

How could you test reinforcement in humans as opposed to animals? Can you design a simple study to ascertain what form of positive reinforcement is most effective with students to ensure they complete school work to the best standard they can achieve? How would you do it ethically? What design would you use? Repeated measures or independent groups? Explain why you have chosen this type of design.

For information on research methods, see Chapter 7.

Types of reinforcement

Although the idea of reinforcement for shaping behaviour is a robust one, the frequency and way in which reinforcement is administered can affect the likelihood of it affecting the behaviour. The continuous reinforcement outlined above is just one way of shaping behaviour. Skinner's work considered how varying the reinforcement had an effect on how the rats learned.

In his work five different types of reinforcement were investigated: continuous reinforcement, fixed interval, variable interval, fixed ratio and variable ratio. What these mean and the effects on behaviour are outlined in Table 5.2 below.

Table 5.2 Common reinforcement schedules, and associated patterns of response and resistance to extinction

Reinforcement schedule	Example	Pattern and rate of response	Resistance to extinction	Example of human behaviour
Continuous reinforcement (CRF)	Every single response is reinforced	Response rate is low but steady	Very low – the quickest way to bring about extinction	1 Receiving a high grade for every assessment 2 Receiving a tip for every customer served
Fixed interval (FI)	A reinforcement is given every 30 seconds (FI 30), provided the response occurs at least once during that time	Response rate speeds up as the next reinforcement becomes available; a pause after each reinforcement. Overall response rate fairly low	Fairly low – extinction occurs quite quickly	1 Being paid regularly (every week or month) 2 Giving yourself a 15-minute break for every hour's studying done
Variable interval (VI)	A reinforcement is given on average every 30 seconds (VI 30), but the interval varies from trial to trial. So, the interval on any one occasion is unpredictable	Response rate is very stable over long periods of time. Still some tendency to increase response rate as time elapses since the last reinforcement	Very high – extinction occurs very slowly and gradually	Many self-employed people receive payment irregularly (depending on when the customer pays for the product or service)
Fixed ratio (FR)	A reinforcement is given for a fixed number of responses, however long this may take, e.g. one reinforcement every ten responses (FR 10)	There's a pronounced pause after each reinforcement, and then a very high rate of responding leading up to the next reinforcement	As in FI	1 Piece work (the more work done, the more money earned) 2 Commission (extra money for so many goods made or sales completed)
Variable ratio (VR)	A reinforcement is given on average every ten responses (VR 10), but the number varies from trial to trial. So, the number of responses required on any one occasion is unpredictable	Very high response rate – and very steady	Very high – the most resistant of all the schedules	Gambling

Variable ratio reinforcement is clearly the most successful for response rate and continuous effect. This is because there is no way of predicting when the next reward is going to be given and so the response rate continues at a high rate. This is the reason why slot machines and other forms of gambling are so successful. If someone does not know the next time they are going to win money they will continue putting money into the slot machine as they will think the next coin could be the winning one.

Skinner's analysis of behaviour

Although influenced by Thorndike, Skinner developed his own terms and described the processes involved in operant conditioning using the ABC of operant conditioning.

So, to analyse any behaviour it is necessary to consider:

1 **Antecedents:** What happens just prior to a behaviour being performed. In the case of the rat it could be a light

2 **Behaviours:** Skinner called these operants and the operant in the rat example is pressing the lever

3 **Consequences:** This is what happens after the operant. It is the result. So, for the rat it might result in a pellet being administered down the chute.

Evaluation

- Behaviourists use scientific methods to investigate human behaviour and there is seen to be credibility in their methods.
- They believe that behaviour is learned and therefore are strong proponents of the nurture side of the nature–nurture debate.
- Their ideas are used widely to help change behaviour which is seen to be negative and to encourage positive behaviour such as behaviour modification strategies used in prisons and schools.
- They do not consider the influence of thought and cognitive processes as they are not observable.
- They do not argue that we have control over our own behaviour, which is deterministic. This means that there are ramifications for legislation, such as the idea of someone not being in control of their actions if they commit a crime.
- Any spontaneous behaviour that occurs in humans is not easily explained by the behaviourists' principles of classical and operant conditioning.
- Behaviourists use animal research in their work and it is argued that this is not appropriate due to the differences in the complexity of human and animal behaviour. The opposing argument is that it is more ethical to test animals in this way than testing humans.

Social learning theory

The basic assumptions of this approach are as follows.

- Behaviour is learned from the environment, so therefore it does not regard genetics as an influence on behaviour.
- Behaviour is learned from observing others and the reinforcement or punishment they receive.

Social learning theory (SLT) is argued not strictly to be a behaviourist approach as it does not look solely at behaviour, it also considers cognitive processes.

Bandura's research

Albert Bandura (born 1925) is a learning theorist but not strictly a behaviourist as his theory also considers the thought processes that underlie our behaviour. He challenges Skinner's idea that reward and punishment will prompt or stop a behaviour automatically. He argues that reinforcers and punishments merely inform the individual of likely consequences and it is down to the individual as to whether their behaviour is affected by the potential consequences. This acknowledgement of thought processes has meant that the theory is sometimes referred to as social cognitive theory. Bandura's basic idea is that we learn behaviour by observing the positive and negative consequences of someone else's behaviour. This means we learn the behaviour vicariously – we don't receive the reward or punishment, the person who is modelling the behaviour does. They are referred to as the role model.

CLASSIC RESEARCH

The Bobo doll experiment – Bandura, Ross & Ross (1961)

Figure 5.9 Interactions with a Bobo doll

Bandura's study was designed to examine the role of a model on influencing an observer's behaviour. This had already been documented by Bandura & Huston, 1961, but Bandura was interested in seeing if the influence continued once the role model was no longer present.

Aims

1 To examine the effect of the continual influence of the model.
2 To examine if the sex of the model influenced same-sex and opposite-sex participants to a differing degree.

Procedure

1 There were 36 male and 36 female participants in the study. Their age ranged from 37 to 69 months, and the mean age was just over 4 years.
2 Two adults, a male and a female, served in the role of model for the experiment. There were eight experimental groups (each with six participants in). Half the groups observed an aggressive role model and the other half saw non-aggressive behaviour from their role model. The groups were further subdivided by gender and whether the model was the same sex or opposite sex of the participants.
3 Participants were put into a room one at a time and observed the adult role model's behaviour (either aggressive or non-aggressive). In the room there was a Bobo doll (an inflatable doll that is weighted at the bottom), a hammer and other toys. The aggressive model had to hit the Bobo doll with the hammer and shout abuse at it at the same time. Examples of the abuse were 'Punch him in the nose', 'He sure is a tough fella' and 'Pow'.
4 After witnessing the behaviour for about 10 minutes participants were taken down the corridor to another room. Initially there was aggression arousal, whereby the participants were taken straight to a room where they were told they couldn't play with the toys as they were being saved for other children, but that they could play with the toys in a neighbouring room. They were then allowed to go into that room with the experimenter (about 2 minutes later) and play with any toys that they wanted.
5 The room contained a range of toys: a 3-foot Bobo doll, a mallet, dart guns, etc. and 'non aggressive toys' such as dolls, crayons and a plastic farm. The participants were observed in that room for 20 minutes and rated for the extent they imitated the behaviour they had just seen.

Results

They found that the children who had observed aggressive behaviour acted more aggressively when observed and that boys acted more aggressively than girls. There was also a greater level of imitation of behaviour if the role model was the same gender as the child.

Conclusion

It seems then that there is a behavioural effect from observing aggressive behaviour and that this behaviour continues after a delay.

Evaluation

The effects of social learning are still only short term in this experiment and it is difficult to see whether there are any long-term effects on the children.

There are issues with interpreting the behaviour as all being influenced by social learning. Most people would hit a Bobo doll as it is designed for this purpose. This affects the validity of the experiment.

○━━━━

RESEARCH IN FOCUS

1 Bandura used observations as his research method. What are the advantages of this method?
2 What are the disadvantages of this method?
3 Are there any ethical issues with Bandura's research?
4 How might Bandura's study have lacked validity?
5 How might Bandura's study have lacked reliability?

For information on research methods, see Chapter 7.

YOU ARE THE RESEARCHER

Bandura's research on the Bobo doll examined the immediate effect of observing a role model and imitation of the behaviour. However, it is criticised for looking at the short-term effects of witnessing aggression.

How would you test for long-term effects other than just putting the children, years later, back in the room with a Bobo doll? How could you test to see how aggressive they were as adults? Ensure your design is ethical!

For information on research methods, see Chapter 7.

Key concepts

The following terms relate to the social learning approach.

Imitation

This is the term used to describe when an individual observes a behaviour from a role model and copies it. The term imitation is more appropriate than copying as the behaviour is often not able to be copied exactly, it is merely a simulation.

Identification

Identification is when an individual is influenced by another because they are in some way similar or wish to be like them. The 'model' is the person with whom they identify. There are many factors influencing the choice of model by someone. These include same gender and ethnicity, higher status and greater expertise. These need not all be present but identification does not occur unless there is a reason.

Modelling

When someone is influential on an individual in some way, they are referred to in social learning theory as a model. If the individual then imitates that person's behaviour later it is called modelling the behaviour. This term is only used when referring to behaviour that is imitated.

Vicarious reinforcement

This is the term used to describe the reinforcement the observer sees the model receiving. They do not receive the reward themselves; they see someone else get it. A reinforcement, such as a reward, makes a behaviour more likely to happen again. When it is vicarious, the person learns by observing the consequences of another person's behaviour, e.g. a younger sister observing an older sister being rewarded for a particular behaviour is more likely to repeat that behaviour herself.

The role of mediating processes

We do not automatically observe the behaviour of a model and imitate it. There is some thought prior to imitation and this consideration is called mediational processes. This occurs between observing the behaviour (stimulus) and imitating it or not (response).

There are four mediational processes documented by Bandura (1977): *attention*, *retention*, *reproduction* and *motivation*.

Attention

For a behaviour to be imitated it has to grab our attention. We observe many behaviours on a daily basis and many of these are not noteworthy. Attention is therefore pivotal in whether a behaviour has an influence on others imitating it.

Retention

The behaviour may be noticed, but it is not always remembered, which obviously prevents imitation. It is important therefore that a memory of the behaviour is formed for it to be performed later by the observer. Much of social learning is not immediate so this process is especially vital in those cases. Even if the behaviour is reproduced shortly after seeing it there needs to be a memory to refer to.

Reproduction

We see much behaviour on a daily basis that we would like to be able to imitate but that is not always possible. We are limited by our physical ability and for that reason, even if we wish to reproduce the behaviour, we cannot. This influences our decision whether to try and imitate it or not. Imagine the scenario of a 90-year-old lady (who struggles to walk) watching *Dancing on Ice*. She may appreciate that the skill is a desirable one, but she will not attempt to imitate it because she physically cannot do it.

Motivation

The rewards and punishments that follow a behaviour will be considered by the observer. If the perceived rewards outweigh the perceived costs (if there are any) then the behaviour will be more likely to be imitated by the observer. If the vicarious reinforcement is not seen to be important enough to the observer then they will not imitate the behaviour.

For example, Natasha, a little girl trying on lipstick, illustrates these processes. Natasha notices her mum putting on lipstick prior to going out for the evening. She then hears her dad complimenting her mum on how she looks. She notices this (attention). She remembers where her mum keeps her make-up and how to open the lipstick (retention). She is also able to apply it (reproduction). She knows she will probably be told off but she wants to get compliments from her dad too and wants to look grown up like her mum, which is more important than the telling off (motivation). In all likelihood Natasha will imitate the behaviour.

- The social learning approach takes thought processes into account and acknowledges the role that they play in deciding if a behaviour is to be imitated or not.

- The approach can successfully explain the initiation of certain behaviours; this has been shown in examples such as why someone would start smoking.

- Learning theory is not a full explanation for all behaviour. This is particularly the case when there is no apparent role model in the person's life to imitate for a given behaviour. This occurs, for example, in the case of psychopathic behaviour in just one individual in a family.

- Social learning theorists use a variety of research methods in their work; this means that they can sometimes be criticised for being unscientific.

INCREASE YOUR KNOWLEDGE

Bandura acknowledged the role of biology in his work on social learning and aggression. He thought that there were biological urges to be aggressive, but that social learning taught the individual how and when to be aggressive.

Taking this into consideration, it can be argued that Bandura's work is a combination of three approaches: learning, biological and cognitive. It is generally seen as a learning approach because it describes a learning process, but the mediating processes are cognitive, and he acknowledges that biological urges and instincts do exist. The biological aspect of his work, however, is not a key element to the theory, whereas the learning and cognitive elements are.

STRENGTHEN YOUR LEARNING

1 What is meant by the term behaviourism?
2 What are the three ways you can learn behaviour included by this approach?
3 What is the difference between classical and operant conditioning?
4 What does vicarious reinforcement mean?
5 What is the difference between negative reinforcement and punishment?
6 What is the role of mediating processes?
7 What is modelling?
8 Explain how schedules of reinforcement affect response.
9 Explain the strengths of the learning approach.

ASSESSMENT CHECK

1 Johnny and Jamie are friends with Spencer. Spencer gets a tattoo of a skull and crossbones on his forearm on his eighteenth birthday and everyone at school said how cool it was. A month later, on his eighteenth birthday, Johnny also gets a tattoo, whereas Jamie, whose parents disapprove of tattoos, says he has no intention of ever getting one.

Explain how the social learning approach would explain why Johnny gets a tattoo and Jamie does not. **[4 marks]**

2 Outline and evaluate one learning approach. **[12 marks]**

3 Copy and complete the table below by writing which definition A, B, C or D describes which term. One definition will be left over. **[3 marks]**

   A Makes behaviour more likely to avoid a negative consequence

   B Makes behaviour more likely to get a reward

   C Makes behaviour less likely due to a negative consequence

   D Makes behaviour more likely to get a negative consequence

Term	Definition (A,B,C or D)
Positive reinforcement	
Punishment	
Negative reinforcement	

4 Describe how Skinner's research contributed to our understanding of learning behaviour. **[4 marks]**

5 Using the classical conditioning process, explain how someone may acquire a phobia of trains. **[3 marks]**

6 Researchers investigating operant conditioning in schools decided to use an independent groups design (Group A and Group B). They decided to use no punishment for late submission of homework with Group A and punishment for late submission of homework with Group B.

The number of late submissions in each group are shown in the table below.

Draw a graph for the results in the table. Ensure the axes are labelled and that there is a title for the graph. **[3 marks]**

Group	Number of late submissions
A	62
B	21

7 Discuss learning explanations of human behaviour. Use at least two alternative approaches as a comparison in your answer. **[16 marks]**

5.4 The cognitive approach

'If the Martians ever find out how human beings think, they'll kill themselves laughing.'

Albert Ellis (1962)

Mental processes

The foundation of the first cognitive school in 1959 by Ulric Neisser signalled the start of the cognitive psychology movement which is a major force in psychology. Cognitive psychologists believe that we must refer to thought processes in order to explain behaviour.

They make the following assumptions.

- Thought processes can be, and should be, studied scientifically. They therefore feel that introspection is too unscientific and that well controlled laboratory studies can investigate what we are thinking.
- The mind works like a computer in that it has an input from our senses which it then processes and produces an output such as language or specific behaviours.
- Stimulus and response is appropriate but only if the thought processes that occur between the stimulus and response are acknowledged (this is a direct criticism of behaviourism).

The study of internal mental processes

Cognitive psychologists endeavour to work out what thought processes are occurring from the behaviour an experiment elicits. They apply the scientific method and have worked out some clever ways in which to examine thought. Although we are aware of our thought processes, there are often times when we are actually unaware of what thoughts led us to behave a certain way and so the experimental conditions used widely by cognitive psychologists are really important in understanding those situations.

An example of lack of awareness is outlined in the Invisible Gorilla experiment below.

CLASSIC RESEARCH

Gorillas in our midst: Sustained inattentional blindness for dynamic events – Daniel J. Simons & Christopher F. Chabris (1999)

This is a classic example of a cognitive experiment designed to test the processes of perception and how they differ from person to person.

Aim

Simons & Chabris' experiment was designed to see how much individuals could be unaware of in their visual field. It seems that focused attention on a particular task could mean that other information could be missed. This experiment set out to test what is missed in a dynamic (moving) scene as previous research had focused on static stimuli.

Procedure:

1 There were 228 observers who watched the films shown. The films showed two teams of 3 basketball players, one team wearing white T-shirts and the other wearing black. An orange basketball was passed between the players and observers were asked to keep a tally of the number of passes. In one condition, the easy one, they were asked to keep a mental score of the number of passes. In the difficult condition they were asked to tally the number of throws and the number of bounces from player to player.

2 There were two types of video, transparent (where the film of the players was altered to be partly see-through) and opaque, where no such effect was used.

3 Half the observers watched films where a woman holding an umbrella walked in amongst the basketball players whilst they were playing. The other half watched films with a man in a black gorilla suit walking amongst the players.

There were therefore four film types:
- Transparent/Umbrella Woman
- Transparent/Gorilla
- Opaque/Umbrella Woman
- Opaque/Gorilla

4 Observers were then asked to immediately write their counts on paper and were also asked several questions, one of which was 'While you were doing the counting, did you notice anything unusual on the video?' Some results were discounted if the counting was inaccurate or the observer was aware of what the experimenters were testing. 192 results were included in the final analysis.

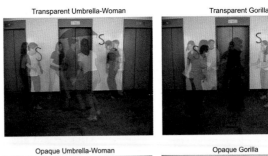
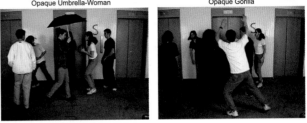

Figure 5.10a–d Stills from the films shown by Simons and Chabris. Figures provided by Daniel Simons.

Results

Simons and Chablis found that:

1 Only 54 per cent of the observers noticed the gorilla or the umbrella-carrying woman (unexpected event)
2 More observers noticed the unexpected event in the opaque condition
3 When the task was harder (transparent) slightly less of the observers noticed the unexpected event.

Conclusion

This seems to indicate that we miss much of what we see in our visual field due to inattention.

Evaluation

The results are robust as the experiment has been modified and rerun on many occasions and similar results found.

The experiment could be criticised for its lack of both mundane realism and ecological validity. The task is not an everyday scenario and the setting means it lacks ecological validity.

(This research was published in *Perception*, 28, 1059–74. See **www.dansimons.com** or **www.theinvisiblegorilla.com** for more information)

ON THE WEB

You can try the experiment, and various modifications of it, by searching YouTube for 'selective attention test' or 'The Monkey Business Illusion'.

However, you know about the gorilla. . . so it won't work on you! Try it on people who are unaware of the experiment.

Find out more from Daniel Simons' website:

www.dansimons.com

The role of schema

Schemas are a cognitive representation of our ideas about a person or situation. They are formed through experience and allow us to predict what may happen in our world. This seems to be important to us as humans.

Our schemas are unique to each individual as their experience of the world is unique to them. This ultimately means that the way we see the world is dependent on what has been experienced (or not), so thinking we all see things the same way is misguided. Our schemas mean we see our own version of reality. There is a cultural effect in that people from the same cultures form similar schemas due to shared experience. However, it is our personal experience that dictates the schemas we form.

KEY TERM

Schema – a collection of ideas about a person or situation formed through experience which helps the individual to understand and predict the world around them

This is best illustrated by an example, and memory lends itself particularly to examining the influence of schemas. This is covered in more detail in Chapter 2 (Cognitive psychology: memory). Bartlett's 1932 'War of the Ghosts' study illustrates how external influences can affect our memory of the event (see page 86).

Theoretical and computer models

Theoretical and computer models can be used to explain and make inferences about mental processes.

Cognitive psychology advocates the use of theoretical models as it supports a scientific approach to enquiry and testing. By taking a behaviour and looking at the thought processes that happen 'behind the scenes', cognitive psychologists will often describe the process in a series of distinct steps. This is well illustrated in memory with models such as the multi-store model of memory (see page 52).

This model has a series of steps which illustrate how a memory goes from sensory input to long-term memory. It shows how memories are forgotten as part of that process, and also how they get to pass on to the next stage. For example, they move from sensory memory to short-term memory when they are paid attention to.

The use of models means that the components can be tested individually and examined in detail. If the data from these experiments does not 'fit' with the model it can be adjusted. It also means that areas of the brain can be identified as specific to certain tasks, which supports the model (but only when it supports the model in question).

One of the core assumptions of the cognitive psychology approach is that the mind functions like a computer. However, how useful that comparison is debatable. There are both similarities and differences (see Figure 5.11 below) but many cognitive psychologists believe that, despite the differences, it is useful for the cognitive psychologist to use this analogy in their work.

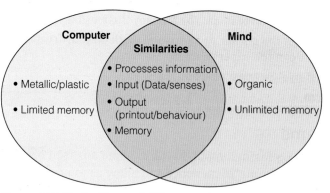

Figure 5.11 Similarities and differences between the mind and a computer

Information-processing model

The information-processing model is one way that cognitive psychologists apply the idea of computational models to the human mind and draws on the similarities between the two. This model dominated research in the 1980s and still has strong influence today.

The model is a three-stage process which is argued to explain behaviours. The general process is outlined below in Figure 5.12.

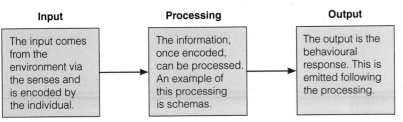

Figure 5.12 The information-processing model

This can be illustrated by an everyday example. Imagine Rob, a young man, is in a supermarket when he sees an old lady struggling to reach the top shelf for a packet of biscuits. He offers to get them down for her and reaches up for them.

The flow diagram in Figure 5.13 illustrates how the information-processing approach would be applied to this behaviour.

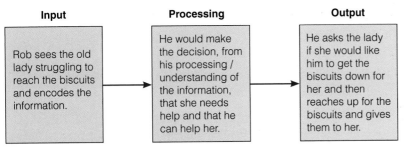

Figure 5.13 An example of the information-processing model

The use of theoretical models is part of this assumption that the human mind is like a computer. The way a computer works is by a series of processing steps, and cognitive psychologists see no reason why behaviour should not be explained the same way. Theoretical and computer models allow them to do this.

The emergence of cognitive neuroscience

Cognitive neuroscience is a discipline that is a combination of several other disciplines, notably cognitive psychology, cognitive science and neuroscience. Its main focus is to look for a biological basis to thought processes, specifically at how the neurons explain those processes.

The discipline has emerged as technology has advanced. This has meant that as scanning machines (see Biopsychology, Chapter 6) have advanced, so too has the ability to investigate how the brain activity might underpin thought.

Originally the discipline of cognitive science emerged from cognitive psychology as the search for biological influences progressed. Cognitive science formed formally at a meeting in the Massachusetts Institute of Technology (MIT) in 1956 where many papers that were presented used rigorous scientific methods. Using the word 'science' at that time distanced the discipline from psychology, which was perceived to lack a scientific stance. The discipline believed that it was necessary to consider physiological reasons for thought and that the mind/computer analogy was important in understanding how we think.

George Miller and Michael Gazzaniga first used the label 'cognitive neuroscience' about twenty years later following the recognition of neuroscience in 1971.Cognitive neuroscientists wanted to bridge the gap between cognitive science and neuroscience, hence the term cognitive neuroscience. The discipline has grown as technology has progressed and continues to be an important discipline today.

Evaluation

- The focus of the cognitive approach is on the importance of thought processes. Thought processes are generally agreed to have an influence on behaviour and have importance for understanding human behaviour.

- The cognitive approach uses experimental methods to research, which means the research has scientific rigour.

- The approach has produced some good descriptions of what processes occur, and this informs treatment (for example, the cognitive theory of depression and CBT, see Chapter 4, page 172).

- The use of laboratory experiments means that the research lacks validity as the thought processes measured could be argued to be artificial due to the context and tasks performed.

- The use of models can be seen as over-simplifying complex processes, for example, the role of emotion is sometimes overlooked.

- The approach is criticised for its comparison of people to computers, seeing people as mechanistic and lacking free will.

STRENGTHEN YOUR LEARNING

1 What is the role of schema?
2 What are three similarities between a computer and the mind?
3 What is the problem with using computer models to explain thought?
4 Explain the strengths of the cognitive approach.
5 What is one difference between the cognitive approach and the learning approach?
6 Explain the weaknesses of the cognitive approach.
7 What is meant by cognitive neuroscience?
8 Explain the information-processing model.
9 Explain the weaknesses of the cognitive approach.

ASSESSMENT CHECK

1 Complete the table below by writing which definition A, B, C or D describes which term. One definition will be left over. **[3 marks]**

   A This comes from the environment and is the first stage of the information-processing model.

   B The format (e.g. visual) our memories are stored in

   C A cognitive representation of our world

   D This could be our behaviour and is the third stage of the information-processing model.

Term	Definition (A, B, C or D)
Schema	
Input	
Output	

2 Outline and evaluate the cognitive approach. **[12 marks]**

3 Explain the difference between cognitive psychology and cognitive neuroscience. **[3 marks]**

4 Joey lacks confidence when he goes on nights out with his friends. Even if a girl he likes comes to talk to him, he doesn't believe that she is attracted to him. His friends try to encourage him, but he doubts that he will ever find a girlfriend.

   With reference to the passage, explain how the cognitive approach would explain Joey's situation. **[4 marks]**

5 Discuss how well the theoretical and computational models can be applied to human behaviour. **[16 marks]**

6 Researchers investigating the cognitive biases of gamblers decided to ask participants to say out loud what they were thinking while playing on a roulette wheel at a casino. They recorded what the participants said using a small microphone. They then analysed the recordings using content analysis.

   Explain why the methodology used could be argued to lack validity. **[4 marks]**

7 Discuss the cognitive approach to understanding human behaviour. Use at least two alternative approaches as a comparison in your answer. **[16 marks]**

SUMMARY

- Wundt's work is some of the first work done under the term 'psychology'. He used introspection in his work to examine the thoughts of his participants.
- Over the years, psychology has emerged as a scientific discipline due to the research methods used to investigate thought and behaviour.
- The biological approach assumes that behaviour is generated by genetics, brain physiology and biochemistry.
- The genotype of the individual is affected by the environment they live in. The product of that interaction is called the phenotype.
- Twin studies can be useful in ascertaining the extent to which genetics influences behaviour. Comparison of the concordance rates of identical and non-identical twins can give us an indication of how much genetics has had an influence.
- Biological psychologists believe that evolution has fine-tuned our behaviour to what is currently displayed. Some behaviours are believed to be adaptive and it is those behaviours that are successful in continuing through generations.
- The nervous system is divided into the central nervous system (the brain and spinal cord) and the peripheral nervous system, which is the nervous system throughout the rest of the body. Neurons are the messengers of the nervous system.
- The endocrine system transmits messages throughout the body using hormones.
- Learning theorists believe behaviour is learned from the environment. This is done in three ways: classical conditioning, operant conditioning and social learning.
- Learning theorists believe that only observable behaviour should be studied and that it is reasonable to use animals to study human behaviour as the same principles apply.
- Classical conditioning is when an association is made between a previous neutral stimuli and a strong emotion.
- Operant conditioning is learning behaviour from consequences received. The most successful way is using positive reinforcement (reward) sporadically.
- Social learning is when behaviour is learned through seeing a role model receive reinforcement for the way they behave.
- Skinner is well known for his work on operant conditioning with rats and pigeons.
- Bandura is well known for his work on observational learning in children using a Bobo doll. It was from this work that his social learning theory developed.
- Cognitive psychology assumes that thought processes underpin behaviour and that the mind works like a computer.
- Schemas are a collection of ideas about the world formed through experience which helps the individual to understand and predict the world around them.
- Cognitive psychologists use theoretical and computer models to understand what thought processes underlie an action or reaction.
- The information-processing model is one such model and likens human thought processes to a computer, with an input which is processed through to an output.
- Cognitive neuroscience has emerged as a discipline from out of cognitive psychology, mainly due to technological advances in brain-scanning technology.

Origins of psychology

The biological approach

The learning approaches

The cognitive approach

Biopsychology for AS and A-level

Introduction

Unsurprisingly, biopsychology as a discipline focuses on explaining behaviour biologically. This can be done in several ways, but the three core ways are: genetics, brain physiology and biochemistry. Chapter 5 (pages 199–204) discussed the use of genetics to explain behaviour. This chapter will predominantly focus on brain physiology and biochemistry.

The basic assumptions of biopsychology were also discussed in the previous chapter, alongside some of the core knowledge which will help you with this chapter. Make sure you are familiar with that content prior to reading and learning this chapter.

This chapter will cover the following areas of the specification:

- The structure and function of bodily systems, for example, the nervous and endocrine systems
- The structure and function of neurons and the synapse
- The fight-or-flight response, including the role of adrenaline.

Please note that the following sections are needed for the **A-level only**:

- The structure of the brain and localisation of function
- Ways of studying the brain
- Biological rhythms: the types and the regulators of the rhythms.

Understanding the specification

- For this part of the specification the emphasis is very much about understanding rather than evaluating. Follow the wording of the specification very closely as, if it is mentioned, it can be asked about specifically.
- You will need to know how to outline *the divisions of the nervous system* including both the central and peripheral (somatic and autonomic) systems but within the peripheral system you could also be asked about the somatic and autonomic divisions.
- You could also be asked about *the structure and function of sensory, relay and motor neurons*.
- Describing *the process of synaptic transmission*, ensuring you can refer to neurotransmitters, excitation and inhibition, is also important to know.
- You will need to know *the function of the endocrine system* including the glands and hormones within the system.
- You need to understand *the systems involved in the fight-or-flight response*, and be able to write about *the role of adrenaline*.

These are the basic requirements of the specification. However, other relevant material is included in this chapter to provide depth and detail to your understanding.

For A-level only:

- In terms of the brain physiology, you should know about *localisation* (particularly the motor, somatosensory, visual, auditory and language centres; Broca's and Wernicke's areas) and *hemispheric lateralisation*. *Split-brain research* is mentioned specifically, as is *plasticity* and *functional recovery of the brain after trauma*.

- You need to be able to describe and evaluate ways of studying the brain. These are specifically named as *scanning techniques* such as *functional magnetic resonance imaging* (fMRI), *electroencephalogram* (EEGs) and *event-related potentials* (ERPs), together with *post-mortem examinations*.

- Finally you should know about *biological rhythms*. You should know how to define and give examples of *circadian*, *infradian* and *ultradian*. You should also understand the difference between these rhythms. Similarly you need to be able to define, describe and evaluate the effect of *endogenous pacemakers* and *exogenous zeitgebers* on the sleep/wake cycle.

6.1 The influence of biological structures on behaviour: the divisions of the nervous system

'Physics investigates the essential nature of the world, and biology describes a local bump. Psychology, human psychology, describes a bump on the bump.'

Willard Van Orman Quine (1969)

The nervous system of humans is divided into the **central nervous system (CNS)** and the **peripheral nervous system (PNS)**.

The CNS comprises the brain and spinal cord and the PNS is the nerves outside the brain and spinal cord. From these two initial divisions, the system divides further.

The CNS

The brain is involved in psychological processes and its main job is to ensure life is maintained. There are many parts to the brain, some of which are more primitive and concerned with vital functioning. Others are involved in higher order thinking such as problem solving and planning.

KEY TERMS

Central nervous system (CNS) – this system comprises the brain and spinal cord

Peripheral nervous system (PNS) – this system includes all of the nervous system throughout the rest of the body

The spinal cord facilitates the transferral of messages to and from the brain to the peripheral nervous system (PNS). It is also involved in reflex actions such as the startle response.

The PNS

The PNS extends beyond the CNS and transmits messages to the whole body from the brain and vice versa. It has two divisions: the somatic system and the autonomic system.

The somatic system's main job is to transmit and receive messages from the senses such as visual information from the eyes and auditory information from the ears. It also directs muscles to react and move.

The autonomic system helps transmit and receive information from the organs and is further divided into two systems: the sympathetic system (which increases activity) and the parasympathetic system (which conserves the body's natural activity levels by decreasing activity or maintaining it). There is more information on the sympathetic and parasympathetic systems later in this chapter (see page 231).

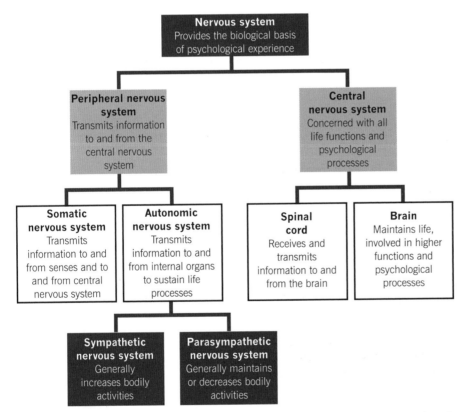

Figure 6.1 Divisions of the nervous system, with an indication of the function of each division

6.2 The structure and function of sensory, relay and motor neurons

Neurons receive information and transmit it to other cells. There are thought to be around 100 billion neurons in the brain and 1 billion neurons in the spinal cord. Neurons are an essential part of a massive communication system within the body.

There are three main types of neurons, all of which have a different role to play. See Table 6.1 which summarises the structure and function of these neurons.

Table 6.1 The three main types of neuron

Neuron type	Function	Structure
Sensory	These neurons tell the rest of the brain about the external and internal environment by processing information taken from one of the five senses.	The cellular structure of all neurons is the same. There are anatomical differences in size depending on their function, e.g. the axons of motor neurons can be very long. 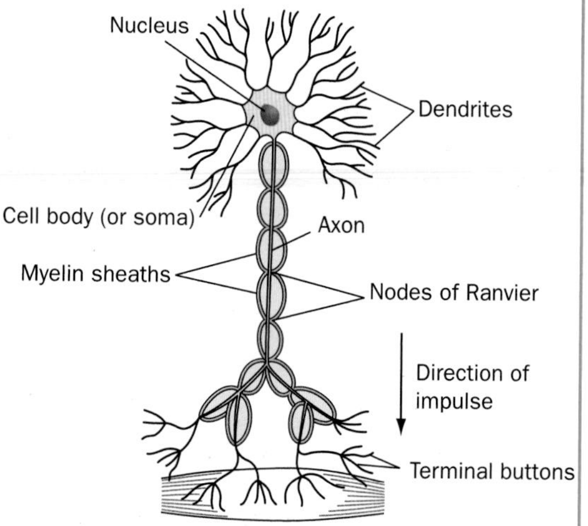
Relay	Relay neurons carry messages from one part of the CNS to another. They connect motor and sensory neurons.	
Motor	Motor neurons carry signals from the CNS which helps both organs, including glands and muscles, function.	

Figure 6.2 The structure of a neuron, showing dendrites, cell body, axon, nucleus, nodes of ranvier and schwann cells

As Table 6.1 states, the structure of the neurons is the same but the components will vary, depending on the role within the nervous system and location in the body.

Figure 6.3 below shows the anatomical differences. Essentially, as sensory neurons only transmit messages, they are known as unipolar neurons. Both motor and relay neurons are multipolar, as they send and receive messages from many sources. This has meant much variation anatomically.

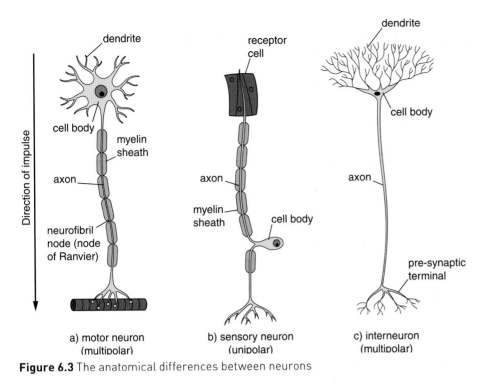

Figure 6.3 The anatomical differences between neurons

In all neurons, the dendrite/receptor cell receives the signal and it then travels through the neuron to the pre-synaptic terminal.

INCREASE YOUR KNOWLEDGE

Santiago Ramón y Cajal (1852–1934)

Cajal was a pioneer in the field of neuroscience and is known for his biological illustrations and work on cell structure and systems.

Cajal had a strict upbringing, often being flogged at school for not paying full attention in Latin class, given just one meal a day and confined in a cell alone.

He wanted to be an artist but his father insisted he study medicine as it was considered to be a more stable profession. His illustrations, however, allowed him to use his drawing skills in his professional life.

He used the technique of using silver salts to stain infant cells and discovered that nerve cells are not actually joined together as first thought. His work has therefore been very influential in understanding the synapse, which is the gap between neurons.

Figure 6.4 Santiago Ramón y Cajal

The process of synaptic transmission

Synaptic transmission is the process for transmitting messages from neuron to neuron. The synapse is a specialised 'gap' between neurons through which the electrical impulse from the neuron is transmitted chemically.

Initially, the electrical nerve impulse travels down the neuron and prompts release of neurotransmitters (chemicals in the brain) at the pre-synaptic terminal. These chemicals are then released into the synaptic fluid in the synapse. The adjacent neuron must then quickly take up the neurotransmitters from the fluid and convert them to an electrical impulse to travel down the neuron to the next pre-synaptic terminal. And so the impulse continues to be transmitted on.

KEY TERM

Synaptic transmission – the process by which nerve impulses are carried across the small gap, the synapse, between one neuron and another. The nerve impulse is an electrical signal which is carried by chemicals called neurotransmitters

This occurs at high speed. For example, when processing visual information, most of the information seems to be encoded in the first 50–100 milliseconds of neuronal activity.

ON THE WEB

Searching YouTube for 'Neuron Synapse' will take you to an animation of how the synapse works. It talks you through excitatory and inhibitory synapse. It will also give you a little extra information if you need it.

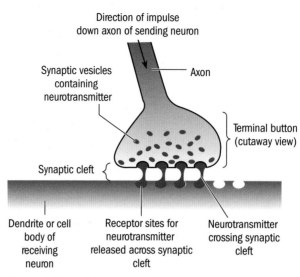

Figure 6.5 A typical synapse between two neurons. The nerve impulse travels from the pre-synaptic neuron, across the synaptic cleft, to the post-synaptic neuron

Research

Yamamoto & Kitazawa (2001) examined why we cannot easily perceive when we are touched in two places simultaneously. So, for example, if someone touches you on your shoulder and your toe at exactly the same time it feels as if each is being touched at a slightly different time. Conversely, you sometimes can't tell, if they are touched at a slightly delayed difference in time, which was touched first. This is argued to be because of the inability of the nervous system to transmit that information accurately as the distance from the brain for the neurons receiving the message is different.

Excitation and inhibition

It should be noted, however, that not all messages prompt activation in the same way. It depends on the 'action potential' of the post-synaptic neuron and the message type received.

Only certain neurotransmitters can 'unlock' a message channel in certain receptors in the post-synaptic neuron. It is a kind of lock and key system. When the right key (neurotransmitter) meets the right lock (receptor) a specific ion channel in the membrane is opened up, a bit like a door. Ions then flow through the membrane into the neuron along their specific pathways. This flooding of ions can cause a 'potential' in the dendrites. These potentials can be excitatory or inhibitory.

- **Excitatory potentials** make it more likely for the neuron to fire and so, if a synapse is more likely to cause the post-synaptic neuron to fire so, it is called an excitatory synapse.
- **Inhibitory potentials** make it less likely to fire and, if the message is likely to be stopped at the post-synaptic neuron, it is called an inhibitory synapse.

A good analogy to understand the role of excitation and inhibition is the pedals of a car. An excitatory potential is like the accelerator and an inhibitory potential is like the brake.

KEY TERMS

Excitatory potentials – increase the chance of a neuron firing

Inhibitory potentials – decrease the chance of a neuron firing

6.3 The influence of neurochemistry on behaviour: the function of the endocrine system

The endocrine system has a series of glands which release chemicals (hormones) throughout the body via the blood and other bodily fluids. This communicates, much like the neurons do, messages to the organs of the body.

There are specialist glands in the body which form part of this system. Their location in the body is shown in Figure 6.6.

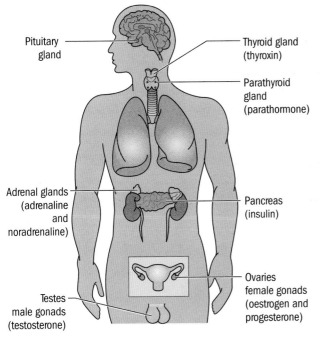

Pituitary gland

Thyroid gland (thyroxin)

Parathyroid gland (parathormone)

Adrenal glands (adrenaline and noradrenaline)

Pancreas (insulin)

Ovaries female gonads (oestrogen and progesterone)

Testes male gonads (testosterone)

Figure 6.6 The endocrine system, showing the major glands in the human body

The functions of several hormones are shown in Table 6.2 below.

Table 6.2 Functions of some glands and hormones

Gland	Function
Pituitary	Some of the hormones released are important for regulating the endocrine system, hence the nickname 'master gland'
Adrenal	An important part of the fight-or-flight response as it facilitates the release of adrenaline
Testes	They facilitate the release of testosterone (male hormone)
Ovaries	They facilitate the release of oestrogen and progesterone (female hormones)

Behaviour is thought to be influenced by hormones, and each hormone is thought to affect behaviour in a different way.

Research

The hormone oxytocin, released by the pituitary gland, is thought to be particularly important for reproductive behaviour. It is released following orgasm, which aids conception, and elicits a feeling of relaxation and calm. Research by Kosfeld *et al* (2005) also found that high levels of oxytocin encourage strong bonding between couples. This is also the case for mother/child bonding (Feldman *et al*, 2007).

Thus it can be seen that hormonal levels can affect behaviour to some extent.

Another example of a behavioural effect from a hormone, adrenaline, is outlined in the following section.

6.4 The fight-or-flight response, including the role of adrenaline

The fight-or-flight response is generated from the autonomic nervous system, specifically the sympathetic branch. It is a reflex response designed to help an individual manage physically when under threat. It is also activated in times of stress as the body perceives stress to be a threat.

The fight-or-flight helps an individual to react quicker than normal and facilitates optimal functioning so that they can fight the threat or run away from it.

This occurs in a series of steps:

KEY TERMS

Hypothalamus – a part of the brain which is located in the centre of the brain and deals with basic survival functions

Adrenal gland – the gland in the adrenal system that releases adrenaline

Adrenal medulla – the central part of the adrenal gland

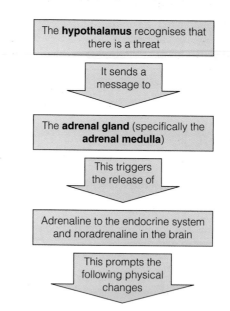

Increased heart rate	To speed up the blood flow to vital organs and improve the spread of adrenaline around the body
Faster breathing rate	To increase oxygen intake
Muscle tension	To improve reaction time and speed
Pupil dilation	To improve vision
The production of sweat	To facilitate temperature regulation
Reduced functioning of the digestive and immune systems	To save energy for prioritised functions, such as running

Figure 6.7 The fight-or-flight response

These physical changes help an individual to fight or run away from the potentially threatening situation.

Evaluation

- Assessing the extent to which biological structures affect behaviour is very difficult. It can be argued that they are merely the 'tools' to make the behaviour happen rather than being the cause. Cause and effect cannot be established in most research. This is because much of the research is correlational. This means that only the relationship between the biological influence and the behaviour can be investigated. For example, research on hormones is problematic for this reason. We can say that there is a relationship between increased relationship intensity and oxytocin levels, but not that oxytocin causes the relationship to be more intense. It is equally plausible that a behaviour such as forming a relationship might mean levels of oxytocin increase, rather than the high levels altering the behaviour.

- The argument that it is the biological structures that underpin behaviour can be seen as reductionist. This means that it attempts to reduce human behaviour and cognitive processes down to biological processes. Within the biological processes there is a further reduction down to a specific component, such as the level of a hormone. Many psychologists argue that this is too simplistic.

- The physical nature of the bodily systems means that research can be said to be scientific as the measures are totally objective and therefore opinion or judgement do not play a part. This increases the reliability of the results.

PSYCHOLOGY IN THE REAL WORLD

A possible clinical use for the calming effects of oxytocin to treat anorexia nervosa – Youl-Ri Kima *et al* (2014)

A small-scale study in the UK found that when administered with doses of oxytocin, sufferers of anorexia nervosa had a reduction in focus of the fat on their bodies and negative images of food.

Anorexia is a complicated illness, with many differing components to it, but the idea that a hormone which occurs naturally in the body could alleviate some of the suffering, is an interesting development.

Professor Janet Treasure, who led the research, made it clear that the research is in its early stages and that there is no 'oxytocin' treatment available for those with the illness. Work is continuing with a view to developing a possible drug treatment.

STRENGTHEN YOUR LEARNING

1 What is the function of a motor neuron?
2 What is the function of a relay neuron?
3 What is the function of a sensory neuron?
4 What is the job of synaptic transmission?
5 What is the difference between excitation and inhibition in neurons?
6 Adrenaline is released from which gland?
7 Does research support the idea that oxytocin has an effect on behaviour?
8 Explain how the fight-or-flight response occurs.
9 Explain one issue with investigating the role of biological structures on behaviour.
10 What is the difference between the central and peripheral nervous systems?

ASSESSMENT CHECK

1 Explain what the function of a neuron is. **[2 marks]**

2 Explain the process of synaptic transmission. **[4 marks]**

3 Copy and complete the table below by writing which definition A, B, C or D describes which term. One definition will be left over. **[3 marks]**

   A This carries signals from the CNS to the muscles and organs.

   B This relays information about the environment.

   C These are only found in the brain.

   D This neuron connects other neurons.

Term	Definition (A, B, C or D)
Sensory neuron	B
Motor neuron	A
Relay neuron	D C

4 Using an example, describe the function of the endocrine system. **[4 marks]**

5 Paul does not like rollercoasters. His mouth goes dry, his heart beats fast and he sweats in the queue while waiting for the ride. With reference to the fight-or-flight response, explain why his body reacts this way. **[4 marks]**

6 Discuss the influence of biological structures on behaviour. **[16 marks]**

7 Research on biological structures is argued to be reliable. Briefly explain why the research is described in this way. **[2 marks]**

8 Outline and evaluate the role of biological structures in explaining human behaviour. **[12 marks]**

6.5 Localisation of function in the brain

The human brain has two hemispheres which are bridged by the corpus callosum. This 'bridge', which is a bundle of fibres, is effectively a communication pathway so that the two hemispheres can exchange information.

Mapping the brain for function, that is which bit does what, is an on-going process, but there is now sufficient evidence to know the function of certain parts of the brain.

KEY TERMS

Localisation – in terms of the brain, this means the part of the brain in which a function is carried out

Contralateral – when the right hemisphere deals with the left-hand side of the body and vice versa

CLASSIC CASE STUDY

An Odd Kind of Fame: Stories of Phineas Gage – Malcolm Macmillan (2002)

The case study of Phineas Gage

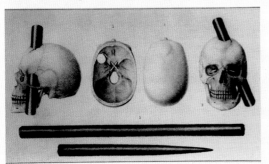

Figure 6.8 The skull of Phineas Gage

Localisation of brain function in the years prior to brain imaging was derived from case studies of people who had suffered brain trauma. One of the most well-known cases was Phineas Gage.

Phineas Gage was a railway worker in the USA, whose job required using dynamite to blast a clear path for railway track construction. He needed to place the dynamite in position and then use a metre-long iron rod with a diameter of one inch (a couple of centimetres) to bed the dynamite in place using sand. The rod was called a tamping iron.

One day, the rod caused a spark and the dynamite blew up, blasting the rod through Phineas' chin and out through the top of his forehead. Immediately after the accident Phineas was conscious and could speak. He was treated by a local doctor but suffered badly over the next few weeks from an infection in the wound.

Eventually he recovered very well physically, with no apparent effect on his functioning other than losing the sight in his left eye. He also obviously had scarring from the injury.

However, psychologically he was a very changed man. Before the accident he was reported to be calm and well-mannered but following the accident he exhibited unreliable, hostile and rude behaviour. He also used vulgar language which he never did prior to the injury.

At that time, there were two schools of thought about the brain. One believed that the brain did not have localisation of function, but that all parts were similar. The other opinion was that it did have localisation. Dr Bigelow from Harvard University subscribed to the first viewpoint, that there was no localisation, and used Phineas' recovery to support that idea. He believed that the rest of the brain had compensated for the damaged part and so therefore the brain was multi-functional throughout. He did, however, largely ignore the personality change.

Conversely, Dr Harlow, the physician who originally treated Gage, believed that there was localisation in the brain and that the area that had been damaged in Gage housed the planning, reasoning and control of the individual. He was proved to be correct in subsequent research into localisation.

(Reference: Macmillan, M. (2002) *An Odd Kind of Fame: Stories of Phineas Gage*. Cambridge, MA: MIT Press)

Hemispheric lateralisation

The brain is **contralateral** (opposite sides) in most people; so parts of the left hemisphere deal with the right side of the body and the right hemisphere does the same for the left side of the body. This means if a person has a stroke in the motor areas of their right hemisphere it will be the left-hand side of the body which is affected by the stroke. It is also the case that what you see in your right visual field is processed by your left hemisphere and although you gather auditory information from both ears, the information from the left ear is dealt with predominantly by the right hemisphere of the brain.

RESEARCH IN FOCUS

1. Give two advantages of using case studies.
2. Give two disadvantages of using case studies.
3. Apart from loss of function, what could account for Phineas' change in behaviour after the accident?

For information on research methods, see Chapter 7.

Taste and smell are also contralateral: taste from your left side of your tongue and smells from your left nostril are processed in the right hemisphere.

Why humans, other vertebrates (and also many invertebrates) are contralateral is not known.

If a function is dealt with by one hemisphere it is said to be lateralised. So the division of functions between the two hemispheres is called **hemispheric lateralisation**. The hemispheres are not symmetrical and this is because the functions of the two differ.

Left hemisphere

For most people their language processing is done in the left hemisphere. Therefore, for many people, if they have a stroke on the left side of their brain, their speech is affected. Areas such as Broca's area and Wernicke's area are found, for most people, on the left side of the brain. This is discussed in more detail later in the chapter (see Language centres, page 237).

Right hemisphere

Recognising

The right hemisphere seems to be particularly dominant for recognising emotions in others (Narumoto *et al.*, 2001). Work has shown that, if a photo of a face that has been split so that one half is smiling and the other is neutral, is shown to someone, the emotion displayed in the left-hand side of the picture is the emotion recognised by the participant (Heller & Levy, 1981). This is probably because their right hemisphere is dominant for this task. Don't forget that your left visual field is processed by the right side of the brain.

Spatial relationships

A case study of a woman who had right hemisphere damage highlighted that the right hemisphere seems more adept at spatial relationships. The woman would often get lost, even in familiar situations, unless she had verbal instructions which contained a distinguishable visual feature to follow such as 'turn right at the red house with the turret'. This suggests that the right hemisphere deals with spatial information (Clarke, Assal & de Tribolet, 1993).

Overall differences

If you ask somebody to look at a picture and to identify the small detail there will be a greater level of activity in the left hemisphere than if they look at the picture holistically (all together), which prompts more activity in the right hemisphere (Fink, Halligan *et al.*, 1996). This suggests that the left hemisphere focuses on detail and the right hemisphere processes overall patterns.

Motor centres

1. Motor cortex

Movement is centred on the primary motor cortex of the brain which sends messages to the muscles via the brain stem and spinal cord. The motor cortex is particularly important for complex movement and not basic actions such as coughing, crying or gagging.

KEY TERM

Hemispheric lateralisation – this is when one hemisphere carries out a particular function

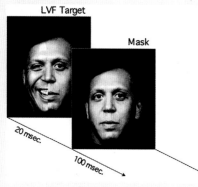

Figure 6.9 An example of the stimuli Narumoto would have used. This image is from Levy, J.,Heller, W., Banich, M. T., Burton, L. A., 'Asymmetgry of perception in free viewing of chimeric faces', 404-419 (1983) *Brain and Coqnition 2/4*

Within the motor cortex there are areas which control specific parts of the body. This is shown in Figure 6.10.

The diagram illustrates the approximate position of the neurons designated to specific areas of the body. Note that there is no relationship between the size of the area of the body and the number of neurons involved. This is due to the complexity of movement in the area dictating how many neurons are needed. For example, although the trunk is a large area of the body, it does not need to complete complex movements, just twisting and bending, so therefore does not need much of the brain to control it.

When the motor cortex instructs an outcome it is the spinal cord and other areas which co-ordinate all the various areas of the body into a movement.

There are other areas of the brain which are involved in movement. These are summarised in Table 6.3 below.

Table 6.3 Areas of the brain involved in movement

Spinal cord and brain	Co-ordinate movements
Premotor cortex	Plans a movement prior to executing it
Prefrontal cortex	Stores sensory information prior to a movement and works out the probable outcome of the movement

2. Somatosensory centres

Somatosensory is referring to the sensation of the body. The somatosensory cortex lies next to the motor cortex in the brain. It perceives touch, so the amount of neuronal connections needed dictates the amount of somatosensory cortex needed for that area of the body. It is clear from Figure 6.10 that touch-sensitive areas such as the face require a larger proportion of the somatosensory cortex than say the trunk, which does not require a high level of sensitivity.

3. Visual centres

Primary visual cortex

The brain has two visual cortices, one in each hemisphere.

The primary visual cortex is in the occipital lobe, which is at the back of the brain. This is seen to be the main visual centre. With that centre, it is specifically an area called Area V1 which seems to be necessary for visual perception. Individuals with damage to that area report no vision of any kind: conscious vision, visual imagery while awake *or* in their dreams (Hurovitz *et al.*, 1999).

The visual information is transmitted along two pathways, one containing the components of the visual field and the other being involved in the location within the visual field.

Research

Occasionally individuals with damage to Area V1 will show 'blindsight'. This is a condition where someone appears qualitatively blind, in that they report no vision, but they can locate objects in a visual field by pointing at them. This seems to suggest that some of the processing in the visual cortex is not conscious (Bridgeman & Staggs, 1982).

The following contemporary case study illustrates this well.

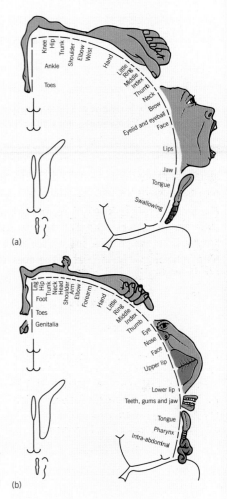

(a)

(b)

Figure 6.10 Representation of different parts of the human body on the motor cortex (a) and somatosensory cortex. Notice that the face and hands take up more than half of the cortices

Visual experience and blindsight: a
methodological review – Overgaard *et al.* (2008)

This case study is about a 31-year-old woman, GR, who experienced the phenomenon called 'blindsight'.

GR had been experiencing headaches over a period of 3 months. These suddenly got worse and she developed blindness in her right visual field. CT scanning showed a haemorrhage in the left occipital lobe.

The brain started to swell more, and a drain was put in to allow the fluid to exit the skull. An operation followed which left her in intensive care. She started to recover function but although she had no injuries to the eyes, the brain was damaged in the visual cortex, which meant she was cortically blind.

Her vision was tested at 3 weeks after the operation. She remained blind a year later.

However, in tests asking her to detect a letter shown on a screen, she could not identify the letter but she did report 'awareness of something', despite *seeing* nothing. This pattern continued with many of the stimuli, and, when tested statistically, there was found to be a significant relationship between awareness of stimuli and accuracy. GR was argued to have blindsight.

This suggests that there may be two types of vision, one conscious and the other unconscious.

4. Auditory centres

Primary auditory cortex

The human brain has two primary auditory cortices, one in each hemisphere.

The primary auditory cortex in both hemispheres receives information from both ears via two pathways that transmit information about what the sound is and its location (in a similar way to how the visual information gets passed to the visual cortex). The information from the right ear goes primarily to the left hemisphere but some is transmitted to the left primary auditory cortex too. This happens in the same way with information from the left ear.

If the primary auditory cortex is damaged it does not lead to total deafness. Sounds can still be heard but if they require complex processing such as music, then this ability is no longer present.

Research

The primary cortex is not just involved with conscious sound. It also processes auditory imagery, so, for example, Meyer *et al.* (2010) found that when people watch silent films their primary auditory cortex in both hemispheres will activate if a door is shut with force, for example, because they are imagining the bang.

5. Language centres – Broca's and Wernicke's areas

In most people, Broca's and Wernicke's areas are in the left hemisphere, and that is where most language processing in the majority of the population is situated.

Broca's area

Broca's work (see the classic case study on page 238) therefore correctly identified the area of the brain responsible for speech production.

Not all words are affected equally in this area of the brain. Nouns and verbs seem relatively unaffected in some patients with damage in Broca's area, but other classes of words, such as prepositions and conjunctions, cannot be spoken. For example, people with Broca's aphasia can't read out loud 'To be or not to be' but can say 'Two bee oar knot two bee' (Gardner & Zurif, 1975).

Mysterious 'Monsieur Leborgne': The Mystery of the Famous Patient in the History of Neuropsychology is Explained' – Domanski (2013)

The case study of Leborgne: Broca's area

Louis Victor Leborgne was the son of a schoolteacher in France and suffered with epilepsy throughout his childhood. He worked as a craftsman and was educated. He eventually lost the ability to speak (other than say the word Tan) and was hospitalised at the age of 30. He stayed in hospital until his death in 1861 at the age of 51.

In the hospital he was treated by a neurologist called Paul Broca. Following Leborgne's death, Broca conducted a post-mortem on his brain. He found a lesion (area of damage) on the left temporal lobe. As this was the only visible site of damage he concluded that it was the area responsible for production of speech, based on the deficit Leborgne exhibited.

This is a robust finding and Paul Broca correctly identified the function of that area. The term Broca's aphasia is used today to describe patients with problems producing speech.

Leborgne's brain has also been preserved and kept in the Musée Dupuytren museum in Paris. It has been scanned using modern day technology and, although the damage is more extensive than that documented by Broca, the area identified as responsible for speech production is correctly localised.

Further information on the case can be seen at: Domanski, C.W. (2013) Mysterious 'Monsieur Leborgne': The Mystery of the Famous Patient in the History of Neuropsychology is Explained. *Journal of the History of the Neurosciences*, 22 (1), 47–52 PMID: 23323531.

RESEARCH IN FOCUS

1. What are the disadvantages of using a post-mortem examination (like Broca's research used) to establish brain localisation?
2. What are the advantages of using post-mortem examination in brain localisation research?

For information on research methods, see Chapter 7.

Wernicke's area

This is a separate area of language processing which seems to have a specific function. In 1874, Karl Wernicke, who worked at a hospital in Germany, found that patients who had damage in an area close to the auditory cortex had specific language impairments. These included the inability to comprehend language and anomia, which is when someone struggles to find the word they need. However, Wernicke noticed that these people did have fluent speech, when they could access the words quickly. This led Wernicke to suggest that the area now called Wernicke's area was important for understanding language and accessing words.

Figure 6.11 shows where these two areas are located.

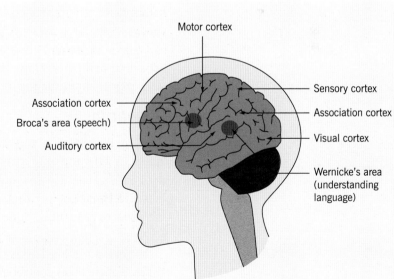

Figure 6.11 Broca's area and other localisation of cortical function

- The holistic theory of brain function argues that localisation of function is largely incorrect. Work by Lashley (1950) on rats' brains did not find a specific area involved in memory. It appeared to be stored all over the brain. This would suggest that the idea of specific areas performing specific functions is a misnomer. However, caution should be used when generalising this to humans, due to physiological differences.

- Evidence from case studies of individuals with brain damage seems to indicate there is both localisation and lateralisation of function. If function was spread out throughout the entire brain there would not be specific deficits such as loss of speech function in people that had suffered damage in some way.

- It can be argued that the fact that rehabilitation can work following brain injury suggests that there is no localisation or lateralisation. If there were task-specific areas then there would be no brain plasticity (function regained by using other parts of the brain). On page 242 the case study of EB, who had his left hemisphere removed during surgery, yet regained most of his language abilities, would seem to imply that there is no lateralisation and localisation of function (in this case language). However, it could equally be argued that as he never fully recovered function there is some localisation with certain areas of the brain. It should also be noted that a case study can only provide evidence, not proof.

Split-brain research

The corpus callosum, as stated previously (page 235), is the link between the hemispheres. In people who suffer from epilepsy, and are not helped by drug treatment, brain surgery is considered as an option because the epilepsy is generated by a focus area in the brain. By removing that area the epilepsy can be eradicated or reduced. However, in a small number of people with drug-resistant epilepsy, there is more than one focus so the areas cannot be removed. This has led surgeons in the past to cut the corpus callosum so that the epilepsy is contained within one hemisphere of the brain. This has the knock-on effect of reducing the number of fits suffered by the patient as the hemispheres rebounding off each other can prompt seizures.

However, although severing the communication between the hemispheres can reduce the effect epilepsy has on someone, there are effects on their behaviour and perception. These 'split-brain' patients can also tell us to some extent about the role of each hemisphere.

Research

Work by Roger Sperry and colleagues (Nebes, 1974) documented the effects on the functioning of these individuals. Their findings are as follows.

- Certain unfamiliar functions such as stringing beads onto a piece of thread cannot be performed, yet very familiar actions such as tying shoelaces can still be done.

- In the first few weeks after surgery the hemispheres act separately, making the person feel like two people in one body (Dimond, 1979). The left hemisphere takes control of situations and suppresses interference from the right hemisphere by using smaller pathways that connect the hemispheres. It is an adaptive process.

- In some patients the hemispheres co-operate with each other. For example, if a colour is shown to the left visual field then the right hemisphere can see it, but the left cannot articulate the colour. As the left hemisphere is responsible for speech, when the person is asked what the colour is the left hemisphere will guess, as it cannot see it. The right hemisphere knows the answer, but cannot speak, so indicates that the answer is wrong by prompting a frown.

- Some patients compensate for the lack of connectivity of the two hemispheres by using strategies such as turning their heads so both hemispheres can take in the environment.

Work conducted has helped understand the function of the hemispheres and how they communicate. However, although there were successes in this line of work the fact that there are two functioning hemispheres has caused issues with competition between parts of the brain in some patients. This was particularly pronounced in the case study of Karen Byrne (see below).

IN THE NEWS

Ψ The Psychological Enquirer

On the other hand

The case study of Karen Byrne was covered in some detail by the BBC film, *Broken Brains*. Clips for the film regarding this case study can be seen via the link below:

www.bbc.co.uk/news/uk-12225163

Karen suffered from epilepsy and at the age of 27, the decision was taken to operate and cut the connection between the two hemispheres by severing the corpus callosum. On waking up from the operation, it became apparent that Karen's left hand functioned separately from the rest of her body.

In the film she is quoted as saying:

'Dr O'Connor said "Karen, what are you doing? Your hand's undressing you." Until he said that, I had no idea that my left hand was opening up the buttons of my shirt. So I started rebuttoning with the right hand and, as soon as I stopped, the left hand started unbuttoning them. So he put an emergency call through to one of the other doctors and said,

"Mike, you've got to get here right away, we've got a problem."

I'd light a cigarette, balance it on an ashtray, and then my left hand would reach forward and stub it out. It would take things out of my handbag and I wouldn't realise so I would walk away. I lost a lot of things before I realised what was going on.'

Karen's left hand was out of control. She has been diagnosed as having Alien Hand Syndrome.

Figure 6.12 Alien Hand Syndrome means the hand functions separately from the rest of the body

This is a rare condition which does not always occur when the corpus callosum is cut in surgery. This was a very unfortunate effect for Karen Byrne.

What this example illustrates is the way that the brain is separated into the two hemispheres. It also shows how movement on each side of the body is lateralised into the two hemispheres. The split-brain patients on the whole managed to ensure their two hemispheres acted in a relatively cohesive way and their limbs acted in a co-ordinated way. This clearly was not the case for Karen Byrne.

As explained, Alien Hand Syndrome does not always occur following brain surgery; in fact, it is very unusual indeed.

Evaluation

- Split-brain research has been useful in understanding the role of each hemisphere and the extent to which they are lateralised.
- It is problematic to assume that evidence is not flawed. The extent to which the split brains were indicative of normal functioning prior to surgery is an issue, especially as the surgery was to treat a problem within the brain. It is also possible that there were other effects during surgery, in addition to the procedure itself.

Plasticity and functional recovery of the brain after trauma

'I tell people whom I want to inform about brain injury to imagine their brain as a dartboard... having speech, thinking, intellect, walking, planning, memory, etc... for areas to be hit. Then close your eyes, grab a random number of darts and throw them at it! The result may be in one area, many areas, a few...who knows?'

Brian Weir, brain injury survivor (1963)

There is no doubt that damage to the brain can be life-changing, and the extent to which it affects an individual depends on many factors including the extent of the trauma and the subsequent care. Almost all people who suffer damage to the brain can make some recovery. New branches of axons and dendrites need to grow within neurons but in some instances the brain adapts to the trauma and finds another way to complete a function. Recovery is not always complete and depends on the level and type of the damage.

IN THE NEWS

Ψ The Psychological Enquirer

Does heading footballs cause brain damage?

There is currently debate in football as to whether children should be prevented from heading footballs due to the potential for brain damage.

In March 2014, the Football Association apologised to the widow of West Bromwich Albion and England striker Jeff Astle for their lack of communication with the family following his death in 2002 at the age of 59.

Jeff Astle was the first footballer to be certified as dead due to brain injury from heading footballs during his career. It was originally thought that he had died from Alzheimer's but a neurosurgeon's report twelve years later ruled that the cause of death was 'boxer's brain', a condition brought about by repeated damage to the head. The heavy leather footballs used whilst Jeff Astle was a professional player are thought to be the reason there was so much damage experienced.

The Football Association will be conducting research into this potential problem.

Some neuroscientists are calling for a ban on heading footballs for all children as they are most at risk of damage. Their brains are very vulnerable to damage due to them still developing and their neck muscles are not strong enough to withstand extra pressure.

The FA released guidelines and rules for treatment of concussed players. They have also recommended baseline testing of players' cognitive faculties annually, similar to the testing conducted in American Football and rugby union. This will allow any potential decline in brain function to be picked up.

This level of damage is less likely to occur in footballers nowadays due to the change in the footballs currently used. However, the example does illustrate that prolonged, low-level damage to the brain has far-reaching effects, and that it is not just occasional accidents to the head that can cause lasting damage.

Figure 6.13 Are headers putting footballers at risk of brain damage?

Plasticity

Plasticity is the ability to replace the function lost by anatomical damage. A cell body can never be replaced, but axons, in some cases, can.

There are three main anatomical ways that the body can replace axon function in the brain after trauma:

Increased brain stimulation

As neurons are damaged there is an effect on the neighbouring neurons as they no longer have input. This happens with the hemispheres too. Although damage may only be on one side, the other hemisphere functions at a lower level too, as it has reduced input. Work by Takatsuru *et al.* (2009), demonstrated that if the undamaged hemisphere is stimulated, recovery from a stroke can be improved.

Axon sprouting

When an axon is damaged its connection with a neighbouring neuron is lost. In some cases, other axons that already connect with that neuron will sprout extra connections to the neuron, replacing the ones that have been destroyed. It is compensating for the loss of a neighbour. This occurs for the most part two weeks after the damage happens. It helps replace function, but only if the damaged axon and the compensatory axons do a similar job. If not, problems can occur with function.

Denervation supersensitivity

This occurs when axons that do a similar job become aroused to a higher level to compensate for the ones that are lost. However, it can have the unfortunate consequence of over-sensitivity to messages such as pain. This increases the pain levels in an individual.

Functional recovery of the brain after trauma

Much recovery after trauma is due to anatomical compensation, brought about by intensive rehabilitation. The brain learns to compensate for function. The brain can be taught to learn how to use the working faculties and function to compensate for the ones that are lost forever (see the contemporary case study below).

CONTEMPORARY CASE STUDY

Is a lone right hemisphere enough? – Laura Danelli et al. (2013)

The boy who learned to speak again after losing his left brain hemisphere

EB, an Italian boy, was operated on at the age of $2\frac{1}{2}$ years to remove a large benign tumour from his left hemisphere. Due to the size of the tumour virtually all of his left hemisphere was removed, and, at that time, all of his linguistic abilities disappeared too. He was right handed and it seems that his language localisation was in his left hemisphere (this is the case with 95 per cent of right-handed people).

He underwent an intensive rehabilitation programme and his language abilities started to improve around the age of 5. They continued to do so over the next three years to the point that no problems of language ability were reported.

Danelli *et al.* (2014) tested him further at the age of 17 to compare his language abilities with 'normal' controls. They found that his right hemisphere had compensated for the loss of the left hemisphere in that he was functioning linguistically well. However, they did find some areas which were not at the expected standard. There were some minor grammatical problems and he was slower at naming objects in pictures.

This led the researchers to conclude that the right hemisphere had compensated following the intensive programme, but that it was never able to compensate fully. When scanning EB's brain, the brain activity was practically identical to the activity in 'normal' controls. This shows (in this case study at least) that hemispheric lateralisation can be compensated for to at least a basic degree by the non-specialist hemisphere.

There should be a degree of caution used in reading too much into case studies, but this example does show that the brain is able to adapt to profound injury, at least in early childhood.

Factors affecting recovery of the brain after trauma

Perseverance

Functional recovery after brain trauma is dependent on assessment and perseverance. Sometimes a function may appear to be lost but that may be because the individual affected may not be trying and takes the view that it is unrecoverable. Animal studies have shown that when a monkey has a 'deafferented' limb (when a limb has lost its sensory input), it will not try to use it. However, if the functioning of the other limbs becomes damaged, then it will have no option than to use the deafferented one. The motor nerves are still connected to the limb, but because the sensory nerve connection is damaged the monkey does not feel as though it can move the limb (Taub & Berman, 1968).

Physical exhaustion, stress and alcohol consumption

When function is recovered in an individual it is important to remember that often the function is used with considerable effort and although the person can do a task, they are often fatigued by the effort. It is similar to walking through deep mud rather than on a tarmac road surface. Other factors such as stress and alcohol consumption can affect the ability to use any function that has been regained (Fleet & Heilman, 1986).

Age

There is a deterioration of the brain in old age and this therefore affects the extent and speed of recovery (Corkin *et al*, 1989). A study by Marquez de la Plata *et al.* (2008) found that, following brain trauma, older patients (40+ years old) regained less function in treatment than younger patients and they were also more likely to decline in terms of function for the five years following the trauma. The contemporary case study of Danelli *et al.* (2013) (page 242) illustrates the extent to which a young brain can regain function following severe damage.

Gender

There is research to suggest that women recover better from brain injury as their function is not as lateralised (concentrated in one hemisphere).

Ratcliffe *et al.* (2007) examined 325 patients with brain trauma for their level of response for cognitive skills to rehabilitation. The patients were 16–45 years old at injury, received rehabilitation at a care facility, and completed a follow-up one year later. None of them had learning problems prior to the trauma. When assessed for cognitive skills, women performed significantly better than men on tests of attention/working memory and language whereas men outperformed females in visual analytic skills. Overall, the results suggest a better recovery for women. However, the results did not control for performance pre-injury, so this could have influenced results.

Research is, however, mixed in this area, so clear overall conclusions cannot be drawn.

Higher education associated with better recovery from traumatic brain injury – Schneider *et al.* (2014)

Aim

Schneider *et al.* investigated whether time spent in education would be a factor in recovery from brain injury.

Procedure

769 people who had suffered head injuries from road traffic accidents and falls were studied. They had all been treated in the emergency room in the hospital and followed a programme of rehabilitation. Their progress was monitored.

Findings

1 Of the 769 participants, 24 per cent did not finish school, 51 per cent had 12 to 15 years of education and 25 per cent had graduated from university, with an undergraduate degree or a higher level of qualification.
2 One year after the injury, 28 per cent of the participants had made a full recovery and were back in education or working.
3 39 per cent of the graduates were left free of disability, whereas of those who had left school early, only 10 per cent made a full recovery.
4 The researchers are not sure why these results arose but argue it may be that more educated people make more effective use of their brains, which strengthens them.
5 They found that similar injuries had very different outcomes, and that one of the factors implicated in successful outcomes was the amount of time spent in education. Schneider suggests that people with an increased cognitive capability might heal in a different way to those who have a low capability – it may be that some people have a greater ability to compensate for function. They are seven times more likely to make a full recovery than people who did not finish school.

Conclusion

People who have remained in education for longer have a greater 'cognitive reserve', which means they are less likely to be left permanently disabled after a head injury. Their brains are better able to maintain function in spite of damage, which makes them more likely to regain function following a brain trauma.

Evaluation

The large sample size for this study means that it shows a general trend in recovery levels overall. However, there are many other factors that could be implicated in the recovery levels and so suggesting it is due to education level is problematic.

Evaluation

- Research has shown that recovery is possible following trauma. There is evidence to show that rehabilitation programmes work successfully.

- In some cases there is no record of functioning level prior to the trauma, so it is difficult to know the extent to which the brain has recovered to pre-trauma levels.

- The ability of the brain to recover varies according to the extent of the damage, the location of the damage, and the individual. For this reason, each case varies vastly and generalisations are difficult to make.

STRENGTHEN YOUR LEARNING

1 What is the function of the motor cortex?
2 What is the function of the somatosensory cortex?
3 What is meant by hemispheric lateralisation?
4 What is meant by brain localisation?
5 What is the difference in function between Broca's and Wernicke's areas of the brain?
6 Where is the brain split in split-brain research?
7 How does split-brain research add to our understanding of the brain?
8 Explain the meaning of brain plasticity.
9 What factors determine the level of recovery of the brain following trauma?
10 What are the limitations of investigating recovery of the brain after trauma?

ASSESSMENT CHECK

1 Explain what hemispheric lateralisation is. [**2 marks**]

2 Outline and evaluate split-brain research. [**16 marks**]

3 Copy and complete the table below by writing which definition A, B, C or D describes which term. There will be one definition left over. [**3 marks**]

   A Area of the brain which deals with what you hear

   B Area of the brain implicated in speech production

   C Area of the brain implicated in understanding language

   D Area of the brain that co-ordinates movement

Term	Definition (A, B, C or D)
Motor cortex	D
Wernicke's area	C
Broca's area	B

4 Outline two findings from split-brain research. [**4 marks**]

5 Joanne is amateur boxer and has sustained a severe blow to her head during a match. She was knocked unconscious and suffered concussion and some damage to her brain. Outline two factors that will affect her chances of a full recovery. [**4 marks**]

6 Researchers investigating recovery rates from brain trauma concluded that men recovered at a slower rate than women, because they spent longer in rehabilitation units. The sample size for the study was six men and seven women.

Explain why the researchers' conclusions may not be valid. [**4 marks**]

6.6 Ways of studying the brain

Functional magnetic resonance imaging (fMRI)

Functional **fMRIs** operate in the same way as standard MRIs but can also show activity as it occurs. MRIs work by recording the energy produced by molecules of water, after the magnetic field is removed. The fMRI uses the same principle, but instead of measuring the energy emitted from water, it measures the energy released by haemoglobin (the protein content of blood). When haemoglobin has oxygen it reacts differently to when it is without oxygen. So, when an area of the brain is active and is therefore using more oxygen, the difference in the amount of energy released by the haemoglobin is detected by the scanner and the change measured. This gives a dynamic (moving) picture. It shows activity about one second after it occurs. It is also accurate to within 1–2 mm in the brain.

KEY TERMS

Functional Magnetic Resonance Imaging (fMRI) – a technique of brain scanning that uses a magnetic field and radio signals to monitor the blood flow in the brain. Areas of the brain that are involved in activities done by the person during scanning have a greater blood oxygenation and flow, so specific brain areas can be linked to specific abilities

Evaluation

- fMRI provides a moving picture of brain activity. This means that patterns of activity can be compared rather than just the physiology of the brain. The dynamic nature of brain activity is important and so the fMRI is particularly useful for this.
- The complexity of brain activity means that interpreting an fMRI scan is problematic. It is a difficult task, made more difficult by the time delay of the scan.
- fMRI machines are expensive to buy and maintain and they require trained operators. This makes research expensive and difficult to organise.
- The sample sizes in studies are often small due to limited availability and funding. The cost per participant is high. This makes results difficult to generalise from.

ON THE WEB

In a programme called *Alan Alda: Brains on Trial* there is a lot of coverage on how brains are studied. The programme is available on YouTube and has been divided up into sections. One section covers how fMRIs work.

You can access the clip by searching YouTube for 'How does fMRI brain scanning work? Alan Alda and Dr. Nancy Kanwisher, MIT'.

INCREASE YOUR KNOWLEDGE

fMRIs are just one method of scanning the brain that is used in research. However, there are other methods available. These methods are also used to gather data for research.

- **CAT scan:** The full name for this method is 'computerised axial tomography', and the technique uses an X-ray beam to produce a picture of the physiology of the brain. The picture is not moving, but can pick up lesions (damage) and unusual brain physiology.
- **PET scans:** the full name for this method is 'positron emission tomography'. It produces a moving picture of brain activity using radioactive glucose which has been injected into the bloodstream. The scanner picks up where in the brain the most glucose is being consumed, as this indicates which areas are the most active. The scan pictures look rather like heat sensor pictures, with red indicating high activity and blue/green showing little activity.
- **MRI scans:** These are magnetic resonance imaging, which use the same technology as fMRIs, but are unable to produce a moving picture.

The availability and cost of these methods dictate which are used for diagnosis and research.

Electroencephalogram (EEG) and event-related potentials (ERPs)

For an **EEG**, electrodes are placed on the scalp and they record the electrical activity of the brain. There can be anything from two to three electrodes to over a hundred. Electrodes measure the activity of the cells immediately under the electrode, so using more electrodes gives a fuller picture. Dement & Kleitman (1957) used this method in their research on the sleep cycle (see page 252).

ERPs use the same apparatus as EEGs, but record when there is activity in response to a stimulus introduced by the researcher. For example, Costa, Braun & Birbaumer (2003) used this method to record responses to nude pictures of both sexes in young people (aged 19–29 years). When asked about how they felt, men generally said they were aroused by the nude female pictures, whereas women mostly reported to have neutral feelings to both male and female nude pictures. However, when Costa and colleagues examined the ERPs of both males and females they found a higher response to opposite-sex nude pictures than reported by the participants. This seems to suggest that this method of measuring activity has greater accuracy than self-reports.

Evaluation

- Both methods are only reasonably accurate for activity measured close to the electrode. This means that the finer detail is missed so this type of method is only suitable for certain research questions.
- EEGs and ERPs are cheaper methods than scanning so they are more widely available to researchers.
- The output from the equipment needs to be interpreted so there is a level of expertise required if a researcher decides to use these methods.
- ERPs are a useful method to test the reliability of self-report answers. They are a useful supplementary method for research, particularly when the area of research is potentially sensitive and open to social desirability bias.

Post-mortem examinations

Post-mortem examinations are when a person's body, including the brain, is examined after they have died. They can be used to see where damage had occurred in the brain and how that might explain behaviour exhibited by the individual prior to death. One of the most famous case studies is Leborgne (see the classic case study on page 238).

Evaluation

- The research is conducted on a dead person so there is no brain activity measured.
- There are issues with comparison of functioning prior to death. It may be that there is little information about how the person managed before they died.
- Some brains may have been affected by the reason for the death (for example, disease).
- There is no discomfort experienced by the individual as they are not alive.

6.7 Biological rhythms

'Our biological rhythms are the symphony of the cosmos, music embedded deep within us to which we dance, even when we can't name the tune.'

Deepak Chopra (2004)

Circadian rhythms

Circadian rhythms are biological rhythms lasting a day (approximately 24 hours). An example is the sleep/wake cycle, which is usually measured by reading the time and regular events like when we eat and go to sleep. Our body clock is regulated by an internal system including such factors as release of hormones like melatonin, metabolic rate and body temperature.

Research

Siffre (1975) peformed a case study of a French man (using himself as the participant) and spent six months in a cave with no natural light or cues as to the day or time. When he woke up he had artificial light to help him navigate within the cave and keep himself busy. His internal body clock was allowed to free-run and it settled into a sleep/wake cycle of between 25 and 30 hours. He lost track of how many days he had been in the cave, believing it to be one month less than he had actually stayed in. He was in the cave for a total of 179 days. This suggests that natural light sources in the environment are vital for keeping the individual to a 24-hour cycle.

Aschoff & Weber (1962) studied participants living in a bunker that had only electric light and no windows. The participants were allowed to turn lights on and off as they wished, so that the light source fitted with their body clocks. Eventually their body clocks settled into a sleep/wake cycle of 25 to 27 hours. This seems to suggest, like Siffre (1975), that we use our natural light source to entrain (or 'adjust') our pacemakers (see below) with the environment and that the 24-hour clock is not in line with our natural bodily rhythms.

Folkard *et al.* (1985) withdrew participants from natural light for three weeks, and changed the time cues to only 22 hours a day without the participants being aware this occurred. Only one participant out of twelve could not adjust to the shortened day. This shows that our natural circadian rhythm is flexible and can differ between individuals.

KEY TERM

Circadian rhythms – biological rhythms that occur every 24 hours

Figure 6.14 Siffre during his time in the cave

249

The effect of endogenous pacemakers and exogenous zeitgebers on the sleep/wake cycle

Endogenous pacemakers

Endogenous pacemakers are rhythms that are from internal bodily systems. They can also be affected by the environment. Research shows that the endogenous pacemakers still function without the cues from the environment, although the circadian rhythm can vary as a consequence (see research on circadian rhythms, page 248).

The suprachiasmatic nucleus (SCN) seems to be the most influential endogenous pacemaker in the body. It is in the centre of the brain and is regulated by light from the environment. It could be argued to be our internal body clock.

The SCN is found in animals and this has therefore facilitated research examining its role. It also means that the extent to which the SCN is influential in regulating biological rhythms can be examined. This would be difficult and unethical in humans. It is argued that research on animals such as this can be generalised to humans.

Research

Ralph *et al.* (1990) removed the SCN out of genetically abnormal hamsters which only had a circadian cycle of 20 hours. They then transplanted the SCN cells into hamsters which had no such abnormality and functioned on the normal 24-hour cycle. Following the transplant the circadian rhythm of the hamsters shortened to 20 hours. This suggests that the SCN is pivotal in regulating the internal body clock.

When the SCN from normally functioning hamsters is removed, Morgan (1995) found that their circadian rhythms disappeared. However, a reversal was possible as when SCN cells were transplanted back in, the rhythm returned. This further supports Ralph *et al.*'s findings that the SCN is all-important in the internal body clock.

Exogenous zeitgebers

Exogenous zeitgebers are cues from the environment that play an important role in regulating time and hence the circadian rhythm in humans. They are a cue for the pacemakers previously discussed and help regulate the body clock so that the individual is synchronised with the environment. Sunlight is an example of a zeitgeber, as are noise, the seasons and the moon.

Entrainment is where there is an adjustment of the body clock in line with the environment. This happens when a traveller crosses time zones as their pacemakers are not synchronised with the environment anymore. Zeitgebers therefore act as cues, allowing the person to adjust.

Research

Campbell & Murphy (1998) monitored the body temperatures of fifteen volunteers who slept in a laboratory. They introduced light to them during the night at a series of intervals by shining a beam of light onto the back of their knees. They were woken at different times and a light pad was shone on the back of their knees. Their circadian rhythms were disrupted by up to three hours. This shows that it is not necessary for light to just enter the eyes to have a physiological effect on the biological rhythms.

Shih-Yu Lee *et al.* (2013) found that light therapy can help mothers of premature or low birth weight babies who are in intensive care. As the environment has low lighting, mothers find that their sleep is disrupted. To compensate for this, fifteen women were given bright light therapy over three weeks and their sleep was monitored. Women receiving the therapy reported an improvement in sleep quality in comparison to a control group. This shows the effect on sleep quality that zeitgebers can have and also the practical applications of the research.

Steel *et al.* (2008) investigated the effects of constant daylight on circadian rhythms by monitoring six participants living in isolation in the Arctic for six weeks. There was constant daylight throughout that time. The participants kept sleep logs. The researchers found that five of the six participants developed a free-running sleep/wake cycle longer than 24 hours. However, they also found that the sleep patterns were individual and there were no synchronised patterns that emerged. This means that social cues may not have a strong effect in the absence of other zeitgebers.

PSYCHOLOGY IN THE REAL WORLD

Chronotherapeutics

The use of light therapy as a clinical treatment for depression is now recognised as an effective and affordable intervention for affective disorders (disorders that affect mood). It can be used as the sole treatment or with drug treatment to maximise success.

Benedetti *et al.* (2007) conducted a study examining the effects of light therapy and sleep deprivation in patients suffering from bipolar disorder. They found that the use of chronotherapeutics reduced two-thirds of the patients' depression inventory score by 50 per cent.

This shows a clear practical implication for research on biological rhythms.

Figure 6.15 Chronotherapeutic lights can help people with depression

Evaluation

- Much of the research can be criticised for external validity. It is often carried out in artificial conditions and therefore the resulting behaviour could be argued to be similarly false.

- Monitoring sleep can also have an effect on the sleep patterns of the participant. This means that the sleep patterns recorded could be a by-product of being monitored rather than the effect of the zeitgeber/pacemaker.

- Using animals in research also raises concerns regarding extrapolation. There are clearly physiological differences which may in turn make generalising to humans problematic.

- Research can be used to develop interventions to help the clinical population. (See Benedetti *et al.* (2007) in Psychology in the real world, above.)

ON THE WEB

It is argued that the body clock of some individuals means they are more alert in the morning and this type of people are called morning larks. Conversely, there are evening owls who function at their best in the evening. The neurogeneticist Dr Louis Ptacek argues this is genetic.

There are tests available to determine whether you function as an evening owl or a morning lark. Try searching using the terms 'body clock test'.

When do you think you function better?

Infradian rhythms

Infradian rhythms last more than 24 hours. An example is the menstrual cycle, which is dictated by the endocrine system. However, this rhythm is not imposed purely by the release of hormones. It is suggested that zeitgebers such as light and odours are also involved. Another example of an infradian rhythm is hibernation, which is an annual rhythm observed in certain animals.

KEY TERM

Infradian rhythms – biological rhythms that occur less than once a day

Research

McClintock & Stern (1998) found that when women received 'odourless compounds' from the armpits of women in the latter half of their menstrual cycle, their menstrual cycle was shortened, presumably by the effect of the other women's pheromones as they approached the end of their cycle. The compounds were transferred by the women wiping a pad, which had previously been wiped across the donor's armpit, above their upper lip. However, if the compounds (which included pheromones) were collected from women at the beginning of their cycle, this had the opposite effect, lengthening the cycle of those who had received the compound. This shows that the menstrual cycle of a woman can be altered by communication via pheromones.

A 1967 study by Reinberg involved a woman spending three months in a cave with only the light of a small lamp. As a result of this her days lengthened to 24.9 hours and her menstrual cycle shortened to 25.7 days. This study shows that the levels of light in the cave could have affected the woman's menstrual cycle. After the study it took her body a year to readjust her menstrual cycle. This research shows how infradian biological rhythms can be influenced by external zeitgebers such as light.

Evaluation

- The effects of pheromones can help explain menstrual synchronicity, whereby groups of women who live together, such as nuns, have menstrual cycles that can become synchronised with each other. The idea of communication via pheromones can neatly explain this phenomenon as there must be something in the shared environment that acts as a zeitgeber.

- It is suggested that there is an evolutionary advantage if this occurs, as it means there could potentially be synchronised pregnancies and that means that childcare could be shared when the babies are born at or around the same time.

- How close women have to live together and for what period of time, for menstrual synchronisation to occur, is not clear. The extent to which pheromones can have an effect still requires research.

- Wilson (1992) challenged the idea of menstrual synchronicity, stating that experimental evidence of its existence was exaggerated.

Ultradian rhythms

Ultradian rhythms are biological rhythms lasting less than 24 hours, like the sleep/wake cycle. Sleep has five stages that occur through the night. These stages can be witnessed throughout the lifespan but vary in length depending on age. Broadly speaking, the complete sleep/wake cycle lengthens with age to 90 minutes.

The stages within the sleep/wake cycle vary in terms of length of time, brain activity and physiological effects. These are summarised in Table 6.4 below:

KEY TERM

Ultradian rhythms – biological rhythms that occur more than once a day

Table 6.4 The sleep/wake cycle

Stage	Length	Brain activity	Physiological effects
One	The length in each stage varies between 5 and 15 minutes.	Less than relaxed wakefulness, but higher than other stages (apart from REM).	Heart rate slows and muscles relax. People are still easily woken at this stage.
Two		Sleep spindles (short bursts of activity) occur on EEG outputs in this stage.	The body continues to relax. It is still easy to wake someone from this stage.
Three		There are less sleep spindles in this stage. EEG outputs show slow delta waves.	The body relaxes still further and people become harder to wake in this stage.
Four	40 minutes.	Delta waves, which are a specific type of brain wave, increase and the level of activity is slower than all other stages.	Metabolic rate, which is the rate food is digested, is low. People are difficult to wake. Growth hormones are released.
REM (rapid eye movement)	15 minutes initially, lengthening throughout the night (with less time spent in other stages).	More brain activity than in any other sleep stage.	Complete relaxation of the trunk. Irregular breathing and heart rate. Probability of dreams.

Over the course of about 90 minutes, a sleeper goes through stages 1–4 and then returns to stage 3, and then stage 2, before going into REM sleep. The sleep cycle then starts again. The number of sleep cycles depends on how long an individual sleeps for. There can be about five full cycles in a full night's sleep.

CLASSIC RESEARCH

The relation of eye movements during sleep – William Dement & Nathaniel Kleitman (1957)

This is a classic study as this work was the first to document what occurs in REM sleep and offer insight into what happens during our sleeping hours.

Aim

To investigate brain activity change throughout night-time sleep.

Procedure

1 Seven adult males and two adult females were the participants.
2 Participants were asked to report to the laboratory at bedtime where they were connected to an EEG. The EEG took measurements throughout their time asleep, all night.

Participants were asked not to drink caffeinated drinks for the day before their sleep was investigated.

Findings

1 Dement & Kleitman found that everyone had periods of REM every night.
2 They also found high incidences of dream recall when participants were awakened during REM periods of sleep. If awakened in the other stages, very few reported dreaming. Participants were woken between 5 and 15 minutes into the start of REM sleep.
3 When looking for a relationship between brain activity and dreams, Dement & Kleitman found that the brain activity of very vivid dreams was different to the less clear dreams.
4 They also found that the rapid eye movements of the participants during REM sleep varied according to the dream type and mirrored their rapid eye movements

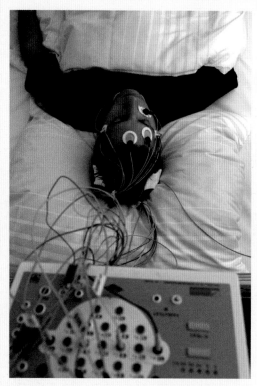
Figure 6.16 Electrodes used to measure brain activity during sleep in research settings

whilst awake and completing a similar task to the one they had dreamt about. For example, one participant exhibited vertical rapid eye movements during his dream. When awoken and asked about the content he reported dreaming about climbing a series of ladders and looking up and down whilst he climbed.

This showed that Dement & Kleitman had identified the stage of the sleep cycle in which most dreams occur.

Evaluation

The research by Dement & Kleitman is seen as robust as there has been much replication of their findings since 1957.

The manner in which data was collected could have caused an atypical reaction from participants and the frequency of occurrence of REM sleep might be different in a non-experimental setting. This would also apply to all subsequent research.

Dreaming is difficult to measure as it is experienced in a state of consciousness where communication is very difficult if not impossible.

Using an EEG is an objective measure and is therefore scientific, so has increased reliability.

Conclusion

From the research it can be concluded that the stages of sleep follow a typical pattern throughout the night, and that dreams mostly occur in REM sleep.

STRENGTHEN YOUR LEARNING
1 What is the function of the SCN?
2 Define what a circadian rhythm is.
3 What is meant by an infradian rhythm? Give an example.
4 What is meant by REM sleep?
5 What is the difference in function between an infradian and an ultradian biological rhythm?
6 How many sleep stages are there?
7 What are the problems with using an EEG to measure sleep patterns?
8 Explain the meaning of the term endogenous pacemakers and give an example of one.
9 Explain the meaning of the term exogenous zeitgebers and give an example of one.
10 Give an example of a practical application of research into biological rhythms.

ASSESSMENT CHECK

1 Explain the difference between ultradian and infradian rhythms. [**2 marks**]

2 Outline and evaluate research into circadian rhythms. [**16 marks**]

3 Copy and complete the table below by writing which definition A, B, C or D describes which term. One definition will be left over. [**3 marks**]

   A Measures the electrical activity of the brain

   B Investigates brains following death

   C Measures the change in energy released by haemoglobin

   D Measures changes in activity in the brain following presentation of a stimulus

Term	Definition (A, B, C or D)
Functional magnetic resonance imaging (fMRI)	
Event-related potentials (ERPs)	
Electroencephalograms (EEGs)	

4 Identify two endogenous pacemakers. [**2 marks**]

5 Explain two issues with using post-mortem examinations to localise function in the brain. [**4 marks**]

6 Researchers decided to compare the brain activity of elderly (70 years old) individuals during sleep with the activity of young adults (11–25 years old). They used EEG measurements for the comparison.

   Explain why the data gathered may lack reliability and validity. [**4 marks**]

The divisions of the nervous system

The structure and function of neurons

The process of synaptic transmission

The function of the endocrine system
The fight or flight response

Localisation of function in the brain and hemispheric lateralisation

Plasticity and functional recovery of the brain after trauma

Ways of studying the brain

Biological rhythms

SUMMARY

- The nervous system is divided into the central nervous system (CNS) and the peripheral nervous System (PNS).
- The CNS consists of the brain and spinal cord, and the PNS is made up of the nervous system of the rest of the body.
- There are three types of neuron: sensory (which transmit information from the senses) relay (which transmit messages) and motor (which help organs and muscles to function).
- The synapse is the gap between neurons. Messages are transmitted chemically across the synapse at high speed.
- Some neurons have potentials that are excitatory (increase the chance of firing) and some are inhibitory (decrease the chance of firing).
- The endocrine system transmits messages around the body using hormones.
- The fight-or-flight response (generated from the autonomic nervous system) helps an individual prepare for quick reaction to a potentially threatening situation.
- The brain has two hemispheres which are connected using the corpus callosum. There are some differences between the roles played by each hemisphere.
- For most people, the left hemisphere deals with language processing, whereas the right hemisphere is dominant whilst processing faces. The left hemisphere seems to focus on detail, whereas the right hemisphere looks at things holistically.
- The motor cortex is responsible for movement and is next to the somatosensory cortex, whose role is perceiving sensation in the body.
- The visual centres of the brain are mostly in the occipital lobe at the back of the brain, whereas the auditory centres of the brain are in the temporal lobes.
- The two language areas are Broca's area, which deals with speech production, and Wernicke's area, which focuses on understanding.
- Split-brain research has been useful in furthering our understanding of the role of the two hemispheres.
- Plasticity is the ability of the brain to recover function after brain trauma. This can be done by regeneration and compensation via intensive rehabilitation.
- Factors affecting recovery of the brain after trauma include: perseverance, exhaustion, stress, alcohol consumption, age and gender. The location and extent of the damage are also very important.
- The brain can be studied using scanning techniques such as fMRI, EEGs and ERPs. Post-mortem examination can also be carried out.
- There are three types of biological rhythm: circadian (these last 24 hours), infradian (these last more than 24 hours) and ultradian (these last less than 24 hours).
- Circadian rhythms are influenced by endogenous pacemakers (such as the suprachiasmatic nucleus, known as the SCN) and exogenous zeitgebers (such as light and sound).
- An example of a circadian rhythm is the sleep/wake cycle. An infradian rhythm is the menstrual cycle, and an ultradian rhythm is the stages of sleep.

Research methods for AS and A-level

Introduction

Research methods are the means by which theories are constructed and tested. There are many types of research methods, each with strengths and weaknesses. Specific focus will be upon:

- Research methods (experimental and non-experimental)
- Scientific processes
- Data analysis.

Understanding the specification

- For research methods, you need to understand *experimental and various non-experimental methods*.
- For scientific processes, you need to understand *the processes involved in designing and carrying out investigations*. This includes ethical considerations and the reporting of investigations.
- For data analysis, you need to be able *to analyse and present data*, including both descriptive and inferential analysis.

These are the basic requirements of the specification. However, other relevant material is included in this chapter to provide depth and detail to your understanding.

IN THE NEWS

Ψ The Psychological Enquirer

The war against the birds

Figure 7.1 A starving Chinese child in the great famine of 1958–61, a disaster caused partly by a lack of scientifically conducted research

In 1958, Chinese leader Mao Zedong made the observation that sparrows always seemed to be feasting on the rice fields. He estimated that each sparrow ate 4.5 kilos of

rice a year, so for every 1 million sparrows that could be killed there would be food for 60,000 people. He therefore announced that all citizens were to participate in a campaign to kill the sparrows, so that food production could be increased and famine avoided. On December 13th The Shanghai Newspaper reported on the start of the 'total war' against the birds; of the waving flags and scarecrows, the whistles and gongs to keep the birds airborne, the poisoning and shooting of sparrows, the destruction of their nests and eggs. Hundreds of millions of sparrows were killed and the bird became nearly extinct. Yet as early as April 1960 it was realised with horror that what the birds had mainly been snacking on were the locust grubs that attacked the rice crop. Without the sparrows the grubs literally had a field day, swarms of locusts rampaged unchecked, and between 1958 and 1961, a period known in China as 'the great famine', it is estimated that up to 60 million people starved to death.

This is an example of the negative consequences that can occur when practical applications are based on flawed evidence. Mao Zedong's intentions were good, but if he had subjected his beliefs to proper scientific research, this disaster would never have happened. Practical applications that truly benefit society should be based upon objective, unbiased research that is capable of being replicated and which has been subjected to peer review to check its credentials. In this chapter we look at the many ways in which psychologists can conduct research, the individual strengths and weaknesses of each, and the techniques that can be employed, so that research is carried out in a responsible manner.

7.1 Research methods

'Equipped with his five senses, man explores the universe around him and calls the adventure science.'
Edwin Powell Hubble (1929)

'Men love to wonder and that is the seed of science.'
Ralph Waldo Emerson (1860)

There are several **research methods** in psychology. Like a golfer selecting the most appropriate club, psychologists choose the most appropriate method for research. No single method is perfect; each has strengths and weaknesses.

The experimental method

The **experimental method** is a scientific method involving the manipulation of variables to determine cause and effect. A variable is any object, characteristic or event that varies in some way. Participants are randomly allocated (without bias) to the different testing groups, so that the groups should be fairly similar. All procedures in an experiment should be standardised (kept the same for all participants).

Figure 7.2 Like a golfer selects the best club to play a shot, psychologists select the most appropriate research method to conduct a study

In an experiment a researcher manipulates an **independent variable (IV)** to see its effect on a **dependent variable (DV)**. For example, caffeine consumption (IV) could be manipulated to see its effect on reaction time (DV).

Operationalisation

Variables must be operationalised; this means clearly defining them so they can be manipulated (IV) and measured (DV). Some variables are more difficult to operationalise, for instance, anger levels. Another problem is that **operationalisation of variables** leads to only one aspect of a variable being measured. However, without accurate operationalisation, results will be unreliable and could not be replicated to check their validity.

Extraneous and confounding variables

Extraneous variables (other variables that could affect the DV) are controlled so that they do not vary across any of the experimental conditions or between participants. Uncontrolled extraneous variables can become **confounding variables** and 'confuse' the results by affecting the DV. For example, if researchers wished to investigate the effect of background music (Condition 1) or silence (Condition 2) on homework performance using two classes, they would have to control a number of extraneous variables, including age, homework difficulty, etc. If these were all controlled, the results would be trustworthy. However, if the participants in Condition 1 were brighter than those in Condition 2, intelligence would be a confounding variable. The researchers could not then be sure whether differences in homework performance were due to the presence of the music or intelligence. Results would be confounded and worthless.

There are three main types of extraneous variables:

1 **Participant variables** – concern factors such as participants' age and intelligence.
2 **Situational variables** – concern the experimental setting and surrounding environment, for example temperature and noise levels.
3 **Experimenter variables** – concern changes in the personality, appearance and conduct of the researcher. For example, female researchers may gain different results from male ones.

Demand characteristics

Conducting research involves interaction between researchers and participants and such interactions can affect research findings.

There are several features of research studies that enable participants to guess what a study is about and what is expected of them. Such **demand characteristics** can involve participants:

- guessing the purpose of the research and trying to please the researcher by giving the 'right' results
- guessing the purpose of the research and trying to annoy the researcher by giving the wrong results; this is called the 'screw you effect'
- acting unnaturally out of nervousness or fear of evaluation
- acting unnaturally due to social desirability bias (see page 266).

The single-blind procedure is a technique that reduces demand characteristics. It involves participants having no idea which condition of a study they are in.

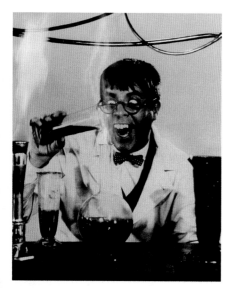

Figure 7.3 The physical appearance of an investigator can unconsciously affect the behaviour of participants in studies

In drug trials, for example, they would not know whether they were being given a real drug or a placebo drug (sugar pill).

Investigator effects

Investigator effects are the ways in which researchers unconsciously influence the results of research and can occur in several ways:

● Physical characteristics of investigators may influence results, such as age or ethnicity. For example, male participants may be unwilling to admit sexist views to female researchers.

● Less obvious personal characteristics of investigators, like accent or tone of voice, can influence results. For example, participants may respond differently to someone with a stern voice.

● Investigators may be unconsciously biased in their interpretation of data and find what they expect to find.

The double-blind procedure is a technique to reduce investigator effects, which involves neither participants nor investigators knowing which condition participants are in. They are both 'blind' to this knowledge. This prevents investigators from unconsciously giving participants clues as to which condition they are in and therefore reduces demand characteristics. For example, in drug trials, the drug and placebo would be allocated in such a way that neither the participant nor the researcher would know who was receiving which.

STRENGTHEN YOUR LEARNING

1 Describe the experimental method in terms of:
   (i) manipulation of variables
   (ii) random allocation
   (iii) operationalisation
   (iv) extraneous and confounding variables.
2 What are:
   (i) demand characteristics
   (ii) investigator effects?
3 How can the risk of demand characteristics and investigator effects be reduced?

Types of experiment

Laboratory experiments

Laboratory experiments, for example Baddeley's (1966) study of encoding in memory (see page 55), are performed in a controlled environment, using standardised procedure, with participants randomly allocated to experimental groups.

Advantages of laboratory experiments

● **High degree of control** – experimenters control all variables and the IV and DV are precisely operationalised (defined) and measured, leading to greater accuracy and objectivity.

● **Replication** – other researchers can repeat the experiment to check results.

- **Cause and effect** – as all other variables are controlled, the effect (change in the value of the DV) must be caused solely by the manipulation of the IV.
- **Isolation of variables** – in the laboratory, individual pieces of behaviour can be isolated and rigorously tested.

Weaknesses of laboratory experiments

- **Experimenter bias** – experimenters' expectations can affect results and participants may be influenced by these expectations.
- **Problems operationalising the IV and DV** – to gain precision measurements can become too specific and not relate to wider behaviour, for example, defining 'getting fatter' as putting on two pounds per week.
- **Low external (ecological) validity** – high degrees of control make experimental situations artificial and unlike real life. Therefore, it can be difficult to generalise results to other settings. Laboratory settings can be intimidating places so people may not act normally.
- **Demand characteristics** – participants are aware they're being tested and so may unconsciously alter their behaviour.

RESEARCH IN FOCUS

Have a look at Baddeley's (1966) laboratory experiment into coding in memory (page 55).
1 Can you identify the IV and the DV?
2 What aspects of this study make it a laboratory experiment?
3 What are the advantages and weaknesses of conducting this study as a laboratory experiment?

Field experiments

Field experiments, for example Bickman's (1974) study of obedience (see page 30), occur in 'real world' settings rather than the laboratory. The IV is manipulated by the experimenter and as many other variables as possible are controlled.

YOU ARE THE RESEARCHER

Construct a field experiment that looks at whether people are more willing to help females or males when asked to change a 20p piece for two 10p pieces.

Why would this be a field experiment rather than a laboratory or natural/quasi experiment? What would be your IV and DV? What type of sample would you be using? Compose a suitable null hypothesis (see page 271) for your study.

Natural and quasi experiments

In **natural experiments** the IV varies naturally; the experimenter does not manipulate it, but records the effect on the DV. For example, Costello *et al.* (2003) was studying the mental health of Native Americans on a reservation. During the study a casino opened, giving an opportunity to study the effect of decreasing poverty on mental health. In **quasi experiments** the IV occurs naturally, such as in a study of gender where males and females are compared. Natural and quasi experiments are often used when it is unethical to manipulate an IV. In such studies random allocation of participants is not possible.

KEY TERMS

Field experiment – experiment conducted in a naturalistic environment where the researchers manipulate the independent variable

Natural experiment – experiment where the independent variable varies naturally

Quasi experiment – where the researcher is unable to freely manipulate the independent variable or randomly allocate the participants to the different conditions

Advantages of field and natural experiments

- **High ecological validity** – due to the 'real world' environment, results relate to everyday behaviour and can be generalised to other settings.
- **No demand characteristics** – often participants are unaware of the experiment, and so there are no demand characteristics.

Weaknesses of field and natural experiments

- **Less control** – it is more difficult to control extraneous variables, so causality is harder to establish.
- **Replication** – since the conditions are never exactly the same again, it is difficult to exactly repeat field and natural experiments to check the results.
- **Ethics** – when participants are not aware that they are in an experiment it incurs a lack of informed consent. This applies more to field experiments, since in natural/quasi experiments the IV occurs naturally and is not manipulated by the experimenter.
- **Sample bias** – since participants are not randomly allocated to groups, samples may not be comparable to each other.

YOU ARE THE RESEARCHER

Design a quasi experiment that assesses whether children who regularly attend day care are more aggressive than children who are raised at home.

Why would this be a quasi rather than a field or laboratory experiment? What would the IV and DV be? Refer to the section on inferential testing (page 301) to work out what type of statistical test you would need. What advantages and limitations would there be compared to a laboratory study?

Observational techniques

Observations involve watching and recording behaviour, for example children in a playground. Most observations are naturalistic (occur in real-world settings), but can occur under controlled conditions, for example Milgram's (1963) obedience study (see page 18).

There are two main types of observation:

1 **Participant observation** involves observers becoming actively involved in the situation being studied to gain a more 'hands-on' perspective, for example Zimbardo's (1971) prison simulation study (see page 13).

2 **Non-participant observation** involves researchers not become actively involved in the behaviour being studied, for example Ainsworth's (1971) Strange Situation study (see page 120).

Observations can also be:

- **overt** – where participants are aware they are being observed, for example Zimbardo's (1971) prison simulation study (see page 13).
- **covert** – where participants remain unaware of being observed, for example Festinger's (1957) study where he infiltrated a cult who were prophesying the end of the world.

Advantages of observational techniques

- **High external validity** – since observations usually occur in natural settings, participants behave naturally and so results can be generalised to other settings.
- **Practical method** – can be used in situations where deliberate manipulation of variables would be unethical or impractical, for example studying football hooliganism. It is useful where co-operation from those being observed is unlikely and where the full social context for behaviour is needed. It is particularly useful when studying animals or children.
- **Few demand characteristics** – with covert observations participants are unaware of being observed and so there are no demand characteristics.

Weaknesses of observational techniques

- **Cause and effect** – causality cannot be inferred, since the variables are only observed, not manipulated, and there is little control of extraneous variables.
- **Observer bias** – observers may see what they want to see, though this can be reduced by establishing inter-observer reliability (see page 264).
- **Replication** – the lack of control over variables means conditions can never be repeated exactly to check the results.
- **Ethics** – if participants are unaware of being observed, issues of invasion of privacy and informed consent arise (though if participants are informed of the study, then there is a possibility of demand characteristics).
- **Practical problems** – it can be difficult to remain unobserved and there can be problems recording behaviour, for example seeing all behaviours exhibited. It can also be difficult to categorise observed behaviours accurately.

Figure 7.4 Observational studies usually involve observing behaviour in real-world settings, for example observations of football hooliganism

Observational design

There are several ways in which data can be gathered in **naturalistic observations**, including visual recordings like videos and photographs, audio recordings, or 'on-the-spot' note-taking using agreed rating scales or coding categories. The development of effective behavioural coding categories is integral to the success of observational studies.

Behavioural categories

Observers agree on a grid or coding sheet on which to record the behaviour being studied. The **behavioural categories** chosen should reflect what is being studied. For example, if observers are interested in the effect of age and sex on the speed of car driving, they might want to develop behavioural categories like those given in Table 7.1.

Rather than writing descriptions of behaviour observed, it is easier to code or rate behaviour using previously agreed scales. Coding can involve numbers (like age of driver) or letters to describe characteristics (like M = male) or observed behaviours (like T = talking). Observed behaviour can also be rated on structured scales, like 1–5 on a scale of 'safe driving'.

Table 7.1 Behavioural categories of driving behaviour

Driver	Sex (M/F)	Age (estimate)	Number of passengers	Observed behaviour	Type of car	Speed (estimate in km per hour)	Safe driving rating 1 = very unsafe 5 = very safe
A	M	55	0	M-P	Ford	40	2
B	F	21	2	T	VW	30	5
C	F	39	3	D	BMW	50	3
D etc.	M	70	0	C	Jensen	60	5

Observed behaviour code

D = Distracted   **M-P** = Using mobile phone

T = Talking   **C** = Concentrating

Sampling procedures

In observational studies it is difficult to observe all behaviour, especially as it's usually continuous. Breaking behaviour down into categories helps, but decisions must also be made about what type of sampling procedure (methods of recording data) to use.

- **Event sampling** – counting the number of times a behaviour occurs in a target individual or individuals.
- **Time sampling** – counting behaviour in a set time frame, for example recording what behaviour is being exhibited every 30 seconds.

Inter-observer reliability

Inter-observer reliability occurs when independent observers code behaviour in the same way (for example, two observers both agree on a score of '3' for safe driving) and lessens the chances of observer bias, where an observer sees and records behaviour in a subjective way (i.e. sees what they want to see). Inter-observer reliability needs to be established before an observation begins and it is easier to achieve if behavioural categories are clearly defined and do not overlap with each other.

RESEARCH IN FOCUS

A 2004 NICHD (National Institute of Child Health and Human Development) study found that children with the longest number of hours in day care had the lowest levels of aggression, suggesting that day care has a positive effect on aggression levels. But an earlier NICHD study found the opposite, using observations made by mothers rather than those made by teachers and carers.

1 Why might these similar studies into the effects of hours of day care on aggression levels, which both used observational techniques, have found such different results?

2 The establishment of inter-rater (or observer) reliability could have created clearer results.

Explain what inter-rater reliability is and how it would be established in this study.

Self-report techniques

Self-report techniques are research methods in which participants give information about themselves without researcher interference.

Questionnaires

With **questionnaires**, respondents record answers to a pre-set list of questions, usually concerning behaviour, opinions and attitudes – for example, Adorno's (1950) F-scale questionnaire (see page 30). Two main types of question are asked:

1 **Closed (fixed) questions** – involve yes/no answers (for example, do you believe in UFOs? 'yes' or 'no') or a range of fixed responses (for example, do you eat meat 'always', 'usually', 'sometimes', 'never'?). Such answers are easy to quantify, but restrict participants' answers.

2 **Open questions** – allow participants to answer in their own words. They are more difficult to analyse, but allow freedom of expression and greater depth of answers. For example, what kinds of music do you like and why?

Advantages of questionnaires

- **Quick** – compared to other methods, large amounts of information can be gathered in a short period. Postal questionnaires can gain relatively large samples for the cost of a stamp while online questionnaires are lost-free.
- **Lack of investigator effects** – questionnaires can be completed without researchers present.
- **Quantitative and qualitative analysis** – closed questions are easy to analyse statistically, while open questions provide richer, fuller detail.
- **Replication** – as questionnaires use standardised questions (the same for everyone), they are easy to replicate. This is particularly true of questionnaires using closed questions.

Weaknesses of questionnaires

- **Misunderstanding** – participants may misinterpret questions. (For example, what is meant by do you 'usually' do your homework?) There can also be problems with technical terms, emotive language and leading questions.
- **Biased samples** – questionnaires are suitable for people who are willing and able to spend time completing them. Certain types of people may be more willing to fill in questionnaires and not be representative of the whole population.

- **Low response rates** – questionnaires are an uneconomical research method as they can get very low return rates.
- **Superficial issues** – questionnaires, particularly those using closed questions, are not suitable for sensitive issues requiring detailed understanding.
- **Social desirability/idealised answers** – participants may lie in order to give answers expected of them (for example, not revealing racist beliefs) or may give answers that reflect how they would like to be, rather than how they actually are.

Questionnaire construction

There are several important considerations in designing questionnaires that people will actually complete and provide useful data to.

- **Aims** – having an exact aim helps, as it is then easier to write questions that address the aim.
- **Length** – questionnaires should be short and to the point, as the longer the questionnaire, the more likely people will not complete it.
- **Previous questionnaires** – use examples of questionnaires that were previously successful, as a basis for the questionnaire design.
- **Question formation** – questions should be concise, unambiguous and easily understood.
- **Pilot study** – questionnaires should be tested on people who can provide detailed and honest feedback on all aspects of the design of the questionnaire.
- **Measurement scales** – some questionnaires use measurement scales to assess psychological characteristics or attitudes. These involve statements on which participants rate levels of agreement or disagreement. See an example below.

Rate your level of agreement with the following statement:				
'Vigorous regular exercise is good for your health.'				
1	2	3	4	5
Strongly agree	Agree	Undecided	Disagree	Strongly disagree

There are usually a number of statements on a particular topic and the answers to these statements are combined to create a single score of attitude strength. However, it is not easy for participants to judge answers, so many choose the middle score. When this happens it is impossible to know whether they have no opinion or cannot decide between their attitudes in both directions. The best known of these attitude scales is the Likert scale (as in the example above).

YOU ARE THE RESEARCHER

1. Compose three open and three closed questions for a questionnaire examining people's smoking habits and attitudes to smoking.

   What type of data would:
   (i) the open questions generate
   (ii) the closed questions generate?

2. Explain how:
   (i) social desirability bias could affect the answers given
   (ii) idealised answers could affect the answers given.

Interviews

Interviews involve researchers asking face-to-face questions, for example Bowlby's (1944) study of maternal deprivation in juvenile thieves (page 134). There are three main types: structured, unstructured and semi-structured.

1 **Structured** – involves identical closed questions being read to participants, with the interviewer writing down answers. Interviewers do not need much training, as such interviews are easy to conduct.

2 **Unstructured** – involves an informal discussion on a particular topic. Interviewers can explore interesting answers by asking follow-up questions. Interviewers need considerable training and skill to conduct such interviews.

3 **Semi-structured** – involves combining structured and unstructured techniques, producing quantitative and qualitative data.

Advantages of interviews

- **Complex issues** – complicated or sensitive issues can be dealt with in face-to-face interviews by making participants feel relaxed and able to talk. This is particularly true of unstructured interviews.

- **Ease misunderstandings** – any misunderstood questions can be explained and individual questions can be adapted so they are understood by all participants.

- **Data analysis** – semi-structured interviews produce both quantitative and qualitative data, which can be used to complement each other. Structured interviews produce quantitative data that can be easily analysed.

- **Replication** – the more standardised or structured an interview, the easier it is to replicate. Unstructured interviews are less easy to replicate but it should be possible for other researchers to review data produced.

Weaknesses of interviews

- **Interviewer effects** – interviewers may unconsciously bias answers, like by their appearance; for example, women may be less willing to talk about sex with male interviewers. Interviews are also subject to demand characteristics and social desirability bias.

- **Interview training** – a lot of skill is required to carry out unstructured interviews, particularly concerning sensitive issues, and such interviewers are not easy to find.

- **Ethical issues** – participants may not know the true purpose of an interview and there is also the danger that participants may reveal more than they wish.

- **Participant answers** – interviews are not suited to participants who have difficulty putting their feelings, opinions, etc. into words.

Design of interviews

Aside from deciding whether to use a structured, unstructured or semi-structured interview and open or closed questions, decisions need to be made about who would make the most appropriate interviewer. Several interpersonal variables affect this decision:

- **Gender and age** – the sex and age of interviewers affect participants' answers when topics are of a sensitive sexual nature.

- **Ethnicity** – interviewers may have difficulty interviewing people from a different ethnic group to themselves. Word *et al.* (1974) found that white participants spent 25 per cent less time interviewing black job applicants than white applicants.

Figure 7.5 Interviews involve answering questions face-to-face

ON THE WEB

A useful video that contrasts a poor interview technique with a good interview technique can be found by searching YouTube for 'How to do a research interview'.

- **Personal characteristics and adopted role** – interviewers can adopt different roles within an interview setting, and use of formal language, accent and appearance can also affect how someone comes across to the interviewee.

Interviewer training is essential to successful interviewing. Interviewers need to listen appropriately and learn when to speak and when not to speak. Nonverbal communication is important in helping to relax interviewees so that they will give natural answers. Difficult and probing questions about emotions are best left to the end of the interview when the interviewee is more likely to be relaxed, whereas initial questions are better for gaining factual information.

Correlational studies

KEY TERMS

Correlational studies – the factors measured in a correlational study to assess their direction and strength of relationship

Co-variables – the variables investigated in a correlation. They are not referred to as the independent and dependent variables because the study is investigating the relationship between them, not trying to show a cause and effect relationship

Experiments look for a difference between two conditions of an IV, while **correlational studies** involve measuring the strength and direction of relationships between **co-variables**, for example Holland's (1967) study of the relationship between locus of control and obedience.

- A **positive correlation** occurs where one co-variable increases as another co-variable increases, for example ice cream sales increase as the temperature increases.
- A **negative correlation** is where one co-variable increases while another co-variable decreases, for example raincoat sales decrease as sunny weather increases.

Scattergrams (also known as scattergraphs) are a type of graph used to display the extent to which two variables are correlated. The measurement of one co-variable goes on one axis and the measurement of the other co-variable on the other axis.

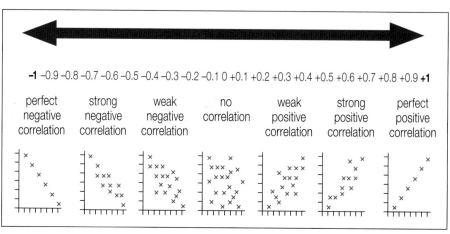

Figure 7.6 Scattergrams and correlation strength

Advantages of correlational analysis

- **Allows predictions to be made** – predictions can be made from correlations, like predicting the number of ice creams that will be sold on hot days.
- **Allows quantification of relationships** – correlations show the strength of relationship between two co-variables. A correlation of +0.9 (90 per cent similarity) means a high positive correlation, while a correlation of –0.1 (10 per cent similarity) indicates a weak negative correlation (see below).
- **No manipulation** – correlations do not require manipulation of variables and so can be used where carrying out an experiment may be unethical.

Weaknesses of correlational analysis

- **Quantification problem** – correlations that appear low (e.g. +0.28) can sometimes be significant (meaningful) if the number of scores is high, while correlations that seem high (e.g. +0.76) are not always statistically significant.
- **Cause and effect** – as they're not done under controlled conditions, correlations do not show causality. Therefore, we cannot say that one co-variable has caused the other.
- **Extraneous relationships** – other variables may influence the co-variables. For example, many holidays are taken in the summertime and people eat ice creams on holiday; therefore, the variable 'holiday' is related to both temperature and ice cream sales.
- **Only works for linear relationships** – correlations only measure linear (straight-line) relationships. For example, correlations cannot show the relationship between temperature and aggression, as it is curvilinear (not a straight line): as temperature increases, aggression levels increase up to an optimum point: then any further increase in temperature leads to a decline in aggression levels.

YOU ARE THE RESEARCHER

Design a correlational study that studies the relationship between age and memory ability. What would be your co-variables and how would you measure them?

Previous research into whether memory declines with age is contradictory. With this in mind compose a suitable correlational hypothesis. What type of graph would you use to plot the data?

Figure 7.7 Is memory ability related to age? A correlational study would answer this question

KEY TERM

Case studies – in-depth, detailed investigations of one individual or a small group

Case studies

Case studies are in-depth, detailed investigations of one individual or a small group. They usually include biographical details, behavioural information and experiences of interest. Case studies allow researchers to examine individuals in great depth. Explanations of behaviour are outlined in subjective ways, describing what an individual feels or believes about particular issues. For example Koluchova's (1972) 'Czech twins' study (see page 133).

Advantages of case studies

- **Rich detail** – case studies provide great depth and understanding about individuals and acknowledge human diversity. Because case studies are about 'real people', they have a feeling of truth about them. Information relates to a real person, not an average gathered from many.
- **The only possible method to use** – case studies allow psychologists to study unique behaviours or experiences that could not have been studied any other way. The method also allows 'sensitive' areas to be explored, where other methods would be unethical, like the effects of sexual abuse.
- **Useful for theory contradiction** – just one case study can contradict a theory. Curtis (1977) reported on the case study of Genie (see page 133), which helped to question evidence regarding critical stages of language development.

Weaknesses of case studies

- **Not representative** – as no two case studies are alike, results cannot be generalised to others. But do we always have to find universal truths of behaviour?
- **Researcher bias** – researchers conducting case studies may be biased in their interpretations or method of reporting, making findings suspect.
- **Reliance on memory** – case studies often depend upon participants having full and accurate memories.

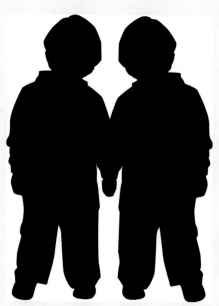

Figure 7.8 Twins can provide fascinating material for case studies

RESEARCH IN FOCUS

In 1972, Koluchova conducted a case study into twin boys who had been severely abused by their stepmother (see page 133).

1 Why was the case study method the only viable way of studying these boys?
2 What advantages and weaknesses of the case study method may apply in this particular study?

STRENGTHEN YOUR LEARNING

1 What similarities and differences are there between laboratory, field and natural experiments?
2 What strengths and weaknesses are there of:
   (i) laboratory experiments
   (ii) field experiments
   (iii) natural experiments?
3 For the following research methods:
   Observations
   Questionnaires
   Interviews
   Correlations
   Case studies
   (i) explain how they work
   (ii) detail their strengths and weaknesses.

7.2 Scientific processes

'The great tragedy of science – the slaying of a beautiful hypothesis by an ugly fact.'

Thomas Huxley (1870)

Aims

An **aim** is a precise statement of why a study is taking place/what is being studied, for example to investigate the effect of caffeine on reaction times. An aim should include what is being studied and what the study is trying to achieve.

Hypotheses

A hypothesis is a precise, testable prediction of what is expected to happen. For example, 'caffeine consumption will affect reaction times'.

- **The experimental/alternative hypothesis** – predicts that differences in the DV will be beyond the boundaries of chance (they will occur as a result of manipulation of the IV). Differences beyond the boundaries of chance are significant differences and this can be incorporated into a hypothesis. For example, 'caffeine consumption will significantly affect reaction times'. Statistical tests are used to see if results are significant (see page 304). The term 'experimental hypothesis' is only used with the experimental method. Other research methods use the term 'alternative hypothesis', but the definition is the same.

- **The null hypothesis** – is 'the hypothesis of no differences'. It predicts that the IV will not affect the DV. Any differences in results will be due to chance factors, not the manipulation of the IV, and will therefore be not significant and this can be incorporated into a null hypothesis. For example, 'there will be no significant difference in reaction times as a result of caffeine consumption'.

One of the two **hypotheses**, null or experimental, will be supported by the findings and thus be accepted, with the other one being rejected.

There are two types of experimental/alternative hypotheses:

- **Directional ('one-tailed') hypothesis** – predicts the direction of the results. For example, 'there will be a significant reduction in the speed of reaction times as a result of caffeine consumption'. It gets its name from predicting the direction the results will go.

- **Non-directional ('two-tailed')** – predicts that there will be a difference, but does not predict the direction of the results. For example, 'there will be a significant difference in the speed of reaction times as a result of caffeine consumption'. Reaction times will be either quicker or slower.

Directional hypotheses are used when previous research suggests that results will go in one direction, or when replicating a previous study that also used a directional hypothesis.

RESEARCH IN FOCUS

Have a look at Ginet & Verkampt's (2007) study of anxiety and memory (page 91). For this study compose a suitable:
- **(i)** directional (one-tailed) hypothesis
- **(ii)** non-directional (two-tailed) hypothesis
- **(iii)** null hypothesis.

Sampling

KEY TERM

Sampling – the selection of participants to represent a wider population

A population is all of something, for example all the grains of sand on a beach. Researchers generally don't have the means to test whole populations, so they use **sampling** (testing part of the population), part of the population. Ideally a sample is representative (contains the same characteristics as the population from which it was taken) and the term target population is used to indicate the group of people the results are targeted at. Psychologists use several sampling techniques, each with strengths and weaknesses.

Random sampling

Random sampling is where each member of a population has an equal chance of being selected. One way to achieve this is to place all names from the target population in a container and draw out the required sample number, while computer programs are also used to generate random lists. This results in a sample selected in an unbiased fashion.

Strengths of random sampling

- **Unbiased selection** – there is no bias in selection, increasing the chances of getting an unbiased and thus representative sample.
- **Generalisation** – as the sample should be fairly representative, results will be generalisable to the target population.

Weaknesses of random sampling

- **Impractical** – random sampling is difficult to achieve, as it is sometimes difficult to get full details of a target population and not all members may be available or wish to take part.
- **Not representative** – unbiased selection does not guarantee an unbiased sample, for example all females could be randomly selected, making the sample unrepresentative and thus the results not generalisable.

Opportunity sampling

Opportunity sampling involves selecting participants who are available and willing to take part, for example asking people in the street who are passing. Sears (1986) found that 75 per cent of university research studies use undergraduates as participants, simply for the sake of convenience.

Strengths of opportunity sampling

- **Ease of formation** – opportunity samples are relatively easy to create, as they use people who are readily available.
- **Natural experiments** – with natural experiments opportunity sampling usually has to be used, as the researcher has no control over who is studied.

Weaknesses of opportunity sampling

- **Unrepresentative** – the sample is likely to be biased by excluding certain types of participants and thus be unrepresentative, so that findings cannot be generalised to the target population. An opportunity sample collected in town during the day on a week day would not include those at work or college.
- **Self-selection** – participants have the option to decline to take part and the sampling technique thus turns into a self-selected sample.

Volunteer (self-selected) sampling

Volunteer or self-selected sampling involves people volunteering to participate. They select themselves as participants, often by replying to adverts.

Strengths of self-selected sampling

- **Ease of formation** – creating the sample requires little effort from the researchers (other than producing an advert), as participants volunteer themselves.
- **Less chance of 'screw you' phenomenon** – as participants are eager to take part there will be less chance of them deliberately trying to sabotage the study.

Weaknesses of self-selected sampling

- **Unrepresentative** – the sample will be biased, as volunteers tend to be a certain 'type' of person and thus unrepresentative, making results not generalisable to a target population.
- **Demand characteristics** – volunteers are eager to please, which increases the chances of demand characteristics, for example participants giving the answer they think is required.

Figure 7.9 Self-selected sampling involves participants volunteering to take part in a study

Systematic sampling

Systematic sampling involves taking every *n*th person from a list to create a sample. This involves calculating the size of the population and then assessing what size the sample needs to be to work out what the sampling interval is. For example, if a company has a workforce of 1,000 employees and a sample of 20 participants is required; then $1000 \div 20 = 50$, therefore take every fiftieth name from the list of employees to form the sample.

Strengths of systematic sampling

- **Unbiased selection** – there is no bias in selection, increasing the chances of getting an unbiased and thus representative sample.
- **Generalisation** – the results are representative of the population unless certain characteristics of the population are repeated for every *n*th person, which is unlikely.

Weaknesses of systematic sampling

- **Periodic traits** – the process of selection can interact with a hidden periodic trait within the population. If the sampling technique coincides with the frequency of the trait, the sampling technique is neither random, nor representative of the target population. For example, if every fifth property in a street is a flat occupied by a young person then selecting participants who live at every fifth property will not gain a representative sample.

- **Not representative** – unbiased selection does not guarantee an unbiased sample, for example all females could be selected, making the sample unrepresentative and thus the results not generalisable.

Stratified sampling

A stratified sample is a small-scale reproduction of a population. It involves dividing a population into characteristics important for the research – for example, by age, social class, etc. Then the population is randomly sampled within each stratum (category). If 12 per cent of the population is between 20 and 30 years old, then 12 per cent of the sample is randomly selected from that age sector.

Strengths of stratified sampling

- **Representative** – as selection occurs from representative sub-groups within a population, the sample should also be fairly representative.
- **Unbiased** – as random sampling is performed upon the sub-groups of a population, selection is unbiased.

Weaknesses of stratified sampling

- **Knowledge of population characteristics required** – stratified samples require a detailed knowledge of the population characteristics, which may not be available.
- **Time-consuming** – the dividing of a population into stratums and then randomly selecting from each can be time-consuming.

ON THE WEB

A simple explanation of sampling methods, including their strengths and limitations, can be found by searching YouTube for 'A-level Psychology – Sampling Methods' (StickyStudies channel).

STRENGTHEN YOUR LEARNING

1 What is the difference between:
    (i) an aim and a hypothesis
    (ii) a directional (one-tailed) and a non-directional (two-tailed) hypothesis
    (iii) an experimental and a null hypothesis?
2 For the following sampling methods:
    Random sampling
    Opportunity sampling
    Self-selected sampling
    Systematic sampling
    Stratified sampling
    (i) explain how they are conducted
    (ii) detail their strengths and weaknesses.

ASSESSMENT CHECK

1 The cognitive interview is designed to improve recall in police interviews. Researchers had some confederates perform a fake assault in front of an audience of witnesses who had replied to an advert to take part in the study. Half were interviewed using the standard police interview procedure and half by the cognitive interview technique. The amount of accurate recall was compared.

   Identify the independent variable and the dependent variable in this study. **[1 + 1 mark]**

2 **a)** Identify one confounding variable that might occur in the above study. **[1 mark]**

   b) Explain how this confounding variable might be controlled. **[2 marks]**

3 Explain how the following might influence the findings from the study. **[2 + 2 marks]**

   (i) investigator effects

   (ii) demand characteristics.

4 Suggest an appropriate non-directional hypothesis for this investigation. **[2 marks]**

5 The above study was a laboratory experiment. Explain one way in which a laboratory study differs from a natural experiment. **[2 marks]**

6 What type of sample was used in the above study? Give one limitation of this type of sampling. **[1 + 2 marks]**

7 A team of researchers used a stress scale to measure the amount of stress that individual workers at a factory experienced and the number of days they were off sick over a 6-month period. The researchers found that as the amount of stress increased, the number of days absent also increased.

   (i) What kind of correlation does this research show? **[1 mark]**

   (ii) Outline one strength and one weakness of using correlational research to investigate the effects of stress on health. **[2 + 2 marks]**

   (iii) What type of graph would be used to display the correlational data? **[1 mark]**

   (iv) Compose a suitable non-directional correlational hypothesis for this study. **[2 marks]**

   (v) Explain how the researchers might have gained a systematic sample for this study. **[1 mark]**

   (vi) Give one strength and one limitation of a systematic sample. **[2 + 2 marks]**

   (vii) The stress scale was given to participants as a questionnaire. Explain one advantage and one weakness of doing this in comparison to an interview. **[2 + 2 marks]**

Pilot studies

Pilot studies are small-scale practice investigations, carried out prior to research to identify potential problems with the design, method or analysis, so they can be fixed. Participants may also suggest appropriate changes, for example, if participants admit that they guessed the purpose of the study and acted accordingly (demand characteristics), changes could be made to avoid this. Pilot studies also identify whether there is a chance of significant results being found.

Experimental designs

There are three main types of experimental design: the independent groups design, the repeated measures design and the matched pairs design.

Independent groups design (IGD)

An **independent groups design** uses different participants in each of the experimental conditions, so that each participant only does one condition (either the experimental or control condition). Different participants are therefore being tested against each other.

Strengths of the independent groups design

● **No order effects** – as different participants do each condition there are no order effects whereby the order in which the conditions are done may have an effect on the outcome (see below).

● **Demand characteristics** – participants do one condition each, therefore there is less chance that they can guess the purpose of the study and act accordingly.

● **Time saved** – both sets of participants can be tested at the same time, saving time and effort.

Weaknesses of the independent groups design

● **More participants needed** – with participants each doing only one condition, twice as many participants as needed as for a repeated measures design (RMD).

● **Group differences** – differences in results between the two conditions may be due to participant variables (individual differences) rather than manipulations of the IV. For example, participants in one condition may be more intelligent than those in another condition. This is minimised by random allocation of participants to each condition.

Repeated measures design (RMD)

In a **repeated measures design** each participant is tested in all conditions of an experiment. Participants are therefore being tested against themselves.

Advantages of the repeated measures design

● **Group differences** – as the same people are measured in all conditions, there are no participant variables (individual differences) between the conditions.

● **More data/fewer participants** – as each participant produces two or more scores, more data is produced compared with an independent measures design (IMD). Therefore fewer participants are needed to get the same amount of data.

Weaknesses of the repeated measures design

- **Order effects** – with an RMD, participants do all conditions and the order in which they do these conditions can affect the results. Participants may perform worse in the second condition due to fatigue or boredom (negative order effect) or perform better due to practice or learning (positive order effect). Counterbalancing can control this, where half the participants do Condition A followed by Condition B, and the other half do Condition B and then Condition A.

- **Demand characteristics** – by participating in all conditions, it is more likely that participants may guess the purpose of the study and act accordingly.

- **Takes more time** – a gap may be needed between conditions to counter the effects of fatigue or boredom. Each condition may also need different materials; for example, in a memory test the same list of words could not be used for both conditions.

Figure 7.10 Identical twins are often used for a matched pairs design, as they form a perfect matched pair

Matched pairs design (MPD)

A **matched pairs design** is a special kind of RMD. Different, but similar, participants are used in each condition. Participants are matched on characteristics important for a particular study, such as age. Identical (monozygotic) twins are often used as they form perfect matched pairs, sharing identical genetic characteristics.

Advantages of the matched pairs design

- **No order effects** – as different participants do each condition there are no order effects.

- **Demand characteristics** – participants do one condition each, therefore there is less chance of them guessing the purpose of the study.

- **Group differences** – as participants are matched, there should be less chance of participant variables (individual differences) affecting the results.

Weaknesses of the matched pairs design

- **More participants** – with participants each doing only one condition, more participants are needed than for an RMD.

- **Matching is difficult** – it is impossible to match all variables between participants and an unmatched variable might be vitally important. Also, even two closely-matched individuals will have different levels of motivation or fatigue at any given moment in time.

- **Time-consuming** – it is a lengthy process to match participants.

> ### KEY TERM
>
> **Matched pairs design** – experimental design where participants are in similar pairs, with one of each pair performing each condition

YOU ARE THE RESEARCHER

Design a laboratory experiment that assesses whether memory recall is affected by the amount of sleep a person has had. How would you do this using an IGD? An RMD? An MPD? Compose a suitable aim and non-directional (2-tailed) hypothesis. Explain how you would attempt to control extraneous variables. How could you reduce the risk of demand characteristics? Explain how you would get a stratified sample for the study.

KEY TERM

Ethical issues – the rules governing the conduct of researchers in investigations

Ethical issues

Ethical issues involve researchers assessing and acting upon all ethical considerations involved in a research study before it is conducted. The main consideration is that the health and dignity of participants should be protected. The British Psychological Society (BPS) has published a Code of Ethics that all psychologists should follow and most research institutions, like universities, have ethical committees which have to approve research projects before they commence. Researchers should also, before conducting research, seek peer advice (advice from colleagues), consult likely participants for their views, consider alternative research methodologies, establish a cost–benefit analysis of short-term and long-term consequences and assume responsibility for the research. If, during the research process, it becomes clear there are negative consequences resulting from the research (like harm to participants), the research should be stopped and every effort made to correct the negative consequences. Any researcher having ethical concerns about a colleague's work should contact them in the first instance, and if their concerns are not met, contact the BPS.

The Code of Ethics includes:

Informed consent – investigators should give participants sufficient details of an investigation that they can make a considered choice as to whether they wish to participate. Parental consent should be obtained in the case of children under 16 years of age. Informed consent cannot be gained from those under the influence of alcohol or drugs or mentally unfit to give consent.

Avoidance of deception – the withholding of information or the misleading of participants is unacceptable if participants are likely to object or show unease once debriefed. Intentional deception over the purpose and general nature of investigations should be avoided. Participants should not deliberately be misled without scientific or medical justification. If deception occurs, informed consent cannot be gained from participants. It is often necessary that participants do not know the purpose of a study in order to get realistic results. In such cases, deception must be dealt with in an ethical manner. There are a number of ways to achieve this:

- *Presumptive consent* – this is gained from people of a similar background to participants in a study. If they state that they would have been willing to participate, then it is deemed that the actual participants would too.

- *Prior general consent* – this involves participants agreeing to be deceived without knowing how they will be deceived. As participants know they will be deceived, this can affect their behaviour.

- *Retrospective consent* – this involves asking participants for consent after they have participated in a study. However, they may not consent and yet have already taken part.

If deception is used, participants must be told immediately afterwards and given the chance to withhold their data from the study.

Adequate briefing/debriefing – all relevant details of a study should be explained to participants before and afterwards. A debrief is important if deception has been used. Participants should leave the study in no worse state than when they started it. Debriefing does not provide justification for unethical aspects of a study.

Protection of participants – investigators have a responsibility to protect participants from physical and mental harm during the investigation. Risk of harm must be no greater than in ordinary life.

Right to withdraw – participants should be aware that they can leave a study at any time, and can even withdraw their data after the study has finished.

Confidentiality/anonymity – participants' data should not be disclosed to anyone unless agreed in advance. Numbers should be used instead of names in published research papers. Confidentiality means that data can be traced back to names, whereas anonymous data cannot, as the researchers collect no names. Confidential data collection is preferable in cases where participants might be followed up later.

Observational research – observations are only made in public places where people might expect to be observed by strangers.

Incentives to take part – participants should not be offered bribes or promised rewards for their participation, as this puts pressure on them to take part.

Figure 7.11 Participants should not be offered money or any other incentives to participate in research studies

ON THE WEB

The British Psychological Society's code of ethics for research with humans can be found in full at:

www.bps.org.uk/sites/default/files/documents/code_of_human_ research_ethics.pdf

The implications of psychological research for the economy

Psychology creates practical applications used in everyday life for the betterment of society. This occurs through conducting research that allows psychology to form such practical applications. Therefore research contributes to the economy in a substantial way, such as by the creation of effective therapies for mental disorders. Ten per cent of people will spend time in a mental institution and about one in three people will receive treatment for mental problems. Effective therapies, developed through research, make huge savings in financial costs, allowing many people to return to work and contribute more fully to the economy. For example, Koran *et al.*'s. (2000) study into the atypical antipsychotic drug, olanzapine (see page 190), found that the drug when combined with the serotonin re-uptake inhibitor fluoxetine had a positive effect upon treatment of resistant forms of OCD – a finding which benefits the economy, as sufferers of OCD can return to work and thus earn money, pay taxes and not incur long-term financial costs upon the health service. Brosnan & Thorpe's (2006) study into the treatment of technophobia by systematic desensitisation (see page 168) could be used in a similar fashion, as could research into behaviourist treatments for phobias (see pages 163–70), cognitive treatments of depression (see pages 172–82) and other biological treatments of OCD (see pages 184–93).

- As well as contributing to the economy by producing a better functioning workforce, psychological research also cuts down on costs to the health service and to policing, the judiciary, the prison service, etc., as psychologically healthy people are less likely to incur costs upon these institutions.

- When conducting research, psychologists need to be aware that ethical considerations come before profit and that psychology should not be used to exploit people, as this has negative consequences. For example, ironic deviance (see page 36) shows us that if individuals believe a source of informational influence is not genuine, they will not act upon that influence. So if psychologists were perceived to advise a practical application because they had been manipulated to do so, people are likely not to trust such an application.

- Psychologists must also take care not to become divorced from the consequences of their research by being in the agentic state and not taking responsibility for their actions, such as by conducting research into psychoactive drugs that are then misused by profiteering drug companies (see Psychology in the real world, page 290). In one of his variations (see page 19) Milgram found that if participants only read out the questions and someone else administered the shocks 92.5 per cent of participants obeyed.

A

Reliability

Reliability refers to consistency. If a study is repeated using the same method, design and measurements, and the same results are obtained, the results are said to be reliable. Reliability can be improved by developing more consistent forms of measurement, using clearly defined operational definitions and by improving inter-observer reliability (see below).

- **Internal reliability** concerns the extent to which something is consistent within itself, for example a set of scales should measure the same weight between 50 and 100 grams as between 150 and 200 grams.

- **External reliability** concerns the extent to which a test measures consistently over time.

Ways of assessing reliability

- **The split-half method** measures internal reliability by splitting a test into two and having the same participant do both halves. If the two halves of the test provide similar results this indicates that the test has internal reliability.

- **The test – retest method** measures external reliability, by giving the same test to the same participants on two occasions. If the same result is obtained, then reliability is established.

- **Inter-observer reliability** (see page 264) is a means of assessing whether different observers are viewing and rating behaviour in the same way. This can be achieved by conducting a correlation of all the observers' scores, with a high correlation indicating that they are observing and categorising behaviour consistently. Inter-observer reliability is improved by developing clearly defined and separate categories of observational criteria.

If results are unreliable, they cannot be trusted. However, results can be reliable, but not be valid (accurate). For example, if you add up 1 + 1 several times and each time calculate the answer as 3, then your result is reliable (consistent), but not valid (accurate).

Validity

Validity concerns accuracy, the degree to which something measures what it claims to. Therefore validity refers to how accurately a study investigates what it claims to and the extent to which findings can be generalised beyond research settings as a consequence of a study's internal and external validity (see below). Validity can be improved by improving reliability (see above) and by improving internal and external validity (see below).

- **Internal validity** concerns whether results are due to the manipulation of the IV and have not been affected by confounding variables. Internal validity can be improved by reducing investigator effects, minimising demand characteristics and by the use of standardised instructions and a random sample. These factors ensure a study is highly controlled, leaving less doubt that observed effects are due to poor methodology.

- **External validity** refers to the extent to which an experimental effect (the results) can be generalised to other settings (ecological validity), other people (population validity) and over time (temporal validity). Milgram's electric shock study lacked external validity, as it is not usual to shock people for getting questions wrong, the study only used male participants and was a product of its time. External validity can be improved by setting experiments in more naturalistic settings.

RESEARCH IN FOCUS

Hofling (1966) performed an obedience experiment in the naturalistic setting of a hospital and found that the authority of doctors was a greater influence on nurses' behaviour than hospital rules.

Explain why initially it seems as if this study has high external validity, but why on closer inspection it seems that it actually has low external validity. (For further guidance, see page 25.)

Figure 7.12 Hofling's study was performed with real nurses in a real hospital setting, but did it still lack external validity?

Ways of assessing validity

- **Face validity** is a simple way of assessing validity and involves the extent to which items look like what a test claims to measure.
- **Concurrent validity** assesses validity by correlating scores on a test with another test known to be valid.
- **Predictive validity** assesses validity by predicting how well a test predicts future behaviour, for example, do school entrance tests accurately predict later examination results.
- **Temporal validity** assesses to what degree research findings remain true over time.

STRENGTHEN YOUR LEARNING

1 Why is it important that research be carried out in an ethical way?
2 Explain what is meant by the following ethical considerations:
Informed consent
Avoidance of deception
Briefing/debriefing
Protection from harm
The right to withdraw
Confidentiality/anonymity
Incentives to take part.
3 How can deception be avoided?
4 What do the following terms refer to:
   (i) reliability
   (ii) validity?
5 Explain what is meant by:
   (i) internal reliability
   (ii) external reliability
   (iii) internal validity
   (iv) external validity.
6 How can each be assessed?
7 Explain what is meant by inter-observer reliability and how it can be achieved.
8 (i) What is a pilot study?
   (ii) Why would one be conducted?
9 For the following experimental designs:
Independent groups design
Repeated measures design
Matched participants design
   (i) explain how they would be conducted
   (ii) detail their strengths and weaknesses.

Features of science

*'No amount of experimentation can ever prove me right;
a single experiment can prove me wrong.'*

Albert Einstein (1920)

KEY TERM

The scientific process – a means of acquiring knowledge based on observable, measurable evidence

Science is a system of acquiring knowledge through a process known as the scientific method (**the scientific process**), which is defined as the observation, identification, description, experimental investigation and theoretical explanation of phenomena.

The scientific method has three parts to it:

1 Observation and description of a phenomenon or group of phenomena

2 Formulation of a hypothesis to explain the phenomena. Use of the hypothesis to predict the existence of other phenomena, or to predict quantitatively the results of new observations

3 Performance of experimental tests of the predictions by several independent experimenters and properly performed experiments.

The prime feature of science is its dependence on empirical methods of observation and investigation. This involves observations based upon sensory information rather than simply upon thoughts and beliefs. Therefore a scientific idea is one that's been subjected to empirical testing by the use of rigorous observations of events and/or phenomena. For science to make sense there must be an explanation of empirically observed phenomena, achieved by developing theories that can be tested and improved by empiricism.

Science therefore involves making predictions, tested by scientific observations (empirical ones). Such observations are made without bias or expectation by the researcher and are performed under controlled conditions. In this way theories and hypotheses are validated (found to be true) or falsified (found to be untrue). It is the belief that this ability to predict and control behaviour under experimental conditions can also be achieved in real-life settings, which makes Psychology opt for science as its selected path towards the acquisition of knowledge.

Replicability

Replicability involves repeating research to check the validity of the results. Therefore research has to be fully and clearly written up so that it can be repeated under identical conditions. Fleischmann & Pons (1989) claimed to have created cold fusion, a way of producing abundant, cheap energy. However, replications of their experimental technique failed to get the same results. They had made an error in their procedure and only by replication were scientists able to realise this.

Objectivity

Objectivity is an important part of empiricism, where observations are made through sensory experience and not from the biased viewpoint of researchers.

Empirically observed phenomena must be objective to be considered truly scientific. To lessen the possibility of unconscious bias, researchers aim to use standardised instructions, operational definitions of observed variables and physically defined measurements of performance, the double-blind technique, etc. If phenomena are observed in a biased fashion, then they are subjective rather than objective, such as a biased interpretation of answers to an interview.

Most bias is unconscious, but there have been incidences of deliberate fraud too. This is important, because practical applications that are based on flawed research could have disastrous consequences. Peer review acts as a 'gatekeeper' to stop the publication of unscientific and flawed research. Replication also helps to show if research findings are valid.

Falsification

Part of the verification (validation) process is the idea of falsifiability, where a scientific theory or hypothesis must be empirically testable to see if it is false. Replication is the accepted way of determining this. Freud's psychodynamic approach is criticised for being unfalsifiable, as Freud placed interpretations on behaviour that couldn't be empirically tested to see if they were untrue.

Popper (1935) proposed the hypothetico-deductive model of science and is credited with advancing empirical falsification into scientific methods and procedures. He argued that no matter how many positive validations of a scientific theory occur through experimental testing, it doesn't prove it as undeniably true. However, one example of **falsification** is enough to render a theory untrue.

Popper sees falsifiability as being the determining line between what is and what isn't scientific.

KEY TERMS
Replicability – being able to repeat a study to check the validity of the results
Objectivity – observations made without bias
Falsification – that scientific statements are capable of being proven wrong

Figure 7.13 Karl Popper is credited with introducing empirical falsification into scientific methods and procedures

Theory construction and hypothesis testing

Popper saw tentative theories as being the first stage of the scientific process. These are used to generate predictions, expressed as testable hypotheses, which are tested by rigorous empirical means, the important point being that science doesn't depend upon chance observations, but on carefully arranged unbiased observations. Therefore initial observations yield up information about the world which is then formulated into theories that try to account for this information. Predictions in the form of testable hypotheses are formulated and experimentally tested, producing data that can be statistically analysed to see if the theory can be refuted or falsified, often leading to adjustments in the theory. This is seen as a process of verisimilitude, increasingly gaining closeness to the truth.

So the scientific method operates as a cycle with set phases:

1 **Inductive phase** – observations yield information that is used to formulate theories as explanations.

2 **Deductive phase** – predictions made from theories, in the form of testable hypotheses, are tested and yield data that is analysed, leading to theory adjustment.

Following this process it then becomes possible to generate laws and scientific principles. Popper reasons that a theory can be accepted as being validated if research evidence supports it, but that one finding of it not being true leads to its falsification. Therefore, although a theory can easily be disproved, it is never a 100 per cent certainty that it is absolutely true.

The most empirically based research method in psychology is the laboratory experiment, which allows causality (cause and effect relationships) to be established.

Other methods of hypothesis testing have reduced capability to determine causality, such as field and natural experiments, but even non-experimental methods can be performed using the scientific method, like naturalistic observations. Objectivity is improved by methods like inter-observer reliability, where researchers make efforts to ensure they observe phenomena in identical, unbiased ways. Therefore results can then be claimed to be valid.

Physics and chemistry are seen as 'hard', objective sciences, but a problem for psychology is that it is regarded as a 'soft science', because it tries to use the deterministic and reductionist principles of science, but due to the subjective subject matter, research can't be carried out with the usual rigorous vigour.

Paradigm shifts

Kuhn (1962) argued that Popper's idea of a scientific method involving induction and deduction isn't how science works. He believed that scientists collect data that fits the accepted assumptions of a science. This creates a type of bias whereby scientists attempt to find examples confirming their hypotheses rather than refuting them, with scientific journals publishing and focusing upon confirmatory examples of research, rather than non-confirmatory ones.

Kuhn referred to this as a paradigm (see page 7), 'a shared set of assumptions about the subject matter of a discipline and the methods appropriate to its study'. Very occasionally a paradigm is replaced with a new paradigm, often emerging from a minority position, for example the acceptance in physics of Einstein's beliefs about the nature of the universe.

Figure 7.14 Thomas Kuhn argued that science advances through paradigm shifts, where an accepted viewpoint is replaced by another

ON THE WEB

A short video clip that explains paradigm shifts through a visual demonstration, using pom-poms and a bottle, can be found on YouTube by searching for 'Kuhn's paradigm shift'.

Kuhn therefore argued that scientific advancement occurs not through the steady progress advocated by Popper, but instead by revolutionary **paradigm shifts**.

It may be the case that Psychology isn't yet in its scientific phase as it has yet to establish its paradigm. The counterview to this is that Psychology has a number of paradigms, such as behaviourism, evolutionary psychology, etc.

Reporting psychological investigations

Progress in science depends on communication between researchers. It is therefore essential to describe the results of research as accurately and as effectively as possible. To get research published in eminent peer-reviewed journals psychologists have to write reports in a conventional manner. This means that reports are written in such a way that replication would be possible, allowing others to repeat the research to check results.

The basic requirements of a report are to communicate:

- what was done
- why it was done
- what was found
- what it means.

There is no single best way to set out a report, but the general format is as follows:

1 Title
2 Table of contents
3 Abstract
4 Introduction
5 Aims
6 Hypotheses
7 Procedure/method
8 Findings/results
9 Discussion
10 Conclusion
11 References
12 Appendices.

1. Title

This should be clear, relevant and fully informative.

2. Table of contents

This is optional, but best included, along with page numbers.

3. Abstract

A summary of the research. The abstract generally consists of two sentences each on the theoretical background (previous research), aims and hypotheses, methodology, results, conclusions and suggestions for future research.

4. Introduction

This details why the study was conducted. General theoretical background, controversies and previous research investigations of the chosen topic are covered. Only relevant material should be used. A 'funnel' technique is used, starting off with a broad theoretical perspective, which then narrows down to the precise study area and leads on to the aims and hypotheses.

5. Aims

The overall aim(s) are stated clearly, precisely and concisely.

6. Hypotheses

The experimental/alternative hypotheses and the null hypothesis are stated, precisely and unambiguously. A justification of the direction of hypotheses (one-tailed or two-tailed) is also included, as is the level of significance, which is normally 5 per cent ($p < 0.05$).

7. Procedure/method

An outline of what was done. All methodological details are reported so the study can be replicated. Materials used in the study, like questionnaires and standardised instructions, are included in the appendices. This section splits into several sub-sections:

Design

Includes:

- choice of method, e.g. laboratory experiment
- choice of design, e.g. independent measures
- choice of techniques, e.g. time-sampling
- identification of variables, e.g. IV, DV and extraneous variables
- ethical considerations.

Participants

Includes sampling details such as:

- target population described in terms of relevant variables, like age, gender, etc.
- sampling method, e.g. opportunity sampling
- actual sample, including how many participants and how they were recruited and selected
- naivety of participants as to the purpose of the study and whether any declined to take part or subsequently dropped out
- allocation of participants to the testing conditions.

Apparatus/Materials

Description of any technical equipment involved and how it was used. Only materials directly relevant to the investigation are included. Any mark schemes, questionnaires go in the appendices.

Standardised procedure

Consists of a step-by-step procedure allowing replication of the study. Includes details of where the study took place, any standardised instructions and debriefing procedures. If instructions are lengthy they can be placed in the appendices and are referenced here. Material detailed in the method section is not repeated here.

Controls

Details of such controls as counterbalancing, random allocation of participants to groups, single- or double-blind procedures, control of extraneous variables, and what steps were taken to avoid bias in the sampling or experimental procedures.

8. Findings/results

Involves a presentation of what was found in terms of the data collected. This occurs as abbreviated or summary versions of the raw data, written in words with the support of tables and/or graphs.

Raw data is referenced here and presented in the appendices. One example answer sheet, questionnaire, etc. is included in the appendices.

Descriptive statistics

Key findings should be described briefly in the most straightforward manner to give readers a chance to 'eyeball' the data.

Numerical statistics, like measures of central tendency (mean, mode or median), measures of dispersion (range, standard deviation) should be included and results summarised in the most appropriate graphical form. Only one graph should be presented for the same data and should be visually clear and not over-complex.

Tables, graphs, etc. should be clearly titled and labelled and units of measurement specified.

Tables should be numbered and titled above the table, figures and graphs below. Labels on axes should be unambiguous.

Inferential statistics

Reasons for selecting a particular statistical test are given, as well as what it tests for. Actual calculations are referenced here, but placed in the appendices.

The outcome of statistical analyses is given along with critical table values of the test, the significance level and whether the test was one-tailed or two-tailed.

The outcome is explained in terms of acceptance and rejection of the experimental and null hypotheses.

9. Discussion

This section explains what the results mean and is broken down into several sub-sections.

Explanation of findings

Key findings are described that relate to the aims and hypotheses. All findings should be presented, including minor ones, unexpected and contradictory ones, plus an explanation of what the findings show and why they occurred.

Relationship to background research

Research is presented and discussed in terms of previous research findings presented in the introduction. Aspects of the design that may account for differences in the findings from previous studies are outlined.

Limitations and modifications

Possible sources of error, like flawed measurement techniques, poor sampling, lack of controls and/or poor procedures, etc. are outlined and discussed. Possible means of rectifying these faults are presented.

Implications and suggestions for future research

Further research studies suggested by the findings of the current one are presented here, as well as other possible ways of testing the hypotheses.

Also presented are any implications and applications that the findings of the present study suggest. Specific suggestions, like using more participants, eliminating confounding variables such as background environmental noise, and improving standardised instructions, are fine provided it is demonstrated that these factors have affected the findings in some way.

10. Conclusion

A concise paragraph is presented that summarises key conclusions drawn from the study.

11. References

Full details are listed of all references cited in the report. This enables others to research the references if desired. The standard format is as follows:

ON THE WEB

Although textbooks relate the main features of important research studies, there is no substitute for reading the original report write-ups. Go to the following link to access the website, 'Classics in the History of Psychology':

http://psychclassics.yorku.ca/index.htm

Read through famous psychology papers, which will be of use elsewhere in your studies, but also to see how research is written up and presented.

- *Journal articles* – Author's surname(s), initial(s), year of publication (in brackets), title of article. Title of journal (in full, italicised). [Online, if applicable, in square brackets] Volume number (part number/month in brackets), page number(s) (p.xx). Available from: URL. [Accessed: followed by the date viewed in square brackets]. For example:

  Shepard, R. and Metzler, J. (1971) Mental rotation of three dimensional objects. *Science*. 171(972), pp.701–3.

- *Books* – Author's surname(s), initial(s) (and 'ed.' or 'eds' if they are the editor/s), year of publication (in brackets), title of book (initial capitals for key words, italicised), edition (if not the first). Place of publication: publisher. For example:

  Wodehouse, P.G. (1917) *The Man with Two Left Feet*. London: Methuen.

- *Chapters in books* – Combines aspects of the procedure for journal articles and books (see above), by giving the author of the chapter and their chapter title first followed by 'in Smith, A. (ed.) …', etc. For example:

  Cohen, G. (1982) 'Theoretical interpretations of visual asymmetries', in Beaumont, J.G. (ed.) *Divided Visual Field Studies of Cerebral Organisation*. London: Academic Press.

12. Appendices

Numbered appendices are provided, containing full instructions given to subjects, raw data, and calculations for statistical analyses, plus other stimulus materials used. Information should be presented clearly and unambiguously.

The role of peer review in the scientific process

Peer review is part of the verification process where research is deemed to be scientifically acceptable or not. It consists of a system used by scientists to determine whether research findings can be published in scientific journals. The peer review system subjects scientific **research papers** to independent scrutiny by scientific experts (peers) before a decision is made about whether they can be published. As such, it acts as a 'gatekeeper' or filter system reducing the chances of flawed or unscientific research being accepted as fact. It operates on the belief that the status of research results is as important as the findings themselves.

There is a growing amount of scientific information being made public, as well as an increasing number of organisations, such as drug companies, promoting and discussing scientific research in public, and it is often difficult to decide which research is worthy of consideration and which is invalid, especially when different scientists argue completely different viewpoints – for example, whether or not climate change is due to human influence.

Over a million research papers are published in scientific journals each year, but although the peer review system is recognised and used by scientists globally as the best means of assessing scientific plausibility, the general public knows little, if anything, about this verification process. However, it is important that the public, especially those who deal with scientific claims, such as patient groups (an example of a patient group for depression is the Black Dog Institute), are aware of and understand peer review if they are to avoid the damage that comes from accepting poor scientific research.

The peer review process

During peer review it is usual for several expert reviewers to be sent copies of a researcher's work by a journal editor. These reviewers report back to the editor, highlighting weaknesses or problem areas, as well as suggestions for

KEY TERMS

Peer review – scrutiny by experts of research papers to determine scientific validity

Research papers – investigation reports written to a conventional format

improvement if necessary. There are generally four options for reviewers to recommend:

1 Accept the work unconditionally
2 Accept it so long as the researcher improves it in certain ways
3 Reject it, but suggest revisions and a resubmission
4 Reject it outright.

Single-blind review

This is the usual form of peer review, which involves the names of reviewers not being revealed to the researcher. The idea is that reviewer anonymity allows for an unbiased review free from interference by the researcher. However, there is the danger that anonymous reviewers may delay the review process to allow them to publish similar research first, and/or hide behind their anonymity to be undeservedly harsh.

Double-blind review

This involves both reviewers and the researcher being anonymous. The idea is that bias based on the researcher's ethnicity, gender, age, etc. will not occur and that research will be peer reviewed fairly and not be based upon the researcher's fame (or lack of it). However, it's likely that the researcher would be identifiable from the writing/research style, etc.

Open review

This involves reviewers and the researcher being known to each other. This is seen as reducing the risk of personal comments and plagiarism (stealing other people's work) and encourages open, honest peer reviewing. However, it may be that deserved criticism is watered down due to politeness or fear of retribution from famous, powerful researchers.

Criticisms of peer review

Critics argue that peer review isn't unbiased. Research occurs in a narrow social world and social relationships within that world affect objectivity and impartiality. In obscure research areas it may not be possible to find persons of sufficient knowledge to carry out a proper peer review. There are even suspicions that some scientists' ability to consider research in an unbiased and professional manner is compromised by them being funded by organisations which want certain research to be seen as scientifically acceptable. Reviewers have also been accused of not accepting research, so that their own studies can be published, and even of plagiarising (copying) research and then passing it off as their own. One way of attempting to address this is to ensure reviewers are anonymous and independent.

A further criticism is that the ability to publish research papers is controlled by elites. Therefore there may be resistance to revolutionary ideas that go against the elite or prevailing views, fitting Kuhn's idea that science doesn't advance steadily, but by one paradigm being toppled and replaced with another.

Peer review is also a slow process, sometimes taking months or even years to complete.

The consequences of false or unscientific research being accepted as true can be serious, not least because many other scientists' subsequent research may be built upon the fact of the original research being accepted as true. Cyril Burt, who falsified research into the heritability of intelligence, was a major figure in the field of intelligence and his research findings, widely accepted by the psychological community as being true, greatly influenced the work of subsequent researchers, who often took his work as a starting point for their own research.

PEER REVIEW

Figure 7.15 Peer review subjects research reports to intense scrutiny to ensure their scientific validity before publication

RESEARCH IN FOCUS

Increasing numbers of psychologists are publishing their research papers privately on the internet without having them subjected to peer review.

1 What are the dangers of conducting scientific research in this way?

2 What negative perceptions of the peer review system may be leading to psychologists doing this?

PSYCHOLOGY IN THE REAL WORLD

Scientific research is supposed to be conducted in a rigorous, unbiased and objective manner, or else the theories and practical applications based upon such research will be flawed, with potentially catastrophic consequences. That is why research has to be conducted in a replicable manner, be capable of being falsified and be subjected to peer review before being published in approved journals.

And yet the accusation remains, from many scientists in the field, that published research is often a world away from these ideals. One problem is that too often too little is revealed, with researchers, for example, not revealing their financial ties to drug companies they are conducting research for when asking participants to enrol in drug testing. Another major problem is that of company funded research; the *New England Journal of Medicine* (1998) reported that 96 per cent of researchers who published positive results for specific drugs had financial ties to the drug manufacturers, while only 37 per cent of researchers publishing critical papers had such ties. And it gets even murkier. Companies often own the data from research and so suppress unfavourable data and only publish favourable results. A drug's effectiveness may be reported, but not the fact that it has toxic side-effects. Another strategy is to bias the way in which research is designed and conducted, for instance comparing a higher dose of a favoured drug against a lower dose of a comparison drug. Those that expose such dark practices can be hit with expensive lawsuits, making future whistle-blowers more unlikely.

Only by having fully independent researchers and all research findings published will we have findings that can truly be trusted. Legislators in Europe have been drafting laws to force companies to publish all their research, including that which shows negative results or dangerous side-effects. However, companies have been financing so called 'patient interest groups' to campaign against such legislation. It seems we are a long way yet from being able to fully trust the research we see published in scientific journals.

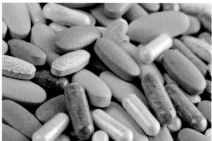

Figure 7.16 Evidence suggests that research is often not as unbiased and objective as it should be

ON THE WEB

For a detailed report of what peer review is and does, including a discussion of the criticisms levelled at the process and the pressures on researchers to act dishonestly, go to:

www.columbia.edu/cu/21stC/issue-1.1/peer.htm

Or, alternatively, look at:

http://science.howstuffworks.com/innovation/scientific-experiments/scientific-peer-review.htm

STRENGTHEN YOUR LEARNING

1 What are empirical methods of observation?
2 What is meant by falsification?
3 How is replication part of the falsification process?
4 Explain what is meant by objectivity.
5 Explain how Popper saw the process of science as working.
6 What is meant by paradigm shifts?
7 Describe the conventional method of writing up practical reports.
8 Why are reports written up in a conventional manner?

ASSESSMENT CHECK

1 Researchers decided to study the behaviour of a young girl who experienced disruption to attachment when she had to go into hospital for a few days. Naturalistic observation of the girl before and after the separation was conducted, with each period of observation lasting for two hours.

   (i) Suggest two behavioural categories the researchers could use to record the girl's behaviour. **[2 marks]**

  (ii) How might the researchers record the girl's behaviour? **[2 marks]**

 (iii) Explain why a pilot study might be carried out before the main observation. **[2 marks]**

  (iv) Explain why the researchers would need to establish inter-rater reliability. **[2 marks]**

   (v) Explain how inter-rater reliability could be established. **[2 marks]**

2 A stratified sample of participants were shown a tray containing 30 unrelated items for 30 seconds, after which time the tray was removed from sight. Half the participants were made moderately anxious, by wearing fake electrodes, which they were told would give them electric shocks for answers they got wrong. The other participants had low anxiety levels, through being told that the fake electrodes were merely monitoring bodily processes. Participants were instructed to recall as many items as possible.

   (i) What were the IV and the DV in this study? **[1 + 1 marks]**

  (ii) What experimental design was used in this study? **[1 mark]**

 (iii) Explain one strength and one weakness of this experimental design in the context of this study. **[2 + 2 marks]**

  (iv) Give one strength and one weakness of the sampling method used in this study. **[2 + 2 marks]**

   (v) Explain two ethical issues the researchers would have to consider. **[2 + 2 marks]**

  (vi) Explain one way in which psychological research might benefit the economy. **[2 marks]**

 (vii) Briefly explain one method the researchers could use to check the validity of the data collected in this study. **[2 marks]**

3 Scientific research should be falsifiable. Explain what is meant by falsification and what researchers should do to ensure that research is falsifiable. **[6 marks]**

4 Explain one reason why research should undergo peer review. **[2 marks]**

5 Detail criticisms of the peer review process. **[6 marks]**

6 Outline the major features of science. **[8 marks]**

7.3 Data handling and analysis

'Data! Data! Data! I can't make bricks without clay.'
Sherlock Holmes (1892)

Quantitative and qualitative data

KEY TERMS

Quantitative data – data occurring in numerical form

Qualitative data – non-numerical data expressing meanings, feelings and descriptions

Quantitative data is numerical (occurs as numbers), like counting the number of stressful incidents in a study, while **qualitative data** is non-numerical (occurs in forms other than numbers), like describing the emotional experience of each stressful incident. Research involves the collection of both quantitative and qualitative data. Qualitative studies tend to produce subjective, detailed, less reliable data of a descriptive nature, whereas quantitative studies produce objective, less detailed, more reliable data of a numerical nature. Although they are different forms of data they can often be used collectively to give stronger emphasis to research findings and a deeper insight.

Qualitative data provides insight into feelings and thoughts that quantitative data cannot, though analysis of such data can be very subjective, based on the researcher's own interpretation. Qualitative data can be converted into quantitative data, though, through content analysis (see page 293) and then be presented in quantitative forms, such as tables and graphs, and be analysed by numerical means such as by statistical tests.

Experiments are seen as producing mainly quantitative data, though qualitative data in the form of opinions/comments from participants can also be gathered. Observations, through the use of behavioural categories and ratings of behaviour, produce quantitative data, while questionnaires produce quantitative data from closed questions and qualitative data from open questions. Similarly, interviews produce quantitative data from structured interviews and qualitative data from unstructured interviews. Correlational data tends to be quantitative, while case studies produce mainly qualitative data.

Table 7.2 Qualitative and quantitative data

Qualitative data	Quantitative data
Subjective	Objective
Imprecise non-numerical measures used	Precise numerical measures used
Rich and detailed	Lacks detail
Low in reliability	High in reliability
Used for attitudes, opinions, beliefs	Used for behaviour
Collected in 'real-life' setting	Collected in 'artificial' setting

ON THE WEB

An illuminating video concerning the differences between qualitative and quantitative data can be found on YouTube by searching for 'Qualitative VS Quantitative Research'.

Primary and secondary data

Primary data refers to original data collected specifically towards a research aim, which has not been published before, while **secondary data** refers to data originally collected towards another research aim, which has been published before. Primary data is more reliable and valid than secondary data, as it has not been manipulated in any way. However, secondary data drawn from several sources can help to give clearer insight into a research area that primary data cannot.

Meta-analysis

Meta-analysis is a statistical technique for combining the findings of several studies of a certain research area, for example Grootheest *et al.*'s (2005) meta-analysis of the heritability of OCD, taken from several twin studies (see page 185). As a meta-analysis involves combining data from lots of smaller studies into one larger study, it allows the identification of trends and relationships that wouldn't be possible from individual smaller studies. The technique is especially helpful when a number of smaller studies have found contradictory or weak results, in order to get a clearer view of the overall picture.

RESEARCH IN FOCUS

Deffenbacher (1983) performed a meta-analysis into the role of anxiety in the accuracy of EWT (see page 91).
1 How was this achieved?
2 Would the researchers be using primary or secondary data?
3 What are the main strengths of conducting a meta-analysis?
4 Can you think of any problems with this type of research?

Content analysis

Content analysis is a method of quantifying qualitative data through the use of coding units and is commonly performed with media research. It involves the quantification of qualitative material, in other words, the numerical analysis of written, verbal and visual communications. For example, Waynforth & Dunbar (1995) analysed 'lonely hearts' columns to find out whether men and women look for different things in relationships.

Content analysis requires coding units to categorise analysed material, like the number of times women commentators appear in sports programmes. Analysis can involve words, themes, characters or time and space. The number of times these things do not occur can also be important.

Table 7.3 Coding units for content analysis

Unit	Examples
Word	The number of slang words used
Theme	The amount of violence on TV
Character	The number of female commentators there are in TV sports programmes
Time and space	The amount of time (on TV) and space (in newspapers) dedicated to eating disorders

KEY TERMS

Primary data – data collected specifically towards a research aim, which has not been published before

Secondary data – data originally collected towards another research aim, which has been published before

Meta-analysis – a process in which a large number of studies, which have involved the same research question and methods of research, are reviewed together and the combined data is tested by statistical techniques to assess the effect size

KEY TERM

Content analysis – a method of quantifying qualitative data through the use of coding units

Strengths of content analysis

- **Ease of application** – content analysis is an easy-to-perform, inexpensive research method, which is non-invasive, as it doesn't require contact with participants.
- **Complements other methods** – content analysis can be used to verify results from other research methods and is especially useful as a longitudinal tool (detecting trends; changes over time).
- **Reliability** – establishing reliability is simple as a content analysis is easy to replicate, through others using the same materials.

Weaknesses of content analysis

- **Descriptive** – content analysis is purely descriptive and so does not reveal underlying reasons for behaviour, attitudes, etc. ('what' but not 'why').
- **Flawed results** – is limited by availability of material, therefore observed trends may not reflect reality; for example, negative events receive more coverage than positive ones.
- **Lack of causality** – content analysis is not performed under controlled conditions and therefore does not show causality.

Thematic analysis

Thematic analysis is a qualitative analytic method for identifying, analysing and reporting themes (patterns) within data, with patterns identified through data coding. Ultimately, thematic analysis organises, describes and interprets data. The identified themes become the categories for analysis, with thematic analysis performed through the process of coding involving six stages:

1 **Familiarisation with the data** – involves intensely reading the data, to become immersed in its content.

2 **Coding** – involves generating codes (labels) that identify features of the data important to answering the research question.

3 **Searching for themes** – involves examining the codes and data to identify patterns of meaning (potential themes).

4 **Reviewing themes** – involves checking the potential themes against the data, to see if they explain the data and answer the research question. Themes are refined, which can involve splitting, combining or discarding one.

5 **Defining and naming themes** – involves a detailed analysis of each theme and creating an informative name for each one.

6 **Writing up** – involves combining together the information gained from the analysis.

Thematic analysis goes beyond just counting words or phrases, and involves identifying ideas within data. Analysis can involve the comparison of themes, identification of co-occurrences of themes and using graphs to display differences between themes.

Descriptive statistics

Descriptive statistics provide a summary of a set of data, drawn from a sample, that applies to a whole target population. They include measures of central tendency and measures of dispersion.

Measures of central tendency

Measures of central tendency are used to summarise large amounts of data into averages ('typical' mid-point scores). There are three types: the median, the mean and the mode.

The median

The median is the central score in a list of rank-ordered scores. With an odd number of scores, the median is the middle number. With an even number of scores, the median is the mid-point between the two middle scores and therefore may not be one of the original scores.

The advantages of the median are:
- It is not affected by extreme 'freak' scores.
- It is usually easier to calculate than the mean.
- The median can be used with ordinal data (ranks), unlike the mean.

The weaknesses of the median are:
- It is not as sensitive as the mean, because not all the scores are used in the calculation.
- It can be unrepresentative in a small set of data. For example:
  1, 1, 2, 3, 4, 5, 6, 7, 8 – the median is 4.

The mean

The mean is the mid-point of the combined values of a set of data and is calculated by adding all the scores up and dividing by the total number of scores.

The advantages of the mean are:
- It is the most accurate measure of central tendency as it uses the interval level of measurement, where the units of measurement are of equal size (for example, seconds in time).
- It uses all the data in its calculation.

The weaknesses of the mean are:
- It is less useful if some scores are skewed, such as if there are some large or small scores.
- The mean score may not be one of the actual scores in the set of data. For example:
  1, 1, 2, 3, 4, 5, 6, 7, 8 – the mean is 4.1 (1 + 1 + 2 + 3 + 4 + 5 + 6 + 7 + 8 = 37. 37/9 = 4.1)

The mode

The mode is the most common, or 'popular', number in a set of scores.

The advantages of the mode are:
- It is less prone to distortion by extreme values.
- It sometimes makes more sense than the other measures of central tendency. For example, the average number of children in a British family is better described as 2 children (mode) rather than 2.4 children (mean).

The weaknesses of the mode are:
- There can be more than one mode in a set of data. (For example, for the set of data 2, 3, 6, 7, 7, 7, 9, 15, 16, 16, 16, 20, the modes are 7 and 16.)
- It does not use all the scores.

KEY TERM

Measures of central tendency – methods of estimating mid-point scores in sets of data

Measures of dispersion

Measures of dispersion provide measures of the variability (spread) of scores. They include the range and standard deviation.

The range

The range is calculated by subtracting the lowest value from the highest value in a set of data.

The advantages of the range are:

- It is fairly easy and quick to work out.
- It takes full account of extreme values.

The weaknesses of the range are:

- It can be distorted by extreme 'freak' values.
- It does not show whether data are clustered or spread evenly around the mean. For example, the range of the two sets of data below is the same (21 – 2 =19), despite the data being very different.

  Data set one: 2, 3, 4, 5, 5, 6, 7, 8, 9, 21

  Data set two: 2, 5, 8, 9, 10, 12, 13, 15, 16, 18, 21

Standard deviation

Standard deviation is a measure of the variability (spread) of a set of scores from the mean. The larger the standard deviation, the larger the spread of scores will be.

Standard deviation is calculated using the following steps:

1 Add all the scores together and divide by the number of scores to calculate the mean.

2 Subtract the mean from each individual score.

3 Square each of these scores.

4 Add all the squared scores together.

5 Divided the sum of the squares by the number of scores minus 1. This is the variance.

6 Use a calculator to work out the square root of the variance. This is standard deviation.

The advantages of standard deviation are:

- It is a more sensitive dispersion measure than the range since all scores are used in its calculation.
- It allows for the interpretation of individual scores. Thus, in Figure 7.17, anybody with an IQ of 121 is in the top 5 per cent from the population, between +2 and +3 standard deviations from the mean.

The weaknesses of standard deviation are:

- It is more complicated to calculate.
- It is less meaningful if data are not normally distributed (see Figure 7.17).

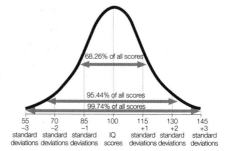

Figure 7.17 Standard deviation: IQ scores

Percentages

Percentages are a type of descriptive statistic that shows the rate, number or amount of something within every 100. Data shown as percentages can be plotted on a pie chart.

Data can be converted into percentages by multiplying them as a factor of 100. For example, a test score of 67 out of a total possible score of 80 would be: $\frac{67}{80} \times \frac{100}{1} = 83.75\%$

Correlational data

Correlational studies provide data that can be expressed as a correlation coefficient (see page 301), which shows either a positive correlation, negative correlation or no correlation at all. The stronger a correlation, the nearer it is to +1 or −1. Correlational data is plotted on a scattergram, which indicates strength and direction of correlation (see Figure 7.6, page 268).

Presentation of quantitative data

Quantitative data can be presented in various ways. Although emphasis is primarily on statistical analysis, data can also be presented through tables that summarise data to reveal findings of interest, as well as visually through **graphs** and charts, pictorial representations of data that allow viewers to more easily see patterns in data. Correlational data are presented via scattergrams, while other types of graphs exist for different types of research data.

Graphs and charts

Bar charts

Bar charts show data in the form of categories to be compared, like male and female scores concerning chocolate consumption. Categories are placed on the *x*-axis (horizontal) and the columns of bar charts should be the same width and separated by spaces. The use of spaces illustrates that the variable on the *x*-axis is not continuous (for example, males do not at some point become females and vice versa). Bar charts can show totals, means, percentages or ratios and can also display two values together, for example male and female consumption of chocolate as shown by gender and age (see Figure 7.18).

Histograms

Histograms and bar charts are somewhat similar, but the main difference is that histograms are used for continuous data, such as test scores, like the example shown in Figure 7.19. The continuous scores are placed along the *x*-axis, while the frequency of these scores is shown on the *y*-axis (vertical). There are no spaces between the bars since the data are continuous and the column width for each value on the *x*-axis should be the same width per equal category interval.

Frequency polygon (line graph)

A frequency polygon is similar to a histogram in that the data on the *x*-axes are continuous. The graph is produced by drawing a line from the mid-point top of each bar in a histogram. The advantage of a frequency polygon is that two or more frequency distributions can be compared on the same graph (see Figure 7.20).

Pie charts

Pie charts are used to show the frequency of categories as percentages. The pie is split into sections, each one of which represents the frequency

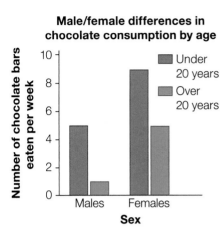
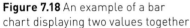

Figure 7.18 An example of a bar chart displaying two values together

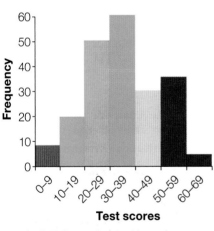

Figure 7.19 Example of a histogram

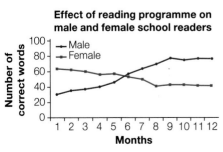
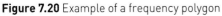

Figure 7.20 Example of a frequency polygon

297

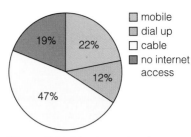

Figure 7.21 Pie chart showing different ways British people accessed the internet in 2010

of a category. The sections are colour coded, with an indication given of what each section represents and its percentage score (see Figure 7.21).

Tables

Results tables summarise the main findings of data and so differ from data tables, which just present raw, unprocessed scores (ones that haven't been subjected to statistical analysis) from research studies. It is customary with results tables to present data totals (though percentages can also be shown) and relevant measures of dispersion and central tendency (see Table 7.4 below).

Table 7.4 Male and female scores on a test of concentration

	Males	Females
Total scores	160	132
Mean	8	6.6
Range	9	13
Number of participants	20	20

ON THE WEB

A video lecture on descriptive statistics in psychology (including inferential testing, probability and Type I and II errors) with easy to follow examples can be found on YouTube by searching for 'AP Psychology Statistics Notes'.

KEY TERMS

Normal distribution – data with an even distribution of scores either side of the mean

Skewed distribution – data that does not have an even distribution of scores either side of the mean

STRENGTHEN YOUR LEARNING

1 What is the difference between:
   (i) quantitative and qualitative data
   (ii) primary and secondary data?
2 What is meant by a meta-analysis?
3 Explain how:
   (i) content analysis works
   (ii) thematic analysis works.
4 Describe the different types of measures of central tendency and measures of dispersion and give the strengths and weaknesses of each.
5 What is:
   (i) the difference between a bar chart and a histogram
   (ii) the similarity between a histogram and a frequency polygon
   (ii) the difference between a results table and a data table?
6 When would a pie chart be used to display data?

Distributions

Normal distribution

The idea of **normal distribution** is that for a given attribute, say for example IQ scores, most scores will be on or around the mean, with decreasing amounts away from the mean. Data that is normally distributed is symmetrical, so that when plotted on a graph the data forms a bell-shaped curve with as many scores below the mean as above it (see Figure 7.22)

There are several ways that data can be checked to see if it is normally distributed:

1 **Examine visually** – look at the data to see if most scores are clustered around the mean.

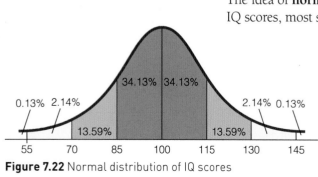

Figure 7.22 Normal distribution of IQ scores

2 **Calculate measures of central tendency** – calculate the mean, mode and median to see if they are similar.

3 **Plot the frequency distribution** – plot the data on a histogram (see page 297) to see if it forms a bell-shaped curve.

Skewed distribution

Unless a distribution of scores is symmetrical, as in a normal distribution, it will be skewed (not have an even distribution of scores either side of the mean). Outliers (extreme 'freak' scores) can cause **skewed distributions**: a positive skewed distribution occurring when there is a high extreme score (or group of scores), with a negative skewed distribution occurring when there is a low extreme score (or scores). Therefore, a positively skewed distribution will contain more low than high scores (the skew having been produced by outlying high scores) and a negatively skewed distribution will contain more high than low scores (the skew having been produced by outlying low scores).

Introduction to statistical testing

One method of analysing data from psychological investigations is the use of statistical tests. One such test is the **sign test**, which is used when a difference is predicted between two sets of data (such as in an experiment), the data is of at least nominal level (see Levels of measurement, page 301) and a RMD has been used. The test assesses the direction of any difference between pairs of scores

Statistical analysis produces an *observed* value, which is compared to a *critical* value in order to determine if the observed value is significant (beyond the boundaries of chance) (see Probability and significance, page 302). The sign test requires observed values to be equal to or less than the critical value to be accepted as significant, allowing the null hypothesis to be rejected (see Interpretation of significance, page 304).

A worked example of the sign test

A food manufacturer wishes to know if its new breakfast cereal 'Fizz-Buzz' will be as popular as its existing product 'Kiddy-Slop'. Ten participants try both and choose which they prefer. One participant prefers the existing product, seven the new product and two like both equally.

Table 7.5 Preferences for breakfast cereals

Participant number	Preference	Direction of difference
1	Fizz-Buzz	+
2	Fizz-Buzz	+
3	No difference	Omitted
4	Kiddy-Slop	–
5	Fizz-Buzz	+
6	Fizz-Buzz	+
7	Fizz-Buzz	+
8	No difference	Omitted
9	Fizz-Buzz	+
10	Fizz-Buzz	+

KEY TERM

Sign test – a non-parametric statistical test used for experiments where data is at least nominal and a repeated measures design has been used

To calculate the sign test:

- Insert the data into a table (see Table 7.5)
- Use a plus or minus sign to indicate the direction of difference for each participant.
- To calculate the *observed value* add up the number of times the less frequent sign occurs (This is *s*). This equals 1 in this case.
- Get the critical value of *s* from a critical value table. This shows the maximum value of *s* that is significant at a given level of probability. To do this you need the value of *N*, the number of pairs of scores, omitting scores with no + or − sign. In this case $N = 8$.
- Work out whether you have used a one-tailed (directional) hypothesis or a two-tailed (non-directional) hypothesis. This affects what the *cv* (critical value) will be – we'll assume here it's two-tailed.
- A significance level of $p \leq 0.05$ is normally used.
- The *cv* is found from a critical values table (see Table 7.6)

Table 7.6 The critical values of *s* in the sign test

Level of significance for a one-tailed test				
	0.05	0.025	0.01	0.005
Level of significance for a two-tailed test				
N	0.10	0.05	0.02	0.01
5	0	-	-	-
6	0	0	-	-
7	0	0	0	-
8	1	0	0	0
9	1	1	0	0
10	1	1	0	0
11	2	1	1	0
12	2	2	1	1
13	3	2	1	1
14	3	2	2	1
15	3	3	2	2
16	4	3	2	2
17	4	4	3	2
18	5	4	3	3
19	5	4	4	3
20	5	5	4	3

N = 8, two-tailed hypothesis, significance level $p \leq 0.05$, cv = 0, observed value s = 1

Therefore not significant, accept the null hypothesis

It might surprise you that seven preferences for one product against one preference for another product isn't a difference beyond the boundaries of chance, but is probably because the sample was too small, i.e. there weren't enough participants to show such a difference.

Analysis and interpretation of correlation

A correlational study produces a correlation coefficient: a numerical value showing the degree to which two co-variables are related. Measurements range from +1 (perfect positive correlation) to −1 (perfect negative correlation). The closer the correlation to a perfect correlation, the stronger the relationship between the two variables. If there is little correlation, the result will be near to zero (0.0).

Data from correlational studies can be analysed with both the Spearman's rho and Pearson's product moment statistical tests (see statistical tests, page 303).

7.4 Inferential testing

Research studies produce data, which in order to be made sense of, has to be analysed. As discussed previously, this can be achieved using descriptive statistics (measures of central tendency and dispersion, graphs, tables, etc.) to illustrate the data. But a more sophisticated means of analysis is the use of inferential statistical tests (**inferential testing**), which allow researchers to make inferences (informed decisions) about whether differences in data are significant ones (beyond the boundaries of chance) that can be applied to the whole target population which a sample represents.

In order to decide which statistical test to use, it needs to be decided:

1 *whether a difference or a relationship between two sets of data is being tested for*
2 *what level of measurement the data is:* there are three basic levels of measurement: nominal, ordinal and interval/ratio
3 *what design has been used:* either IGD or RMD (including MPD, as it's regarded as a type of RMD).

Levels of measurement

Nominal, ordinal and interval/ratio data are ranked in relation to one another, getting gradually more informative each time. The mnemonic NOIR (Nominal, Ordinal, Interval/Ratio) can be used to remember this order. The level of data produced by a research study affects which statistical test will be chosen.

- **Nominal data** – involves counting frequency data, for example how many days of the week were rainy or sunny? Tally charts are used to record this type of data. Nominal data is the crudest, most uninformative type of data. For example, although we might know how many days were sunny/rainy overall, nominal data doesn't show how rainy or sunny each day was hour-by-hour.

- **Ordinal data** – involves ranking data into place order, with rating scales often being used to achieve this. Ordinal data is more informative than nominal data, but still lacks being fully informative. For example, the finishing places in an athletics race, first, second, third, fourth, etc., show which athletes are better than others, but don't inform us about the distances between individual athletes. The distance between first and second may be shorter than between second and third. Similarly, one person's subjective rating of 7 may be very different to another's rating of 7.

- **Interval/ratio data** – standardised measurement units like time, weight, temperature and distance are interval/ratio measures and are the most informative and accurate form of measurement, as they use equal

KEY TERM
Inferential testing – statistical procedures that make predictions about populations from mathematical analysis of data taken from samples

ON THE WEB

A useful video explaining inferential testing and critical values can be found by searching for 'Inferential Tests, Alpha Probabilities and Critical Values'.

Figure 7.23 The finishing places in a running race, first, second, third, fourth and so on, provide an example of ordinal level data

measurement intervals, for example one second in time is the same length as any other second in time. Interval and ratio data are classed together, as they apply to the same statistical tests, but the difference between them is that interval data has an arbitrary zero point, whereas ratio data has an absolute zero point. For example, zero degrees temperature doesn't mean there's no temperature (interval data), whereas someone with zero pounds in their bank account would have no money (ratio data).

Selecting an inferential test

Once it has been determined (i) whether a difference or a relationship is being sought between two sets of data, (ii) what level of measurement has been used, and (iii) whether an IGD or a RMD has been used, the appropriate statistical test can be selected. (See Table 7.7.)

Table 7.7 Choosing an appropriate statistical test

Nature of hypothesis	Level of measurement	Type of research design	
		Independent (unrelated)	**Repeated (related)**
Difference	Nominal data	Chi-squared	Sign test
	Ordinal data	Mann-Whitney U test	Wilcoxon (signed-matched ranks)
	Interval data	Independent t-test	Related t-test
Correlation	Ordinal data		Spearman's rho
	Interval data		Pearson product moment

RESEARCH IN FOCUS

1 What statistical test would you use to analyse the data from Jenness' (1932) study of conformity (see page 5)?
You'll need to decide if a difference or a relationship was being sought, what design was used and what level of measurement was used.
2 Do the same thing for Bond & Smith (1996) (see page 10), who found a positive correlation between conformity rates and the size of the majority influence.

Probability and significance

When differences and relationships are found between sets of data it is important to determine whether such differences and relationships are significant ones, beyond the boundaries of chance.

If a coin is tossed 100 times, then by the law of averages there should be 50 heads and 50 tails. However, it might be 52 heads and 48 tails, meaning there's a difference between the two sets of data, but is it beyond the boundaries of chance? Probably not, but how is the cut-off point determined between the two sets of data being significant or insignificant? 55 heads to 45 tails? 60 to 40? This is where the idea of **probability** comes in.

Figure 7.24 If a coin is tossed 100 times, the expectation would be for 50 heads and 50 tails, but what ratio of heads and tails would be deemed beyond the boundaries of chance?

Probability is denoted by the symbol p and concerns the degree of certainty that an observed difference or relationship between two sets of data is a real difference/relationship, or whether it has occurred by chance. It is never 100 per cent certain that such differences and relationships are real ones, i.e. beyond the boundaries of chance. This is why it's impossible to prove something beyond all doubt, so an accepted cut-off point is needed; in psychology, and in science generally, a significance (probability) level of $p \leq 0.05$ is used. This means there's a 5 per cent possibility that an observed difference or relationship between two sets of data isn't a real difference, but that it occurred by chance factors. This is seen as an acceptable level of error.

On certain occasions a stricter level of significance may be needed, for example if testing out untried drugs or in new research areas. Then a **significance level** of $p \leq 0.01$ might be used, meaning there's a 99 per cent certainty that an observed difference/relationship is a real one, but there's still a 1 per cent chance that it occurred due to chance factors. An even stricter level of $p \leq 0.001$ would mean there's a 99.9 per cent certainty of a real difference/relationship, but there's still a 0.1 per cent chance that it occurred by chance.

Type I and Type II errors

A **Type I error** occurs when a difference/relationship is wrongly accepted as a real one, i.e. beyond the boundaries of chance, because the significance level has been set too high. This means the null hypothesis is wrongly rejected. An example, would be if a pregnancy test revealed a woman to be pregnant and she wasn't. With a 5 per cent significance level this means, on average, for every 100 significant differences/relationships found, five of them will have been wrongly accepted.

A **Type II error** occurs when a difference/relationship is wrongly accepted as being insignificant, i.e. not a real difference/relationship, because the significance level has been set too low (for example, 1 per cent). This means that the null hypothesis would be wrongly rejected. An example would be if a pregnancy test revealed a woman not to be pregnant when she was.

The stricter the significance level is, the less chance there is of making a Type I error, but more chance of making a Type II error and vice versa. One way to reduce the chance of making these errors is to increase the sample size.

A 5 per cent significance level is the accepted level, as it strikes a balance between making Type 1 and Type 2 errors.

Statistical tests

- **Sign test** – used when a difference is predicted between two sets of data, the data is of at least nominal nature and RMD has been used
- **Chi-squared** – used when a difference is predicted between two sets of data, the data is of at least nominal level and an IGD has been used. It's also possible to use Chi-squared as a test of association (relationship).
- **Mann-Whitney** – used when a difference is predicted between two sets of data, the data is of at least ordinal level and an IGD has been used.
- **Wilcoxon signed-matched ranks** – used when a difference is predicted to occur between two sets of data, the data is of at least ordinal level and a RMD or MPD has been used.
- **Independent (unrelated) t-test** – used when a difference is predicted between two sets of data, the data is normally distributed, the data is of interval/ratio level and an IGD has been used.
- **Repeated (related) t-test** – used when a difference is predicted between two sets of data, the data is normally distributed, the data is of interval/ratio level and a RMD or MPD has been used.

- **Spearman's rho** – used when a relationship (correlation) is predicted between two sets of data, the data is of at least ordinal level and the data are pairs of scores from the same person or event.
- **Pearson product moment** – used when a relationship (correlation) is predicted between two sets of data, the data is normally distributed, the data is of at least interval/ratio level and the data are pairs of scores from the same person or event.

Interpretation of significance

Statistical analysis produces an observed value, which is compared to a critical value in order to determine if the observed value is significant (beyond the boundaries of chance). Critical value tables need to be referenced, taking into consideration such information as whether a hypothesis is directional or non-directional (one-tailed or two-tailed), the number of participants or participant pairs (N) used and what level of significance, for example 5 per cent, is being used.

The Mann-Whitney and Wilcoxon and sign tests require observed values to be equal to or less than the critical value to be accepted as significant, allowing the null hypothesis to be rejected. The Chi-squared, independent (unrelated) t-test, repeated (related) t-test, Spearman's rho and Pearson product moment tests require an observed value to be equal to or greater than the critical value to be accepted as significant, allowing the null hypothesis to be rejected.

Table 7.8a Critical values of chi-square for a two-tailed (non-directional) test. Chi-square is significant if it is equal to or greater than the table value

df	0.20	0.10	0.05	0.02	0.01	0.001
1	1.64	2.71	3.84	5.41	6.64	10.83
2	3.22	4.6	5.99	7.82	9.21	13.82
3	4.64	6.25	7.82	9.84	11.34	16.27
4	5.99	7.78	9.49	11.67	13.28	18.46
5	7.29	9.24	11.07	13.39	15.09	20.52
6	8.56	10.64	12.59	15.03	16.81	22.46
7	9.8	12.02	14.07	16.62	18.48	24.32
8	11.03	13.36	15.51	18.17	20.09	26.12
9	12.24	14.68	16.92	19.68	21.67	27.88
10	13.44	15.99	18.31	21.16	23.21	29.59
11	14.63	17.28	19.68	22.62	24.72	31.26
12	15.81	18.55	21.03	24.05	26.22	32.91
13	16.98	19.81	22.36	25.47	27.69	34.53
14	18.15	21.06	23.68	26.87	29.14	36.12
15	19.31	22.31	25.0	28.26	30.58	37.7
16	20.46	23.54	26.3	29.63	32.0	39.29
17	21.62	24.77	27.59	31.0	33.41	40.75
18	22.76	25.99	28.87	32.35	34.8	42.31
19	23.9	27.2	30.14	33.69	36.19	43.82
20	25.04	28.41	31.41	35.02	37.57	45.32
21	26.17	29.62	32.67	36.34	38.93	46.8
22	27.3	30.81	33.92	37.66	40.29	48.27

23	28.43	32.01	35.17	38.97	41.64	49.73
24	29.55	33.2	36.42	40.27	42.98	51.18
25	30.68	34.38	37.65	41.57	44.31	52.62
26	31.8	35.56	38.88	42.86	45.64	54.05
27	32.91	36.74	40.11	44.14	46.96	55.48
28	34.03	37.92	41.34	45.42	48.28	56.89
29	35.14	39.09	42.69	46.69	49.59	58.3
30	36.25	40.26	43.77	47.96	50.89	59.7

Table 7.8b Critical values of chi-square for a one-tailed (directional) test

df	0.10	0.05	0.025	0.01	0.005	0.0005
1	1.64	2.71	3.84	5.41	6.64	10.83

Table 7.9 Mann-Whitney: critical value table of U for a one-tailed (directional) test at p = 0.005 and two-tailed (non-directional) test at p = 0.01. Dashes indicate no decision is possible at the stated level of significance. For any N1 and N2 the observed value of U will be significant if it is equal to or less than the critical values shown

N1

N2	1	2	3	4	5	6	7	8	9	10	11	12	13	14	15	16	17	18	19	20
1	-	-	-	-	-	-	-	-	-	-	-	-	-	-	-	-	-	--	-	-
2	-	-	-	-	-	-	-	-	-	-	-	-	-	-	-	-	-	-	-	-
3	-	-	-	-	-	-	-	-	0	0	0	1	1	1	2	2	2	2	3	3
4	-	-	-	-	0	0	1	1	2	2	3	3	4	5	5	6	6	7	8
5	-	--	-	-	0	1	1	2	3	4	5	6	7	7	8	9	10	11	12	13
6	-	-	-	0	1	2	3	4	5	6	7	9	10	11	12	13	15	16	17	18
7	-	-	-	0	1	3	4	6	7	9	10	12	13	15	16	18	19	21	22	24
8	-	-	-	1	2	4	6	7	9	11	13	15	17	18	20	22	24	26	28	30
9	-	-	0	1	3	5	7	9	11	13	16	18	20	22	24	27	29	31	33	36
10	-	-	0	2	4	6	9	11	13	16	18	21	24	26	33	31	34	37	39	42
11	-	-	0	2	5	7	10	13	16	18	21	24	27	30	39	36	39	42	45	48
12	-	-	1	3	6	9	12	15	18	21	24	27	31	34	37	41	44	47	51	54
13	-	-	1	3	7	10	13	17	20	24	27	31	34	38	42	45	49	53	56	60
14	-	-	1	4	7	11	15	18	22	26	31	34	38	42	46	50	54	58	63	67
15	-	-	2	5	8	12	16	20	24	29	34	37	42	46	51	55	60	64	69	73
16	-	-	2	5	9	13	18	22	27	31	36	41	45	50	55	60	65	70	74	79
17	-	-	2	6	10	15	19	24	29	34	39	44	49	54	60	65	70	75	81	86
18	-	-	2	6	11	16	21	26	31	37	42	47	53	58	64	70	75	81	87	92
19	-	0	3	7	12	17	22	28	33	39	45	51	56	63	69	74	81	87	93	99
20	-	0	3	8	13	18	24	30	36	42	58	54	60	67	73	79	86	92	99	105

Table 7.10 Mann-Whitney: critical value table of U for a one-tailed (directional) test at p = 0.01 and two-tailed (non-directional) test at p = 0.02. Dashes indicate no decision is possible at the stated level of significance. For any N1 and N2 the observed value of U will be significant if it is equal to or less than the critical values shown

N1

	1	2	3	4	5	6	7	8	9	10	11	12	13	14	15	16	17	18	19	20
1	-	-	-	-	-	-	-	-	-	-	-	-	-	-	-	-	-	-	-	-
2	-	-	-	-	-	-	-	-	-	-	-	-	0	0	0	0	0	0	1	1
3	-	-	-	-	-	0	0	1	1	1	2	2	2	3	3	4	4	4	5
4	-	-	-	-	0	1	1	2	3	3	4	5	5	6	7	7	8	9	9	10

N2	1	2	3	4	5	6	7	8	9	10	11	12	13	14	15	16	17	18	19	20
5	–	–	–	0	1	2	3	4	5	6	7	8	9	10	11	12	13	14	15	16
6	–	–	–	1	2	3	4	6	7	8	9	11	12	13	15	16	18	19	20	22
7	–	–	0	1	3	4	6	7	9	11	12	14	16	17	19	21	23	24	26	28
8	–	–	0	2	4	6	7	9	11	13	15	17	20	22	24	26	28	30	32	34
9	–	–	1	3	5	7	9	11	14	16	18	21	23	26	28	31	3	36	38	40
10	–	–	1	3	6	8	11	13	16	19	22	24	27	30	33	36	38	41	44	47
11	–	–	1	4	7	9	12	15	18	2	25	28	31	34	37	41	44	47	50	53
12	–	–	2	5	8	11	14	17	21	24	28	31	35	38	42	46	49	53	56	60
13	–	0	2	5	9	12	16	20	23	27	31	35	39	43	47	51	55	59	63	67
14	–	0	2	6	10	13	17	22	26	30	34	38	43	47	51	56	60	65	69	73
15	–	0	3	7	11	15	19	24	28	33	37	42	47	51	56	61	66	70	75	80
16	–	0	3	7	12	16	21	26	31	36	41	46	51	56	61	66	71	76	82	87
17	–	0	4	8	13	18	23	28	33	38	43	49	55	60	66	71	77	82	88	93
18	–	0	4	9	14	19	24	30	36	41	47	53	59	65	70	76	82	88	94	100
19	–	1	4	9	15	20	26	32	38	44	50	56	63	69	75	82	88	94	101	107
20	–	1	5	10	16	22	28	34	40	47	53	60	67	73	80	87	93	100	107	114

Table 7.11 Mann-Whitney: critical value table of U for a one-tailed (directional) test at p = 0.025 and two-tailed (non-directional) test at p = 0.05. Dashes indicate no decision is possible at the stated level of significance. For any N1 and N2 the observed value of U will be significant if it is equal to or less than the critical values shown

								N1												
N2	1	2	3	4	5	6	7	8	9	10	11	12	13	14	15	16	17	18	19	20
1	–	–	–	–	–	–	–	–	–	–	–	–	–	–	–	–	–	–	–	–
2	–	–	–	–	–	–	–	–	–	–	–	–	0	0	0	0	0	0	1	1
3	–	–	–	–	0	1	1	2	2	3	3	4	4	5	5	6	6	7	7	8
4	–	–	–	0	1	2	3	4	4	5	6	7	8	9	10	11	11	12	13	13
5	–	–	0	1	2	3	5	6	7	8	9	11	12	13	14	15	17	18	19	20
6	–	–	0	1	3	5	6	7	8	10	11	13	14	16	17	19	21	22	25	27
7	–	–	1	3	5	6	8	10	12	14	16	18	20	22	24	26	28	30	32	34
8	–	0	2	4	6	8	10	13	15	17	19	22	24	26	29	31	34	36	38	41
9	–	0	2	4	7	10	12	15	17	20	23	26	28	31	34	37	39	42	45	48
10	–	0	3	5	8	11	14	17	20	23	26	29	33	36	39	42	45	48	52	55
11	–	0	3	6	9	13	16	19	23	26	30	33	37	40	44	47	51	55	58	62
12	–	1	4	7	11	14	18	22	26	29	33	37	41	45	49	55	57	61	65	69
13	–	1	4	8	12	16	20	24	28	33	37	41	45	50	54	59	63	67	74	76
14	–	1	5	9	13	17	22	26	31	36	40	45	50	55	59	64	67	74	78	83
15	–	1	5	10	14	19	24	29	34	39	44	49	54	59	64	70	76	80	85	90
16	–	1	6	11	15	21	26	31	37	42	47	53	59	64	70	75	81	86	92	98
17	–	2	6	11	17	22	28	34	39	45	51	57	63	67	75	81	87	93	99	105
18	–	2	7	12	18	24	30	36	42	48	55	61	67	74	80	86	93	99	106	112
19	–	2	7	13	19	25	32	38	45	52	58	65	72	78	85	92	99	106	113	119
20	–	2	8	13	20	27	34	41	48	55	62	69	76	83	90	98	105	112	119	127

Table 7.12 Mann-Whitney: critical value table of U for a one-tailed (directional) test at p = 0.05 and two-tailed (non-directional) test at p = 0.10. Dashes indicate no decision is possible at the stated level of significance. For any N1 and N2 the observed value of U will be significant if it is equal to or less than the critical values shown

N1

N2	1	2	3	4	5	6	7	8	9	10	11	12	13	14	15	16	17	18	19	20
1	–	–	–	–	–	–	–	–	–	–	–	–	–	–	–	–	–	–	0	0
2	–	–	–	–	0	0	0	1	1	1	1	2	2	2	3	3	3	4	4	4
3	–	–	0	0	1	2	2	3	3	4	5	5	6	7	7	8	9	9	10	11
4	–	–	0	1	2	3	4	5	6	7	8	9	10	11	12	14	15	16	17	18
5	–	0	1	2	4	5	6	8	9	11	12	13	15	16	18	19	20	22	23	25
6	–	0	2	3	5	7	8	10	12	14	16	17	19	21	23	25	26	28	30	32
7	–	0	2	4	6	8	11	13	15	17	19	21	24	26	28	30	33	35	37	39
8	–	1	3	5	8	10	13	15	18	20	2	26	28	31	33	36	39	41	44	47–
9	–	1	3	6	9	12	15	18	21	24	27	30	33	36	39	42	45	48	51	54
10	–	1	4	7	11	14	17	20	24	27	31	34	37	41	44	48	51	54	58	62
11	–	1	5	8	12	16	19	23	27	31	34	38	42	46	50	54	57	61	65	69
12	–	2	5	9	13	17	21	26	30	34	38	42	47	51	55	60	64	68	72	77
13	–	2	6	10	15	19	24	28	33	37	42	47	51	56	61	65	70	75	80	84
14	–	2	7	11	16	21	26	31	36	41	46	51	56	61	66	71	77	82	87	92
15	–	3	7	12	18	23	28	33	39	44	50	55	61	66	72	77	83	88	94	100
16	–	3	8	14	19	25	30	36	42	48	54	60	65	71	77	83	89	95	101	107
17	–	3	9	15	20	26	33	39	45	51	57	64	70	77	83	89	96	102	109	115
18	–	4	9	16	22	28	35	41	48	55	61	68	75	82	88	95	102	109	116	123
19	–	4	10	17	23	30	37	44	51	58	65	72	80	87	94	101	109	116	123	130
20	–	4	11	18	25	32	39	47	54	62	69	77	84	92	100	107	115	123	130	138

Table 7.13 Critical values of T for the Wilcoxon signed matched ranks test. Values of T that are equal to or less than the table value are significant

Level of significance	for a	two-tailed	(directional)	hypothesis
	0.10	0.05	0.02	0.01
Level of significance	for a	one-tailed	(non-directional)	hypothesis
N	0.05	0.025	0.01	0.005
5	0			
6	2	0		
7	3	2	0	
8	5	3	1	0
9	8	5	3	1
10	10	8	5	3
11	13	10	7	5
12	17	13	9	7
13	21	17	12	9
14	25	21	15	12
15	30	25	19	15
16	35	29	23	19

17	41	34	27	23
18	47	40	32	27
19	53	46	37	32
20	60	52	43	37
21	67	58	49	42
22	75	65	55	48
23	83	73	62	54
24	91	81	69	61
25	100	89	76	68

Table 7.14 Critical values table for Spearman's rank order correlation coefficient test. Values of rs that are equal to or exceed the table value are significant

Level of significance	for a	two-tailed	(non-directional)	hypothesis
	0.10	0.05	0.02	0.01
Level of significance	for a	one-tailed	(directional)	hypothesis
N	0.05	0.025	0.01	0.005
4	1.0			
5	.9	1.0	1.0	
6	.829	.886	.943	1.0
7	.714	.786	.893	.929
8	.643	.738	.833	.881
9	.6	.7	.783	.833
10	.564	.648	.745	.794
11	.536	.618	.709	.755
12	.503	.587	.671	.727
13	.484	.56	.648	.703
14	.464	.538	.622	.675
15	.443	.521	.604	.654
16	.429	.503	.582	.635
17	.414	.485	.566	.615
18	.401	.472	.55	.6
19	.391	.46	.535	.584
20	.38	.447	.52	.57
21	.37	.435	.508	.556
22	.361	.425	.496	.544
23	.353	.415	.486	.532
24	.344	.406	.476	.521
25	.337	.398	.466	.511
26	.331	.39	.457	.501
27	.324	.382	.448	.491
28	.317	.375	.440	.483
29	.312	.368	.433	.475
30	.306	.362	.425	.467

Table 7.15 Critical value tables for Pearson's product moment correlation test. The P value of Pearson's product is significant if it is equal to or greater than the table value. Degrees of freedom = pairs of scores minus 2

Level of significance	for a	one-tailed	(directional)	hypothesis
	0.02	0.025	0.005	0.0005
Level of significance	for a	two-tailed	(non-directional)	hypothesis
N	0.1	0.05	0.01	0.001
4	.9	.95	.99	.999
5	.805	.878	.959	.991
6	.729	.811	.917	.974
7	.669	.754	.875	.951
8	.621	.707	.834	.925
9	.582	.666	.798	.898
10	.549	.632	.765	.872
11	.521	.602	.735	.847
12	.497	.576	.708	.823
13	.476	.553	.684	.801
14	.458	.532	.661	.78
15	.441	.514	.641	.76
16	.426	.497	.623	.742
17	.412	.482	.606	.725
18	.4	.468	.59	.708
19	.389	.456	.575	.693
20	.378	.444	.561	.679
21	.369	.433	.549	.665
22	.36	.423	.537	.652
23	.352	.413	.526	.64
24	.344	.404	.515	.629
25	.337	.396	.505	.618
26	.33	.388	.496	.607
27	.323	.381	.487	.597
28	.317	.374	.479	.588
29	.311	.367	.471	.579
30	.306	.361	.463	.57

Table 7.16 Critical value table for the T-test (independent and related t-tests). To be significant T should be equal to or greater than the table value. Degrees of freedom (df) for a related T-test = $N - 1$. Degrees of freedom for an independent T-test = $N1 + N2 - 2$

Level of significance	for a one-tailed	(directional)	hypothesis
	.1	.05	.025
Level of significance	for a two-tailed	(non-directional)	hypothesis
df	.2	.1	.05
1	2.0	6.314	12.706
2	1.895	2.92	4.303
3	1.644	2.353	3.182
4	1.533	2.132	2.776
5	1.487	2.015	2.571
6	1.446	1.943	2.447
7	1.41	1.895	2.365

8	1.4	1.860	2.306
9	1.389	1.833	2.262
10	1.376	1.812	2.228
11	1.368	1.796	2.201
12	1.364	1.782	2.179
13	1.358	1.771	2.16
14	1.355	1.761	2.145
15	1.349	1.753	2.131
16	1.343	1.746	2.12
17	1.338	1.74	2.110
18	1.336	1.734	2.101
19	1.334	1.729	2.093
20	1.332	1.724	2.086
21	1.328	1.721	2.08
22	1.327	1.717	2.074
23	1.325	1.714	2.069
24	1.323	1.711	2.064
25	1.321	1.708	2.06
26	1.318	1.706	2.056
27	1.316	1.703	2.052
28	1.314	1.701	2.048
29	1.312	1.699	2.045
30	1.31	1.697	2.042

STRENGTHEN YOUR LEARNING

1 What are the features of:
   (i) normal distribution
   (ii) skewed distribution?
2 Explain what is meant by inferential testing.
3 What is meant by the following levels of measurement:
   (i) nominal
   (ii) ordinal
   (iii) interval/ratio?
4 What three criteria should be considered when choosing a statistical test?
5 With reference to probability what is meant by a significant difference/relationship?
6 What are Type I and II errors and when do they occur?
7 What is meant by a critical value?

Required mathematical skills in AS and A-level psychology

The entries with purple-coloured bullet points are for A-level only.

Arithmetic and numerical computation	• Recognise and use expressions in decimal and standard form e.g. converting data into decimal form to construct a pie chart
	• Use ratios, fractions and percentages e.g. calculating percentages of categories in an observational study
	• Estimate results e.g. estimating the range for a set of data

Handling data	• Use an appropriate number of significant figures e.g. expressing a correlation coefficient to two or three figures
	• Find arithmetic means e.g. calculating the means in two experimental conditions
	• Construct and interpret frequency tables and diagrams, bar charts and histograms e.g. selecting and sketching an appropriate graph from a set of data
	• Understand simple probability e.g. explaining the difference between 0.05 and 0.01 levels of significance
	• Understand the principles of sampling as applied to scientific data e.g. explaining how to obtain a random sample
	• Understand the terms mean, median and mode e.g. selecting most appropriate measure of central tendency for a set of data
	• Use a scatter diagram to identify a correlation between two variables e.g. plotting two co-variables on a scattergram
	• Use a statistical test e.g. calculating a non-parametric test using data from an experiment
	• Make order of magnitude calculations e.g. estimating mean test score for many participants on the basis of overall total score
	• Distinguish between levels of measurement e.g. stating which level of measurement has been used in a study
	• Know the characteristics of normal and skewed distributions e.g. indicating the position of the mode from a set of scores
	• Select an appropriate statistical test – e.g. selecting and justifying choice of inferential test for a study
	• Use statistical tables to determine significance e.g. using statistical tables to state whether an observed value is significant
	• Understand measures of dispersion, including standard deviation and range e.g. explaining why standard deviation may be the most useful measure of dispersion for a set of scores
	• Understand the differences between qualitative and quantitative data e.g. explaining how qualitative data could be converted into quantitative data
	• Understand the difference between primary and secondary data e.g. stating whether data is primary or secondary data
Algebra	• Understand and use symbols e.g. stating a level of significance using the appropriate symbols
	• Substitute numerical values into algebraic equations using appropriate units for physical quantities e.g. inserting appropriate values from a set of data into a statistical test
	• Solve simple algebraic equations e.g. calculate the degrees of freedom for a statistical test
Graphs	• Translate information between graphical, numerical and algebraic forms e.g. constructing a bar chart from a set of scores
	• Plot two variables from experimental or other data e.g. sketching a scattergram using correlational data

Table 7.17 Algebraic and statistical symbols

Symbol	Symbol name	Symbol	Symbol name
=	Equals	Σ	Sum of
>	Greater than	U	Calculated value of Mann-Whitney U
<	Less than	r_s	Spearman rank correlation coefficient
$\geq$	Greater than or equal to	r	Pearson correlation coefficient
$\leq$	Less than or equal to	T	Calculated value of T (Wilcoxon signed-matched ranks test)
p	Probability	S	Calculated S (signed ranks test)
μ	Population mean	t	Calculated values of related and unrelated t-test
σ	Standard deviation	$x^2\chi^2$	Chi squared statistic

ASSESSMENT CHECK

1 Use the data in the table below to create a results table showing male and female total scores, mean scores and ranges. **[6 marks]**

Male participants	Concentration test score (out of 10.0)
1	5.0
2	6.2
3	7.3
4	8.1
5	6.3
6	4.0
7	7.1

Female participants	Concentration test score (out of 10.0)
1	5.0
2	6.2
3	7.3
4	8.1
5	6.3
6	4.0

2 What graph would be appropriate to use with this data? Explain your answer. **[1 + 2 marks]**

3 Which statistical test would be used to analyse the data? **[1 mark]**

4 Give three reasons for selecting this test. **[3 marks]**

5 Outline one strength and one limitation of standard deviation. **[2 + 2 marks]**

6 What is meant by the following? **[2 + 2 marks]**

   (i) a Type I error

   (ii) a Type II error?

7 Explain why a 5 per cent significance level is the accepted level of significance in psychological research. **[2 marks]**

8 Describe the features of normal distribution. **[3 marks]**

9 Explain how primary and secondary data differ from each other. **[2 marks]**

SUMMARY

- Several research methods exist. No single method is perfect; each has strengths and weaknesses.
- The experimental method involves manipulation of an independent variable (IV) to determine its effect on a dependent variable (DV) and through the use of controlled conditions is able to establish causality.
- Observations measure behaviour occurring in naturalistic settings, though they can also be conducted under controlled conditions.
- Questionnaires are a self-report method where participants give written answers to pre-set questions.
- Interviews are a self-report method involving answering face-to-face questions.
- Correlational studies measure the strength and direction of relationships between co-variables.
- Case studies involve detailed investigation of one individual or a small group.
- Content analysis quantifies qualitative data by categorising material into coding units.
- Thematic analysis is a qualitative analytic method for identifying, analysing and reporting patterns within data.
- The scientific process involves generating and testing hypotheses upon a sample of participants.
- There are three main experimental designs: the IGD, the RMD and the MPD, each having its strengths and weaknesses.
- Research should be conducted under ethical guidelines in order to protect the health and dignity of participants.
- Reliability refers to consistency, with internal reliability concerning how consistent things are within themselves and external reliability concerning the extent to which measures are consistent with other measures of the same thing.
- Validity refers to accuracy, with internal validity focusing on whether results are due or not to the manipulation of an IV, and external validity referring to the extent to which results can be generalised to other settings.
- Replicability involves a study being able to be repeated exactly to check the validity of its results.
- Empiricism involves objectivity; where observations must be made without bias.
- Falsification involves a scientific theory being empirically testable to see if it is untrue.
- Paradigm shifts involve revolutionary shifts in scientific beliefs.
- Psychological reports involve research being written up in a conventional manner that permits replication.
- Peer review involves scrutiny of research by experts to assess its suitability for publication.
- Data analysis involves the scrutiny of research findings to assess research aims, and involves a number of techniques centred upon both quantitative and qualitative data.
- Descriptive statistics summarise data findings in terms of measures of central tendency and dispersion, as well as through graphs and tables.
- Inferential testing involves the use of statistical tests to draw conclusions applicable to whole populations from data taken from representative samples.
- Probability and significance concern the likelihood of research findings being beyond the boundaries of chance.

Glossary

Abnormality – a psychological or behavioural state leading to impairment of interpersonal functioning and/or distress to others

Active processing – subjecting information to deep and meaningful analysis

Adrenal gland – the gland in the adrenal system that releases adrenaline

Adrenal medulla – the central part of the adrenal gland

Affectionless psychopathy – an inability to show affection or concern for others

Agentic state – the way in which an individual may obey an order, perhaps to do something that they see as 'wrong', because the individual hands over the responsibility for the outcome of the action to the authority figure. The individual sees themselves as acting as an agent for the authority figure and therefore does not feel responsible

Aim – a precise statement of why a study is taking place

Androcentrism – a bias in psychological research in which a male perspective is over-emphasised at the expense of a female one

Anxiety – an unpleasant state of emotional arousal

Articulatory process (AP) – part of the phonological acoustic store, allows sub-vocal repetition of information within the store

Attachment – a two-way, enduring, emotional tie to a specific other person

Authoritarian personality – this title describes a person who holds rigid beliefs, is intolerant of ambiguity, submissive to authority and hostile to those of lower status or members of an out-group

Autonomous state – opposite side of the agentic state, where individuals are seen as personally responsible for their actions

Beck's negative triad – a model of the cognitive biases which are characteristic features of depression. The triad consists of three elements, pessimistic thought patterns, about the self, the world and the future

Behavioural categories – dividing target behaviours into subsets of behaviours through use of coding systems

Behavioural approach – the perception of phobias as occurring through learning processes with treatments based upon modifying maladaptive behaviour through substitution of new responses

Biological approach – the perception of OCD as determined by physiological means with treatments based upon chemical means

Bipolar depression – a form of depression characterised by periods of heightened moods and periods of despondency and hopelessness

Capacity – the amount of information that can be stored at a given time

Case studies – in-depth, detailed investigations of one individual or a small group

Central executive (CE) – component of the WMM that oversees and co-ordinates the components of working memory

Central nervous system (CNS) – this system comprises the brain and spinal cord

Chunking – method of increasing STM capacity by grouping information into larger units

Circadian rhythms – biological rhythms that occur every 24 hours

Classical conditioning – occurs when a response produced naturally by a certain stimulus, becomes associated with another stimulus that is not normally associated with that particular response

Coding – the means by which information is represented in memory

Cognitive approach – the perception of depression as determined through maladaptive thought processes with treatments based upon modifying thought patterns to alter behavioural and emotional states

Cognitive dissonance – an unpleasant feeling of anxiety created by simultaneously holding two contradictory ideas

Cognitive interview (CI) – a procedure for police questioning of witnesses that promotes accurate, detailed recall of events

Compliance – publicly, but not privately, going along with majority influence to gain approval

Confederates – (also known as pseudo-participants and stooges) individuals who pretend to be participants or researchers in research studies, but who are actually playing a part

Conformity – yielding to group pressure (also known as majority influence)

Confounding variables – uncontrolled extraneous variables that negatively affect results

Content analysis – a method of quantifying qualitative data through the use of coding units

Context-dependent failure – a form of CDF where recall occurs in a different external setting to coding

Continuity hypothesis – the idea that there is consistency between early emotional experiences and later relationships

Contralateral – when the right hemisphere deals with the left-hand side of the body and vice versa.

Correlational studies – the factors measured in a correlational study to assess their direction and strength of relationship

Co-variables – the variables investigated in a correlation. They are not referred to as the independent and dependent variables because the study is investigating the relationship between them, not trying to show a cause and effect relationship

Critical period – a specific time period within which an attachment must form

Cross-cultural studies – comparison of findings from people of different cultures

Cue-dependent forgetting (CDF) – a type of forgetting based upon a failure to retrieve the prompts that trigger recall

Cultural relativism – the way in which the function and meaning of a behaviour, value or attitude are relative to a specific cultural setting Interpretations about the same behaviour may therefore differ between cultures

Cultural variations – differences in child-rearing practices and attachment types between different cultural groupings

Cupboard love theory – the belief that attachments are formed with people who feed infants

Dehumanisation – degrading people by lessening their human qualities

De-individuation – a state in which individuals have lower self-awareness and a weaker sense of personal responsibility for their actions. This may result from the relative anonymity of being part of a crowd

Demand characteristics – features of a piece of research which allow the participants to work out its aim and/or hypotheses. Participants may then change their behaviour and so frustrate the aim of the research

Dependent variable (DV) – the factor measured by researchers in an investigation

Depression – a mood disorder characterised by feelings of despondency and hopelessness

Deprivation – long-term disruption of an attachment bond

Deviation from ideal mental health – failure to meet the criteria for perfect psychological wellbeing

Deviation from social norms – behaviour violating accepted social rules

Dispositional explanation – the perception of behaviour as caused by internal characteristics of individuals

Drug therapy – the treatment of OCD through chemical means

Duration – the length of time information remains within storage

Electroencephalogram (EEG) – a method of measuring brain activity using electrodes on the scalp

Ellis' ABC model – an explanation that sees depression occurring through an activating agent, a belief and a consequence

Endocrine system – this is the system which affects the transfer and secretion of hormones throughout the body

Endogenous pacemakers – internal body 'clocks' that regulate biological rhythms such as regular times of sleep linked to levels of light. Examples include the suprachiasmatic nucleus and the pineal gland

Enhanced cognitive interview (ECI) – an advanced method of questioning witnesses that overcomes problems caused by inappropriate sequencing of questions

Episodic buffer – component of the WMM that serves as a temporary store of integrated information from the central executive, phonological loop, visuo-spatial sketchpad and LTM

Episodic memory (EM) – a form of LTM for events occurring in an individual's life

Ethical issues – the rules governing the conduct of researchers in investigations

Event-related potentials (ERPs) – a method of measuring brain activity in response to a stimulus (using the same equipment as EEG)

Excitatory potentials – increase the chance of a neuron firing

Exogenous zeitgebers – external stimuli, such as levels of light, temperature and social cues, which influence biological rhythms

Experimental method – a research method using random allocation of participants and the manipulation of variables to determine cause and effect

Extraneous variables – variables other than the IV that might affect the DV

Eye-witness testimony (EWT) – evidence provided by those recalling an event who were present when the event took place

Failure to function adequately – an inability to cope with day-to-day living

Falsification – that scientific statements are capable of being proven wrong

Field experiment – experiment conducted in a naturalistic environment

where the researchers manipulate the independent variable

Flooding – a behavioural therapy used to remove phobias through direct confrontation of a feared object or situation

Forgetting – the failure to retrieve memories

Genetic explanation – the perception of OCD as transmitted through inherited factors

Genotype – the genetic make-up of an individual

Graphs – easily understandable, pictorial representations of data

Hemispheric lateralisation – this is when one hemisphere carries out a particular function

Hormones – chemicals secreted by the endocrine system in to the blood and other bodily fluids

Hypothalamus – a part of the brain which is located in the centre of the brain and deals with basic survival functions

Hypotheses – precise testable research predictions

Identification – public and private acceptance of majority influence in order to gain group acceptance

Imposed etic – using techniques that are only relevant to one culture to study and/or draw conclusions about another

Imprinting – a form of attachment where offspring follow the first large moving object

Independent groups design – experimental design in which each participant performs one condition of an experiment

Independent variable (IV) – the factor manipulated by researchers in an investigation

Individual variables – personal characteristics that affect the degree to which individuals yield to group pressures

Inferential testing – statistical procedures that make predictions about populations from mathematical analysis of data taken from samples

Informational social influence (ISI) – a motivational force to look to others for guidance in order to be correct

Infradian rhythms – biological rhythms that occur less than once a day

Inhibitory potentials – decrease the chance of a neuron firing

Inner scribe – part of the VSS, stores information about the physical relationships of items

Institutional care – childcare provided by orphanages and children's homes

Interactional synchrony – the co-ordinated rhythmic exchanges between carer and infant

Interference/Interference theory (IT) – an explanation for forgetting when similar material is confused in recall from the LTM

Internal working model – a cognitive framework used to understand the world, self and others, that acts as a template for future relationships based on an infant's primary attachment

Internalisation – public and private acceptance of majority influence, through adoption of the majority group's belief system

Inter-observer reliability – where observers consistently code behaviour in the same way

Interviews – self-report method where participants answer questions in face-to-face situations

Introspection – a technique pioneered by Wilhelm Wundt, the father of modern psychology, to gain insight into how mental processes work. People were trained to report in detail on their inner experiences when presented with a stimulus such as a problem to solve or something to be memorised

Investigator effects – a research effect where researcher features influence participants' responses

Ironic deviance – the belief that other people's behaviour occurs because they have been told to do it lowers their informational influence

Laboratory experiment – experiment conducted in a controlled environment allowing the establishment of causality

Learning theory – the belief that attachments develop through conditioning processes

Legitimacy of authority – the degree to which individuals are seen as justified in having power over others

Localisation – In terms of the brain, this means the part of the brain in which a function is carried out

Locus of control (LoC) – the extent to which individuals believe that they can control events in their lives

Long-term memory (LTM) – a permanent store holding limitless amounts of information for long periods

Matched pairs design – experimental design where participants are in similar pairs, with one of each pair performing each condition

Measures of central tendency – methods of estimating mid-point scores in sets of data

Measures of dispersion – measurements of the spread of scores within a set of data

Meta-analysis – a process in which a large number of studies, which have involved the same research question and methods of research, are reviewed together and the combined data is tested by statistical techniques to assess the effect size

Milgram paradigm – experimental procedure devised by Stanley Milgram for measuring obedience rates

Minority influence – a type of social influence that motivates individuals to reject established majority group norms

Misleading information – information that suggests a desired response

Mnemonics – techniques that promote memory recall

Modified cognitive interview (MCI) – an amended form of the CI

Monotropic theory – used by John Bowlby to suggest that the infants have an inbuilt tendency to make an initial attachment with one attachment figure, usually the mother. He suggested that this tendency has an evolutionary origin

Monotropy – an innate tendency to become attached to one particular adult

Morality – decisions and behaviour based upon the perception of proper conduct

Multiple attachments – the formation of emotional bonds with many carers

Multi-store model (MSM) – an explanation of memory that sees information flowing through a series of storage systems

Natural experiment – experiment conducted in a naturalistic environment with a naturally occurring independent variable

Naturalistic observations – surveillance and recording of naturally occurring events

Negative reinforcement – a behaviour is more likely to reoccur because of avoidance of negative consequences

Neural explanation – the perception of OCD as resulting from abnormally functioning brain mechanisms

Neuron – a nerve cell which transfers information throughout the nervous system

Neurotransmitters – chemicals within the cerebral (or brain) fluid that transmit signals

Normal distribution – data with an even distribution of scores either side of the mean

Normative social influence (NSI) – a motivational force to be liked and accepted by a group

Obedience – complying with the demands of an authority figure

Objectivity – observations made without bias

OCD – anxiety disorder characterised by persistent, recurrent, unpleasant thoughts and repetitive, ritualistic behaviours

Operant conditioning – learning occurring via reinforcement of behaviour, thus increasing the chances of the behaviour occurring again

Operationalisation of variables – the process of defining variables into measurable factors

Paradigm shifts – revolutionary changes in scientific assumptions

Peer review – scrutiny by experts of research papers to determine scientific validity

Peripheral nervous system (PNS) – this system is the accompanying system running throughout the body which acts with the central nervous system

Personality – the combination of characteristics that forms an individual's distinctive nature

Phenotype – the characteristics shown by a person that have occurred because of their genes and the environment

Phobias – anxiety disorders characterised by extreme irrational fears

Phonological loop (PL) – component of the WMM that deals with auditory information

Pilot studies – small-scale practice investigations

Positive reinforcement – a behaviour is more likely to re-occur because of positive consequences

Post-event discussion – information added to a memory after the event has occurred

Primary acoustic store (PAS) – part of the phonological loop, stores words heard

Primary data – data collected specifically towards a research aim, which has not been published before

Privation – never having formed an attachment bond

Proactive interference – a form of interference that occurs when past memories inhibit an individual's full potential to retain new memories

Probability – the likelihood of events being determined by chance

Procedural memory (PM) – type of LTM for the performance of particular types of action

Punishment – a behaviour is less likely to reoccur because of negative consequences.

Qualitative data – non-numerical data expressing meanings, feelings and descriptions

Quantitative data – data occurring in numerical form

Quasi experiment – where the researcher is unable to freely manipulate the independent variable or randomly allocate the participants to the different conditions

Questionnaires – self-report method where participants record their own answers to a pre-set list of questions

Reactance – rebellious anger produced by attempts to restrict freedom of choice

Reciprocity – the interaction of similar behaviour patterns between carer and infant

Reliability – the extent to which a test or measurement produces consistent results

Repeated measures design – experimental design where each participant performs all conditions of an experiment

Replicability – being able repeat a study to check the validity of the results

Research methods – the means by which explanations are tested

Research papers – investigation reports written to a conventional format

Resistance to social influence – the ways in which individuals attempt to withstand perceived attempts to threaten freedom of choice

Retrieval – the recall of stored memories

Retrieval failure – an explanation for forgetting when material is stored in the LTM but cannot be consciously recalled as a result of a lack of retrieval cues to 'jog the memory'

Retroactive interference – a form of interference that occurs when newly learned information interferes with the recall of previously learned information

Sampling – the selection of participants to represent a wider population

Schema – a collection of ideas about a person or situation formed through experience which helps the individual to understand and predict the world around them/a readiness to interpret sensory information in a pre-set manner

The scientific process – a means of acquiring knowledge based on observable, measurable evidence

Secondary data – data originally collected towards another research aim, which has been published before

Self-actualisation – used by Abraham Maslow in the humanistic approach to psychology. It refers to a state in which people achieve their full potential. He suggested that every person has a motivation to achieve this

Self-report techniques – participants giving information about themselves without researcher interference

Semantic memory (SM) – type of LTM for meanings, understandings, and other concept-based knowledge

Sensitive period – a best time period within which attachments can form, though they still can form with more difficulty outside this period

Sensitive responsiveness – recognising and responding appropriately to infants' needs

Sensory register (SR) – a short-duration store holding impressions of information received by the senses

Separation – short-term disruption of an attachment bond

Separation anxiety – the degree of distress shown by infants when parted from attachment figures

Short-term memory (STM) – a temporary store holding small amounts of information for brief periods

Significance levels – statistical criteria determining if observed differences/ relationships are beyond the boundaries of chance

Sign test – a non-parametric statistical test used for experiments where data is at least nominal and a repeated measures design has been used

Situational variables – features of an environment that affect the degree to which individuals yield to group pressures

Skewed distribution – data that does not have an even distribution of scores either side of the mean

Social change – the process by which society changes beliefs, attitudes and behaviour to create new social norms (expected ways of behaviour and thinking)

Social releasers – innate, infant social behaviours that stimulate adult interaction and care-giving

Social roles – the parts individuals play as members of a social group, which meet the expectations of that situation

Social support – the perception of assistance and solidarity available from others

Standard police interview (SPI) – the established method of police questioning

State-dependent failure – a form of CDF where recall occurs in a different internal setting to coding

Statistical infrequency – behaviours that are rare

Status – an individual's social position within a hierarchical group

Stimulus discrimination – when a stimulus is not associated with the conditioned response as it is too different from the original stimulus

Stimulus generalisation – when a stimulus becomes generalised to other related stimuli which are also associated with the conditioned response

Stranger anxiety – the degree of distress shown by infants when in the presence of unfamiliar persons

The Strange Situation – the accepted observational testing method for measuring attachment types

Synaptic transmission – the process by which nerve impulses are carried across the small gap, the synapse, between one neuron and another. The nerve impulse is an electrical signal which is carried by chemicals called neurotransmitters

Systematic desensitisation – a behavioural therapy for treating anxiety disorders in which the sufferer learns relaxation techniques and then faces a progressive hierarchy of exposure to the objects and situations that cause anxiety

Systematic processing – analysis based upon critical thinking

Temperament hypothesis – the idea that the nature of infants' attachments is due to innate personality factors

Thematic analysis – a method of qualitative research linked to content analysis, which involves analysing text in a variety of media to identify the patterns within it. A coding system may be needed sort the data and to help to identify patterns

Two-process model – the perception of phobias as acquired through classical conditioning and social learning, with their maintenance upheld through operant conditioning

Type I errors – when a difference/ relationship in a data set is accepted as a real one but is in fact not

Type II errors – when a difference/ relationship in a data set is rejected, but actually does exist

Ultradian rhythms – biological rhythms that occur more than once a day

Unipolar depression – a form of depression occurring without mania

Validity – the extent to which results accurately measure what they are supposed to measure

Visual cache (VC) – part of the VSS, stores information about form and colour

Visuo-spatial sketchpad (VSS) – component of the WMM that deals with visual information and the physical relationship of items

Working memory model (WMM) – an explanation that sees short-term memory as an active store holding several pieces of information simultaneously

Index

A

Abed & Pauw (1998) 188
Abel & Bauml (2013) 78
Abernethy (1940) 79
abnormality, definitions of 146–52
    deviation from ideal mental health 150–1
    deviation from social norms 147–8
    failure to function adequately 148–9
    statistical infrequency 151–2
Abrams et al. (1990) 4, 5
Abramson et al. (1978) 173
Abu Ghraib 19
active processing 96–7
Adams, Douglas 146
Adorno et al. (1950) 30, 265
adrenaline 231, 232
adult relationships 139–42
advertising 12
affectionless psychopathy 134
agency theory 27–8
aggression 14, 108, 187, 202, 213, 269
agoraphobia 155
aims of scientific processes 271
Ainsworth (1971) 120–1, 262
Ainsworth et al. (1978) 120–1
Ainsworth, Mary
    attachment types 119–20
    biographical details 122
    Strange Situation 120–2
algebra 310–11
algebraic symbols 310–11
Alien Hand Syndrome 241
Alkhalifa (2009) 66–7
Alkhalifa, Ashaa 66
Allen & Levine (1971) 34
Altemeyer (1988) 30–1
alternative (experimental) hypothesis 271
Alzheimer sufferers 73
amnesia 52, 60, 61
anaclitic depression 134
androcentrism 22–3
animal attachment studies 109–13
    imprinting 90, 110–12, 119
    isolation and social interactions 112–13
animal phobias 155
Anokhin (1973) 59, 60
anonymity 279
anorexia nervosa 233
anterograde amnesia 60
anti-conformity 33
antidepressants 157, 170, 181, 189, 190, 191
anxiety 11, 90–2: see also obsessive-compulsive disorder (OCD); phobias
arbitrary inferences 172
Arendt, Hannah 17
arithmetic 310
articulatory process (AP) 64
Asch (1955) 4–5, 6–7, 8, 9, 49

Asch (1956) 10, 34
Aschoff & Weber (1962) 249
Asch, Solomon 6
assisted suicide 44
Astle, Jeff 242
Atkinson & Shiffrin (1968) 52
attachment 101–42
    Ainsworth's Strange Situation 119–27
    animal studies 109–13
    Bowlby's maternal deprivation hypothesis 109, 113, 129–38
    caregiver–infant interactions 102–9, 119, 126, 127, 144
    influence on childhood and adult relationships 138–42
    learning theory 115–16, 144
    monotropic theory 116–19, 144
attachment theory 127
attention 215
attentional bias 166
attributional style questionnaire (ASQ) 173–4
auditory centres 238
authoritarian personalities 30
autonomic nervous system 203, 227, 232
autonomous state 27
autonomy 151
Avant & Knudson (1993) 11
avoidance responses 154, 155, 163, 164, 165, 166
Avtgis (1998) 35
axons 228, 229, 230, 242, 243
Azar (2007) 72–3

B

Baddeley (1966) 55, 260
Baddeley (1986) 64
Baddeley (1996) 60, 63
Baddeley (2000) 65
Baddeley, Alan 55, 67
Baddeley et al. (1975) 64
Baddeley & Hitch (1974) 63
Baddeley & Hitch (1977) 78
Bagby (1922) 165
Bahrick et al. (1975) 59, 60
Baltes & Kleigl (1992) 96
Bandura, Albert 213, 216
Bandura & Huston (1961) 213
Bandura, Ross & Ross (1961) 213
bandwagon effect 12
bar charts 297
Barlow (2002) 169
Barrett (1997) 131
Bartlett (1932) 85–6
Baumrind (1964) 21
Beck (1987) 172–3
Beck depression inventory (BDI) 175
Beck depression inventory version 2 (BDI-II) 179
Beck's negative triad 172–3, 175
Beevers, Clasen, Stice & Schnyer (2010) 174
behavioural categories 263–4

behaviourism (learning theory) 115–16, 144, 206–12
    classical conditioning 115, 163, 164–5, 167, 206–8
    operant conditioning 115–16, 163–4, 165, 208–12
    see also systematic desensitisation (SD)
Bekerian & Bowers (1983) 88
Belsky (1999) 123, 141
Belsky et al. (2009) 108
Belsky & Rovine (1987) 118
Benedetti et al. (2007) 251
Bergquist et al. (1999) 190
Bernier & Miljkovitch (2009) 108
Bialik, Mayim 115
bias 23, 166, 261, 262, 263, 266, 267, 270, 283
biased samples 265
Bickman (1974) 30, 261
Billings, Josh 85
Binstock, Melissa 184
biological approach to psychology 199–204
    basic assumptions 200
    biological structures 202–3
    genes, influence on behaviour 200–2
    neurochemistry 203
biological preparedness 167
biological rhythms 249–54
    circadian rhythms 249–52
    infradian rhythms 252
    ultradian rhythms 253–4
biopsychology 204, 225–54
    biological rhythms 249–54
    brain study methods 247–8
    endocrine system 203, 231–2
    fight-or-flight response 231, 232–3
    localisation of brain function 235–45
    nervous system 226–7
    neurons 203, 228–30, 243
bipolar (manic) depression 156, 158, 175, 251
Blass (1991) 35
blindsight 237–8
Bobo doll experiment 213
bodily contact 103–4
Bogdonoff et al. (1961) 5
Bolzan, Scott 52, 60
Bombeck, Irma 102
Bond & Smith (1996) 10
Bottoms, Sharon 138
Bounton (2007) 166
Boury et al. (2001) 175
Bowlby (1944) 134, 267
Bowlby (1969) 130
Bowlby, John 105, 107, 109, 116
    biographical details 122
    maternal deprivation hypothesis 109, 113, 129–38, 144
    monotropic theory 109, 116–19, 144
Bradley & Baddeley (1990) 82
brain function, localisation of 235–45
    functional recovery after trauma 243–5
    hemispheric lateralisation 235–6, 243